THE JEWS
IN NEW SPAIN

THE JEWS IN NEW SPAIN

FAITH, FLAME, AND THE INQUISITION

by Seymour B. Liebman

UNIVERSITY OF MIAMI PRESS
Coral Gables, Florida

FRONTISPIECE: *Francisca de Carvajal de Matos being disrobed before the inquisitors. Reproduced from* El Libro Rojo

Designed by Bernard Lipsky

Manufactured in the United States of America

*This book is dedicated to
my devoted wife Malvina*

Contents

Illustrations

Acknowledgments

No study and its published result comes to fruition without the help of many others. I especially wish to thank Professor Nahum N. Glatzer and Beacon Press for permission to quote from *Faith and Knowledge*, Dr. Enrique Rivas for the translations of some of the liturgy used by the Iberian Jews in New Spain, and Dr. Richard E. Greenleaf, who offered encouragement in the early days of my research when few believed that there were sufficient records to prove the existence of a Jewish community in New Spain. I am indebted to Drs. Jacob R. Marcus and Stanley F. Chyet of the American Jewish Archives, who graciously complied with my requests for copies of documents that they had or could procure. All translations unless otherwise noted are by this author.

This book is dedicated to my wife. It is but small evidence of my eternal indebtedness for her belief in me, her dedication to me, her zealousness in reading and correcting numerous drafts of the manuscript, and for the countless indefinable ways her help is constantly manifested. Second only to the lives of those who people this book, she was my greatest inspiration.

There is a further note of dedication. It is to the thousands of Jews in the colonial era whose blood and bones hallow the ground of Mexico. Their graves are unmarked. No tombs or monuments have been erected for them. They opted for Judaism at the risk of their lives. It is hoped that some day some synagogue poet will emulate for the Jews of New Spain the liturgical poem written by Kalonymous ben Yehuda for the eleventh century martyrs of the Rhine region:

Yes, they slay us and they smite,
Vex our souls with sore affright;
All the closer cleave we, Lord,
To Thine everlasting word.
Not a line of all their Mass
Shall our lips in homage pass;
Though they curse and bind and kill,
The living God is with us still.
We still are Thine, though limbs are torn;
Better death than life forsworn.
From dying lips the accents swell,
"Thy God is One, O Israel";
And bridegroom answers unto bride,
"The Lord is God, and none beside,"
And, knit with bonds of holiest faith,'
They pass to endless life through death.

It behooves modern Mexican Jewry to remember those who preceded them to the shores of New Spain. When a prayer for any Jewish martyr or group of martyrs is recited in Mexico, let not the contemporary Mexican Jew forget Mexico's own who died for the sanctification of the name of God as did all those martyrs who preceded and followed them.

THE JEWS
IN NEW SPAIN

Introduction

THE HISTORY of the Jews is suffused with trag-
edy. There are tragedies other than those of persecution, loss of life,
rapine, or desecration of holy places. It is tragic that there are dark
or unknown periods of Jewish history, whole eras from which apparently no writings or documents have survived.

When such dark periods encompass certain ancient epochs, as
from the fifth to the second century B.C.E., Before the Common Era,
there is little that can be done other than to search for data and
sources that may have escaped attention. When records do exist and
their presence is known and nothing is done to study them, such lack
of research about a segment of the Jewish people also borders on
tragedy.

The *Ramo de la Inquisición*, Inquisition section, of the *Archivo
General de la Nación*—The Mexican National Archives—has thousands of original documents that reveal and portray the daily events
of the lives of countless Jews who were the victims of *El Tribunal
del Santo Oficio de la Inquisición en México*, the Court of the Holy
Office of the Inquisition in New Spain. Yet today few people have
any knowledge of the Jews who lived in New Spain prior to 1821.
Lucien Wolf, president of the Jewish Historical Society of England,
wrote many years ago:

> The work of the more ambitious branches of the Holy Office . . .
> in America has only been made known to us piecemeal; and with
> reference to the conspicuous individuals or specially romantic
> cases. For social data relating to the great body of Marranos the
> records have not hitherto been studied.[1]

Jews have inhabited New Spain without interruption since 1521, but there has been no continuity of any one community. Immigration has been episodic rather than continuous except within certain periods, such as from 1580 to 1640 and after 1862. The immigrants came in waves from various European points of origin and from the Canary Islands, the Azores, and the Middle East.

Mexico was a colony of Spain from 1521 to 1821 and was then known as Nueva España, New Spain. It was administered by a viceroy. The viceroyalty included all of modern Mexico, Central America, the Philippines, and the southwestern portion of the present United States. The jurisdiction of the Holy Office extended over the same territory. The name México was used during the colonial period for what we now know as Mexico City, which served as the capital, viceregal seat, and the location of the base of the Inquisition in New Spain.

The presence of Jews in New Spain during the three centuries under study was illegal except for a few decades. For three hundred years there was no such thing as Mexican citizenship. *Criollos*, children born in New Spain of Spanish parents (even of nobility), were barred from holding any office above the municipal level. The English word "creole" is used as a translation of criollo but has other meanings as well as that of a white person born of Spanish parents in the New World. All positions of importance, civil as well as clerical, were reserved for the *gachupine*, or Spanish born. By the eighteenth century the term gachupine became opprobrious.

The Jews who practiced their faith during the colonial era did so secretly, although in all generations there were nonobservant and rebellious Jews. Some married out of the faith regardless of whether the spouse was white or *mestizo* (mixed) ancestry. There is no record of marriage with Indians. When Mexico attained its independence in 1821, Catholicism was decreed the sole or state religion. The Church, however, no longer imposed strict regulations on non-Catholics and it began to be involved in the struggle to retain its supremacy, monopolies, and wealth.

During the colonial period most Jews were Sephardim, the name for those who inhabited or stemmed from the Mediterranean area. They were primarily of Spanish or Portuguese origin, and are referred to as Iberian or Hispanic Jews. There were others from Europe and elsewhere, but they were a minority of the Jews in the New World.

The principal immigration from 1821 to 1875 came from north of the Pyrennees. From 1870 to 1915 there was an influx from the eastern Mediterranean areas, the Middle East, provinces of the Ottoman Empire, and from North Africa. Since 1917 the Ashkenazim or East European Jews from countries such as Poland, Russia, Latvia, Estonia, Germany, Austria, and France have constituted the majority of immigrants.

The events that touched the lives of Mexican Jewry are divided into the epochs of Central American and Mexican history: the colonial era, 1521-1820; the period of independence, 1821-1862; the Maximilian era, 1862-1867; the post-Maximilian and Porifiro Díaz era, 1867-1911; and the post-revolutionary period to the present, 1917-1970. World War I as much as the bloody Mexican Revolution of 1910 to 1917 caused immigration to Mexico to drop to a mere trickle. A deluge of immigrants occurred between 1923 and 1930, and stopped then because of a severe economic depression as well as the months of overt anti-Semitism, which came to an end in June, 1931. There was another small wave of western European Jews who came between 1935 and 1939.

The Mexican Jew of today is not the descendant of the Jews of the colonial times. Few Jews are descendants of the European immigration of the nineteenth century. The descendants of the colonial Jews have assimilated and converted. Some admit their Jewish ancestry. Many of the descendants of the European immigrants who came between 1862 and 1910 have also converted or dropped Judaism.

It has often been written that the Mexican is the product of two cultures: Indian and Spanish. He is also the product of several faiths: Islam, Catholicism, Judaism, Protestantism, and the paganism of the autochthonous. His Judaism came not only during the sixteenth and seventeenth centuries from Iberian forebears but also in modern times from Jews who emigrated to Mexico from Europe and the United States.

World Jewry draws a distinction between Sephardim and Ashkenazim. In modern Mexico there are Jews who divide themselves according to places of geographical origin even though they are now Mexican citizens. Many of their children and grandchildren, native-born Mexicans, follow the same division. The Ashkenazim recognize subdivisions of those from Austria (the *Galitzianer*); those from Poland, Russia, and the now nonexistant Baltic states of

Lithuania, Latvia, and Estonia (the *Litvack*); the Germans; and the Hungarians. The Sephardim have their own community, and the Arab or Oriental Jews are divided into the Aleppo and the Damascus congregations.

There has been some interest in the so-called Mexican Indian Jews. These people's pseudo-exoticism fostered by myth, legend, and historical ignorance pique the curiosity of many American tourists, but they are neither Indians nor Jews and have been discussed at length elsewhere.[2]

Jews swarmed to the shores of New Spain after the conquest of 1521. Why did they come? Their presence in Cuba and Hispaniola (the island now divided between Haiti and the Dominican Republic) prior to 1521 was illegal, as it subsequently was in New Spain. To begin to understand the answer to this question and to innumerable other allied questions requires an understanding of Spanish history with relation to the Christian Spaniard, the Jewish Spaniard, and Sephardic Jewry in general. The Spanish Sephardic Jew must be differentiated from the Ashkenazi Jew.[3]

Spain, as we know the nation, did not come into being until 1516. Jews resided in the various kingdoms that comprised the geographical area of what is modern Spain. After 1492, and to a greater extent after 1580, Jews traveled back and forth between Portugal and Spain. Between the end of the fifteenth and the early nineteenth centuries, Jews had no political rights or even rights of residence in Spain, and none in Portugal from 1497 to 1773. Since it is difficult to denote a Jew of those times either as Spanish or Portuguese, the term "Iberian Jew" is used unless necessity compels a more specific description.

The psyche and the customs of Hispanic Jewry are not generally known. The work of Israel Abrahams of Cambridge University, *Jewish Life in the Middle Ages*, valuable as it is, must be judged on the basis of the time in which it was written, 1896. Sociology, cultural anthropology, psychology, and ethnography were then unknown areas of study. Abrahams treated European Jewry in the Middle Ages as if it were a homogeneous group. He noted minor differences among the Jews of various parts of Europe but failed to recognize the environmental and historical influences on the mentality and general mores of the various Jewish communities. He reported what the people did as Jews, but very little of what they did or how they lived as Spaniards. James Finn, in his work on the Sephardim, acknowledged the variances among Jews:

> The general histories of modern Jews have treated of them as one people *per se*, without adequate consideration of how difficult and differently must have been modified the Judaism of Granada in the twelfth century, or of Castile in the fourteenth century, from that of the same period amid the ferocity and unlettered ignorance of Poland and Muscovy. In Spain, his people [the Sephardim] acquired a degree of nationality not found in other countries, and this again assumed peculiar diversities of circumstances under the three great ascendancies of the Goths, the Arabs and the Inquisition.[4]

While Hebrew was the international language of correspondence among the rabbinate of the various countries in the Middle Ages, and religion the tie that bound all of the Jews together, the differences in mores were effects that stemmed from great ethnic influences. These ethnic influences were primarily secular. The history of the Jews in New Spain for the first three hundred years would have been entirely different if the majority had come from Germany or England or even from France. The Hispanic Jew was *sui generis*.

As a prelude to understanding Spanish history, Américo Castro observed that "the history of Spain has for centuries consisted— among other things—of a tendency to live in disagreement with itself.[5] There was a discordant variety of Hispanic peoples, and it is impossible to know Spanish history without knowing the role of the Jews therein. José Amador de los Ríos begins his *Historia social, politica y religiosa de los judíos de España y Portugal* with these words:

> It is difficult to open the history of the Iberian Peninsula, whether civil, political, religious, scientific or literary, without stumbling on each page over some act of the memorable name of the Hebrew nation which has been dispersed among the generations for 2,000 years. The chronicles of the kings, the histories of the cities and of the religious orders, and family annals are all filled with events in which people of Israel played, more or less, active and direct roles.[6]

If there were such a thing as *the* Spaniard, *the* Jew was the Spaniard in every sense of the word. He possessed all the virtues and vices of the Hispanic people. Salvador de Madariaga makes this point in writing that the Jews of 1492 "left behind a deeply judaized Spain; and they went abroad no less hispanified."[7]

No society was more pluralistic than that of the Iberian Peninsula. The Spanish historian Rafael Altamira stated that the present Spanish people is neither Iberian, nor Celtic, Latin, Arab, Jews, or Visigoth, and that physically and mentally they are the result of the interminglings and cross influences of all the ethnic factors of their history.[8] He could have added Berber, Gaul, and many others who lived on the peninsula at the same time.

It has been said that Africa ends at the Pyrenees. The Pyrenees did not serve as an insurmountable barrier to those coming from the north. Its passes and the Bay of Biscayne served as entrances by land and sea for the invaders from the north. The peninsula's eastern ports served as reception centers for those who came from the Middle East and other parts of the Mediterranean. The diffusion of bloods and cultures helped to create a people which is still in the process of evolving into an indigenous folk.

Castilian is not the language of all the people of the country known as Spain, although it is generally understood. The Basques have their own tongue. Catalans still dream of greater autonomy. Local chauvinism is almost tantamount to divisiveness in national loyalty.[9] If these conditions exist today, how much more marked must they have been during the period from the seventh to the sixteenth centuries. If the Spaniard's ancestry and milieu made him inscrutable and emotionally complex, then we may appreciate the same traits in the Iberian Jew who became the New World colonial Jew.

This work is not to be considered the definitive history of the Jews in New Spain. No one knows better than the author the extent of work yet to be done on the colonial era. There are hundreds of thousands of pages of colonial documents to be read and studied, and hundreds of Mexican Christian families whose ancestors were of Jewish stock to be interviewed. It is hoped that scholars will enter the field and contribute to the expanding knowledge of this period of Jewish history that has been dark for centuries and from which the cobwebs are now being dusted.

My goal has been to give a panoramic view and to reflect not only the trials, tribulations, and vicissitudes but also the joys and, in a smaller measure, the daily lives of the people who created this history.

The task of depicting Spain, the Spaniards, and the Spanish Church in its attitudes toward the Iberian Jew presents many problems. One is that of making qualitative judgments on events and people almost five hundred years after the occurrences. Another is the difficulty of finding adequate words to confine the mercurial Spaniard—either Jew or Christian—within the context of meaningful phrases. A third is the necessity of throttling one's own emotions and remaining properly objective while examining the evidence of history. I acknowledge the assistance of the opinions and conclusions of many others in my endeavors.

It is helpful to clarify who was defined as a Jew in the colonial era. In this history I have considered a Jew to be a direct descendant of a Jewish mother (the Orthodox or traditional view) who adhered to the rites and customs of Judaism. Because of circumstances, outward Catholic professions and practices are disregarded. Allegiance to the Jewish faith and the observance of its ritual, e.g., the Sabbath, circumcision, festivals, koshering meat, praying, and the risking of lives by doing so merited the people's claim to be considered Jewish. The people so defined carried on Jewish tradition surreptitiously for almost three centuries. They had material gains and high posts at their command and stood to lose all, including their lives, if discovered to be adherents of the Law of Moses.

Boleslao B. Lewin makes a distinction between converts who adopted Catholicism in order to remain in Spain after 1492 but clung secretly to Judaism and those who were forcibly converted in Portugal in 1497. The first group he labels "marranos" and the second "crypto-judios," or secret Jews.[10]

I have not used the word marrano, as this word was never used by the Inquisition officials nor is it found in the official and clerical correspondence studied. It appears that this term, which literally means swine, was first used by Jews of medieval Spain to designate Jewish apostates who were sincere converts to Christianity. Such people are called *meshummadim* in Hebrew. Involuntary converts—people who were baptized through force or fear—are termed *anusim* in Hebrew. Later the word marrano came to be used to describe a person who was baptized or who professed Christianity publicly but who practiced Judaism secretly. The preferred terms, however, are crypto-Jew or secret Jew.

Two American Jewish historians, each holding a rabbinical degree, have their own definitions of a Jew. Jacob R. Marcus of Hebrew Union College wrote to this author (February 2, 1961): "I would consider as Jews only those Marranos whose parents were Jews. In other words, I would accept as Jews people in the second generation. The first generation would include those who were actually converted." Salo W. Baron of Columbia University stated, "Any one born to Jewish parents or . . . to a Jewish mother was considered a Jew; a Jew remained a Jew even if he . . . converted himself to another faith, but subsequently repented." He then added that he recognizes as a Jew anyone born of mixed parentage who declares himself as a Jew and is accepted by his neighbors as a Jew.[11]

Those who went to the New World from the Iberian Peninsula and are regarded herein as Jews would fit the classifications of the historians just quoted. The Jews of the colonial era were accepted as Jews by the recognized and openly professing Jews of Curaçao, Jamaica, and distant Italy.

According to Baron, the historian "must also sometimes rather arbitrarily decide whether to include in his narration the story of a Jewish convert to Christianity before and after his conversion."[12] Those colonials who lived as Jews, considered themselves Jews, and had the necessary ancestry are considered in this history as people of the Hebrew faith. Not included are those who were sincere converts to Christianity and who had divorced themselves from other Jews and their affairs. Adherence to the legacy of Jewish custom or disavowal of this faith is the line of distinction between those who are included and those excluded.

The case of Bernardo López de Mendizabal illustrates this distinction. In 1660 to 1661 he was the Spanish governor of a province (now New Mexico) in Nueva España. He was arrested and tried before the Inquisition in Mexico on many charges, one of them for being a Jew. His grandmother had been a Jewess and had been burned at the stake in Spain. López de Mendizabal had studied for the priesthood, was a great liberal in many respects, and was anticlerical during his regime. The Jewish practices attributed to him were having his bed linen changed on Fridays, washing and changing to clean shirts on Fridays, not going to confession for almost two years, and rarely attending church services. He protested his innocence and died before judgment was rendered. There is no record of his participation in Jewish practices or association with other Jews. So while mentioned in the Inquisition records as a Jew because of the charge against him, he will not be considered or counted among the Jews of New Spain.

The word "community" also requires clarification. There were groups of Jewish people with ties of friendship or places of common origin who assembled for festivals or prayer or discussions. No printed rules and regulations for the conduct of a cohesive communal group have been found, but there were synagogues and places for group worship. The use of a messenger to call people to services or for an extraordinary or special meeting has been revealed. Much more than that can be deduced from testimony at Inquisition trials.

The inquisitors were concerned with individuals and not with institutions. According to their rationale, if all Jews were burned or exiled, Jewish institutions and communal activities would cease. The incrimination by the accused involved only names and acts of other individual Jews. There is nothing to indicate any attempt by the inquisitors to ascertain the existence of any communal organization.

The colonial Jewish communities were not unified, and there does not seem to be any connection between the principal ones of Veracruz, Mexico City, and Guadalajara. The Jews did know their coreligionists in other parts of the country and visited and communicated with them.

Confusion often arises when encountering the names of members of one family and noting the dissimilarity in the family name among parents and siblings. Among the peoples of New Spain, Jew or Gentile, many, if not the majority did not bear their fathers' patronymics. Most Christians who came, especially in the sixteenth century, wanted to be considered a *hidalgo*, descendant of nobility. The word hidalgo stems from *hijo de algo*, a son of someone—in this instance someone who was important. The word is similar to the title of English knighthood, Sir. The use of "de" in Spanish names is used to indicate such status. Since many of the early conquistadors and colonizers were not of noble lineage, a change of name facilitated the adoption of a fictitious ancestry. Many others adopted the names of illustrious or wealthy relatives if they lived in the vicinity.

It is not uncommon to find brothers who bore different family names. Very often children bore only their mother's maiden name. For similar and additional reasons, the Jews practiced the same customs. Many Jews entered Spanish New World colonies with forged passports or without any license. They often had to secrete their true identities, especially if other members of the family, past or present, had been pursued by the Inquisition Tribunals of Spain or Portugal.

The difficulty in tracing Jewish genealogies is further compounded by the same names being used by numerous people. For example, three persons bearing the name Francisco de Acosta lived in New Spain between 1620 and 1646. A people whose wits had been sharpened by adversity and constant pursuit and whose ingenuity in concealing their tracks and identity was great must have found expedient the practice of several people adopting identical names. Sometimes one person fifteen or twenty years younger than another used the name of the elder in the expectation of outliving the elder, whose death would be unpublicized; confusion of identity would act as a protective shield for the younger.

Thus we find records of two or more persons simultaneously bearing such names as Hector de Fonseca, Isabel de Campos, Gabriel Arias, Beatriz Enríquez, Juan López, Clara Henríquez, Manuel Días, and Manuel Rodríguez. The same patronymics existed in the Canary Islands, Peru, Holland, and other parts of the New World. In spite of popular opinion, Pérez, Méndez, or other names ending in "ez" were not distinctly Jewish. In New Spain the most common Jewish name was Rodríguez, but it was most common also for Christians, as was López, which ranked second among the Jews. Ironically, we also note that there were Jews named Juan Bautista and María de la Cruz (John Baptist and Mary of the Cross). Many family names were those of towns in Spain or Portugal.[13]

Poor and variable spelling causes much confusion. Isaac became Acach or Acaz; Mordecai changed to Mardofay, and Chasdai to Azday or Hizde. Differences in spelling proper names are to be noted among members of the same extended family. The Portuguese often substituted "s" for "z" and dropped many accents over the vowels.

Many Jews had a secret name among his coreligionists, not merely one such as "David ben [son of] Solomon," but often a complete name. Ferdinand de Medina was known among the Jews as

Alberto Moises Gómez, and Cohen was the secret patronymic for Antonio Váez Henríquez.

Others had secret first names but maintained the family names. *Licenciado* (Dr.) Manuel de Morales was known among the Jews as Abraham Morales, and Isabel Correa was known as Rebecca Correa. Those who had biblical first names usually made no change; hence Simón, Rafael, Daniel, etc. Some adopted new names after departure from Spanish colonies. Thomas Rodríguez Pereira changed his name to Abraham Israel Pereira after his arrival in Holland. He wrote *La Certez del Camino* and dedicated it to the God of Israel as an expiation of his previous sins in living as a Christian.

Jews also bore aliases. The Spanish consul in Amsterdam wrote to the Spanish ambassador in the Hague in the seventeenth century, "It is the custom of members of the nation [Jews] to take as many names as they please either for the sake of deceit or in order not to bear that name so as to jeopardize their parents who are known by that name in Spain."[14]

Manuel Belmonte was also known as Isaac Núñez; Juan Pacheo de León as Salomon Machorro; Nicholas Olivera y Fullana as Daniel Jehudra; Pedro López as Simón Fernández; and Thomas de Pinedo as Isaac de Pinedo. These names and aliases were garnered from the Inquisition records of those apprehended. Jorge Serrano adopted "de Alferez" from someone in Brazil. After escaping from a sentence to the galleys (he had been sentenced in Lima) he came to New Spain and adopted the name of Jorge de Espinosa. How many thousands of persons existed whose religious identity remains successfully hidden to this day must remain conjectural.

For Jews there was another cogent reason for not bearing the names of either of their parents. All those penanced by the Inquisition for *judaizante* or some variation of that charge, as well as other heretics, had his or her sanbenito hung on the walls of the Mexico City cathedral after completing the period during which it was to be worn. This practice was initiated in Mexico City in 1527. On each sanbenito was placed the name of the penitent, the date of his sentence, and the nature of his crime. When Pedro Moya de Contreras officially inaugurated the formal Tribunal of the Holy Office of the Inquisition in 1571, he found many garments on the walls. His attorney, Alonso Hernández de Bonilla, proceeded to make a permanent record, as complete as possible, of the earlier proceedings. Subsequently the space on the walls became inadequate and tabillas were substituted for the full garment. Children of penitents, at any rate, often had good reason to secrete their identity and ancestry.

Wives frequently and for various reasons didn't carry their husband's names; for example, Leonor Machado, daughter of the famous Antonio Machado, was married to Gonzalo Rodríguez de Molina, but she never bore his name.

The false involvement of non-Jews as Jews by perjured testimony and the testimony of Jews given under torture or duress while in the cells of the Inquisition have been the subject of debate among historians. There are some American Jewish historians who place little or no credence in the proceedings of the Inquisition trials, especially for the purpose of identifying Jews. Some of these skeptics are not able to paleograph or decipher Old Spanish and have not had recourse to original documents. On the other hand, authorities such as Henry C. Lea, Richard E. Greenleaf, I. S. Revah of the Colege de France, Haim Beinart of the Hebrew University of Jerusalem, and Pilar León Tello of the Archivo Historico Nacional in Madrid, to name but a few conversant with Inquisition documents, take an almost opposite position. They all believe that *procesos* (records of trial proceedings) should be read with caution and that not every charge of being a Jew or being a practitioner of Jewish rites need be true, but whenever the confessant enumerated his personal observance of Jewish practices, this can be fully accepted as proof. They also agree that whenever a report of a circumcized male appears, it was a fact.

Not all Jews charged with judaizing were examined by physicians to ascertain whether they had been circumcized. When the mark was observed by the examiners, the explanations subsequently given by some of the prisoners about this "Mark of the Covenant" ranged from ignorance of its existence to that offered by Juan Franco, a jeweler, in 1536. His case was initiated on the charge of sorcery. Franco stated that the operation of circumcision was performed by a barber in Puerto Rico "to alleviate the effects of veneral disease which he contracted from an Indian woman there."[15]

There was nothing to be gained by admitting to the Inquisition that one was a Jew if one were not. Every person knew that the fate of being a Jew was not ameliorated by confession except that early full confession removed the sentence of the stake.

Spanish Catholics knew little about their own faith, and yet some writers would impute to them a knowledge of Judaism. A non-Jew conceivably might admit under torture that he was a Jew, but the inquisitors required more than a personal confession. If one admitted being a Jew he had to name other Jews in the community and list their religious observances. A non-Jew could not do this.

The question of the amount of credibility to be given to the Inquisition prisoner's own testimony must have been presented more than one hundred years ago to General Vicente Riva Palacio. This erudite historian wrote:

> . . . but in these causes, it is clearly evident that the accused observed the Law of Moses; the declarations of the prisoners, their accomplices and of the witnesses, the written documents and the books added to the *procesos* demonstrate that these people knew and observed the laws and ceremonies of the Jews [judíos]; and in no other manner can one understand how they were able to give such detailed and exact explanations of the fasts, the ablutions, the observance of the Sabbath, and of the Psalms and of the prayers that they recited, because regardless of the greatest torture to which you can subject a man or woman, he or she could not give information of rites and ceremonies of a faith of which he has no knowledge. The similar phraseology of the accused in their confessions, for the historian, is proof of their familiarity with the Mosaic religion.[16]

Haim Beinart, in his excellent article "The Records of the Inquisition as a Source of Jewish and Converso History," stated: "Drawing aside the veil of Christianity that the Conversos were forced to don, we find them living a real Jewish life. From the words of the witnesses a picture emerges whose reliability cannot be doubted, confirming that the compulsion imposed on the Conversos by the Christian world in Spain, and afterwards in Portugal, could not stifle the longing of the faithful to live as Jews."

Perjury was one of the most serious charges made by the Inquisition because it was an attempt to deceive the Holy Office. Servitude in the galleons was the normal punishment for perjurers. Few dared claim to be Jews if this were not the truth.

The usual charge that appears on the flyleaves of the sixteenth century and early seventeenth century procesos involving those considered as Jews was "judaizante." This is usually defined as one who practices Jewish rites. A study of the procesos reveals that in New Spain the word was synonymous with Jew, as evidenced by the fact that the words judío and judaizante were used interchangeably by the Inquisition with respect to the same individual.

The absence of extended discussion on the Jewish cultural life as distinguished from the religious aspects of their lives should not indicate that it has been overlooked or is completely nonexistent. Other than the half dozen books written in Spanish mentioned later in connection with specific people, there were in the seventeenth century only two books in Hebrew which were popular and in use. The first was the Vatable Bible, edited by Francisco Vatable, a professor of Hebrew at the Royal College of France, and published by Robert Etienne in 1545. It had a Hebrew text based on the Vulgate Bible and that of León of Judah.

The second book is important because it is the first Hebrew grammar written in the New World. Compiled by a monk, the first edition was printed in Spain; a later edition was printed in New Spain in 1676. The explanatory portions were in Latin, and most of the exercises were taken from the New Testament. A few Jews found it useful in teaching Hebrew to their children, especially since it was a safe book to own.

José de J. Nuñez y Dominguez, in his article "Los Judios en la Historia y Literatura Mexicanas," discusses at great length the numerous Mexican authors who used the Jews in New Spain as their theme, as their leading characters, or treated their faith as an important topic. He wrote that "in almost all classes of histories of Mexico, references to Jews are made. This evidences that they were so important that they gave inspiration to the pens of renowned intellectuals so that their deeds passed to posterity."[17]

The relationships between most Christians and the Jews in New Spain were friendly. The number of those delating against Jews was insignificant, although many knew the religious identity of their Jewish neighbors. As a result, the efforts of the Church to create an anti-Jewish popular feeling were not too successful.

The sources consulted in the preparation of this work included the original documents of the branch of the Spanish Inquisition that operated in New Spain. The techniques and procedures used by this institution are not generally known and, since they play an important role in the history of the colonial period, they warrant explanation. Also, when a foreign language is integral to a field of study, terms and spelling frequently need clarification.

Cognates can create confusion. Two examples leap to mind. In the area of general Mexican colonial history, and particularly in the history of the Jews in the colonial era, the word "alias" is found in the report of almost every individual mentioned in this book. In Old Spanish, "alias" meant "formerly known as." It is in this sense that it is herein used.

The second example is the use of the word "relaxed." The Spanish verb "relejar" is translated in English as "to relax." However, in the colonial period in the New World, the Spanish verb also meant "to deliver a capital offender from an ecclesiastical court [the Inquisition] to the secular criminal tribunal." There is no single English word that describes this action. Since the Church did not want the guilt of "effusion of blood" on its hands, when Inquisition officials decided that a prisoner should go to the stake, the prisoner was relaxed—turned over—to the secular royal authorities, who executed the final sentence.

Spelling presents another problem. The amanuenses of the Inquisition Tribunals devised their own forms of shorthand reporting. The Inquisition trial proceedings, or procesos, are, in the main, verbatim reports of examination by the question and answer method. The abbreviations used by the amanuenses became systematized by the 1600's. Spelling, however, was not consistent; "b" and "v" were used interchangeably and such spellings as Thomas instead of Tomas actually appear in the original documents. Sometimes accent marks appear and sometimes they are absent.

The transliteration of Hebrew words as spoken by the Jewish prisoners and as written down by the Inquisition secretaries makes it difficult at times to ascertain what these words were. The difficulty is compounded by the fact that by the late seventeenth and eighteenth centuries many Hebrew words were mispronounced by the prisoners themselves or had been jargonized by the Jews in New Spain.

We have followed the American usage for the word auto-da-fé, which is variously written as auto-de-fé, auto da fe, etc., by the Spanish, Portuguese, and French.

In Mexico, an Inquisition sentence condemning one to life imprisonment rarely meant that the sentence would be carried out,

even when the words "without pardon" were appended to the judgment, since the Suprema in Spain could commute the sentence. The
jailer had to be reimbursed for feeding prisoners who were incarcerated in the cells, and since the prisoner's funds and property were
sequestered by the inquisitors such funds were used for this purpose
as well as being absorbed by the Holy Office. It was expedient,
therefore, to shorten some sentences. In practice, "life imprisonment" usually resulted in incarceration for periods from three to six
years. Sentences shorter than life imprisonment usually meant confinement elsewhere than prison.

A glossary has been appended to facilitate an understanding of
numerous references in the text with which some readers may not be
familiar. Publication data are not given in the notes but are included
in the bibliography. Material in the author's *Guide to Jewish References in the Mexican Colonial Era: 1521-1821* is complementary and,
while not indispensable to understanding this history, may be of
help to those who wish to pursue studies in this field.

Appendix A contains translations of the summarizing accounts of
seventeenth century autos-da-fé and notes on the persons involved.
Except for the procesos, these accounts constituted a major source
of information for the author. After 1600 each auto-da-fé had an
official historian, always a monk and usually a Jesuit. The account of
each auto was called a *relación* and was usually printed. The antipathy to Judaism and the biases of the narrators are often evident in
the relaciónes.

1

Departure from Spain

AUGUST, 1492, is the momentous month that changed the history of the Jews, of Spain, and of the world. Christopher Columbus set sail for the unknown West, the kingdoms of Castile and Aragon began the final steps to unify under one monarchy all the kingdoms of the Iberian Peninsula except Portugal, and the Jews were expelled from Spain. The combination of these events marked the beginning of Spain's meteoric rise as a world empire and foreshadowed its ultimate reduction to a second or third rate power.[1]

Columbus sailed from Palos, Andalusia, on August third, with three ships manned by a total company of about ninety, among whom were at least six Jews. One of these had recently converted to Catholicism. Others in the crew may also have been Jewish or of Jewish parentage. Strangely enough, in a time when no venture was undertaken without the presence of a representative of the Church, no monk or priest sailed with Columbus on his first voyage.

On August second, the day before Columbus' caravels weighed anchor, many other ships had sailed eastward, rather than toward the west, from Cádiz, a port almost adjacent to Palos. The passengers of these ships numbered in the thousands. They were not seeking any new routes to India. Their glances were turned landward. Their reluctant departure was marked by sobbing, wailing, and the murmuring of prayers. They were filled with consternation and doubt as to what the future held in store for them.

These were the Jews whose last hope of remaining in the land of their birth had been extinguished. Their sorrow was intensified because their departure fell on *Tisha B'ab* (the ninth day of the Hebrew month of Ab), the traditional day of fasting to commemorate the destruction of the First and Second Temples in 586 B.C.E and 70 C.E., respectively. It had always been a day of ill omen for Jews. Now, because of the Decree of Expulsion of March 31, giving them only four months to leave, they were finally being forced from their native land.

Many Jews had already left Spain. The total number expelled is variously estimated from 200,000 to 800,000 persons. A few historians give figures in excess of a million, but these approach incredibility.[2] Father Mariana, a Jesuit, stated:

> The number of Jews that quitted Castile is not known; most authors say they amounted to 160,000 families, and some say they amounted to 800,000 souls; undoubtedly an immense multitude. This induced many persons to condemn the resolution adopted by ... Ferdinand in expelling so profitable and opulent a people, acquainted with every mode of collecting wealth.[3]

Moreover, 12,000 families went to Navarre, where King Juan Labrit ordered his frontier commander to admit any Jews expelled from Castile and Aragon and to afford them safe transit and every possible accomodation because he termed the Jews a docile people who could easily be brought to reason.[4] Pope Alexander VI offered them asylum in the papal dominions and subsequently wrote to all the Italian states to grant the exiles of Spain and Portugal the same privileges as resident Jews enjoyed.

Those who boarded the ships in Cádiz with the pitifully small bundles of their remaining possessions had awaited the proverbial eleventh hour, hoping that gold and silver might accomplish what pleas to reason, justice, and humaneness had not been able to achieve. Their Catholic majesties, Isabella of Castile and Ferdinand of Aragon, were known to have yielded to the sound of ducats and maravedis in the past. As late as 1491, Ferdinand and Isabella had permitted the Jews of Zamora to pay for the privilege of complaining against Dominican attacks.[5]

Heinrich Graetz related how two Jews, Isaac Abravanel[6] and

Abraham Senior, hoped to persuade Isabella and Ferdinand to change their Decree of Expulsion. Isaac was a pious and learned Jew, and he and Senior had served their rulers as late as 1488 in important fiscal matters. Abravanel counted among the Christian nobility many friends who were prepared to second his plea for a revocation of the decree. Ferdinand was on the verge of accepting when Tomás de Torquemada, the Inquisitor General and confessor to the queen, interjected himself. He raised a crucifix aloft and cried, "Judas Iscariot sold Christ for thirty pieces of silver, your highnesses are about to sell Him for 300,000 ducats. Here He is, take Him and sell Him."[7]

The Decree of Expulsion was signed at Granada. The Jews could take neither gold, silver, money, nor such forbidden items of export as jewelry and articles containing jewels. They sold vineyards for bolts of cloth and their houses and lands for asses to carry their remaining possessions to some boundary or port.

The Decree of Expulsion is interesting not only for what it says but for what was left unsaid. The main charge against Jews was that "there were some bad Christians [converted Jews] who Judaized and apostatized from our Holy Catholic faith. . . ." and that many had become Christians but had maintained relations with the stubborn (unconverted) Jews who had continued to practice Jewish customs. For a century, many false charges and accusations had been made against the Jews and their faith. None of these charges were repeated in the command to leave or be baptized.

The vessels carrying the exiles sailed east to Italy, Turkey, and North Africa. They were carrying those who had not been among the fortunate 100,000 permitted to enter Portugal and remain there for eight months after July, 1492 (at an exorbitant price exacted by King John II), or those who sought safety in the neighboring kingdom of Navarre or in Provence.

Many Jews remained in Spain but they were no longer called Jews—they had embraced Christianity. They, and those who preceded them to conversion, numbered a million or more. Many had voluntarily embraced the daughter faith of Judaism and had become sincere Christians. Some had been forced into conversion by fear or violence. Others chose this alternative to leaving and intended to observe Judaism secretly. They were called *hebreo-cristianos* (Hebrew Christians), *nuevo cristianos* (New Christians), *conversos* (converts), and, later, *marranos* (swine).

Those who left by ship, refusing to abandon their faith, were truly *am shay choreff* (a stiff-necked people), a biblical term applied many times to the Jews. They were leaving the land that they loved as passionately as did any Christian Spaniard. They were leaving a country that their forefathers had inhabited for almost two millenia; the graves of their fathers and grandfathers were embedded in its soil. They had enriched Spain materially and culturally. and, as a group, were more responsible than any other for the fact that Spain was on the verge of being the greatest sixteenth-century empire. The Hebrews of Segovia, prior to abandoning their homes, spent three days in the cemetery "watering with their tears the ashes of their fathers."[8]

Little did they realize that Columbus' ships were pointing in the direction that many of them would subsequently follow—and that their children and children's children would pursue in their search for surcease from persecution—to a land in which they could speak their mother tongue, Spanish. These people and their descendants were destined to be the first permanent Jewish residents on the North American continent. They were to create the first Jewish community in New Spain. Some were fated to be the forefathers of Jewish martyrs who were sought out by the Inquisition in the New World and who experienced there the licking flames of the stake.

The Jew had been subjected to persecution in different parts of Iberia intermittently over hundreds of years prior to 1492. In spite of this he had a deep attachment to the culture, language, and soil of what is now Spain. What was his character, what were his customs, and why was he what he was? The early New World Jews are inexplicable if we do not understand their ancestors, the Spanish or Hispanic or Iberian Jews.

Spain became a nation between 1475 and 1516. Gregorio Marañon describes the Spanish Empire of 1556 as follows:

Phillip II began to govern his vast Empire which was not old, not favorable, not united; one of the Italian Ambassadors, Suriano, wrote that the King of Spain has many kingdoms but they are distinct or apart from each other, while the King of France has only one kingdom which is obedient to him. The subjects of the King of Spain are richer . . . but those of the King of France are more disposed to serve their Monarch.[9]

The attachment of the Jews to their soil is best illustrated by a quotation from Yitzhak (Fritz) Baer's *Die Juden im Christlichen Spanien* taken from the trial of Francisco de Cáceres before the Inquisition in Spain shortly after 1500. Cáceres had left Spain and then, like many others, outwardly accepted Christianity and returned to his native land. He was arrested for still practicing Jewish rites and was asked why he had returned contrary to law. His reply was:

> If the king, our lord, should order the Christians to become Jews or else to leave his realm, some would become Jews and others would leave; and those who left, as soon as they saw their sad plight, would become Jews so they could return to their native place, and they would be Christians and pray like Christians and deceive the world; in their hearts and wills, they would be Christians.[10]

The attachment of the Jews to their native land was in part evidenced by their continued use of their mother tongue; this became a heritage passed on from father to sons who never knew Spain through personal experience. Salvador de Madariaga expressed it well: "Wherever they went they founded Spanish or Portuguese colonies . . . The Spanish or Portuguese Jews spoke the languages of their native countries . . . with purity, took part in literature, and even when conferring with Christians could do so on equal terms with manliness and without fear or servility."[11]

Américo Castro wrote that the history of non-Hispanic Europe could be written without assigning the Jews any position of prominence, but not so with Spain because, for its five most decisive centuries, Spanish history was Christian-Islamic-Judaic. He termed the Judaic portion "The Supremacy of the Despised."

Jews may have inhabited the Iberian Peninsula since the time of King Solomon. Isaac Abravanel in his commentaries on Zechariah stated that ancestors of his and another family had resided in Seville during the time of the Second Temple. He contended that the charge of deicide could not be leveled at Iberian Jewry because of their residence in Spain, weeks of travel from the scene of the crucifixion. He pleaded to no avail. Others place the Jews there at the time of the Babylonian conquest in 596 B.C.E. Elias Haim Lindo wrote that after the defeat of Bar Kochba's revolt in 135 C.E. a large number of Hebrew prisoners were transported from Judea, "some say as many as 50,000 families, thus greatly increasing the Hebrew population of those Roman provinces."[12]

When conversions were induced by physical fear or the fear of the loss of children or for economic expediency, especially between 1391 and 1492, the Church naïvely accepted the act of conversion and ignored the background of the new convert.

The Jew was no uncivilized person or illiterate, as were so many other converts taken from the ranks of pagans and Moors. The Jew stemmed from a people who had decreed universal, free, and compulsory education. Since they had a background of learning and a veneration of education and the Scriptures, the Church should have made an effort to bring the converts wholeheartedly and intelligently into its midst. To the medieval Church, however, the quantity of converts was more significant than the quality of their knowledge. The failure of the Church to educate, rather than indoctrinate by coercion, was its undoing in making true Christians of many Jewish converts. As Cecil Roth put it, "baptism had done little more than to convert a considerable portion of Jews from infidels outside the Church to heretics inside it."[13]

A brief summary of events, decrees, and actions taken by the Christian rulers of the various Hispanic kingdoms concerning their Jewish subjects prior to 1492 will illustrate the highlights of the crescendo in religious persecution and show that it ranged over much but not all of the peninsula. In no one place were the uprisings against the Jews continuous or of long duration; persecution was sporadic and shifted from place to place. For these reasons the Jews began to be inured to the conduct and threat against them and against their faith.

During the period from the eighth to the eleventh century, it was primarily Judaism that was the object of attack rather than the individual Jew. From 1096 to 1391, the attackers were as often as not non-Spaniards. It was only in 1391 that the game of "Jew hunting" and "Jew baiting" began to be played in deadly earnest by the clergy and members of the Spanish Church.

The Jew had learned to wait out the early storms. At the outset, barring his doors was sufficient to stave off the marauders. Later, walls and gates encircled the *juderías*, the Jewish ghettos, and served as a communal defense. That the situation was deteriorating with the passing of time was not realized by the Spanish Jew. He assumed an impassivity, an inner nonvulnerability to threats and sporadic assaults. His insensibility or apathy to the gathering storm clouds was predicated upon the illusion that "it can't happen to me." He or his forebears had managed to escape or elude the wrath of those incited to hate by religious zeal. He had acquired a mental immunization to the venom that was being dispensed with the intention of destroying him. The Jew left no explanation of why he failed to take early preventive measures or to leave his homeland voluntarily while he could still take his possessions with him.

The sequence of events that culminated in the decree of 1492 also reveals the pattern of what Gordon W. Allport labeled "Rejection of Out-Groups." Allport states that "violence is always an outgrowth of milder states of mind" and traces the progression: "antilocution → discrimination → physical violence."[14] He asserts that the outbreak of violence has been prepared by certain steps which begin by "categorical prejudgment" with the victim group being typed. Verbal complaints follow, suspicion and blame become ingrained, and often discrimination is then enacted into statutes.

By the time of the last step, the in-group must have been exposed to economic privation, a sense of low status, and political unrest due to national or international developments. This leads to emotionalism, a sense of futility, and inner strains that require a catharsis and a desire to erupt and flail out recklessly, especially against minorities. The people are now prepared to succumb to mob hysteria. Impulses to violence are therefore justified by the standards of the group. The "normal brakes" between verbal agression and physical violence are removed. This classical progression outlined by Allport is limned most clearly by the sequence of events in Spain.

King Recarred, upon succeeding to the Visigothic throne (586-601), pledged adherence to the Nicene Creed and made Catholic orthodoxy supreme. At the Council of Toledo, May 25, 627, the bishops pronounced an anathema upon those who failed to accept the Nicene Creed. It prohibited Jews from having Christian wives, concubines, or slaves. Yaacov Vainstein suggests that the Kol Nidre prayer inaugurating Yom Kippur, the most awesome day of the year for Jews, was composed during the reign of King Recarred because of his persecution of his Jewish subjects.[15]

During the reign of King Sisebut, the *Feuro Juzgo* (Visigothic Code) was proclaimed in 612. This law heralded an era of persecution that culminated 880 years later in the expulsion of 1492. The

Fuero Juzgo marked the first Decree of Expulsion. It provided that within one year any Jew who had not been baptized or had not had his children and slaves baptized should be stripped, receive 100 lashes, forfeit his property to the king, and be exiled. Death was decreed for observing the Passover, the Sabbath, and other Jewish holy days. Circumcision and *kashrut* (the ritual preparation and eating of permitted foods as outlined in the Bible) were prohibited. Eating pork was made mandatory.

After the tenth century, commerce and agriculture were carried on for the Castilians either by their slaves or by Jews or Moors. War was the preoccupation of the Castilian.[16] Labor became a sign of the inferior races and was beneath the dignity of the Spanish freeman. This attitude was reflected in the New World in the sixteenth century. Hernán Cortés, the conqueror of Mexico, said, when offered a liberal grant of land on which to settle, "I came to get gold, not to till the soil like a peasant."[17]

From the tenth to the fourteenth century, a brand of Catholicism developed in Spain that assumed different hues from that of Rome. It has been said that Spanish Catholics after the twelfth century outdid the papacy in their Catholicity. Because of the difference, we shall refer to the Roman Church as an entity separate from the Spanish Church. The latter gave lip service to the Bishop of Rome and sought his intercession, but followed his edicts, bulls, braves, etc., only when it so pleased the clergy and the various monarchs. The Church in the New World during the colonial period was a replica of the Spanish Church.

The renewal in the thirteenth century of the earlier Fuero Juzgo and the creation of other laws were attempts to segregate Jews from the general community. The ruling classes wanted to divert to the Jews the animosities which the serfs, slaves, and peasant class felt under the new feudal system. For centuries, the Jew had been painted as a witch, sorcerer, heretic, and an associate of Lucifer and all demons; as a person of foul odor that could never be washed away; as a poisoner of wells and streams; as a defiler of the Host and one who required the blood of Christians (especially children) for the making of *matzot* (unleavened bread) and for magic potions of all kinds. These charges were all repeated in New Spain in the seventeenth century.

Some of the reasons why the hundreds of thousands of Jews had not left the Iberian Peninsula prior to 1492 have been mentioned. Many thousands of Jews did leave after 1391. They joined Jewish colonies in the Maghreb (North Africa), Salonica, and other places in the Ottoman Empire.

Many of the wealthy who had not departed regarded themselves as indispensable. They were tax-farmers, agents for the nobility, and served in various commercial roles. The Jew failed to comprehend the alignment of the crowns and the masses against the marquis, dukes, and other feudal lords. The Spanish rulers of Castile and Aragon were determined to absorb all other kingdoms and then to invest themselves with all the rights of absolute monarchs.

The persecutions and pograms of 1391 and 1412 incited and led by Fernan Martínez and Fray Vincent Ferrer respectively were the fruit of religious intolerance that had been on the increase for centuries. Vulgar prejudice and the constant preaching by the clergy had passed all bounds of human and religious dignity. Benefitting by hindsight, it is easy to see that the Jews should have known that their days in Spain were numbered.

The establishment of the Holy Office of the Inquisition by the bull of Pope Sixtus IV on November 1, 1479, and the appointments of inquisitors on September 17, 1480, and February 11, 1492 (Tomás de Torquemada was in this group) should have indicated to all non-Catholics that events of great portent were to occur. The activities of the inquisitors between 1482 and 1491 were extensive and significant. Thousands of crypto-Jews were burned at the stake. The smoke of the burned flesh lay as a pall over the land and the stench pervaded the nostrils of many Catholics who protested to the crown and the pope—but in vain.

Again, with hindsight, it can be seen that Torquemada and his associates had to find a scapegoat. They required excuses for their failure to achieve religious unity in Spain. The Jew, as ever, was available. They reasoned that the expulsion of Jews would remove a strange faith and a people who attempted to prevent apostasy and who even swayed many converts back to Judaism.

The failure of the Jews and their leaders to realize the ultimate purpose of Torquemada and their misplaced confidence in the power to bribe Church and secular officialdom gave them a sense of security. They took no steps to avert what should have appeared to be inevitable. The Decree of Expulsion was tragic for Jewry but was no less a tragedy for those whose acts, now termed bigotry, were considered blessed zeal for their faith in 1492. In any monolithic structure or institution, a weakness or defect in any one area or place results in the maladjustment of the whole.

2

Prelude to New Spain

ALTHOUGH COLUMBUS made his momentous discovery of the New World on October 12, 1492, this fact did not become known to the Old World until his return to Spain in 1493. Despite the slow means of communication and the difficulties involved in the financing and staffing, and the hazards of such journeys, the ensuing five years saw ships from Europe making frequent voyages to the islands of Hispaniola and Cuba.

The intrepid Spaniards, undaunted by the massacre of Columbus' first settlement, were inspired by romantic tales of fortune awaiting them. Brigantines and caravels brought newcomers by the tens, twenties, thirties, and more. There were no women or children with the conquerors. Women constituted but ten percent of those who came during the next quarter of a century. So great was the dearth of Spanish women for wives that polyandry may have existed. During the period from 1536 to 1569, eighteen Spanish women were charged with bigamy by Church officials who acted as inquisitors. We know of one, Ana Hernández, who had four husbands.[1] Native women served as servants and bedmates for the conquistadors, and interracial unions were frequent because of this shortage of females among the immigrants.[2]

New settlements and cities were small. The total number of Spanish immigrants to the New World is estimated at 300,000 for the colonial period of three hundred years. This does not include Negro slaves from Africa and Oriental slaves from Japan and the Philippines.[3]

Jews were present in the New World even during the early periods of settlement. They came in spite of all obstacles and under false identities. Many of the Jews went to Hispaniola, which was settled first because the discovery of gold had been made there. It was the seat of the first Spanish governor in the Indies; Cuba was developed a little later.

> From the discovery of America the right to emigrate to the New World was reserved, except for a short interval under the emperor Charles V [1516-1556], to peninsular Catholic Spaniards! . . . The preparation of forged licenses became a profession in itself, and when punishment was made more severe the principal effect was to increase the price of these papers and develop the ingenuity of brokers and buyers. Unlicensed Spaniards [Jews and Moors] as well as foreigners got over secretly . . . Jews, Moors and heretics were from the very beginning—from the days of Christopher Columbus—excluded from the New World . . . [Jews slipped through] and managed to live unmolested in loosely organized communities.[4]

The actual number of Jews who came remains unknown. Some of the few figures available concerning the total white population show that in 1545 there were 1,385 Spanish settlers in Mexico.[5] Ricardo Albanes wrote that the Marquis of Guadalcazar made an investigation of the Jewish population and found that in the middle of the sixteenth century there were three hundred Jews in Mexico City and its environs.[6] This high number (almost twenty-five percent) should not be surprising and is corroborated by other sources. From Francisco Fernandez del Castillo we learn that in the 1550's in the Spanish colony in Mexico City there were more Jews than Catholics and there was a Grand Rabbi.[7]

Many Jews attempted to disguise their identity as non-Catholics. A Lutheran (the generic term for Protestants in New Spain in the sixteenth century) could be admitted to reconciliation quite rapidly unless he were an Englishman caught on a pirating expedition. The non-English, nonpolitical Lutheran was not subjected, as were the Jews, to the pressure of revealing the identity of other heretics, and their punishment was generally not as severe as that meted out to Jews.

Another obstacle in ascertaining the number of Jews is that the indices and flyleaves of the Inquisition documents do not always reveal that those apprehended were Jews. Many were arrested for blasphemy or for belonging to the sect of *Alumbrados,* and these charges appear in the index and flyleaves.[8] During the course of a trial, the charges may have been changed to being Jews or practitioners of Jewish rites. The Index of the Mexican National Archives lists the case of Francisco de Tejera, charged with blasphemy. He was a Portuguese Jew arrested in Toluca in 1560 for blasphemy and for spitting on a cross. It was only by reading the whole proceso that the information that he was a Jew was obtained. To gain a more accurate estimate of the number of Jews arrested by inquisitors from 1527 to 1800 would require study of each proceso in the 1,553 volumes in the Inquisition Section of the Mexican National Archives. Even these volumes do not contain all the *expedientes* (files), procesos, and data of the Inquisition. Many other documents have been located in other countries, many are still in the possession of private persons, and many have been inadvertently destroyed by fire.

In the Inquisition records many Jews were simply called Portuguese, as the terms Portuguese and Jewish were sometimes synonymous. Many of the itinerant friars were not learned and were so intent on converting the Indians or indulging their own physical appetites that they overlooked the presence of Jews.[9] Also, many of the leading clergy were descendants of Jews and may have been touched by a mercy unknown to other Christian colleagues in not revealing the Jews' presence.

Jews came to New Spain from many places: Leghorn, Pisa, Ferrara, Dublin, Salonica, Bordeaux, Rouen, and Amsterdam. I. S. Emmanuel reports that navigation and sailing were the principal occupations of the Jews of Curaçao in the seventeenth century.[10] Some of them traded or settled in Mexico. Portugal used to punish its Jews in the 1500's by exiling them to Brazil or the newly discovered West Indian islands.[11] Many of these people also came to Mexico. Many traveled from the east coast of South America (from Brazil or Argentina) to Chile and Peru and then migrated to New Spain.[12] Mexico City appeared to have been the goal of many who lived in other parts of the New World.

After 1580, there was a veritable exodus of Jews to New Spain

Tomás de Torquemada, first Inquisitor General

from the Iberian Peninsula, especially Portugal.[13] Long before that
time, however, Jews already had been arriving from many ports
along the coasts of Portugal and northern Spain. In 1529, Charles V
permitted ships to sail directly to the Americas from Coruña, Bay-
ona, Aviles, Laredo, Bilbao, San Sebastian, Barcelona, and Malaga in
order to encourage emigration and trade.[14] This condition continued until December, 1573.

In addition to the relaxation of the rule that all vessels had to have licenses from Spain's governmental bureau in charge of international commerce, the Casa de la Contratación in Seville, municipal authorities in many places were lax in enforcing regulations about departure and entry of vessels. These ships carried forbidden passengers and goods. Even after 1573, there were illicit sailings from northern ports.[15] The Mexican historian Alfonso Toro wrote, "As the Jew and Judaizers were numerous among the colonizers of New Spain, the scarcity of the records [pertaining to Jews in mid-sixteenth century procesos] is no doubt due to the ignorance of the judges more than anything else."[16]

Major studies have been and are still being pursued on the immigration to the New World during the sixteenth, seventeenth, and eighteenth centuries. Juan Friede has illustrated the difficulties, if not impossibilities, of compiling any list that represents a major portion of the immigrants. He cited clandestine emigration, which, judging by all indications, was very appreciable, and indicated that there was well-founded suspicion that whole shiploads of these clandestine emigrants went to America under the guise of soldiers, sailors, and servants. These last three categories required no licenses or exit visas. Friede estimated that the three-volume *Catálogo de pasajeros a Indias* represents only fifteen percent of the "total number of passengers who traveled . . . in the first half of the sixteenth century."[17] Vicente Riva Palacio stated, "The number of Jews in New Spain must have been very great because in spite of the great precautions which were taken to hide their religion and of their making boasts of their Catholicism, many families fell into the power of the Holy Office."[18]

The absence of authoritative statistics plagues not only the historian seeking precise data on Jewry but also on general demography in the New World during the colonial period. We can only estimate such numbers. By the end of the sixteenth century, the Inquisition became a detested institution in the New World and the inquisitors the objects of scorn and hatred. In 1581, Peruvian bishops dared to write to Spain that they disrespected *(desairasen)* the Inquisition.

The Mexican Fernando Benítez notes the sharp differences of character and outlook that divided the peninsular Spaniard in the New World from the American-born, the criollo. This was evidenced by the "markedly changed attitudes and psychology of the conquistadors and their immediate descendants."[19] The American-born Spaniards expressed feelings and resentments against the mother country. It may be said that they did not love the Jews more but that they loved Spain and all it represented less.

Accounts of chaos and near anarchy that reigned in the New World and existed in the Spanish administration of colonial affairs, especially prior to 1535, constitute reams of pages in histories and need not be repeated here. The brutality of many of the conquistadors, early colonizers, and some of the military rulers and provincial administrators (such as Pedro de Alvarado and Nuño de Guzman) cause revulsion. The desecration of the sacraments of Catholicism by many of its ordained priests, monks, and disciples constitutes black pages in Church history. R. de Lafuente Machain conservatively states that "they were very distant from models of religiosity and of morals."[20] Cecil Roth aptly wrote, "As one reads the pages of Jewish history, one wonders more and more how it was possible that it was the Jews, not their oppressors, who are legendarily considered to be actuated by sordid motives."[21]

Spanish colonial policy in general was on an *ad hoc* basis. It was contrived, without foresight, to meet exigencies.

> It was dictated by two utterly conflicting interests . . . the ecclesiastical and the economic. Add to this this primary reason . . . the fact that Spain drifted into the colonizing business with no adequate machinery of government, under a rigid and cumbersome absolutism, complicated by the interference of favorites and the readiness of every despot to give ear to all tale-bearers, the wonder is that anything constructive was ever accomplished . . . The island [Hispaniola] race perished because they could not support the burden of the harsh and parasite class imposed upon them.[22]

The prohibition against the entry of Jews into the New World appears in many decrees. On September 16, 1501, Ferdinand and Isabella instructed Fray Nicolas de Ovando that "Moors, Jews, heretics, reconciliados, and New Christians are not to be allowed to go to the Indies [the Caribbean islands]." On September 15, 1522, Emperor Charles V decreed in Valladolid that "recent Jewish converts" were to be prohibited from going to the Indies. The first edict specifically barring heretics and Jews from going to New Spain was in 1523.[23] This was later included in the Law of the Indies (*Ley 15, titulo XXVI* of Book IX). Similar decrees were issued periodically

thereafter for almost three hundred years. The last one was that of
September 16, 1802, in Mexico.

In spite of all these decrees and all the efforts of the Inquisition,
as J. Horace Nunemaker wrote:

". . . thumbing through all the lists are the ever recurring cases of
the Jews, whose presence in America seemed almost a mystery to
the Ministry of the Indies in Spain . . . The Inquisition tracked
them down in whole families, member by member, but could
never seem to wipe them out or convert them all.[24]

The Bishop of Puerto Rico complained in a letter of November
26, 1506, about Portuguese ships coming with merchants, "mostly
Hebrews." In 1510, the Bishop of Cuba complained that every boat
from Spain was bringing Jews, New Christians, and heretics.

Hispaniola ran dry of both gold and Indian slaves, and Cuba then
became the center of settlement. Some conquistadors established
farms and haciendas. Cities began to spring up all over the island.
The traffic in slaves—Negro and Indian—grew rapidly, and some
Jews were engaged in this trade as agents for the royal families of
Spain and Portugal.

Fray Bernardo Buil, a prelate of the Dominican order, arrived in
Cuba at the end of 1493 with inquisitorial powers under special au-
thorization. Little is known of his early activities as an inquisitor. It
is likely that he was occupied primarily in conversions and upholding the faith. This was the pattern adopted by the friars in New
Spain for the entire colonial period. The denunciations of the Jews
to the Inquisition by monks, regardless whether Franciscan, Jesuit,
or Carmelite, were few. They were devoted to the salvation of Indian souls, the repression of Indian reversion to paganism, and the
performance of sacraments. They and the secular clergy were battling each other even as the various orders were battling among
themselves.

The lack of reporting the presence of Jews by the clergy, regular or secular, was offset by paid spies of the Inquisition and the
Spanish debtors of Jews who knew that a speedy way of disposing
of a persistent creditor was to report him to inquisitors. In addition,
there were always a few religious zealots. In 1508, the proctors who
were sent to Spain to represent the colonists before the court and

the king's councilors complained that "the natives were being cor-
rupted by their [the Jews'] teachings."[25]

It is interesting to speculate why the Jews should have risked discovery by imparting the Mosaic laws to the Indians. These lessons
were taught on innumerable instances. The first theory is that it was
a matter of self-defense. The first Indian disciples very likely were
slaves owned by the Jews. The Indian, who would detect the Jew
in non-Christian religious rites, might have been prompted to report
the oddities to others, including members of the clergy. By estab-
lishing a bond of religious fraternity, sealed with drops of blood
pricked from fingers, the Jew may have hoped to seal the lips of the
Indian. Blood was of great religious significance to the Aztecs in
particular.

A second hypothesis is that the crypto-Jews may have thought
that teaching Jewish principles to Indians would create a feeling of
resentment in them against Christian masters. The lessons consisted
primarily of ridiculing Jesus as the Messiah since he was born the
son of a carpenter and a poor girl and was crucified. This concept
contrasted with the Indians' remembrance of the colorful and be-
jewelled raiment and exalted status of their priests, who served also
as the embodiment of gods. Quetzalcoatl was a high priest and god
at Tula. The Indians' pagan purgatory was of four years duration
and was without fire and brimstone. To accept Christ was to accept
concepts of hell and damnation. The Jews also taught that a slave,
while yet a slave, had to be treated more kindly than many Christians treated their slaves. The Jews also preached that the Law of
Moses was better than that of Christ.

Some writers have stated that the Inquisition did not take jurisdiction over nonbaptized Jews and that such action was barred by
the rules of the Holy Office. These authors have overlooked the Inquisition rule:

> Although Jews, Idolaters, Mohammedans, and Infidels of other
> Sects are not ordinarily subject to the judgment of the Holy In-
> quisition, in many cases which are also expressed in the Bulls of
> the Supreme Pontiffs, they may be punished by the Holy Office.
>   The Jews, if they were to deny those things of the Faith which
> are common to them and to us Christians, as that God is one,
> eternal, omnipotent, Creator of the Universe, and others of the
> same kind:

If they were to invoke or consult devils, or do sacrifice to them or offer incense, or make prayer, or perform any other act of reverence to them for any purpose whatever, and if they should teach and induce others to do the like:

If they were impiously to say that our Saviour Jesus Christ were a mere man, or a sinner, and that His most Holy Mother was not a Virgin, or any like blasphemy:

If by any means they were to induce a Christian to deny the Holy Faith:

If they were to prevent any Hebrew, or any other Infidel who wished to become a Christian, or were to advise or induce him not to do so:

If they were to possess, conceal, or suffer to be seen Talmudic or other condemned or prohibited Jewish books or prohibited Christian books, or magical writings, and other books of writings tacitly or expressly containing heresies or errors against the Sacred Scripture of the Old Testament, or contumelies, impieties, blasphemies against God, the most Holy Trinity, Our Saviour, the Christian Faith, the most blessed Virgin Mary, the Angels, Patriarchs, Prophets, Apostles, and other saints of God, against the most Holy Cross, the Sacraments of the New Law, the Holy Catholic Church, the Apostolic See, and against the faithful, especially Bishops, Priests, and other ecclesiastical persons, or against the Neophytes who have been lately converted to the Holy Faith, or that contain immodest and obscene narratives:

If they should make jest of Christians, and in despite of the passion of our Lord, in the Holy Week, or at any other time should crucify a lamb, a sheep, or anything else . . .[26]

On June 2, 1517, Cardinal Jiménez de Cisneros delegated inquisitorial powers to all the bishops of the Indies to seek out and prosecute all Jews and Moors in "the New World." With the appointment in 1519 of Bishop Alfonso Manso and the Dominican Pedro de Cordova as inquisitors of the Indies, many Jews residing in the Indies thought that the time had come to move. Some of the young and hardy sought refuge in the militia and armed forces. Others sought to join adventurers or discoverers. In 1519, Cortés prepared to sail to search for the land west of Cuba, which Juan de Grijalva discovered in 1517, and some Jews joined his crew. While Grijalva met disaster, Cortés met Doña Marina and a survivor of the 1517 expedition. Together they founded Veracruz and then marched triumphantly to Tenochtitlán (now Mexico City) and ended the hegemony of the Aztec Empire.

In 1520, Governor General Diego Vasquez of Cuba sent a force to New Spain to capture Cortés because he had proceeded without Vasquez' consent. Cortés defeated Pánfilo Narváez, the leader of the expedition, and invited Narváez' followers to join him for God and gold. Among them were several Jews who had fought with Cortés and aided him in the conquest of Mexico that was completed on August 13, 1521.

3

The Mexican Iberian Jew

One of the great enigmas of Jewish history is why there were Jews in New Spain at all. Rabbis of this time in North Africa and Holland differentiated between Jews who could not leave their homelands and therefore indulged in duplicity to conceal their religious convictions and those Jews who remained although they could have left. There is no question that many could have left New Spain in the seventeenth and eighteenth centuries. During that period they not only failed to leave, but many additional Jews came to New Spain from lands where freedom of religion existed. They came from North Africa, Holland, and the Italian states that tolerated Judaism, as well as from Spain and other Spanish possessions.[1] They knew that they courted danger by coming to New Spain.

The inquisitors apparently never asked why they came, and the confessions never included any explanations or answers. We know that some Jews had plans to leave, but there was always a debt to be collected, another ship to come in, or another transaction to be completed. They knew it was wrong to remain and hide their religious convictions, yet only a few departed.

Yannai, an early Medieval Hebrew poet, wrote these lines:

> Not everyone who is loved, is loved.
> Not everyone who is hated, is hated.
> Some are hated below and loved above . . .
> Hated we are, for you we love, O Holy One.

Nahum N. Glatzer comments, "Those who . . . doubted the reality
of this 'love above' left the community of Israel. Those who remained did so in the daily and hourly affirmation of that love; they
did so, prepared to bear the paradox of the concluding line of Yannai's poem."[2]

It has been said that it is impossible to psychoanalyze the dead,
yet the procesos—the testimonies recorded almost verbatim—of the
trials of the Jews before the inquisitors, may be compared to a tape-
recording of voices from the past. From the minutes of the trials
much can be learned of the psyches, values, characteristics, and customs of the Mexican colonial Jew. These are primary sources that
are extremely valuable to the historian. Histories are the scholarly
interpretations of the facts of history. The procesos are the raw ma-
terials of history.

Jews came to New Spain with Hernán Cortés in 1521, less than
thirty years after the Decree of Expulsion. By 1540, Bishop Juan de
Zumárraga had apprehended a few Jews, but many others were living in various parts of the land. The Jews in New Spain in the early
sixteenth century were either those expelled from Spain or from
Portugal, or were descendants of expellees.

With the exception of the differences in faith and those caused
by religious intolerance, the Jew was very similar culturally to his
non-Jewish compatriot. The Jew, because of religious persecution
and the necessity to practice his rites and customs secretly and at
great peril to his life, as well as the lives of his wife, children, and
friends, "evolved a hardness and cunning with which the Holy Office in Mexico could not cope."[3]

Salvador de Madariaga refers to the "love-hatred" of the Jew
toward Spain because of the Decree of Expulsion. In *Englishman,
Frenchman, Spaniard*, he classifies the Spaniard as a man of passion,
a person who yields to his emotions first. The hatred of the Jew
towards the Church is well illustrated by the comment of the Inquisition attorney in a trial of a Jew in the 1640's, "so that the living
hatred which these miserable and obstinate Jews carried in their
perfidious hearts openly manifested itself."[4]

The Iberian Jew was possessed by "love-hatred" and was a man
of passion. He chose to live in the Spanish Colonial Empire when he
could have found safety and freedom of conscience in North Africa, the papal states, the city-states of Italy, or in the Ottoman Em-

pire. He could have lived in the Low Countries after 1596, or in Germany or Poland. But he loved his country and its mother tongue, Spanish or Portuguese; he loved its ways, its people, and its land. He hated its state religion and showed great disrespect for Christianity by world and deed.

For example, as early as 1536, Gonzalo Gómez, who resided in Michoacán, over 130 miles from Mexico City, was accused of placing a cross on the roof of a hut on his farm, hanging strings of chili peppers on the arms of the cross to dry, and of breaking the arms of three crosses on his farm on Good Friday,[5] among other things. The custom of beating images and crosses that had been practiced in Spain was continued in Mexico.[6] Who but a Spanish Jew would seek to vent his spleen upon a wooden image in which he did not believe? Negro slaves in Mexico were also accused of this practice, but the Jew was credited with more education, sophistication, and rationality than the African slave brought from a presumably primitive, polytheistic culture.

The enforced duplicity of publicly professing Catholicism while secretly practicing Judaism created a dual existence. For such a Jew, the necessity of hiding his faith, not only from his Christian friends and neighbors but even from his Indian household servants and Negro slaves, must have warped the fibers of his being. To have to live a lie and practice dissimulation before one's inferiors must have been galling to the class-conscious Spanish Jew who paraded and preened himself as did any hidalgo.

The Jew of the Iberian Peninsula who came to Mexico was not the fawning, cringing, beak-nosed Jew of the anti-Semitic stereotype of the east European Jew of the nineteenth and twentieth centuries. He was a Sephardic Jew. The Sephardim of Spain stressed the purity of their families and descent from the Judean royalty of the times of King David.[7] He was generally tall and proud of bearing. His women were comely, and frequently their dark hair was contrasted by their blue eyes. One 1651 document in the Mexican National Archives is a receipt given by a ship captain at Veracruz for thirty-eight Jews who were being deported from Mexico to Spain where they were to serve sentences in the Inquisition cells. The physical descriptions of these prisoners are detailed and facilitate the creation of vivid mental pictures of their appearance.

Many of the women were as brave and daring as the men, and

Forms of the badge worn by medieval Jews. Adapted from
Jewish Encyclopedia, *Vol. 2, 1902.*

some were impetuous and capable of throwing caution to the winds.
There were, of course, also some men and women who valued their
own lives above those of their parents or spouses. Some men so
feared pain that they disclosed the names of other Jews merely at
the threat of torture. Animosities and interfamily strifes were pursued by Inquisition officials and resulted in the disclosure of the
faith of other Jews. Common problems, trials, and viscissitudes were
a cohesive force but yielded to *ad hominem* antagonism which led
some to the stake, others to the galleys, and many to exile and perpetual jail. H. J. Zimmels notes that Sephardi communities in the
Middle Ages exhibited two special features: an inclination to domi-
neer over others and to quarrel among themselves.[8]

The Jewish people were God-fearing and superstitious. Superstition played a role as great, if not greater, in their lives than did the
ethics and morality of Judaism. They often had their newborn in-
fants baptized and then washed the babies' heads when they returned
home from the church. (The earliest colonial records reveal that in
1527, Hernando Alonso used wine to wash off the baptismal water
from the head of his infant son.) The Jews respected learning, they

admired it, and they sought learned husbands in Italy for their daughters, yet we find few individuals noted for scholarly attainments. We find no literary figure or poet comparable to the fifteenth century Jew Santob de Carrion or any biblical exegetes.

The Reverend Dr. Solomon Gaon in his essay, "The Sephardi Character and Outlook," offers an explanation—or defense, as one chooses—of the anomaly in his people's character during the Inquisition period:

> Surely the Marranos realized the great risks that they were running by accepting the dominant faith outwardly while inwardly remaining faithful to the faith of their fathers. For themselves and for their children, especially during the Inquisition, they assumed a life of constant danger and fear which could eventually lead to a life of extreme martyrdom. Their integration in the country of their birth made them feel that in order to be able to return to their faith in more favorable conditions, they could accept a temporary compromise.[9]

It must not be forgotten that these people remained Jews even after they were reconciled, knowing full well that a second arrest meant going to the stake.

With the exception of the learned professions, such as medicine and law, and the skilled trades, such as cobbling, dyeing, wine making, and prescription filling, we find the Jews engaged in the routine occupations common to the colonials in New Spain: many were small merchants, shopkeepers, and itinerant peddlers.

They failed to distinguish themselves in any of the liberal arts except for Luis de Carvajal, *el Mozo*, who wrote poetry and liturgy between 1586 and 1595. Some might include as cultured figures those who were descendants of Jews but neither professed nor practiced the faith of their parents. Sor Juana Inez de la Cruz, a distinguished poetess and essayist, is reputed to have Jewish ancestry. The hermit Gregorio López was an author, and several authorities claim that he was a Jew. Fray Bernardino de Sahagun, the New World's first anthropologist, was the son of the Jewish family Ribero. However, he and Sor Juana were members of religious orders and were pious Catholics.

The intellectual practicing Jew was handicapped. He could not write, much less publish, his thoughts on Judaism. He risked expo-

sure if he owned any books in Hebrew—even the Old Testament.
He read the Prophets in Latin, had a Spanish translation of Deuteronomy, and used the Psalms in Spanish. A few persons did have col-
lections of Spanish translations of Hebrew prayers. The Inquisition
in New Spain was more Catholic than its superior in Spain. The
book of Flavius Josephus, *Bello Judaico*,[10] and two volumes on *Customs of the Israelites and Christians* were barred as late as 1802 and
1805 respectively.[11] The Jew in New Spain had meeting places,
however; one such was the store of Baltazar Díaz Santillan, which
has been compared to an academy where discussions on Jewish law
were held.

The resourceful New World Jews learned how to adapt the Dominican Day Book and the Books of Penitential Psalms for their own
religious use by omitting the recital of the "Gloria Patri." Word of
mouth, the ancient Jewish Oral Tradition, was the mainstay of Jewish learning for over two centuries. We know that Francisco Luis
at the age of seventy discussed the Old Testament with his cellmates
(1644-1649), referring to many passages in it and using the names
of the patriarchs, prophets, and their sons and descendants. He was
admired for the knowledge that he had acquired without formal
studies. He had been taught orally by parents, relatives, and friends.

Manuel Méndez de Miranda was found by the inquisitors in 1649
"to be well read in the Holy Bible . . . [he] regularly discussed the
lives of the patriarchs and the prophets of the Old Law." In connection with this fifty-five year old circumcized Jew, who had been
born in Lisbon and was a trader in Veracruz, it should be noted that
he, among many others, "kept Saturdays as holy days, neither buying nor selling on those days." His father, Sebastian Méndez, had
been a lawyer in Lisbon, and he was a first cousin of Sebastian Vas
de Azevedo, who is later discussed.

The search for letters or correspondence between the Jewry of
New Spain and that of other communities has been almost fruitless.
The few documents found reveal little of value to shed light on the
life of the people in the Spanish colonies. We know that there was
considerable exchange, since Jews of Holland, France, Italy, and the
Ottoman Empire knew the whereabouts of New World Jewish
community leaders. Some trial proceedings, such as that of Manuel
Días Enrríquez, reveal the receipt of letters from Holland.[12]

Although the word "synagogue" connotes a place of communal

prayer by Jews, it usually also implies a particular kind of building housing such accoutrements as an ark containing Torah scrolls and embellished by artistic representatives of Judaic sancta. In New Spain, the synagogue was a room in a private home or a space set aside in a store or a warehouse. The area was devoid of all trappings or indicia of a synagogue, even devoid of the eternal lamp or scroll of the Law. These places of prayer fall into Rabbi Milton Steinberg's definition: ". . . many a synagogue is little more than a bare room . . . for it is the Jewish teaching concerning God that, since He is present everywhere, He may everywhere be invoked."[13]

In New Spain, the synagogue was the focal point of communal life, as it was in Spain. The number of places of worship varied with the times. In the middle of the seventeenth century, there were about fifteen congregations in Mexico City and environs, at least three in Puebla, at least two each in Guadalajara and Veracruz, and one each in Zacatecas and Campeche. It is probable that there was at least one each in Merida, Monterrey, Guatemala, Nicaragua, and Honduras.

Charity was as lavish then as it is in the modern Mexican Jewish community. No appeal for distressed overseas brethren went unheeded. If the local impoverished observed Jewish rites, there was usually a generous, wealthy Jewish matron who dispensed largesse. During the colonial period, messengers came from as far as Palestine to raise money to aid distressed Jews in the Holy Land and to ransom Jews captured by pirates and sold as slaves. The messenger, always a man learned in Jewish law, had to spend time in each community teaching and studying with the people before leaving with the funds he had raised. This custom was called *farda*. Moslems had a similar practice.

The Jew of New Spain did not live in a particular quarter. He was found in all urban centers as well as in rural areas. He withstood religious assimilation because of his inner dedication to the faith of his forefathers. Judaism was his religious tradition, and veneration for tradition was inbred in him. Religious necessity drove him to share his time more with other Jews than with non-Jews. He had a superiority complex; Ibn Verga reports the apocryphal story of a Christian called Thomas who proved to King Alfonso that "all Jews of his kingdom were of royal descent."[14]

We find no trace of a *Bet-Din*, the Jewish tribunal that adjudges civil cases between Jews and also rules on religious disputes and questions. There were men who could read the scroll of the Law, among them Juan Cardoso, alias Gabriel Peregrino. Between 1550 and 1650, many Jews were called rabbis by the Inquisition. At least one was undoubtedly a rabbi, Simón Montero. He studied Judaism in Provence, Leghorn, Pisa, and in the Jewish quarter in Rome, where he was circumcized and ordained in 1639.

Francisco Rodrígues de Matos was termed a rabbi by the Inquisition officials in 1589. If they were correct (which is doubtful) he has the distinction of being the second or third rabbi in the Americas. His contemporary, Manuel de Morales, a learned Jew, acted as a rabbi. Jewish encyclopedias and scholars such as Cecil Roth have declared that Isaac de Aboab was the "first rabbi in America," from 1642 to 1654. Roth wrote, however, that "Francisco Rodrígues de Matos was described as a rabbi and dogmatizer or teacher of the Jewish religion."[15] The records reveal that Rodríguez de Matos was neither a rabbi nor a learned Jew. He never had his son Baltasar circumcized, nor had he taught him much about Judaism. Even if Aboab's honor had been confined to South America, it might be questioned. Manuel Bautista Pérez, burned in Lima in the auto-da-fé of January 23, 1639, was called a rabbi by the Inquisition as well as by Ricardo Palma[16] and José Toribio Medina.[17]

An unnamed "Grand Rabbi" has been reported in the Jewish colony in Mexico City about 1550. It appears that the title "rabbi" was used frequently by the inquisitors, being accorded to several persons whose only qualification was that they knew a little more about Judaism than the average crypto-Jews who were rigid followers of ritual. Duarte de León Jaramillo is one such example.

The characteristics of the Jews in New Spain changed several times during the ensuing four hundred years because of changes in environment, the lapse of time, and the nature of the immigration. Jewish immigrants came from all parts of Portugal except the extreme south and principally from the western part of Spain and from the north, where they or their ancestors had been residents.[18]

Some have contended that Spanish Jewry of the fifteenth century was spiritually decadent. "The morale of the people had been undermined by centuries of well-being."[19] Assimilation was rampant, and many Jews of the peninsula found little difficulty with conscience in converting, but the remnant who remained were strong in adherence to their faith.

The Jews of New Spain were better educated than their non-Jewish neighbors, and morality was often a distinction between the Iberian Jew and Christian. Ullick Ralph Burke wrote: "the absence of any social stigma attached to illegitimate birth was one of the noted features of Spanish society in the Middle Ages . . . For a long time, birth out of wedlock was no disgrace in Castile." Abraham A. Neuman added a note to the foregoing: "In contrast, for one Jew to impute illegitimate birth to a Jew during the same period was punished by fasting, flagellation and the dispensing of charity."[20]

The word "illegitimate" was in fact rarely used for Christian children born out of wedlock. They were more often called "natural children." In sharp contrast to the Jewish immigrants to the New World, the Christians are thus characterized by Mariano Picón Salas:

> . . . it is a well-known fact that most of the Spaniards who came here were low, hardened types much given to every kind of vice and sin . . . gangs of commoners, members of an impoverished lower nobility, and disinherited bastards who formed a tidal wave of conquerers . . . distasteful to him [the Spaniard] were purely commercial motives.[21]

For several centuries, the Sephardim did not follow the injunction of Rabbenu Gershom that Jews cease practicing polygamy. The learned rabbi was an Ashkenazi, and his edict was ignored by the Sephardi Jews. The Sephardim of Spain and Portugal used their house servants, slaves, and other willing females as concubines. Offspring from such relationships were often recognized as equals with the children of the first wife. The Portuguese Jews in Amsterdam in the seventeenth century continued this practice even though polygamy was then against the law.

As the decades passed, the Jewish immigration became preponderantly Portuguese. Cecil Roth comments that the Spanish New Christians were "of the weaker sort who had embraced Christianity in order to save their lives."[22] Issue must be taken with this statement because of the origins and subsequent activities of the Jews in New Spain. Some of the most devout and venturesome were New Christians who were born in Seville and other parts of Spain. It is interesting to note that the term "New Christians" was still used for those born in Spain and Portugal in the sixteenth and seventeenth centuries, one hundred years or more after the Decree of Expulsion.

Many of them were the children or grandchildren of Jews burned at the stake in Spain between 1550 and 1600.

During the sixteenth and early seventeenth centuries the Jews in New Spain were accepted without animosity by the general populace because they served a function and role which the Spaniard was unable or unwilling to assume. They were merchants, peddlers, itinerant salesmen, and importers. The virus of hate cast into the winds by the Spanish clergy did not infect all Catholics. For example, Juan de León Plaza, constable of the Inquisition cells, formed a partnership in 1602 with Antonio Méndez, a reconciled Jew. He also engaged in business with and borrowed and repaid money from others convicted of being Jews. We know also of several cases in which Catholics concealed the presence of Jews, hid them, aided in their escape, and flaunted the warnings of the Holy Office.

The charge has consistently been made that the Sephardic Spanish Jews of this period were ostentatious. It should be indicated that this characteristic was not confined to the people of the Hebrew faith. Fernando Espejo wrote concerning Cardinal Pedro de Mendoza, who died in 1495, that "he was a son of his times, ostentatious and refined, genteel and good hearted."[23]

4

Customs in New Spain

THE JEWS in colonial Mexico lived an almost schizophrenic existence. Incessant pressure to play a dual role and the fear of betrayal or disclosure of their true faith was joined with their hope for the coming of the Messiah to redeem them as Moses had redeemed their forebears in Egypt. These conditions afford important clues to the anachronisms in their conduct and to their customs, many of which were indigenous to them.

The hope for redemption and the prayer for the coming of the Messiah was almost a daily ritual. Without their belief in the imminence of the Messiah, they would have abandoned Judaism. While each hoped that the Redeemer would come in his own day, there was no surrender to despair in the thought that he might not. If their prayers for his speedy coming were not answered, they could still die happy in the expectancy that he would come during the days of their children.

This hope for a Messiah had been with the children of Israel for almost 2,000 years prior to 1492, and it continues to this day as a prayer. It was especially fervent during times of stress and persecution and was very strong in New Spain until the eighteenth century. As successive "Messiahs" rose, were exposed, and hopes were cast to the ground with the revelations of their falsity, a new hope arose almost instantly. Disillusionment was the result of revelation of fraudulent claims, but the concept and expectation remained strong.

The dichotomy of their existence created for Jews a strong feeling of living in sin. Outwardly, they had to profess and practice Christianity because they wanted to live. They refused to seek out martyrdom deliberately, but many played the role of martyr bravely when their Judaism was discovered by the Inquisition.

The narration or disclosure of his faith to a child was sometimes delayed until he was thirteen years old or older. Some siblings did not reveal their Judaism to each other. Many families sent one son into one of the religious orders as proof of their devotion to Catholicism, and some monks never knew the true faith of their parents or family. This custom was also practiced in other lands by crypto-Jews.[1]

FASTING

The sense of sin, however, was not to be denied. Many Jews frequently attempted to find refuge, compensation, or penitence through fasting. "The Marranos imposed these penances upon themselves to expiate their sin of outward adherence to the Roman Catholic Church."[2] There were fasts on Yom Kippur, also called *El Gran Día de Ayuno* (The Great Day of Fast) and *El Día del Perdon* (The Day of the Pardon), *Tisha b'Ab*, and for three days before Purim, *Ta'anit Ester* (The Fast of Esther). Many fasted on Mondays and Thursdays. The latter fasts and those preceding Purim were observed only from sunrise to sunset.

Except for the fast on Yom Kippur, that of Purim was the most important. For Jews who can practice their religion freely, this holiday is most gay. It marks the rescue of the Jews while they lived in Persia in the pre-Christian era from the machinations of their archenemy Haman, who had plotted their total destruction. A Jewish girl, Esther, was married to King Ahashueros, who did not know her faith. When Haman secured the king's permission to slaughter all the Jews in the realm, Esther knew that she would have to reveal her faith and plead for the lives of her coreligionists. Esther preceded the day for her plea by a three-day fast. The New World Jews found a parallel between Esther's conduct and their own, with the Inquisition the counterpart of Haman and themselves that of Esther.

As she revealed her faith at the final moment of peril, so did they reveal their faith when they were in the clutches of the Inquisition. Their confessions usually saved them from the stake.

While Jews throughout the world regarded Purim as a joyous day, there were no reports of any festivities in New Spain because the Jews there still kept secret their faith; they lived under the sword of Damocles and prayed for a happy ending for themselves. They prayed for a miracle which would liberate them from the fear of the Inquisition. They recited Psalm 22, which begins, "My God, my God, why hast Thou forsaken me . . ." Fasting was prevalent not only in expiation of sins but also as an expression of thanks to the Almighty for deliverance from some evil or horrendous event.

The assumption of stricter obligations than prescribed by Jewish law was a centuries-old custom in Spain. The thirteenth-century Talmudist Jonah Geronde wrote of penitential tracts that gave conditions for repentance that required a severe regimen in which great emphasis is laid on the elements of sorrow and grief, fasting and weeping.[3] Iberian Jews sought suffering and self-denial as a means of salvation. This concept was borrowed from Catholicism.

The prophet Zechariah had proclaimed that if the Jews of his time would observe four particular fast days, they would be harbingers of joy and gladness and cheerful seasons.[4] In the seventeenth century, Juana Enríquez dispensed charity to all those who had fasted on Yom Kippur and before Purim. She traversed the streets seeking those Jews who had abstained from food and drink on the appropriate days and gave them monetary rewards. This custom was enunciated by Mar Zutra who declared in the fourth century that "the merit of a fast day lies in the charity dispensed."[5] Rabbi Jacob Ben Asher stated that he was a holy person who practiced fasting when he had no physical disabilities to prevent it.[6] Ultimately fasting became an end in itself. María Gómez issued invitations to her home to attend a fast, and some Jews, Luis de Tristan for one, boasted of the number of their fasts. Ana de León, the last surviving sister of Luis de Carvajal, *el Mozo*, was noted as "a most accomplished performer of fasts." In 1640, her fasts were credited with bringing many people to an understanding of the better life. Some fasts were observed openly by stating that they were in honor of the Virgin of Carmen; a church in her honor was located in the outskirts of Mexico City.

Many subterfuges were employed by those desiring to fast and to conceal the fact from their servants. One deception practiced was to send the servants on a lengthy errand at dinner time; usually the main meal was at two or two-thirty in the afternoon. When the servants returned the Jews would be sitting with toothpicks in their mouths. Another subterfuge was to exchange visits with other Jews and ask the servants to get something they claimed had been forgotten at the house of the guest. Stomach disorders were another ruse adopted to avoid eating. Gómez de Medina testified in 1646 that his master and mistress would commence an argument when they sat down at the table and then announce that they could not eat because of the excitement. This pseudo-dispute was a pretense to avoid eating on fast days.

HOLY DAYS

The Sabbath

Attendance for many at community services on Friday at sunset inaugurating the Sabbath appears to have been infrequent. Many more Jews attended a late Saturday afternoon service to mark the conclusion of the Sabbath. Someone usually spoke at these services. The sermon consisted of comments on a portion of the Torah. The recital of some of the Davidic psalms, some of which had been set to music, replaced the synagogue prayers of other lands where prayer books were plentiful and religious tolerance existed.

While the Jews usually were multilingual (many spoke Spanish, Portuguese, and one or more Indian tongues), many of their prayers were in Portuguese. The following was a favorite:

Quen canta, seu mal espanta;	*He who sings will drive away*
Quen chora seu mal aumenta:	*his sorrows;*
Eu canto para espalbar	*He who cries will make them*
A paixao que me altormenta.	*worse:*
	I sing in order to dissipate
	The suffering that torments
	me.

Yom Kippur

This "Day of the Great Fast" was the holiest day of the year for all Jews regardless of the degree of their religious observance. It was observed on the tenth day of the Hebrew month *Tishre*, which coincides with most of the month of September. In Guadalajara, however, a dispute arose as to the exact day for observance. Some wanted to follow the lunar calculations while others said that, in case of doubt, it should be celebrated on the tenth day of September.[7]

The ritual of preparation for the awesome day consisted of bathing on the previous day, changing all of one's clothing, and dining on fish and vegetables. Meat was not permitted. Some, if not all, clothing was new; even the poorest member of the community purchased at least one new garment to wear. The women lit candles, which were placed on a clean cloth. There is mention of seven-armed candelabra, the traditional menorah, which was lit prior to the commencement of the communal services inaugurating the Sabbath. The normal practice of lighting Sabbath candles consisted of putting the candlesticks on a clean cloth under a table covered with a black tablecloth. This was done to prevent them from being seen by outsiders. It appears that for the eve of Yom Kippur, however, some women placed them on the table. The women who did this placed candles on the table for several nights prior to Yom Kippur so that when the Great Day arrived the candles were accepted without curiosity by servants and Christian neighbors who might see them.

Candles were expensive, but even the poor permitted them to burn out completely on Yom Kippur instead of snuffing them out as on ordinary nights. Prayers were recited until after midnight, and some Jews prayed intermittently all night. Children old enough to pray did so but were excused and sent to bed between nine and ten o'clock. The number of congregants in each place varied. The average number was between fifteen and twenty-five. A larger number would have aroused suspicion, yet there may have been exceptions. Simon Váez may have had as many as eighty persons on his hacienda, some of them staying for twenty-four hours or longer.

Prayers were not recited all day on Yom Kippur. Some who found fasting difficult would go for a walk in the Alameda, and some stayed in bed. Some of those who went for a walk did so with toothpicks in their mouths to deceive Christians. The public use of toothpicks at the end of the meal was considered proper. Those who stayed in bed claimed stomach ailments that required abstention from food. The fast was broken after three evening stars appeared in the sky, with a meal similar to that of the eve of the Holy Day.

Lesley Byrd Simpson notes that Spaniards ate fish and eggs prior to fast days.[8] The Jew has always adopted the mores of his country, except when those conflicted with his religion. The custom of eating eggs, fish, and vegetables before and after fasts might have stemmed from the Spaniards.

The orthodox Yom Kippur custom of asking forgiveness from friends and relatives with whom one had quarreled during the year was observed. There is a touching tale of how Margaret de Rivera, a grown woman, on the eve of the Holy Day in 1642 came to her mother, Doña Blanca, with whom she had had differences, and kneeled, kissed her hand, and pleaded for forgiveness. After all the members of the family had apologized to each other and been forgiven, they embraced. The grandmother blessed them all saying, "God bless you and make you good."

The trial record of Gabriel de Granada is one of the sources of information on Yom Kippur customs. As a boy of thirteen he had been taught this prayer just before Yom Kippur of 1642:

> *Lord, my soul called upon Thee to deliver me from the fire and flame that I may not be burned or scorched. Here am I in this desert, turned into a plant [servato] where great trouble shall overtake me. Into thick darkness shall they cast me where neither brother nor cousin can aught avail me. One thing, my God, shall I ask of Thee, that Thou remember my soul and deliver it at the mouth of a cave and going out at a door, and that I may not amuse myself except in counting the Stars of Heaven or throwing water in the Sea.*
>
> [Translated by Col. David Fergusson]

In the earlier years, especially at the end of the sixteenth century, the book *Consejos de Salomon* (Wisdom of Solomon) was a source of consolation, study, and prayers. This book was safe to use since it was an important product of Alexandrian thought and made many references to the New Testament. It is referred to in the Epistles of Paul and was available in Spanish.

Shavuot

The holiday Shavuot, celebrating the giving of the Ten Commandments to Moses on Mount Sinai, is not mentioned in the Edict of Faith. This edict was posted on Church doors by Inquisition officials and listed the customs and holy days of non-Catholic heretics so that the faithful could detect the observers. The three most holy festivals for Jews are Passover, Shavuot, and Succot, and they are so listed in the Bible. The omission of Shavuot by the Inquisition is extraordinary. In the article "Ritos y costumbres de los hebreos espanoles," by Ramón Santa María, the holiday is not listed. It is not mentioned by name in the procesos of the seventeenth century except in that of Mariana de Carvajal and her brother Luis de Carvajal, *el Mozo*.

Luis called Shavuot *Pascua de la Primicias*[9] (Festival of the First Fruits, which is one of the names of this holiday; in Hebrew it is *Hag Habbikurim*). This holy day is known as Pentecost to Christianity. It falls on the fiftieth day after the beginning of Passover. Mariana de Carvajal stated, incorrectly (unless the amanuensis erred), that it came forty days after Passover. She and her family observed it only by prayers.

Passover

The holiday of Passover celebrates the liberation of the Jews from Egypt, under the aegis of Moses. In Spanish, it was called *Pascua de Cordero*, Festival of the Lamb. It is also referred to as *Pascua de Los Panes Acimos*, Festival of the Bread without Yeast and *Pascua del Pan Cenceño*, Festival of the Unleavened Bread. It opens with the evening meal, called seder, inaugurating the holiday. This festival was of great significance because it marked the release of the Jews from Egyptian bondage. To the colonial Spanish Jew, the inability to practice his faith openly and freely was a form of spiritual slavery.

There is a lack of data on the prayers used but there is much on the physical observance. No Haggadah, the special story read on Passover for over a millenium, has thus far been revealed as being in use. Luis de Carvajal read to his family the portion of the Book of Exodus that related the story before the Passover meal.

A prayer referred to in several procesos was the "Song of Moses" (not to be confused with the Canticle of Moses), which was recited by the Israelites after crossing the Red Sea and having observed the destruction by drowning of their Egyptian pursuers (Exodus 15:1-

18.) Again, one can perceive the analogy between the New World Jews who hoped to escape the clutches of the Inquisition (Egypt) and their enslavers, the inquisitors (Pharaoh). While other literature read by the Jews is discussed in connection with various individuals, one psalm must be noted at this point. This is Psalm 10 of David, which begins:

> *Why standest Thou afar off, O Lord?*
> *Why hidest Thou Thyself in times of trouble?*

This psalm has been termed the "Prayer of the Oppressed" by the Reverend Dr. A. Cohen. The psalm concludes:

> *Lord, Thou hast heard the desire of the oppressed*
> *Thou dost make their heart firm,*
> *Thou wilt cause Thine ear to attend*
> . . . .
> *That man who is of the earth may be terrible no more.*

Chapter 12 of Exodus sets forth the commandments and directions by which the people of Israel were to observe the future anniversaries of their redemption from bondage. These directions were followed literally by Jews in New Spain, at danger to their lives because the observances revealed their religious identity. The directions commence with the command for each householder to take a lamb without blemish (Mexican Jewry chose white lambs, although there is no such requirement); the lamb was to be slaughtered before dusk and its blood put "on the two side posts and on the lintel" of the houses where the lamb was to be eaten. The Edict of Faith mentions this custom. There is Talmudic authority for smearing the blood on the interior of the doors rather than on the outside. Many if not all Jews in New Spain placed the blood on the inner side of the entrance.

Exodus 12:8 states "And they shall eat the flesh in the night, roast [*sic*] with fire, and unleavened bread; with bitter herbs they shall eat it." Parsley and lettuce were commonly used, as they are to this day. The lamb was to be roasted whole and not divided, "and thus shall ye eat it; with your loins girded, your shoes on your feet, and your staff in your hand . . ." (verse 11). There is no description of the female garb, but we do know that men wore long cotton white robes, pulled their belts tightly about their waists, and held large wooden staffs in their left hands. They ate standing up, as did the ancient Israelites. Although the Bible instructed that anything of the lamb that remained was to be burned with fire, some Jews gave the remains to their Christian neighbors; there were few who followed the command about eating a lamb and burning anything left over.

Fasting, often observed only from sunrise to sunset, had become so ingrained that many thought that every holiday had to be accompanied by a fast. Consequently, there were some who fasted on one day during the week of Passover in addition to the fasts on Mondays and Thursdays.

Passover was usually observed for only seven days in accordance with the biblical injunction, although the eight-day period was known and followed by some. Observant Jews in New Spain performed no work on the first and seventh days of Passover. There was a strict abstention from leavened bread. The baking of *pan cenceño* (matzot) was practiced. In the sixteenth century, some men ate tortillas in lieu of matzot when traveling during Passover.

Some people made their own matzot but there also were some Jewish bakers. There was a Jewish doctor in Peru in the seventeenth century who prescribed matzot for many Christian patients with stomach disorders. When Passover came, he ate only pan cenceño and contended he was having trouble with his own stomach.

Miscellaneous observances and rites

The minor monthly festival of *Rosh Hodesh* (New Moon) was noted in the three principal Jewish communities in New Spain. It served as their guide for the advent of the holy days. The blessing of the New Moon and the few prayers at the evening services at its appearance are mentioned in one proceso. Constant association with Catholic practices produced hybrid rites among the Jews. New customs developed that were influenced by the outward allegiance to Christianity. Acculturation is plainly evident. At times, there was a syncretism or confusion, as in the testimony in the trial of Hernando Alonso in 1528. He refused to permit his wife to go to church during the forty days after giving birth to a child. In Alonso's mind, the biblical injunction[10] applied to non-Jewish places of worship as well as synagogues.

Not only was there a syncretism and borrowing of Christian

practices, but the possibility exists that Indian practices were also absorbed into Jewish ritual. In the 1647 confession of Francisco de León, we read of a female visitor who stayed at the home of his parents. She prayed with a cloth wrapped about her interlocked hands. Elsewhere he spoke of communal prayers and stated that some men also observed this custom. In the absence of any Jewish source for such a custom, one is compelled to look among the customs of non-Jews. It was not a Catholic custom, but there is a noted statue of a Mayan woman, called the "Caracol," which depicts her with a cloth over her interlocked hands.

The Apocrypha was held in equal reverence with the Old Testament. Recital of passages from the Bible was a common form of prayer. There were innumerable repetitions of the same prayers due to the limited number of prayers that were known. There were no prayer books, and newcomers from abroad were eagerly questioned for new prayers.

Prayers were sometimes borrowed from the Catholic liturgy. Luis de Carvajal, *el Mozo* converted the monk Francisco Ruiz de Luna to Judaism while they were cellmates in 1589. These two would recite together a psalm which began *"Magnus Dominus et Laudabillis"* and which they translated into Spanish: *Grande es El Senor, digno de alabar pues ami, el pecador, quiso alumbra.*[11] In the seventeenth century, Juana Tinoco composed some prayers and also paraphrased many Christian hymns and much of the liturgy so that they were suitable for Jewish use. A person passing the synagogue and hearing the hymnal music might be deceived into thinking that a group of Christians were engaged in a religious observance or a rehearsal for the coming Sunday. To aid in the deception, the names of Jesus and Mary were retained in one or two places.

Luis de Carvajal, *el Mozo* and his siblings substituted aliases for the names of Jesus and Mary, but these aliases were used in curses and imprecations. Christ was called Juan Garrido and the Virgin, Mariafernández *(sic)*.

Abraham A. Neuman in his history, *The Jews of Spain,*[12] states that there was a marked divergence prior to 1492 between the moral standards of the Jewish communities of northeastern Spain (Catalonia, Aragon, and Navarre) and those of Castile and León. One of the factors contributing to these differences undoubtedly was the role played by two Ashkenazi rabbis who served in northeastern Spain, Simón ben Adret and Simón ben Zemah Duran. Since Neuman did not define morality, it may be assumed from the tenor of his work that he used the term in the context of adherence to religious customs. The divergences may be analogous to the modern differences between Orthodox and Conservative practices, the former hewing strictly to the old tradition and the Conservative making accomodation to modernity.

These distinctions in attitudes toward religious practices become important for an understanding of Jewry in New Spain after 1580. We lack precise information of the places in Spain from which the emigrants came prior to 1580. After that date, however, the main areas from which Iberian Jews emigrated were Portugal, western Spain (especially Extremadura), and Seville. These people, except the Portuguese, were far removed from the influence of the rabbis and learned men of northeastern Spain, and consequently the differences in moral standards were even more marked than they were prior to 1492.

Among the differences were less literal observances of the laws for the preparation of meat, a longitudinal rather than circular circumcision administered when the youth was in his teens, and ethnic customs not necessarily decreed by religion. These variations were also motivated by the desire to preserve Judaism under conditions where it was barred. What Cecil Roth wrote concerning Spanish Jews applies equally to Mexican colonial Jewry: "The popular conception of a subterranean Judaism, entirely cut off from the outer world, but in secret clinging with the utmost fidelity to every jot and tittle of ancestral rites and ceremonies, is obviously untrue."[13]

The following list fairly well summarizes the beliefs of Jews in New Spain at the end of the sixteenth century, as culled from reading numerous procesos.

1. That the Law of Moses is the true law. It was sometimes referred to as "the Law that God gave to Moses on Mount Sinai."

2. That this Law was written by God with His fingers on the tablets which He gave to Moses.

3. That one should love only God and not venerate any images since this is prohibited by the Commandments of the Law.

4. That one might not eat pork nor anything of the pig, and that

only the flesh of animals which chewed the cud is permitted; also prohibited is fish without scales. All fowl have to be decapitated and the blood drained. No animal blood or suet may be eaten.

5. That *Pascua* (*Pesach* or Passover) falls on March 14. (Actually, observance of this holiday is not on a fixed date because the Hebrews use the lunar calendar to mark their holy days. Furthermore, *Pesach* never falls as early as March 14.) To deceive Christians, the word *Phase* (of unknown origin) was substituted for the name of Passover.

6. That the Sabbath was observed from the setting of the sun on Friday until after sunset on Saturday. During the Sabbath no kind of work was performed. Clean shirts were worn, "similar to the custom of Christians on Sunday." The Sabbath is a reminder of the creation of the world and that God rested on the seventh day after completing his work. Psalms of praise are to be sung, no fires should be lit, and only those foods prepared prior to the advent of the Sabbath may be eaten.

7. That on the Great Day of Pardon, God judged all beings. This day falls on September 10 (another incorrect date) and is observed by fasting.

Some of the customs observed in New Spain during the sixteenth and seventeenth centuries were almost *sui generis*. Many of these practices were employed during prayer. They included praying with outstretched arms[14] or with arms crossed upon the chest; or with hands overlapping below the chest and covered with a cloth; or with the left hand over the eyes and the right hand over the heart during the recital of the Shema (Deut. 6:4-9, Hear O Israel the Lord our God the Lord is One), and praying on the knees. They did follow tradition in always facing east—toward Jerusalem—while praying.

Antonio J. Texeira of the province of Guatemala in 1642 claimed that secret Jews believed principally in one positive precept, the observance of the Sabbath, and one negative precept, refusal to worship images; and that the intent to observe Mosaic law to the best of one's ability sufficed for the deed.

Jews observed a fast for Judith (the woman who slew Holofernes, Judith 12:13); this has no modern counterpart. When unleavened bread was unavailable for Passover, they ate tortillas since they are made without leavening. They felt that this was proper although the matzot were preferable and traditional.

The preparations for the Sabbath included the cutting of finger and toe nails; the clippings had to be kept together and burned. The use of clean sheets and clean shirts or blouses was de rigeur for the Sabbath. This custom had the sanctity of a religious commandment. Despite the inability to carry out full religious observances, the colonial Jew revered Jewish law and respected the necessity to observe as much as possible. They did nothing to reform the Jewish law and Oral Tradition to make it compatible with their way of life.

The theology of Mexican Jewry was not profound, being the tattered fabric salvaged from persecution and anti-Semitism. There were many adaptations from Christianity, e.g., the use of saints, the concept of purgatory, praying on the knees, etc. Hope lay in the coming of the Messiah and in the belief that the messianic era would be the result of Jewish devotion to Mosaic laws. The negative aspect of the religious doctrine was the antipathy to and, at times, hate of Catholicism and the believers in Christ. Jews were as superstitious as were adherents of Spanish and Mexican Catholicism. Religion in colonial times was not the inspiration for ethics, morality, and love of fellow men.

The custom of sending one son into the Church was confined to Iberian Jewry. Among the last families of New Spain who observed this practice was that of Garci González Bermeguero, who arrived in Mexico in 1559 and was burned at the stake October 11, 1579. One of his sons was an Augustinian. Rodríguez de Matos, whose family was called Carvajal after his brother-in-law, sent his son Gaspar into the Dominican Order while the family still lived in Spain. One of the reasons for discontinuing this custom may have been that the Mexican-born child of Spanish parents was a criollo. Only Spanish born, gachupines, could aspire to positions above that of a parish priest or monk, or of municipal officer in civil life. The status of a second-class citizen with consequent disabilities was imposed on all born in the colonies regardless of the status of their parents. As state and Church were one and the same in many respects, Catholicism differentiated between the children of Christ depending on place of nativity.

The Jew in New Spain did follow his Iberian forebears in his ardent desire to prosyletize and to bring back into the fold of Judaism those who were converts or the descendants of converts. These people who risked their lives by preaching a return to the original faith or to the "dead laws of Moses," as the Inquisition termed it, were known as *dogmatistas* (dogmatizers).

Dogmatizers were quite numerous and active until the end of the seventeenth century. Lack of knowledge of their presence after 1700 should not imply that they no longer continued their practices. The attitudes of the inquisitors and the changes in their primary field of interest after 1700 may account for the absence of reports on dogmatizers.

The zeal of the dogmatizers to bring apostates back to Judaism did bring some Jews before the Inquisition. Their words are reminiscent of their dead ancestors of the fourth century. Rabbi Dr. Joseph H. Hertz quotes a Palestinian rabbi of that era: "Strange are those men who believe that God has a son and suffered him to die. The God who could not bear to see Abraham about to sacrifice his son but exclaimed, 'Lay not thine hand upon the lad,' would He have looked on calmly while His son was being slain and not have reduced the world to chaos?"[15]

Thirteen centuries later, on April 24, 1614 in the city of Zacatecas, Cristóbal de Herrera was accused before the Holy Office of saying that if Jesus were the Messiah promised by the Law, as foretold by the prophets (that an Infant King would come), and if Jesus were the Messiah and a son of a carpenter and of a María, why was he born in a "passageway," and if he were Christ, the Messiah, why did he have to flee to Egypt and let himself die on a cross?[16] The witnesses against Herrera said that the above words were uttered with contempt and in the presence of another witness who was a Knight of Christ. All witnesses testified and Herrera admitted that they were talking about eight Portuguese who were arrested in Oaxaca for teaching the Law of Moses to the Indians.

Herrera denied the interpretation imputed to his words. He stated that he had said that it was a wonder that the Portuguese more than other men of the Spanish nation should "fall into Judaism and believe that the Messiah had not been born since Christ had been born poor in a crib and was the son of a carpenter and a María who was a poor young woman and that he was astonished that they [Portuguese] would not believe in miracles . . ."

Everyone admitted that Cristóbal de Herrera was a learned man. He seemed to be familiar with the Old and New Testaments. His parents came from Jérez de la Frontera, Spain, from which many New Christians had emigrated to Mexico. Although the attorney for the Holy Office recommended prosecution "for being a Jew," there is no record of any subsequent proceedings against Herrera.

Marriage

Many of the wealthier Jews in New Spain sought husbands for their daughters in the Jewish communities of Pisa, Ferrara, Livorno (Leghorn), and Amsterdam. In these cities, there were aspirants for the hands of Mexican Jewesses. Manuel Alvárez de Arellano, an international trader in the seventeenth century, was entrusted with the responsibility of investigating the families of marital aspirants and for locating eligible sons-in-law for prospective New World brides.

The Jews in New Spain wanted to be sure that their children not only did not marry out of the faith but that the non-Mexican spouse was devout, adhered to ritual, and was learned. In accordance with the old Spanish custom, and especially after 1605, many brides were as young as thirteen and fourteen years of age. Documents studied tell that one woman, Catalina Henriquez, was twelve and another, Clara Rivera, had married when she was thirteen. Doña Clara had made over three hundred fasts before she died in the Inquisition cells in 1644. Inéz Pereira had her first child in 1641 when she was fifteen years old. Catalina de Enríquez had her thirteenth child when she was thirty-five years old and her oldest son was then seventeen. A Sephardic father could enter into a marriage contract for his daughter until she was twelve. After that age, her consent was required.

When no rabbi was in New Spain, the couple would solemnize their marriage by a written contract in the presence of their families and friends. This contract was in accordance with Jewish law. The couple would then have a Catholic ceremony. Later, when a rabbi was available, he would repeat the marriage ceremony and add his prayers for blessings for the couple.

The best man and the matron of honor also drank from the nuptial glass of wine that was almost indispensable for the marriage ceremony. The rabbi would throw the empty wine glass into the air and permit it to fall to the ground and break into pieces. A honey cake was the traditional part of the wedding meal, and it was eaten at the outset as a first course. Poultry was the usual main course.

CIRCUMCISION

Circumcision was generally observed as it is traditionally practiced among Jews. There were two variations, however, one fairly common, and the other known to have been practiced by the family of Duarte de León Jaramillo in the 1630's. The first variation consisted of having the cut run longitudinally along the male genital instead of around the organ. Whether any rabbinic sanction existed for such practice is unknown. It was obviously an attempt to comply with the law in having every Jewish male bear the Mark of the Covenant as directed by God to Abraham (Genesis 17:14), while changing the manner of the operation so as to deceive Christians and, in particular, inquisitors. The Franciscan Motolinía, who resided in Mexico in the early and middle sixteenth century, commented that the male organ of the Indian was cut between the skin and the flesh, that this rite was traditionally performed on unmarried youths in their early teens, and that it was called circumcision. Since it is clear that Jews borrowed customs from the Christians and also from the Indians, it may be that their change from a circular to a longitudinal cut was an adaptation. While the foregoing may be considered a tenuous theory, the sharing by Jew and Indian of the custom of cutting the male prepuce may have created some bond between them.

Most Jewish prisoners contended that the mark was a scar and not the result of a religious circumcision, or that they did not know it existed. Some novel explanations were given for circumcision by those who admitted that they had been knowingly operated upon. In 1642, Pedro Fernández de Castro, alias Juan Fernández de Castro, admitted that the cut had been made in the orthodox manner in Ferrara, Italy. It was done, he said, to please a Jewess named Esther with whom he desired to have sexual relations.

The Inquisition usually ordered the physical examination of a Jew by a committee of three or four doctors at the close of the trial proceedings. Circumcision served as corroborating evidence. A study of one hundred cases chosen at random, about half of which involved men who were circumcized and others who were without the mark, fails to reveal any weight being given to those who were circumcized; the uncircumcized Jew received no lighter penalty than he who had been circumcized.

The operation was usually performed on boys between the ages of nine and fourteen. There are several cases of self-circumcision by adults. A rare case of deviation from the traditional manner of circumcision was recorded for the family of Duarte de León Jaramillo, who adhered to Jewish rites devoutly. The males prayed three times daily—upon arising, at ten o'clock in the morning, and at dusk. The mother prayed an hour before sunset on Fridays while sitting at the window facing east. There is no indication of what prayer book she used, the nature of her prayers, or other details that would be of interest. The father, who was intolerant of lapses from fasting, had a store that was used as a synagogue. The oldest son had been circumcized in the traditional fashion on the eighth day after his birth. When the mother was arrested by the Inquisition, Duarte took his younger sons and three daughters into a shed and cut a very small piece of flesh from the left shoulder of each. On October 5, 1646, his son Francisco de León testified that his father had said that "their mother had been imprisoned as a punishment because the sign of the Law was not on the children."[17]

There is no record of any prayers being said upon the occasion or any blessing being made. The story was corroborated by the siblings of Francisco. One of the grisly aspects revealed by the testimony was that the piece of flesh removed "was toasted and eaten" by Duarte. There is no biblical or other Jewish source for any such practice. Maybe the father wanted his children to bear the Mark of the Covenant in a place that would not be identified as Jewish. There is no theory for such action on the female members of his family.

RELIGIOUS DIETARY CUSTOMS

The slaughtering of fowl was done in accordance with Jewish law. The sharpness of the knife and its examination was punctiliously observed. Attention to the sharpness of the knife as an identifying custom is noted in the Edict of Faith. There is no record of salting of meat prior to 1640. This may have been because salt was not plentiful in New Spain and was very costly. But the biblical command that reads "Only be sure that thou eat not the blood: for the blood is life . . . Thou shalt not eat it, thou shalt pour it out upon the earth as water" (Deut. 12:23-24), was obeyed.

Women often acted as slaughterers of the fowl. Those who had new slaves or servants or those who sought to hide their customs from the household servants would wait until the servants had retired to their quarters for the night. About ten-thirty in the evening they would then decapitate the fowl and hang them by their legs so that the blood would run down and drip into a pan of water. The mistress would arise at about four-thirty in the morning, before others were awake, and spill the contents of the pan into the ground and bring the fowl into the house. The meat was washed several times in warm water in order to drain off the blood.

There are a few references to men slaughtering animals but no description of the method employed or any other details. Evidence is plentiful of the practice of *landrecilla* (porging), the removing of the thigh vein and the fat about it. This practice is derived from Genesis 31:33, which reads, "Therefore the children of Israel eat not the sinew of the thigh vein because he [the angel who wrestled with Jacob] touched the hollow of Jacob's thigh." The fat was removed and discarded and hidden so that no traces could be found. The custom of porging led to the disclosure of the religion of many Jewish women by Christians who knew that it was a Jewish practice. There is one case of a man who complained about the quality of the meat because the landrecilla had not been removed. He was reported to the Inquisition by a non-Jew who overheard the remark. It was thus revealed that the complainant was a Jew.

The major portion of the diet of the Jews consisted of fish, eggs, olives, and vegetables. These foods comprised the meals especially before and after fasts and during mourning periods. It may be that the Jews chose these foods since they are not of the categories of either milk or meat and require no special or ritual preparation for consumption but could be eaten at any time.

The above-named foods were prepared in vegetable oil so that they did not fall into the categories of milk or meat products as would happen if they were prepared with butter or meat fat. *Ada-*

fina (*el ani*, in Aragon), a sort of stewed meat or fricassee, was the common meat dish. Eating with neighbors or with Christian friends was fairly frequent. Christians also made stews of meat, but they often included pork. When eating with Christians, some Jews picked out the pieces of swine meat and dropped them to the floor if some animal, such as a dog or cat, was about, or just kept pushing them to the side of their platter, thereby leaving them for the last. Then the Jew would say that he could not eat any more. Such refusals to eat pork also resulted in the arrest of some Jews.

Orthodox observance forbids eating any food prepared in dishes in which nonkosher products had been prepared. Eating pieces of beef which have been cooked together with pork is a violation, since kosher products are made ritually unfit for Orthodox Jews by being in the same pot with the other meat. Antonio Caravallo, whose house was used as a synagogue on Friday nights and Saturdays, never ate bacon or stored it in his house. However, to dissimulate and hide their Judaism, his wife would buy bacon and serve it when they had non-Jewish guests. After the guests departed, he and his wife would forcibly regurgitate to remove the forbidden food from their stomachs.

Chocolate was the favorite drink. Chocolate (a Nahautl word borrowed by the Spaniards and later by the English) was an Indian drink and was prepared without milk. It was whipped with water until it became frothy and was an important staple for all residents of New Spain. This was a useful beverage for Jews since it could be used with both meat and dairy products.

The Friday night meal was occasionally preceded by the attendance of males at communal religious services. In one place of worship there was an embroidered representation of Moses with jewels encrusted on the cloth. Before eating, hands were washed and the appropriate blessing recited. This meal, heavier than usual, consisted of fish, fried or in another form, small home-baked breads with salt sprinkled on top, some meat delicacy, and wine. The wine for Friday nights was old vintage. Dessert frequently consisted of *halvah*, a confection that is made from ground nuts.

Some Jews engaged in a superstitious practice of eating only chickens which were all brown or all black; there had to be a total absence of even one feather of another color.

The fruit *membrilla* (quince) was a favorite of all. Ruy Díaz

Nieto lived on this fruit and cheese for months while he was in the secret cells in 1603. There is no description in any trial records of the nature of the cheese consumed.

Amin, a broth, was used for the sick and faint and by women during pregnancy. In the trial records of Micaela Enríquez many interesting customs are narrated, and it can be deduced that she and her mother prepared *shmira matzot*, the unleavened bread which is made from the earliest wheat and requires special blessings.[18] The matzot were described as round and about six inches in diameter, the same size as a tortilla. Her parents were Antonio Rodríguez Arias and Blanca Enríquez. She was married to Sebastian Cardoso, who had been born in Seville. Her parents were referred to as *rabinos* and as rabbinical dogmatizers (rabbis who attempt to reconvert Jewish apostates to Judaism).

Elena de Silva, also known as Elena López, was another pious woman who made matzot.[19] Prior to Passover in 1641, she and her daughter, Isabel, were surprised by a Catholic neighbor while they were making the unleavened bread. They lied about what they were making and were obliged to let the neighbor taste some. The woman became nauseated, but they convinced her that it was just bland unbaked dough.

During the 1630's and 1640's, the Montoya family was the principal supplier of matzot in Mexico City. The matzot were distributed throughout the city by Rodrigo Tinoco, who also acted as sexton or beadle for one of the Jewish communities prior to 1643. In the other parts of New Spain, the baking of matzot was done by the housewives themselves.

The aforementioned Elena de Silva observed the Jewish law of attending funerals and providing meals for the bereaved during the first period of mourning, during which they sat on the floor. At one of the suppers, a Jewess refused to eat a rice dish sent by Elena, saying that it had been cooked in a lard pot. Elena's mother replied, "It has no lard. My daughter cooked it, may God give her good fortune."

While doing research in Yucatán in 1965, Enrique Gottdiener, the director of Bellas Artes and a professor of history at the university in Merida, confirmed that marranos had lived in and about Merida during the colonial period. He also indicated that there were three dishes which were indigenous to the area and which are of Jewish origin:

Pan trenzada (braided bread) is found in almost all modern Merida bakeries. This is identical with *challa*, the bread which is found only in those Mexican cities that have Jewish communities. Some Yucatecan bakers throw a piece of the dough into the fire, as do Orthodox Jewish women who bake their own bread as a survival or reminder of the sacrifices made in the Jerusalem Temple.[20] The Yucatecan bakers do not appear to be aware of the origin of this custom.

Frijol con puerco (beans with pork). Substitute beef for pork and one has a culinary concoction with the identical ingredients and made in the same manner as *el ani* or *adafina* or *chulent* (the eastern European name). It is usually made preceding the Sabbath and remains in the oven for a day or more.

Pan de pomuch and many of the soups in Yucatán follow old Sephardic recipes. Gottdiener contends that all of the foregoing exist in Yucatán because many of the servants and cooks during the colonial period worked for crypto-Jews in Yucatán, and the recipes have been handed down during the past three centuries.

One of the delicacies of the early seventeenth century in New Spain was *alfajor* (also *alaju*). This is a concoction made of almonds, walnuts, honey, etc. It is still popular among European and American Jews and is traditionally served at the beginning of the Jewish New Year.

The Orthodox washed their hands before eating and their hands, eyes, and mouth after eating. On Saturdays, the pious ate only those things cooked or prepared on the previous day, "in remembrance of the creation of the world and God's order to rest." Bread was sliced before Friday sunset so that no cutting of the bread was done on the Sabbath.

Funeral and Mourning Customs

Since the Edict of Faith (p. 96) lists those customs most commonly observed in the event of death and mourning, they need not be reiterated. Some additional customs appear as family rites when certain individuals are discussed later in this book. Among those not in the edict are the use of linen imported from Rouen for funeral shrouds. They were considered the best because there were several Jewish-owned factories in Rouen manufacturing this linen.

During the mourning period immediately following the funeral, the family of the deceased refrained from eating any meat because of the statement in Deuteronomy 26:14, "I have not eaten thereof in my mourning . . ." While this statement refers to meats offered as sacrifices in the days of the Temple, the Jews in New Spain interpreted it literally.

A circumcized Franciscan monk was discovered to have been a descendant of Jews and a believer in Judaism. He was tried by the Holy Office and was reconciled in 1785. He, however, was determined to die as a Jew and therefore left instructions concerning the rites to be followed after his death: flushing the body internally, shaving the body, and clothing it in a shroud made according to the biblical command (Deut. 20:11) only of wool, linen, or flax. The premature discovery of these instructions caused his second arrest and resulted in his being sentenced to the stake in 1795. At the last moment, the inquisitors changed his punishment to perpetual jail. They may have been mortified at the thought of the consequences when the populace might learn that a Jewish believer had been found under the cassock of a Franciscan monk.

The custom of pouring out all water that had been drawn and lodged in jars in the place where a death had occured was a means of announcing that a death had taken place without making people become bearers of bad tidings. It is also possible that Psalm 20, with which the people were very familiar and which states in verse 15, "I am out like water . . . ," moved them to this practice. Such pouring out of water in the house of death is, however, an ancient superstition observed by many peoples.

The preparations for the burial of Francisco Rodríguez de Matos were made in the presence of his son Luis, Catalina de León, Francisca Núñez (wife of the tailor Juan de Nava), and a Negro slave, Luis:

> The body was washed, nails cut, hair cut, and a shroud with a tunic of Rouen linen then was placed on the body of the corpse. They placed a gold coin under the body, a candle was lit, and a jar of water and a washcloth were left in the room so that the soul of the departed would be able to wash and dry. There was also deposited nearby some simple food and an egg without salt. Upon the completion of all these rituals, they recited prayers.[21]

Antonio López Blandon, a practicing Jew, died about 1632 and was buried in a crypt in the cathedral in the vestments of a Franciscan monk. Many other crypto-Jews were interred in the cathedral and other churches in and about Mexico City.

There was another custom that may have been adopted from some of the Indians. In the mouth of the deceased, if he were poor, was placed a piece of grain or barley or a piece of broken pearl. A piece of a broken coin or gold was used if he were wealthy. Among the Indians, "a piece of jade was put into the mouth upon burial to represent the heart; a commoner received only a common green stone."[22]

From the 1625 trial of Tomas Treviño de Sobremonte, we learn that blessings from the deathbed were highly cherished. When a member of the family died, fish constituted the principal dish during the mourning period for the bereaved.

The first period of deep mourning lasted for seven or eight days, but general mourning was observed for one year. Money was left by the deceased for charitable distribution, or the family, from their own funds, gave money to the poor who were observers of the Law of Moses. Recipients were supposed to fast for the sake of the soul of the deceased. Quite often gifts were sent to nonfamily members to pray for the deceased. These friends sometimes attended the mourners and fasted for a full day.

The bodies of deceased women were flushed and washed by women. For a time in the seventeenth century, one or two women acted as burial attendants even for deceased men. This is understandable since the fear of detection became obsessive after 1642. Women could carry on the necessary procedures in the protection of the home while men attended to their daily business routines without being missed and questioned.

Interment was always made in the cathedral or churches because of the subsurface waters underlying the entire capitol. Mourners always placed some virgin soil in the coffin before it was sealed. In San Angel, now part of Mexico City but then a separate municipality, the convent of Our Lady of Carmen was a favorite burial place.

As is still practiced today by most Jews, hard boiled eggs were eaten upon the return from the funeral after washing the hands before entering the house. The egg, being round, represents the cycle of life and, being hard boiled, is a reminder of the tribulations of life. The trial records of Gabriel de Granada state that the distributor of the eggs to the mourners stood on one foot.[23] Fried eggs and chocolate were sent later by friends. For the initial week of mourning, friends delivered and served all the meals to the family of the deceased.

Defying the Church

Slips of the tongue in public sometimes betrayed a Jew reviling the Church and Christ. Most defiances, however, were exhibited in grimaces and gestures. The gesture of holding fingers to the nose in church was used by Jews and often identified them. The most common manner of exhibiting contempt and soul-burning hatred of Christianity was the beating of images of Christ and breaking images of saints. The striking of images of Christ on the Cross was almost a universal practice throughout Spain and in every part of the New World under Spanish dominion.[24]

The practice was first discovered by the Inquisition in 1532. In that year Michael Rodríguez and his wife Isabella Martínez Albarez were accused of having struck the image of Christ with a whip and having insulted it in various ways as if to revenge themselves upon it for all the evils which the Christians made the Jews suffer.

As a result of deliberately breaking the arms of a crucifix, the Rivera family was implicated before the Inquisition. Their arrest in 1642 ultimately led to the involvement of almost one hundred other Jews.

The beating of statues was carried over into New Spain. There are several cases in which this practice is revealed. It was usually followed by those quite orthodox in their religious practices. Notable among these was the family of Duarte de León Jaramillo. His sons, Francisco and Simón, testified about this custom in 1647.[25] The father would bring down from the living quarters to the counter of his store a crucifix about eighteen inches long and place it face down on the counter. Then, for about an hour, the crucifix was beaten with straps and was told that "its law was not good." Rosaries were also broken.

There were two other analogous rites in Mexico. One was followed by a Jewish shoe repair man who put small crosses between the heels and the uppers of shoes so that the customer would be treading on a cross. Another storekeeper placed a cross under the threshold leading to his store and all Jews would deliberately step on it and thus identify themselves.

In 1696, Pedro Carretero, alias Pedro de la Vega, was convicted of being a Jew and sentenced to public scourging and to servitude in the Philippine galleys for six years without pay. He testified that he and four others used to beat an ivory crucifix on Fridays. Each lashed the image of Christ thirteen times and defamed his powers as a god. The Sephardic Jew was obsessed by hatred of the Church and all its ritual and symbolism. These gestures acted as a catharsis and sublimation for pent-up emotions. Christ epitomized the cause of his troubles.[26]

Superstitions

The lives of the Jews in the middle of the seventeenth century were heavily tinged with superstitious beliefs and practices. Among these were the following:

1. A bed had to be made tidily with the sheets pulled straight. If not, the souls of the dead might lie on them and torment the sleeper.

2. The hair of single young women had to be dried well after washing and put into buns, or no gentlemen would woo and marry them.

3. A girl could capture a man by giving him a powder made either of a toasted swallow or the brains of a cow.

4. A matza placed on the head would cure a headache. It was also carried in a small pouch suspended from the neck as an amulet.

5. Clothes worn inside out would bring misfortune.

6. Hands folded on top of the head would bring misfortune.

7. Amulets were used to ward off catastrophes.

Some of the superstitions among the Jews of that time are revealed by funeral practices and events. At the services prior to interment, men and women covered their heads and observed silence for one hour during which they silently prayed and commended the departed to the Almighty. They requested a revelation to one of those present indicating whether the departed was in purgatory or heaven. (New World Jewry adopted the concept of a purgatory from their Christian neighbors.) On more than one occasion during the 1630's, Tomas Treviño or his mother-in-law, Ana Gómez, both noted for their piety, would announce that they had had such a revelation showing the soul of the departed to be in heaven. Cocks crowing in the pre-dawn hours were considered an evil omen.

5

The Spaniard and the Spanish Inquisition

THE INTOLERANCE of Christian Spaniards came to flower in 1481. It had been bred on "an exasperated feeling against the Jews . . . which had shown itself . . . in plunder and murder of multitudes of that devoted race [which, with the Moors] was hated by the mass of the Spanish people with a bitter hatred . . . and of both it was taught by the priesthood, and willingly believed by the laity, that their [the Jews] opposition to the faith of Christ was an offense against God, which it was a merit in his people to punish."[1]

Henry C. Lea described Spain of the fifteenth century as a land suffused with a fanaticism plus greed and envy.[2] Henry B. Parkes wrote that the Spaniard "was a Catholic . . . for whom the adherents of the other religions were the enemies of God, deserving to be persecuted and plundered . . ."[3]

The two words which best describe the Spaniard are ambivalent and mercurial. He was an individualist but required leadership. Salvador de Madariaga wrote that the Spanish psyche abounds in conflicting tendencies. He used pairs of words to illustrate these: hard and human, resigned and rebellious, energetic and indolent. He then summed it up in three words, "humanism, individualism, and amorality."[4] He defined humanism as "an attitude to judge the whole man which leads to personalism and envy."

While the Jew of the legends taught by the Church did not resemble the Jew whom the local people knew, first his forced recession from social intercourse and then his gradual segregation from society and the distinctive badge and clothing he was compelled to wear began to make him appear, to the medieval mind, what he was not. Even though the Reformation and Renaissance were aborning in the thirteenth and fourteenth centuries and their rustlings heard and felt by the Jews, the Spanish masses were still mired in ignorance and superstition and impregnated with absolute credulity in spirits and demons. They were constantly cautioned that only the Church could serve as a defense against the evils which were poised to beset them. The fact that the Jews did not accept Jesus as the Messiah and that they believed that the Messiah was yet to come was contorted by the Church into the interpretation that the Jewish Messiah, when he came, was to be anti-Christ.

In order to arouse hate, the Church propagated reports that Jews threw stones at churches, beat and threw refuse at images of Christ and the saints and made lewd gestures to images; that converts to Judaism had to knife a crucifix, etc. Some of these charges were repeated by the Inquisition against Jews in New Spain in the seventeenth century.[5]

The Spanish Church was a totalitarian power. Its hold on the masses was complete. It did not tolerate differences or independence of thought or action. In the words of Lord Acton, "power corrupts and absolute power corrupts absolutely." The Church fostered the Inquisition in the belief that it would be an instrument for religious unification through its autos-da-fé and thus suppress all heresies. Ferdinand and Isabella perceived religious utility of the Inquisition as well as its potential for political unification and economic advantages through confiscation. Long before its creation, Peter II of Aragon in 1197 decreed the death penalty for heresy. Pope Innocent III justified capital punishment because "heresy was equivalent to treason." This pope sanctioned the Albigensian Crusade of 1212-1220 that marked the beginning of the monastic Inquisition in the thirteenth century.

If in the twentieth century, Miguel Unamuno, Spain's great philosopher and literary figure, could say, "I am not a modern man.

Civilization and science are repugnant to me," what could the fifteenth century Spaniard have been? Margaret T. Rudd commented on Unamuno, "Probably, as he once said, he was Spain, the very essence of her quixotic spirit."[6]

The words of Thucydides and Polybius well mark Spanish Christendom's figurative crucifixion of Jew, Moor, and heretic. Thucydides wrote that "to power nothing is inconsistent which is expedient." This aptly describes the role of the Church in the era prior to the Reformation. Polybius said that "public crimes which go unpunished do not differ from private except in quality and extent." But there were none to point the finger at the Church.

THE HOLY OFFICE OF THE INQUISITION

The institution known as the Holy Office of the Inquisition has existed, in a general form, from the sixth century until recent times. Its functions normally rest within the episcopal powers of every bishop, who is the guardian of the faith within his diocese. We are here concerned with the Spanish Inquisition, which was "destined to discourage and check that intellectual freedom without which there can be no wise and generous advancement in any people."[7]

The severity of the practices of the Holy Office encouraged a great amount of fraud and falsehood. George Ticknor wrote that it strains the credulity to read the eyewitness accounts of what was transpiring in Spain. He notes that "it is only by reading . . . that it is possible to learn how much the Spanish character was impaired and degraded by this hatred, inculcated during the nine centuries, seventh to sixteenth."[8]

The monarchs as well as the people lost remembrance of the vital role played by Jews in the history of their kingdoms. This forgetfulness permitted a "wave of aggressive intolerance and terrorism to sweep through the people stirred up by vulgar prejudice and by preaching of some Catholic clerics."[9]

Inevitably some Jews continued to convert. From the Jewish point of view, there were two main groups of converts. The *anusim*, forced ones, were regarded as still being within the pale of Judaism. Many rabbis asserted that it was the duty of Jews to bring this group back into the fold. In prayers for the welfare of the Jewish community the anusim were specifically mentioned,[10] and it was deemed meritorious to assist them in their attempt to escape from Christianity. The second group were *meshummadim*, voluntary converts, who had no desire to return to Judaism. The Christians called Judaizing Christians (those who tried to reconvert meshunmadim) "alboraycos." This word came from al-Borak, the name of the miracle horse presented to Mohammed by the angel Gabriel.[11] The animal was neither horse nor mule and neither male nor female. The Christians compared each organ of the Jew with that of the beast. Such comparison may have arisen from the charge that sexual relations with a Jew were called sodomy since the Jew was considered not a human being but an animal.

Only jurisdiction over heretics was originally given to the inquisitors, but later it was extended to even include Jews who had never converted. The monks who administered the Inquisition legalized this concept by the process of vitiating the role of Christianity as a daughter faith of Judaism, substituting "proof" that Christianity antedated the beginning of revealed history and that Christians were the true descendants of the people of the Old Testament. The Jews, therefore, were heretics because of willful departure from the true religion. Even Martin Luther referred to the baptism of Jews as a "return to their natural religion."[12]

Salo W. Baron described the Church's anomalous position of calling an unbaptized Jew a heretic as a rationalization of the concept that:

> Mankind as a whole is but the mystic body of Christ. In this corpus Christi are included not only Christians but also infidels. In it each corporate group, each *universitas* has a special funtcion, as of a special organ within the human body. The Jewish community, also a member of this universal body, must be maintained as such a *universitas*, apart, with as much separation and segregation . . . as possible . . . This formula is the more remarkable, the more uncontested the general theory and practice of intolerance became in the Christian world.[13]

This rationalization is significant. Originally, the unbaptized Jew was beyond the jurisdiction of the Holy Office. He was detested because he was accused of undermining the faith of the converts. Owing to forced baptism of children under fourteen, especially in

Portugal between 1498 and 1503, and acts of barbarism, there were hundreds of thousands of feigned conversions. These pseudo-converts were said to frequently seize the opportunity of "returning to their vomit as does the dog." (This pungent expression was favored by the Church and the prosecuting attorneys for the Inquisition. Even Rabbi Simon ben Zemach Duran used it when speaking of anusim who did not escape when they had the opportunity.)[14]

Ferdinand and Isabella intended the Spanish Inquisition to be a national institution owing obedience to the crown rather than to Rome. In 1483, they formed the *Consejo de la Suprema y General Inquisicion* (shortened hereafter to Suprema) with an Inquisitor General to preside and to have full power of appointment. Tomás de Torquemada was the first to hold the chair. The council had six other members. On November 29, 1484, he and his associates drew the *Instrucciones de Sevilla*, in 1488 the *Instrucciones de Valladolid*, and in 1498 those of Avila, all of which, together with amendments, became known as the *Instrucciones Antiguas*.[15]

The inquisitors were so disliked that in February, 1510, Ferdinand found it necessary to write letters calling on officials and gentlemen to give inquisitors and their staffs lodging at current prices and not to assail them, under penalty of 50,000 maravedis fine. To quote from Henry C. Lea: "Thus, notwithstanding the Spanish abhorrence of Jews and heretics, the dread which the Inquisition inspired was largely mixed with detestation, arising from its abuse of its privileges in matters wholly apart from its functions as the guardian of the faith."[16] A popular saying of the sixteenth century was *con el rey y la inquisición, chiton!* (keep silent as to the king and the Inquisition). The Inquisition considered itself a house of health.[17]

THE TRIBUNAL OF THE HOLY OFFICE

The Tribunal of the Holy Office of the Inquisition was unique and independent of the Catholic Church. It had branches throughout Spain and, after 1571, in Mexico City, Cartagena, Lima, Santiago de Chile, and Buenos Aires. The geographical jurisdiction of each Tribunal was coequal with that of the viceroyalty in which it was located. The Tribunal in New Spain ultimately became known as the "autonomous Inquisition" because it so often acted independently of the Suprema in Seville. The Inquisition imbedded into Mexican jurisprudence the presumption in criminal law that the accused is guilty and has the burden of proving his innocence.

Inconsistency was one of the Inquisition's outstanding characteristics. Not every inquisitor was a demonic sadist. Not all the inquisitors made women bare themselves to the waist for the rack or public scourging or used their power to seduce or rape, although many did.[18] Many performed their functions, voted harsh punishments, and then relented. Relenting was sometimes induced by the sweet sound of ducats clinking against each other in a leather pouch. Inquisitors in New Spain knew that exile or banishment from the Indies was an order with which there was rare compliance. Life imprisonment usually meant serving an indeterminate term. The two sentences that permitted no mitigation were those of burning at the stake or serving as an oarsman on the galleons that plied the oceans from Spain to Veracruz and from Acapulco to the Philippines. Most of the inquisitors knew that there was more breach than observance of the Instrucciones Antiguas. After 1571, Dominicans served as inquisitors in the New World.

Apologists for the Holy Office claim that it was a divine creation. They explain that God was the first inquisitor and that the first trial at which he presided involved Adam and Eve after their fall. His final judgment on them consisted of exile, with permission to wear skins instead of fig leaves to cover their nudity. These skins were said to be the first sanbenitos. (It is said that when Voltaire heard the foregoing story, he remarked that while it did not prove that God was the first inquisitor, it did prove that he was the first tailor.)

The Spanish Inquisition operated under the *patronato real,* the 1508 papal grant of power over the Church to the Spanish throne. The papacy ceded to Spanish kings the right to collect tithes, censor papal communications, and to make all clerical and secular appointments to the Church and the Inquisition. The Holy Office owed nominal allegiance to the Holy See, but it operated apart from it when it so chose, even in disregard of papal wishes. It was *imperium in imperio.*

LIMPIEZA DE SANGRE

The concept of purity of blood, *limpieza de sangre,* became very important in Spain after 1449. Purity of blood meant that one's ancestors in paternal and maternal lines were "old" Catholics. The rise to power of Jewish converts in the Church or the court made the "old" Christians envious and jealous. Despite papal letters of Pope Nicholas V declaring that all Christians were to be equal regardless of their ancestry or date of personal baptism, the old Spanish Catholics resented the New Christians.

In 1488, all holy orders in Spain were closed to children and grandchildren of converts. One of the causes for this action was the discovery, in 1485, that a Jeronomite monk was an unbaptized Jew.[19] Gregorio Marañon wrote that a certificate of limpieza de sangre was easily obtained although the blood had not been very clean; and also that many known converts had positions of responsibility, including positions in the Holy Office where the purity of one's ancestry was demanded.[20] The Inquisition held that a person contaminated with Jewish blood carried the devil within himself. Valeriu Marcu even mentions a medical test given to Juan Huarte de San Juan to determine his faith.[21]

The requirement for the certificate of limpieza de sangre was important in the New World because Jews, Moors, and their descendants as well as those penanced by the Inquisition were legally barred from the Indies. This only made more expensive the cost of breves and forged papers needed for emigration.

PROHIBITED BOOKS

The Council of Toulouse (1229) decreed that laymen were prohibited from reading the Scriptures in the vernacular. Thereafter, the Talmud was adjudged guilty of containing anti-Christian passages. The list of prohibited books grew as the years passed. In 1559, the eighth Inquisitor General, Don Ferdinand Valdez, Archbishop of Seville, published his catalogue of prohibited books; this included all Hebrew books and those in other languages treating Jewish customs. As a result, the four-volume *History of the Jews* by Samuel Basnague, in French, was condemned in Mexico City,[22] and in 1805, the two volume work *Customs of the Israelites and Christians* was seized.[23]

The Mexican inquisitors were more severe than those of Spain. Even books bearing the *nihil obstat* of the Bishop of Burgos in the

Burning of the Talmud and other Hebrew books. Painting of San Domingo de Guzman by Berruguete. Original in Museo del Prado

eighteenth century were condemned in Mexico. When the Jesuits in New Spain had their feud with Bishop Juan de Palofox y Mendoza of Puebla, in the 1640's, the index of prohibited books of the Jesuits included the treatises of this bishop.

THE EDICT OF FAITH

The Edict of Faith was read in churches to give heretics and those who knew of wrongs against the faith as described in the edict an opportunity to secure absolution by making confession within a prescribed number of days. In cities where the Holy Office sat regularly, the edict was placed on all church doors on a Sunday during Lent.

Lea wrote that this act "elevated delation to the rank of high religious duty; it filled the land with spies and it rendered every man an object of suspicion, not only to his own family."[24] The fifteenth century Jesuit historian Mariana characterized the cautious reserve found among Spaniards as an heirloom of the Inquisition.

Inquisitors were instructed to visit every town within their respective jurisdictions at least once each year. There were *comisarios* (agents) throughout their areas who gathered evidence in the intervening periods. The edict promised secrecy to informers and prosecution to those who aided or concealed heretics. Hearsay was as valid as personal knowledge. Any individual who knew or heard of any violator, alive or dead, present or absent, or of any deed or utterance of any word or opinion "heretical, suspect, rash, ill-sounding, scandalous, or heretically blasphemous," was to report to the Tribunal or the local comisario within six days. The deed or word could have been done or said thirty or forty years prior. There was no statute of limitation for matters involving the faith.

The following is an almost literal translation of the Edict of Faith read in New Spain (words in brackets have been interpolated for clarification). It begins, "We, the Inquisitors, Against Perverse Heresy and Apostasy in this City and Archbishopric of Mexico [and] the States and Provinces of New Spain, New Galicia, Guatemala, Nicaragua, Yucatan, VeraPaz, Honduras, the Philippine Islands and their Districts and Jurisdictions of Apostolic Authority. . . ." Then follows the admonition and a list of all the customs of those who follow the Law of Moses, Islam, Lutheranism [references to Lutheranism began to appear in the edicts of the latter part of the sixteenth century], Diverse other Heresies, Solicitation of women by confessors or clerics for sexual relations, Treason to the King, Bigamists, Astrologists, Necromancy, Sorcery with herbs, powders, and so on.

The section relating to Judaism reads as follows:

It is useful or you may have had the opportunity to know or have known or heard said that someone or some persons had observed some Sabbaths in honor and in accord with the Law of Moses, donning clean blouses and other clothing of holidays, putting clean tablecloths on the tables and clean sheets on the beds in honor of the said Sabbath, not having fire or any other thing [burning], observing this from Friday afternoon. Or that they had cleansed and drained blood from meat into water. Or that they had porged [removed the vein] from the leg of the lamb or other kinds of meat, or that they decapitated the fowl or birds which they slaughtered saying certain words [but] first testing the knife on the finger nail to see if there were any nicks, and [then] covering the blood with earth. Or that they have eaten meat except by necessity during Lent or on other days prohibited by the Holy Mother Church and believing that eating meat was not a sin. Or that they had fasted on the Grand Fast Day [Yom Kippur] which they call the [Day of] Pardon or that they went without shoes on that day. Or if they recited the prayers of Jews and on the eve [of Yom Kippur] they asked each other's pardon, or fathers putting their hands on their son's heads in order to sanctify them either saying nothing [sic] or asking of God that they may be blessed in order that they may serve the Law of Moses and his ceremonies. Or if they fast on the Fast of Queen Esther or on the Fast of Rebeazo [Tisha B'ab] which they call the destruction of the Holy Temple, or other fasts of Jews during the week as on Mondays or on Thursday, not eating on these days until the appearance of the stars at nightfall, and on these nights they do not eat meat and they bathe on the day before the said fasts, cutting their [finger and toe] nails and the ends of their hair, catching and burning them. Reciting Jewish prayers [while] raising and lowering the head and turning the face to the wall; and before they pray they wash their hands with water or earth; dressing themselves in garments of serge or silk or woolen or linen, [praying] with certain cords or straps suspended from the head with certain knots [phylacteries], or celebrating the Festival of Unleavened Bread beginning with the eating of lettuce, celery, or other greens on those days. Or observing the Feast of the Little Huts [Succot], putting on the huts green branches or embellishments, eating at each other's [huts]. Or the Festival of the Candles [Hanukkah], burning one after another until ten [*sic*] candles are lit and after they have begun to burn reciting Jewish prayers on those days. Or if they bless the table according to the custom of the Jews [either *Kidush* or the prayer over bread at the commencement of the meal], or if they drink *caser* [kosher] wine, or if they make a blessing [*boracha*], taking the glass of wine in their hand, saying certain words over it and giving it to each one to take a swallow, or if they eat only meat decapitated by a Jew or if they eat at their table with the [other Jews] or [only] from their food, or if they recite the Psalms of David omitting Gloria Patri, or if they hope for the Messiah and say that the Messiah promised in the Law has not come and that he is to come and they hope for him in order to be taken from captivity as in the past and that he will take them to the Promised Land. Or if some woman waits forty days after giving birth before entering the Temple for the Ceremonies according to the Law of Moses [Leviticus 12:2, 3, 4]. Or if when children are born they are circumcised or they are given Jewish names and they are called by them. Or if they rub off the Holy Water or wash after Baptism where the Oil and Holy Water had been put. Or on the seventh [*sic, septena*] night after the birth of a child, they take a vessel with water, throwing into it gold, silver, a misshapen pearl, wheat, barley, or other things, [then] washing the child in this water reciting certain words. Or having made guardian angels or fairies [*hadas*] for their sons. Or if some of them are married according to the Jewish manner. Or if they make a parting of their ways which is when some person goes on a separate road [a married couple living apart]. Or if they bear Jewish names. Or if at the time when they take the dough to make the challah [*hala*] they burn some [they throw a piece of the dough into the fires] as a sacrifice. Or if when some person is at the point of death, he turns to the wall to await death and then [the corpse] is washed with warm water, shaving the beard and under the arms and other parts of the body, and attiring it with clean linen, underdrawers, and shirt and cover, which is folded over the top, and putting a pillow with virgin soil under the head, or money in the mouth, or a misshapen pearl or some other thing. Or singing some funeral dirge or throwing out the water from the large jars and emptying all the containers with water in the house of the deceased and all other houses of the area as a Jewish custom; eating fish and olives on the floor behind the doors; no meat because of sorrow of their loss; not leaving the house for one year in accordance with the observance of the laws. Or if they are buried in virgin soil or in a Jewish cemetery. Or if some have converted to be Jews. Or if some have said that the Law of Moses is as good as the Law of our Redeemer Jesus Christ.

NOS LOS INQUISIDORES

Contra la Heretica Pravedad, y Apoſtaſia en eſta Ciudad, y Arzobiſpado de Mexico, Eſtados, y Provincias de la Nueva-Eſpaña, Nueva-Galicia, Goathemala , Nicaragua , Yucatán , Vera-Paz , Honduras, Iſlas Filipinas, ſus Diſtriƈtos, y Juriſdicciones. Por Authoridad Apoſtolíca, &c.

 Todos los Vecinos,

y moradores, eſtantes, y reſidentes en todas las Ciudades, villas, y Lugares de nueſtro Diſtriƈto, de qualquier Eſtado, Condicion, Preeminencia, ô Dignidad, que ſean, exemptos, ô no exemptos, y cada uno, y qualquiera de Vos, à cuya noticia viniere lo contenido en eſta nueſtra Carta en qualquiera manera , ſalud en Nueſtro Señor Jesu-Christo,

Edict of Faith read in New Spain in 1639. Courtesy of
Academy of Franciscan American History

2

CHRISTO, que es verdadera falud. Y à los nueftros Mandamientos que mas verdaderamente fon dichos Apoftolicos, firmemente obede-cer, guardar, y cumplir. = Hazemos faber, que ante Nos pareció el Promotor Fifcal del Santo Oficio, y nos hizo Relacion, dicienno: Que bien fabiamos, y nos era notorio, que de algunos dias, y tiem po à efta parte por Nos en muchas Ciudades, Villas, y Lugares de efte nueftro Diftrido, no fe havia hecho Inquificion, ni Vifita General. Por lo qual no havian venido á nueftra noticia muchos delicio s que fe havian cometido, y perpetrado contra nueftra Santa Fé Ca-tholica, y eftaban por punir, y caftigar, y que de ello fe feguia defervi-cio á Nueftro Señor, y gran daño, y perjuicio à la Religion Chriftia-na, que Nos Mandaffemos, è hizieffemos la dicha Inquificion, y Vi-fita General, leyendo para ello Edidos publicos, y caftigando los que fe hallaffen culpados, de manera que nueftra Santa Fé Catholica fiem-pre fueffe enfalzada, y aumentada.

Y Nos vifto fu pedimento fer jufto, queriendo proveer cerca de ello lo que conviene al fervicio de Dios Nueftro Señor : MANDA-MOS dar, y dimos la prefente para Vos, y cada uno de Vos en la dicha razon, para que fi fupieredes, ò entendieredes, ò huvieredes vifto, ò oído decir, que alguno, ò algunas perfonas, vivos, prefentes, ò aufen-tes, ò difuntos, hayan hecho, ò dicho, ò creído algunas opiniones, ò palabras hereticas, fofpechofas, erroneas, temerarias, mal fonantes, efcandalofas, ò blafphemia heretical contra Dios Nueftro Señor, y fu Santa Fé Catholica, y contra lo que tiene, predica, y enfeña nueftra Santa Madre Iglefia Romana, lo digais, y manifefteis ante Nos.

COnviene à faber, fi fabeis, ò haveis oído decir, que alguna, ò al-gunas perfonas hayan guardado algunos Sabados por honra, guarda, y obfervancia de la Ley de Moyfen, viftiendofe en ellos ca-miffas limpias, y otras ropas mejoradas, de fieftas, poniendo en las meffas manteles limpios, y echando en las camas fabanas limpias, por honra del dicho Sabado, no haciendo lumbre, ni otra cofa alguna en ellos, guardandolos defde el Viernes en la tarde. O que hayan purga-do, ò defebado la carne que han de comer, echandola en agua por la defangrar. O que hayan facado la landrecilla de la pierna del Carne-ro, ò de otra qualquier Res. O que hayan degollado Reses, ò Aves que han de comer atraveffadas, diciendo ciertas palabras, catando primero el cuchillo en la uña por vér fi tiene mella, cubriendo la fan-gre con tierra. O que hayan comido carne en Quarefma, y en otros dias prohibidos por la Santa Madre Iglefia, fin tener neceffidad para ello, teniendo, y creyendo, que la podian comer fin pecado. O que hayan ayunado el ayuno mayor, que dicen del perdon, andando aquel dia defcalzos. O fi rezaffen oraciones de Judios, y à la noche fe de-

deman-

This translation was made from the edicts of December 19, 1639, and October 15, 1795, both of which were read in New Spain and which are identical except for the spelling of a few words. They were printed in the thousands, read in churches, and nailed on the church doors. Although the signs of Judaism were listed at length, the document is interesting for what is missing as well as for what it contains. The word *hebreo* was never used, only *judío* or *judaycas* appéars. In the list of Jewish holidays, Rosh Hashona and Shavuot are significant by their absence. While the word "Sabbath" is present, there is no mention of lighting of candles or attending synagogue services on the Sabbath. Nothing is mentioned of a Talmud, a Torah scroll, a mezuzzah, a tallit (prayer shawl), or books such as *Clave de Salomón* or *Espejo de Consolación*.

Espejo de Consolación

On the Saturday of the week preceding the reading of the edict, a public proclamation was made requiring all inhabitants to attend church to hear the anathema under pain of excommunication and fifty ducats fine. On the awesome Sunday, there were no sermons preached in any other churches of the town. After six days, at high mass, all those who had failed to confess or report others and who were suspected of the breaches of faith, heresy, or other crimes listed in the edict were considered to have been excommunicated. The proceedings in pronouncing the anathema upon the culprits were enough to strike terror into the most hardy, and it requires no great effort to gauge the effect on the religiously fanatic or superstitious of colonial times.

The clergy marched into church with a cross bedecked in black and placed it on the altar, flanked by two flaming torches. During the reading, the clergy stood as soldiers, with eyes straight ahead, lips pursed, and in profound silence while the following was intoned:

> We excommunicate and anathematize, in the name of the Father and of the Son and of the Holy Ghost . . . all apostate heretics from our Holy Catholic faith, their supporters and concealers who have not revealed them, and we curse them that they may be accursed as associates of the devil and separated from the bosom and unity of the Holy Mother Church. We order all the faithful . . . to curse them so that they may fall into the wrath . . . of Al-

mighty God. May all the curses and plagues of Egypt which befell Pharaoh come upon them because they disobey the commandments of God! May they be accursed wherever they be, in the city or in the country, living or dying! May the fruits of their land be accursed and the cattle thereof! May God send them hunger and pestilence to consume them! . . . May the devil be at their side! . . . May they be driven from their homes and their enemies take their possessions! May their wives and children rise against them and then be turned into orphans and beggars with none to assist them! . . . May they be accursed with all the curses of the Old Covenant and the New! May the curse of Sodom and Gomorrah overtake them and its fire burn them. May the earth swallow them like Dathan and Abiram for the sin of disobedience! May they be accursed as Lucifer with all the devils of hell where may they remain with Judas and the damned forever, if they do not acknowledge their sin, beg mercy, and amend their lives.[25]

The people responded "Amen," the clergy chanted, and the great bells tolled as for a death. The torches were extinguished by plunging them into the basin of the holy water as the priests said, "As these torches die in the water, so will their souls in hell!"

Confession under the edict had to be full and complete. Not only personal heresies were to be disclosed but those of others as well. It was assumed that confessants were sincere and their confessions genuine since they, as good Catholics, would not want any heretic, regardless of relationship to them, to escape the clutches of the Holy Office. The absolution granted was no bar to subsequent arrest and condemnation if the confession had not been complete. Such a defective confession made during an Inquisition trial was called a *diminuto*. Inquisition canons did not recognize the plea of "double jeopardy."

THE INQUISITORIAL PROCEEDINGS

Eduardo Pallares wrote his book to gather "irrefutable proof of the injustices of inquisitorial proceedings (many of them infamous and atrocious) in order to show that the Holy Office as an institution deserved the curses of all human lovers of true justice and the liberty which God had granted to man."[26] The persecution and punishments of the Inquisition were so severe that officials and private persons close to the throne made vehement protests, and there were indignant critics of the abuses of Inquisition practices at every stage of its history.[27]

Arrest, Sequestration, and Audiences

Proceedings were normally begun by the arrest of the heretic, usually after midnight, with immediate sequestration of all of his personal property. The edict of September 2, 1561, consisted of eighty-one provisions or articles. Appendix B lists the most pertinent provisions of this edict, which was the body of law that governed the Inquisition Tribunals overseas. Taking possession of all of the prisoner's personal property deprived him of the means of securing assistance and beggared his family.

The property sequestered was a great source of income for the Holy Office and, at times, lined the pockets of the inquisitors themselves. The sequestered property was used to defray the cost of the prisoner's food, barber's services, and the fees of those who administered torture. All charges were deducted even if the case were ultimately suspended or the prisoner was acquitted. Sequestration was total. It included furniture, clothing, and linens. The secret cells were usually bare. The prisoner was permitted to retain for his cell a bed, two sheets, a pillow, a blanket, and two complete sets of clothing including undergarments. The food was of poor quality and the subject of constant complaint. Prisoners were permitted to have food brought from the outside, but this did not reduce the daily food charge. During the seventeenth century in New Spain, servants brought food (some kosher) from the homes of their Jewish masters. Sometimes messages were concealed in the food.

The evils of sequestration could be visited upon innocent grandchildren even decades after the death of a grandparent from whom the child may have inherited property.[28] Antonio Puigblanch wrote:

> . . . the death of the accused is not a barrier against the fury of the Inquisition, or the grave an asylum against its inexorable persecutions. The memory of him who died upright in the opinion of all is pursued with malignity, even a century after he had ceased to exist, if after the lapse of time anyone seeks to avenge himself or take an interest in his defamation. His bones are dug out of his grave and burned . . . while his property is wrested from its present possessors.[29]

Without fail, the question was put to prisoners, "when did you begin following the dead Law of Moses?" The significance of the question was usually lost upon the prisoners. Many, if not most, Jews would ascribe the beginnings to their early ages when they were under the influence of their parents. From the date of the observance of heretical rites, the prisoner lost all rights to property thereafter acquired. It was a cut-off point to fix the date from which all the prisoner's property could be acquired by the Holy Office. Such property could be traced into the hands of previous and innocent purchasers. A husband could be made to surrender the dowry he received years previously from his wife if she were accused of judaizante. In one case in New Spain, that of Simón Váez, the Holy Office demanded not only the amount equal to the dowry but also one-half of his fortune because this had been accumulated as a result of the investments made with the funds that he received when he and his wife had been married twenty years previously.

The prisoner could not select his own attorney. After the first audience he was offered a choice of one of three lawyers nominated by the inquisitors. Independence of action by the advocates for the defense was beyond reason. His task was to encourage the prisoner to confess. Lawyers were barred from conferring privately with their clients and were sworn to secrecy.

Sentences of those to be burned were announced the night before the official auto-da-fé. This obviated appeals to Spain or Rome or attempts to invoke intercession. The prisoner was not advised of the charges against him either at the time of his arrest or at the first or second hearing. He was compelled to guess the charges and declare what he thought to be the causes of his arrest. The prosecuting attorney filed his written accusation (a form of indictment minus names and dates) after the third hearing or audience.

If the prosecuting attorney had not sufficiently proved the accusation, he then requested that the prisoner be tortured. The right of the accused to call witnesses was limited. New Christians, family, servants, infamous persons, and anyone could testify for the Holy Office, but the aforementioned as well as relatives and employees could not testify in favor of the accused. The inquisitors in New Spain paid lip service to the rule that the testimony of two witnesses was required for each salient fact. In practice, a single witness sufficed for arrest and torture, and the testimony of even the vilest person was welcomed without discrimination.[30]

Technically, the accused was to have three audiences within the first days after his arrest. At the first he was admonished to tell the truth without concealment of anything he may have said or done contrary to the Catholic faith. For full disclosure, he was promised leniency, and for noncompliance he was threatened with great severity. While still ignorant of the specific charge against him, he was told that the Tribunal never apprehended anyone without sufficient proof and therefore voluntary confession was for his best interest.

The hearing room was quite bare. In Mexico, usually two or three inquisitors were present. There was a couplet about this in New Spain, *"Un Santo Cristo, dos candelbros, / un pobra y dos majaderos"* (One holy Christ, two candles, / one poor devil and two scoundrels).[31] During the seventeenth century in New Spain periods between imprisonment and final sentencing ranged from three to thirteen years.

The accused was warned that any physical injury that he sustained while under torture was the result of his own doing. In the public autos, "great care was also taken that no prisoner made his appearance maimed or bruised by torture."[32] We know of one prisoner who needed four years to recuperate from the maiming sustained under torture before he was taken to an auto for his punishment.

That many of the inquisitors were corrupt and venal was revealed by the Visitador Pedro de Medina Rico.[33] His report on the inquisitors in Mexico City in the seventeenth century is discussed in Chapter 13.

The inquisitors had secretaries, *fiscales, familiars*, wardens, notaries, and other necessary assistants. The *fiscal* served as a superior clerk of the court and he also acted as prosecuting attorney. He drew accusations, advised the inquisitors, marshalled the evidence, and kept the records in order. He was used as a bogey man—that is, the accused was constantly threatened with what the fiscal would do if he did not confess. One threat was that the attorney would present a formal accusation in which he would demand torture and relaxation for the accused.

The familiar served as a deputy for the inquisitors. Each maintained an office in an outlying area of New Spain, made investigations in his area, and filed denunciations in the capital, where the inquisitors determined what action was to be taken.

*Inquisitor's table. Photograph from the House
of the Inquisition, Lima, Peru*

The warden was the jailer and vested with the responsibility of guarding the prisoners in their cells, reporting all incidents in the cells to the inquisitors, and acting as an eavesdropper for them. There were no female jailers. Moral depravity was evidenced by some male wardens. It is true that they were deterred by the threat of the death penalty for violating the rights of female prisoners, but the threat was not completely efficacious in attaining the desired ends. Cases of rape and seduction have been reported. Many male prisoners had no hesitation in requesting better food, medical services, and slight improvements in their physical surroundings, and these pleas were often heeded by the inquisitors.

TESTIMONY

Audience chambers had a *celosia*, a jalousy, peep-hole, or lattice-work device through which a witness could peer without being seen. These may still be seen in Puebla in Mexico and the Casa de la Inquisición in Lima, Peru. Testimony from trials of other people could be introduced against prisoners, who did not have the opportunity to cross-examine the witnesses. The prisoner was never told the name of the witnesses, and the testimony presented may have been ten or fifteen years old. When the testimony was "published" (submitted in evidence to the inquisitors), a garbled summary, so as to secrete any clues that might reveal the identity of the witness, was read to the prisoner.

Testimony against "the memory and fame" of accused deceased persons could be adduced many years later. The statute of limitations or bar to sequestration of property was recognized only if good Catholics, not lineal descendants of the deceased, had had possession of the accused's property for fifty or more years.

The defenses available to accused heretics were *tachas*, enmity or other disability of the witness, and *abonos*, proof of good moral character and religiosity. While there were some acquittals, the Inquisition seldom was that unequivocal; more often there was an order of suspension, thus leaving a degree of uncertainty for the record.

THE AUTO-DA-FÉ

The auto-da-fé was the ceremony accompanying the pronouncement of judgment by the Inquisition and was followed by the execution of the sentences by the secular authorities. It was intended to instill fear into the observers.

It began with a procession of monks, the leading royal officials, and those to be penanced. The day of a general or public auto was always held on a Sunday or other holy day. Lent was a favorite period, as was the period preceding Christmas. These were fiesta days and people came from miles around; one risked suspicion by absence. The proceedings began at sunrise and, if there were long sentences and many penitents, sometimes continued into a second day. The stench of burning flesh and the screams of the few who had not been permitted strangulation by the garrote added awesome effects. The auto was intended to be a replica of the scene of the ultimate Day of Judgment. It was devised to inspire awe for the mysterious authority of the Inquisition and to impress on the populace a total abhorrence of heresy.

Sanbenitos. From Stockdale's The History of the Inquisition

The parade was called the Procession of the Green Cross. The Green Cross, the emblem of the Holy Office, was used by Dominicans (originally known as the Militia of Christ) and was carried at the head of the procession. Green denoted hope for the salvation of the souls about to be penanced. The Mayordomo of the *Cofradia* (brotherhood) carried a large white cross.

Those to be burned at the stake carried green candles and wore *corazas* with flames painted on them. The coraza was a high conical cap similar to that used as a dunce cap many years ago in schools. The term "coraza" has also been defined as a miter. Those to be burned or scourged wore halters about their necks.

The most important garment worn by the penitents was the sanbenito. There were four classes of sanbenitos, but all were made of coarse cotton or linen and were put on over the head. For those to be relaxed, black sanbenitos with pictures of flames, and sometimes demons pushing the heretic into hell, were worn. Those to be reconciled and merely flogged wore a simple sanbenito with two bars and a green cross. Those to abjure *de vehementi* wore garments with one bar behind and one diagonal bar in front. Negative penitents (those who refused to admit the crime of heresy or Judaism) wore garments with flames and demons on a yellow ground and with hoods.

Sanbenitos had to be worn in the streets over one's clothing for a prescribed period of time. The effect of the sanbenito was to make the wearer a pariah. Ricardo Palma wrote that "people fled from him as if he were a pestilence."[34] In New Spain during the 1650's a certain Jew who had been condemned to wear a sanbenito for five years doffed it and was hailed before the Tribunal for noncompliance with his sentence. His defense was that he, a fencing master, could not earn his living while wearing it because he was shunned by the gentility.

SENTENCES AND RECONCILIATION

Sentences were given either *con méritos* or *sin méritos*. The former meant that a review of the proceedings of the entire trial was read aloud at the auto-da-fé, with special stress upon the misdeeds of the culprit. *Sin méritos* meant a very brief report or, sometimes, merely a brief statement of the offense for which the accused was appearing in the auto-da-fé.

All persons not sentenced to the stake were "reconciled." Those reconciled appeared in the auto with candles in their hands, dressed without girdles or caps in a habit of yellow cloth on which were two red bands forming a St. Andrew's cross. They abjured; they knelt during the reading of a short catechism comprising the creed and replied, "Yes, I believe" to each statement of dogma of the faith.

Their sentences were then imposed. The punishments meted out included one or a combination of such penances as abjuration, scourge or vergüenza, the wearing of sanbenitos, consignment to the galleys, servitude as soldiers in remote lands, and imprisonment.

Those penanced for heresy, including those reconciled, were deprived of all rights to hold public office or to be a grocer, apothecary, physician, surgeon, bleeder, broker, merchant, notary, scrivener, or advocate. He or she could not wear gold, silver, coral, pearls, or other precious stones; garments of silk, camlet, or other finery; or ride a horse or bear arms. These prohibitions extended to the third generation.

This was the welcome back into the bosom of the Church. There were rare cases of second and even third reconciliations. Effigies of the dead were also admitted to reconciliation.

After completion of the sentence, the sanbenito was hung on the wall of the cathedral. In New Spain, when wall space was at a premium, *tabillas*, small rectangular strips of cloth with the accused's name, the date of the sentence, and the type of sin, were substituted for sanbenitos.

Abjurations

Abjurations, denial or disavowals under oath, were impressive ceremonies. To abjure *de levi*, the accused faced a large cross with his hands on the Gospels, and swore that he accepted Catholicism as the sole, true faith and that he pledged eternal allegiance to the faith and obedience to the pope. He promised to denounce and persecute any who opposed Catholicism and vowed "to fulfill with all his strength" any penance imposed upon him.

To abjure *de vehementi*, the oath was phrased in stronger words, was presented in writing, and was signed by the prisoner. In addition, the accused had to agree to be treated as "relapsed" (a repetition of heretical practices) with all attendant penalties (an irrevocable sentence of burning) if he ever again strayed.

Abjuration was mandatory if there were only "semi-proof" of guilt, even though torture had not extracted a confession. The instructions held that "abjuration for light or vehement suspicion is a measure to inspire fear for the future rather than punishment for the past."

Scourge and Vergüenza

For the sentence of scourging, lashes were applied by a public executioner, using a *penca* (leather strap). A halter placed around the neck of one to be scourged had knots which indicated the number of lashes he or she was to receive—one knot for each hundred lashes.

The culprit, regardless of sex, was forced to bare to the waist, wear a coraza bearing the inscription of his offense, and ride on an ass during the scourging. Mounted familiars and a notary or secretary, preceded by the town crier proclaiming the orders of the inquisitors, made up the small entourage. Sometimes there was also an official known as the *notario de azotaciónes* (notary of scourgings); in one city such an official received an annual salary of 2,500 reales to keep a record of the number of lashes administered. Two hundred lashes was the usual number given the prisoner, and there was no mercy because of age or sex. A brutalizing effect on the populace must have resulted from these wholesale exhibitions of floggings.

Vergüenza (literally, shame) entailed a similar ceremony but the lashing was omitted. In both scourging and vergüenza, the culprit had to wear the *pie de amigo* (an iron instrument used to keep the head of the person erect). A *mordaza* (gag) was sometimes also used so that a penitent who might be a hardened blasphemer could not create a scandal by uttering oaths and imprecations.

The Galleys

The sentence of consignment to the galleys was the result of a plan by King Ferdinand to save money by using prisoners as oarsmen on galleys traveling between Spain and Sicily. The practice started in Castile in 1503. Pope Alexander VI sanctioned this punishment on May 26, 1503; such approval by the Holy See was needed to still the protests and shock of the populace. In 1506, it was decreed that clerics, women, and men over sixty years old were to be exempt from this penance. From 1527 to 1529 the use of penitents as oarsmen was completely prohibited. After 1529, however, penitents again labored on ships plying their way from Veracruz to

Spain, a trip of sixty to ninety days each way, and from Acapulco to the Philippines, a trip of six to nine months.

There are no records of the mortalities incurred on the galleys. In 1567, the ambassador from Venice commented that the Spanish navy was weak because it was manned by slaves, that the ill treatment of crews was notorious, and that many men died for the lack of the necessities of life.[35] In that same year, 1567, the Suprema ordered that the period of service in the galleys had to be a minimum of three or four years. Even *buen confidentes* (free and prompt confessors) were sent to the galleys, where some captains kept the men beyond the prescribed period of servitude.

The Inquisition in New Spain spared penitents of noble blood from this ignominious, slow death. They were usually ordered to serve as soldiers in distant lands or in jail "without pay." The sentences to the galleys also usually appended the words "without pay" to the orders. By the eighteenth century in New Spain, sentences to *presidios* (jails), especially jails in the Philippines, were substituted for sentences to the galleys.

Imprisonment

Women were usually sentenced to serve without pay in hospitals or houses of correction run by the Church. Such "penitential prisons" were often convents or monasteries, and in some, discipline was comparatively lax. Some prisoners were permitted to seek outside employment and had to report only at night.

Some sentences were to secular presidios or royal jails. Sentences of imprisonment were for varying periods, up to incarceration for life.

The Stake

The Inquisition rendered no judgments of blood, although it did grant indulgences to those of the general public who contributed wood for the funeral pyres. Execution by burning was a matter for secular law.[36] Canon law declared that princes and their officials must promptly punish all heretics delivered to them by the Inquisition, under pain of excommunication. Those found guilty of heresy were turned over to the secular arm of the crown for the punishment that was mandatory—the stake. The sentencing civil magistrates did not have the privilege of reading the transcript of the testimony before the Inquisition.

José Toribio Medina quoted from a Mexican newspaper article of 1870 that summed up well the opinion about the Holy Office:

> It seems that it is not necessary to say more to prove the uselessness of the Inquisition than to cite its opposition to the maxims of the Evangelists or Apostles, the illegality of its judgments, and the evils of its mode of proceeding in everything.[87]

6

New Spain: 1521-1571

MEXICAN JEWRY is older than that of the United States. The North American Jewish community was founded in 1654. The refugees who fled from Recife, Brazil, to escape the inquisitorial wrath, some of whom ultimately sought haven in New Amsterdam, were preceded to the shores of the Western Hemisphere by other refugees from Cuba, Puerto Rico, Spain, and Portugal. These people first came to New Spain in 1521 and continued to arrive regularly thereafter. The word "Mexico" will now be used more specifically to indicate Mexico City.

Among Cortes' company in Mexico in 1521 were Gonzalo de Morales, also known as Francisco de Morales,[1] and Hernando Alonso. Some students contend that the two men were brothers, but there is no clear evidence to substantiate this claim. Gonzalo did have a brother, Diego de Morales, who was also one of the first arrivals in Mexico.

Hernando Alonso was the first Jewish martyr in New Spain. He was burned at the stake on October 17, 1528, a short seven years after the Conquest. Alonso had a partner, Bartolomé de Morales, in the business of supplying meat to the city from 1525 to 1527. Morales was never charged with heresy, judaizing, or other violations. It may be pure coincidence that he bore the same family name as Gonzalo de Morales, who also was sent to the stake at the same auto-da-fé with Hernando Alonso.

Alonso's rapid rise to fortune illustrates the opportunities available in New Spain for the enterprising. Cattle, lamb, and pigs were unknown in Mesoamerica prior to the coming of the Spaniards. These animals were imported from Cuba, Puerto Rico, and Hispaniola, where they had been brought earlier from Spain. Part of the booty which Alonso had received as one of Cortés conquistadors was a farm at Actopan, eighty miles north of Mexico, where he raised cattle and lambs for sale in Mexico.

Alonso's military activities had not ceased in August, 1521. Subsequently he fought under Gonzalo de Sandoval in the Panuco area three hundred miles northeast of Mexico and in Guanajuato two hundred miles west of Mexico. Although these forays consumed much time, Alonso's venture into cattle raising was so successful that in March, 1524, he was able to bid to supply meat for the city and underbid his competitor. Cattle was bought by the city fathers and then slaughtered and sold by them at retail. Alonso sold mutton, beef, and pork. He was a pioneer in this trade, and his participation in cattle ranching was a contribution to the development of the new land.

Alonso must have had political influence. His last bid of March, 1528, was not subjected to the competitive bidding that had been the practice in previous years. Part of his influence may have been due to his third marriage. His wife, Beatriz de Ordaz, a beautiful woman many years his junior, was a sister of Diego de Ordaz, another conquistador. The rarity of the presence of any Spanish women and the conquistadors' own families in the very early years made this kind of marriage unusual.

Alonso was, at best, a peripheral Jew; we know that his religious practices were minimal. His third wife apparently was a convert or a daughter of converts. When Alonso told her that she could not go to mass on Sunday because "in your present [menstrual] condition you would profane the Church," she replied, "These are old ceremonies of the Jews which are not observed now that we have adopted the law of evangelical grace." No proceedings were commenced against her, not even deportation for being in the country in violation of the decree barring children of converts. None was instituted against Alonso's children by prior marriages, by then adults also living in Mexico.

The case of Gonzalo de Morales throws light on the existence of religious persecution in Puerto Rico. De Morales was reported to Fray Vincente de Santa María, the acting inquisitor in New Spain, by the same Bishop Manso of Puerto Rico who had condemned Gonzalo's sister to the stake for Jewish practices in Santo Domingo. Under torture she had revealed that she and her brother had flogged a crucifix. After Gonzalo was arrested in Mexico, testimony that he had urinated on a crucifix was offered against him.

Richard E. Greenleaf has speculated on the possibility that Alonso and Gonzalo de Morales were burned at the stake because of politics, while two other Jews, Diego de Ocaña and Diego de Morales were reconciled. The two martyrs were pro-Cortés, and the others were either violently anti-Cortés or nonparticipants in the controversy raging in the colony at that time. Ocaña had stronger identity as a Jew than Alonso; he was known to be a member of the Jewish family Zuárez de Benedeva of Seville.

Diego de Morales, who was not even deported, seemed to lead a charmed life. He was arrested in 1525 for blasphemy, did public penance, and paid a fine. In 1538 he was arrested in Oaxaca for suspicion of being a Jew, abjured, and did public penance. He was rearrested in 1558 for the same offense in Guatemala and again abjured, did public penance, and paid for a mass.[2]

Ocaña died in 1533 and left a considerable estate, part of which went to the Church. It may be that his protest that he had been unjustly accused as well as his bequest to the Church were to avoid further investigation of his true faith. The name of his wife, Beatriz Núñez, and the names of all of the other members of his family except one are names that were known as primarily Jewish names at that time.

A proceso discloses that Ocaña wore a long coat and a round hat similar to the clothing worn by the Jews of Poland and Lithuania in the seventeenth to the twentieth centuries. Moslems wore long coats (called caftan, an Arabic word also used by the Jews but with "k" substituted for "c") and round hats even in Spain. No explanation for Ocaña's wearing these garments has been found. The caftan as Jewish garb existed in the Ottoman Empire in Turkey in the sixteenth century.

Sixteenth century caftan and hat worn
by Turkish Sephardi Jews

The Jewish and Christian men who colonized the New World were rugged Spaniards who did not fear man or God. Their relationships with the Deity took the form of superstitious prayers for deliverance from harm on the eves of battle, and their remembrances of God were often vocalized in the blasphemy that poured forth from their lips. The majority of the Inquisition cases in New Spain from 1534 to 1571 dealt with blasphemy and bigamy. Morales had concubines, as did most Spaniards. Ethics and morality motivated the lives and behavior of the early Jews in Mexico as little as they did the Christians.

Fray Vicente de Santa María, a Dominican, was the first person sent, in 1528, to try cases involving the faith. A royal decree in 1527 had ordered all "who were descended from Jewish or Moorish parents or grandparents, up to the fourth degree, who had been burned at the stake or required to wear a sanbenito . . . to leave New Spain within six months and [upon failure to do so] were to lose one-half of their fortunes."[3] Bernal Díaz de Castillo reports that only two departed; of these, one, a scribe presumed to be Diego de Ocaña, returned within a year, bringing his Castillian wife with him. We know that there were more than two Jews in Mexico at the time. It is noteworthy that the illegal presence of those apprehended was punished only by a fine.

The 1528 auto-da-fé took place in front of the Cathedral of Santiago de Tlaltelolco. Tlaltelolco was an Indian religious site where a magnificent pyramid had stood. Atop the pyramid Aztec priests had sacrificed brave warriors and torn beating heart from breast to placate their gods. In 1528, Jewish blood and ashes began to mingle in the soil with those of the indigenous population of Tenochtitlán. Attendance of the entire city's population at this auto-da-fé was obligatory under threat of excommunication.

From 1528 to 1534 there is a record of only one trial of a Jew. The explanation for this abatement in cases may be found in European history. The spiritual hegemony of Catholicism was being threatened and the physical realm was being decimated. These years fall during the Reformation and the growth of Protestantism. Sultan Suleiman II (1520-1566) of the Ottoman Empire had captured Belgrade and Rhodes, and his further advances into Europe seemed imminent.

Charles I of Spain was also the Holy Roman emperor known as

Charles V. Although a grandson of Ferdinand and Isabella, he was not a Spaniard but a Habsburg; he introduced this dynasty into Spain. In the early years of his reign the sport of Jew-baiting seemed to have fallen into disfavor and almost desuetude. Adrian VI became pope in 1524 and did not share the anti-Jewish attitudes of the College of Cardinals, who deplored the lack of zeal in "making war on the Jews, putting heretics to death . . ."[4] Among the factors that might account for the benign treatment of Jews outside of Spain proper were the loans obtained by Charles V from a Portuguese bank founded by the husband of Doña Gracia Méndez Nasi (a famous Jewess of the sixteenth century whose financial connections were extensive) and the influence possessed by Benvenida Abravanel, wife of Samuel, who was the son of Isaac Abravanel.

During the same era, David Reubeni appeared in Rome. He was a Jewish adventurer claiming to come from the East. Reubeni was received by the pope and sought munitions for his brother, whom he alleged to be a "King of Jews" in Arabia. Reubeni promised that a Jewish army would be raised to fight against the Turks if the Christians would supply them with arms. Reubeni received letters from the pope addressed to all Catholic kings and left for Portugal to seek aid from King John III (1521-1557). Italian and Iberian Jewry were thrilled to learn of a heretofore unknown Jewish kingdom and of the royal or ambassadorial treatment accorded to one of their coreligionists.

A young Portuguese, inspired by the stories and rumors, dropped his dual role of a Catholic-Jew and became an openly professing Jew. He abandoned family and official post and, becoming filled with the ardor of a visionary, came to believe that he was the long prayed-for Jewish Messiah. He took the name Shlomo (Solomon) Molko. His fame also spread, and he, too, was received in Italy with honor by personages of importance, including the pope. Both he and Reubeni, however, made enemies among Jews and Christians. Their undoing has been attributed in great part to another Jew, Dr. Jacob Mantino.[5]

Before their undoing, however, John III did nothing for Reubeni because he realized that there was an anachronism between helping a Jewish king and persecuting Jews and New Christians within his own realm. Molko died at the stake in Rome. Reubeni was taken to Llerena, Spain, and was there tried and convicted by the Inquisition and burned about 1535. Llerena and the surrounding area held a large crypto-Jewish population, some of whom emigrated to New Spain after 1535.

During the times of Pope Adrian VI (1522-1523), Pope Clement VIII (1523-1534), and Pope Paul III (1534-1550) there was an abatement of persecution of the Jews in the Iberian Peninsula. During the earliest years of the 1530's, Portuguese New Christians had an emissary in Rome who succeeded in securing a papal brief forbidding any action to be taken against conversos. On April 7, 1533, a bull of pardon was issued "which provided New Christians with amnesty for all past offenses in matters of faith" and granted leave to committers of future infractions to justify their acts before the papal nuncio.[6] Thousands of ducats were paid to cardinals and the papal nuncio but, in spite of bribes and due to the change of heart of Charles V, previous temperate bulls were revoked on May 23, 1536.

The collapse of Reubeni and Molko as false Messiahs, the new victory over the Turks at Tunis by Charles V, and the resurgence of religious zeal against Jews contributed to the revival of the search for Jews in New Spain. In Portugal the creation of the Inquisition along Spanish lines was ordered, and tribunals were established at Coimbra, Evora, and Lisbon. By 1540 the first major auto-da-fé was held in Lisbon, and a new need for Jews to emigrate became apparent. The New World seemed the beckoning hope.

In 1528, Bishop Juan de Zumárraga had come to New Spain; later he was named Apostolic Inquisitor. He organized a tribunal and began to ferret out Jews. His methods were in accordance with canon law, and his judgments were tempered with mercy. While he served, a royal decree was issued on August 22, 1534, reminding the officials of the Casa de Contratación that "it was forbidden for reconciled persons, or sons or grandsons of persons burned at the stake, or newly converted from Moors or Jews, to go to our Indies."

While Zumárraga had jurisdiction to prosecute all matters of the faith under his episcopal powers, he began no proceedings against any Jews until September, 1536. His first case involving a Jew was against Gonzalo Gómez, a reconciliado from Spain, who was living in Michoacan, about two hundred miles from Mexico.[7] Of the thirteen counts filed against Gómez, those of Jewish content were that he observed the Jewish Sabbath, and that when traveling he stopped on Friday and resumed his trip on Sunday. He was a circumcized convert, and his parents and family had been reconciled in Spain. The other charges were profanation of crosses and that he used to invite Indians and Spaniards to use his barn, the same building used by itinerant clergymen for mass, as a bordello. Gómez escaped with abjuration, reconciliation, and fine of 400 gold pesos—a tremendous sum.

The earliest colonial Jews were undistinguished by learning, morals, or skills, as were their Christian contemporaries. The later arrivals were nonadventurous and were accompanied by wives and families. They brought farm implements and, as Jews, were better versed in their faith. Some of those who flocked to New Spain were termed dogmatizers by the inquisitors. Their attempts to proselytize made them masters of circumspection in normal conversation. Sometimes such talk, however, led them to the Inquisition. In 1589, such talk was the undoing of Isabel de Carvajal, and in 1594 Manuel de Lucena was arrested for a similar unsuccessful effort.

Colonial Jews seemed determined to undermine the faith both of Christians and of Indians. Juan de Baeza was tried in 1540 for circumcizing Indian children with his fingernails.[8] He was also noted for his detestation of Catholicism. Zumárraga let him off with a monetary fine. Loathing of Christianity was evidenced by many others apprehended during the period from 1536-1543. Nineteen cases were instituted against the Jews by Zumárraga.[9]

From the cases tried by Archbishop Zumárraga we can see the beginning of the first Jewish communal efforts. In one such case, Francisco Millán testified before Zumárraga that the Jews generally knew each other and that some of them ate together and observed their dietary laws. Some of them either had worn sanbenitos in Spain or their parents had worn them.

The records also reveal that they did not confine their habitations to a particular part of any city in New Spain, although many who had come from Jérez de la Frontera in Spain resided in the capital. Gómez lived in Michoacan; other Jews lived in Zultepec, Puebla, Pachuca, and elsewhere. The religious practices were those that did not require overt acts that were easily observable, such as the ritual slaughtering of fowl or cattle. Their religion was observed more in acts of abstinence, such as refraining from eating pork products or working on the Sabbath. Brief prayer services were conducted in homes, never with too many in attendance at one place. Boys and men prayed with caps on their heads. Since Spanish peasants removed the caps from their heads only in church or in bed, the Jew who wore his cap for religious purpose was not bizarre.

Primary sources of information are the facts gleaned from reports of inquisitors' questioning, the scope of the interrogation, and the answers given. It is certain that some people, when compelled to talk through torture or threat of torture, involved other Jews. A few utilized the occasion to seek vengeance on non-Jews whom they regarded as enemies. There is little question that Francisco Millán sought vengeance upon some Christians by claiming that they were Jews. Millán's father had been drawn and quartered in Seville, and many of his relatives (as well as those of other Jews then in New Spain) had been reconciled in Spain. Millán's wife and six children were still in Jérez de la Frontera at the time.

Millán had come to Mexico in 1536. Although he was practically illiterate, he was knowledgeable about Jewish customs and had been circumcized. He had not been baptized. He was reported to the Inquisition as a result of a story told by his Moorish maid and concubine to a wine dealer. She said that she had been told by a former Indian slave of Millán that Millán had flogged an image of Mary, had broken two crosses, and that he had demanded that Mary return money that had been stolen from him. Millán confessed as he was being disrobed in the torture chamber. He was to have been tortured "without effusion of blood, mutilation, or breaking of any limb."

Millán had sold the Indian slave a month before he was denounced to the inquisitor. She had been taken first to Oaxaca and then to Peru, so her testimony was unavailable. Millán's punishment was the total confiscation of his property, exile, and spiritual penance of standing on a scaffold during mass with a candle in his hand and then kneeling at the altar rail while consuming the Eucharist. His public abjuration was on Cananea Sunday, March 2, 1539, after which he was to wear a sanbenito over his clothes whenever he went out of his house until the Suprema in Seville or the king granted leave to remove it.

The requirement for Millán's exile was to be fulfilled by his taking the first ship to Spain. (There is no mention of who was to pay for the passage since Millán had no more money.) Richard E.

Greenleaf, in his epilogue to the summary of the trial, comments, "Like many other banished heretics who had been reconciled, Francisco Millán did not leave Mexico." He was seen in Taxco in July, 1539, "as a beggar wearing a sanbenito—but under his clothes," later in Zultepec, and after that in Toluca, still begging. It is interesting to contemplate why, having defied the inquisitors by not going to Spain, Millán wore the sanbenito at all—and why under his clothes.

Another aspect of Inquisition judgments requires amplification. At the conclusion of article on Millán, Greenleaf notes that the confiscation of Millán's property, including his inn or tavern, netted the Inquisition little because of suits by Millán's creditors, and he adds, "It may have been true that some of the debts were fabricated and that monies were actually held in trust for Millán or his relatives by those who pressed suit."[10] There is little question that many debts allegedly owed by Jews were claimed to thwart the confiscation of property by the Holy Office.

When the Inquisition sequestered the property of a prisoner, the first charges against the cash and the money realized on the sale of the prisoner's personal property were expenses while in prison. Then came the claims of creditors. They were not compelled to await the outcome of the trial; they could file claims and commence suit if their claim was questioned. The Inquisition did not desire to impose hardships on Christian creditors. If the wife of the prisoner were a Christian, she could file a claim against the sequestered property for the recovery of her dowry. Some secret Jewesses risked their safety by such action and recovered their dowries. Some escaped detection for a long time—in one instance over twenty years.

The Jews knew the procedures of the Inquisition. They also knew the suddenness with which arrests took place. They did whatever they could to forestall the loss of their goods and estate. The custom arose of their carrying on their books debts owed to other Jews, and they gave promissory notes and other evidences of indebtedness to members of their families and trusted friends. Sometimes these promissory notes were undated. One unfortunate incident arose from this practice. When Agustín de Roxas was arrested in 1642[11] and his property seized, his half-brother Juan de Roxas filed a claim predicated on a promissory note.[12] But Juan made a slight error. In dating the instrument, he made the date subsequent to that of Augustín's arrest. (Juan's later arrest was not due to this error; he had previously been informed against.) There is no question, however, that his punishment was aggravated by his unsuccessful perjurious attempt to get some of his brother's funds, which ultimately benefitted the Inquisition.

The end of Zumárraga's epoch was marked by his ordering an important Indian cacique (chief) to be burned alive at the stake. This resulted in indignation in clerical as well as secular circles in Spain and his removal as Apostolic Inquisitor. Francisco Tello de Sandoval succeeded Zumárraga, but he completely neglected his inquisitorial responsibilities because of his duties as *visitador* (a one-man investigation committee of affairs of the viceroyalty and other official posts). After Tello de Sandoval's departure in 1547, the bishops and prelates of the various orders regained their inquisitorial powers under the bull *Omnimoda*.

From 1544 to 1574, there are only a few cases before the Inquisition, but subsequent events prove that Jews had been streaming into New Spain. "The Jewish community continued to grow [after 1540] in Mexico City [and] Pachuca . . . and the *conversos* discreetly practiced the old rites in private. It was not until the last two decades of the sixteenth century that the Tribunal of the Holy Office made a concerted effort to eradicate the Judaizantes. Again the effort failed, because the converted Jew had evolved a hardiness and cunning with which the Holy Office could not cope."[13]

Three interesting cases during the quiescent period are worth noting. Juan de Astorga, arrested in 1554, was a clogmaker who inserted crosses between the cork and the sole of the shoes he made. The proceso indicates that he was a Jew, and that his act was considered analogous to the breaking of images. Blas Mosqueras, in 1556, was discovered to be a Jew after he struck a priest.[14] In 1570, there is the first report of an English Jew, Antonio Saña, in Mexico, who was arrested "for being a Jew who practiced the Law of Moses."[15]

On August 14, 1543, the clerk of the Inquisition, Juan Muñoz de Parris, prepared for Tello de Sandoval a list that was supposed to include the names of all children in New Spain of those burned at the stake or reconciled.[16] Nothing happened to any of those named as a result of this list, even though it was prepared pursuant to an order of Prince Philip, who became King Philip II of Spain in 1556. This list contains no outstanding figures or scions of noble families.

Ethnic minority groups are always concerned with the role that their members played in the history of a country and the contributions that they made to its culture and development. Jews have pointed to their impressive achievements in fields of scholarship and science. Their psychological need to point with pride is an understandable result of a history of self-defense against the attempts of the Church in the past and the anti-Semite of the present to discriminate, persecute, and to depict the Jews as foreigners in the nations of which they have long been citizens.

The comment of the sixteenth century Peruvian, Pinto of Lima, that seventy-five percent of the white, Spanish population of Peru in the sixteenth century had Jewish blood in their veins applied almost equally as well to those in New Spain. Laerte de Ferreira, of the same era, also stated that the conquerors themselves were bearers of Jewish blood. The Spaniards of New Spain and Peru came from the same peninsula and from the same stock. Numerous works list the great percentage of the Iberians whose ancestors were Jewish. Pinto further claims that it was the Jews and their descendants who introduced the concepts of social justice into the New World.

Padre Angel María Garibay, Canon of the Basilica of Guadalupe of Mexico City, on November 27, 1961, gave an address in the Palacio de Bellas Artes entitled "Jews in Mexico in the Sixteenth Century." The renowned Franciscan scholar presented a list that covered most of the greatest figures in the first century of Mexican colonial history outside of the field of government.

Among those mentioned were a number of monks. Heading the list was Bernardino de Sahagún, a Franciscan whose works of over fourteen volumes comprise the greatest source of knowledge on the Nahuatl language, the customs of the Aztecs and other tribes, and their pre-Conquest history. Father Sahagún was the greatest anthropologist of his century. He founded the Colegio de Santa Cruz de Tlaltelolco, and his works have been translated into practically every civilized tongue. He was of the Ribero family, the son of a Jewish mother and father who turned the son over to the Church in order to save him from persecution. Garibay wrote in *Novedades*

(April 18, 1961) that the disclosure of Sahagún's ancestry *"lo que no ha de dar gusto a algunos antisemitas"* (will not give pleasure to some anti-Semites).

Diego de Durán, another Franciscan, wrote a history of Mexico in 1556 which rates among the important sources of information. He was the "natural child" of a Jewish father and a mestiza mother. We do not know whether she was Jewish. Garibay believes that the Dominican Gabriel García was a Jew, but qualified the statement by adding that he had no definite proof. In the same category were Fray Luis de León and another Dominican, Luis de Granada.

To complete his tabulation of Jews or those of Jewish descent in monastic orders, Garibay spoke of Gregorio López, who has been beatified as Beato Gregorio. Of this famous Mexican, Garibay said that he was *"enigmatico, pero se reconoce que es judio"* (as odd as it may appear, however, it is acknowledged that he is a Jew). Gregorio is the author of the *Apocalypse of St. John*, but his outstanding work was in the field of medicine. Rafael López, the head of the Mexican National Archives in 1935, attributes the beatified hermit's vast knowledge of medicinal plants to his being one of the "sons of Israel," and said that in his *Book of the Apocalypse*, he always stressed a continuing hope for the second coming of the Messiah.[17]

While Vicente Riva Palacio makes no mention of Jewish parentage for Gregorio in discussing the obscurity of his birth and lineage, others have not hesitated to identify the famous hermit of San Sebastian as a Jew. Among these was his contemporary, Luis de Carvajal, *el Mozo*, who stated unequivocally during his second trial in 1596 that Gregorio was a Jew. Mariano Cuevas, the Jesuit historian noted for his anti-Protestant and anti-Jewish comments, adopts young Louis' characterization. Ricardo Albanes, another anti-Semite, in his *Los judíos a través de los siglos* also concurs in the Jewish classification of Gregorio.

Among the laity listed by Garibay as Jews or children of Jews were Martín López,[18] a conquistador with Cortés who was a master carpenter (and under whom Hernando Alonso served in building ships in 1521) and Enrico Martínez. Martínez established the first printing plant in the capital in the 1530's. He was of German or Italian origin.

In addition to those named, there is another illustrious son of Jewish parents, Francisco de Vitoria, who, after serving as Bishop of

Gregory Lopez. As reproduced in México á
través de los siglos, *Vol. 2*

Tucumán in what is now Argentina, was elevated to post of Archbishop of Mexico and later served as Archbishop of Charques in
Spain. Archbishop de Vitoria was one of the children of Duarte
Núñez and Gracia Núñez, acknowledged as Jews.[19] The presence
of these personages, as well as several others—not all of whom could
have been unaware of the religion of their parents—may have

*Fr. Francisco de Vitoria. Original painting at
the University of Santo Domingo*

played some role in the extreme laxity of enforcement of decrees against Jews and prosecution for Jewish practices.

During the middle and latter part of the sixteenth century, there were many monks and minor officials in Spain and New Spain who were preaching, teaching, or practicing the Law of Moses. Fray Luis de Valdecagnas, a Franciscan and descendant of Jews, was accused in the auto-da-fé of March 15, 1562, at Murcia for preaching the "dead Law of Moses." His companions for similar offenses were Alberto Xuarez and Pablo d'Ayllon, who were aldermen or sheriffs; Pedro Gutiérrez, town councilman; Juan de Sotomayor; Francisco Guillén, a merchant; Juan de Santa Fé; and Juan de León.[20] In 1583 Licenciado Alonso Ruiz, a canon and Vicar General, was convicted in New Spain of being a Jew. We know that he was a great-grandson of Julio Alvarez, also a Jew.[21]

In the 1550's, New Christians paid inquisitor Capodiferra 1,800 cruzados per annum for pardons. In 1554, Pope Julius III sarcastically said that papal nuncios were sent to Portugal to enrich themselves.[22] In 1567, Pope Pius V, at the request of Inquisitor General Espinosa, authorized the absolving publicly or privately for three years of "the Judaizing New Christians" of Murcia and Alcaraz.[23] No fines were to be imposed. There is no question that bribery was the key to leniency; Henry C. Lea even includes some popes as recipients of such favors.

The thirty year quiescent period was marked by the attempts of Jews in Portugal to modify the severity of Inquisition procedures so that the accused could be told the names of their accusers and witnesses. In a memorial to King John of Portugal in 1547, four Jews stated that Portuguese Jews would leave the country unless the long decreed pardons and the requested modifications were put into effect. The modifications were denied, but the pardons were granted to those who recanted Judaism. This situation lasted for a short while, and then the Inquisition in Portugal resumed its efforts, which further stimulated the Jewish hegira to the New World.

A translation of the Inquisition's summary of the content of some blank verse in the possession of Juan Bautista Corvera (also Cervera), of Guadalajara, New Spain, who was tried in 1564 for heretical propositions and judaizante, serves to illustrate the propaganda of the Jews.

If the law given by God to Moses was good, as it undubitably was, there was no reason to change it, especially as Jesus Christ himself had said that he had come to the world in order to fulfill it, and this being so, the persecution which was being made of the Jews and their God was unjust; on the other hand, if there were a change of the Law of Moses, in spite of its being good, such a change itself would be illogical.[24]

Toro concludes that Bautista Corvera had to be a Jew or a New Christian. Bautista Corvera was born in Toledo, Spain, in 1530. His parents were conversos. He wrote many sonnets and couplets, as well as a play that is believed to be the first theatrical work performed in Mexico. His verses were widely disseminated throughout New Spain.[25] Corvera's trial and acquittal gives evidence that there was a strong anti-Church sentiment and that the bishops looked on the anti-Church writings with indulgence. Corvera was a friend of the bishops of Guadalajara, Tlaxcala, and Mexico, and the Bishop of Guadalajara interceded in Juan's behalf.

A noted authority of Mexican history is alleged to have said that the history of Mexico consists of legends with copious footnotes. Luis González Obregon's *México Viejo* is subtitled *Noticias históricas, tradiciones, leyendas y costumbres* (Historical Notes, Traditions, Legends, and Customs).[26] Chapter XI is entitled "The Virgin of Pardon." González Obregon relates it as a legend. The story concerns a painting made by a Jew which was over the altar of the cathedral in Mexico. Rafael Heliodoro Valle refers to the same painting in his article "Judíos en México" and cites two authorities for the authenticity of the painter.[27] The artist's Flemish name was Simon Pereyns (Pereyns or Perines in Spanish); under the latter name he was arrested in Mexico in 1568 for blasphemy. Although Valle and others contend that he was a Jew, he was reconciled and thereafter painted for the Church. The painting over the Great Altar at the Huejotzingo church is also by Perines and dates from 1586, according to the *Mexico City Bulletin* of February 2, 1962.

Alfonso Toro summarized the first fifty years of Mexican Jewish colonial history as follows:

In spite of the legal prohibitions we found that many Israelites went to the New World, that they had a role in its conquest and discovery, as also in the foundation of the colonial society; thus one finds them in all social classes and playing a role in the professions and offices. . . . As the Jews and practitioners of Jewish rites *(los judíos y judaizantes)* were in great numbers among the early population of New Spain, it is undubitable that the lack of procesos involving the observance of the Law of Moses is due to the ignorance of the judges more than to any other cause; since among those [cases] of blasphemy there were many Jews who escaped with light penalties only because careful investigation was not made about their beliefs or because they did not look suspicious to the judges.[28]

For over thirty years, from 1541 to 1571, Judaism was practiced openly in New Spain. Juan Castellano, who was in the auto-da-fé of 1590, had been in Mexico for forty-eight years. García Gonzalo Bermeguero, who was burned at the stake in 1579, had been an acknowledged practicing Jew for over twenty years prior to his arrest. There is no question that Jews had been smearing blood on their doorposts on the eve of Passover in New Spain without molestation for many decades.

7

The New Jewish Settlement:
1571-1596

THE QUARTER of a century from 1571-1596 was momentous in Mexican Jewish history. It began with the inauguration on November 4, 1571, of *El Tribunal del Santo Oficio de la Inquisición,* with Don Pedro Moya de Contreras as Chief Inquisitor. For the period after 1571, the terms Inquisition, Tribunal, and Holy Office will be used interchangeably and are synonymous, unless otherwise indicated. The Holy Office superceded the bishops, who previously had inquisitional powers, in matters of faith. The era ended with the most famous auto-da-fé of the century on December 8, 1596. The advent of the new Tribunal, with all its attendant display of power and the exercise of that power, even over the viceroys, was intended to bring order out of the religious chaos that existed in the colony. It also served to secure the authority of the Church over that of the local secular rulers and was intended to purge Jews and Judaism from New Spain and other parts of the Spanish Empire.

The events leading to this era must be placed against the developments of the preceding decades. The schisms within the Church were many. Protestanism had become independent. It had dared challenge the power of Rome and had won. Luther was no longer alone in his revolution; Calvin, Zwingli, and others were engaged in reform movements. Erasmus the humanist, Thomas More, and Lefevers d'Etaples were among many who remained Catholic but "were in revulsion against the worldliness and corruption of the Church."[1] The Treaty of Augsburg of 1555, signed by Emperor Charles V, was a recognition of Protestanism as a state religion in northern Europe.

In an era when there never was a clear demarcation between Church and state, changes in one understandably produced changes in the other. The House of Habsburg became the active head of the "New Catholicism" that began to emerge. New monastic orders came into being. The most prominent of these was the Society of Jesus, founded in 1540 by the Spaniard Ignacio de Loyola. The Jesuits became the soldiers of the Church and were the power behind many of the proceedings of the Council of Trent. The Catholic Church also decided to revive and reinvigorate the Inquisition. Its greatest successes were in Italy, Spain, and Portugal, places where Protestantism had made little or no inroads.

Philip II ruled Spain from 1556 to 1598. He saw the loss of part of Flanders and knew that he had to take determined and forceful steps as the most important secular Catholic leader. Reports of attacks by English pirates on New Spain and other Spanish colonies in the New World reached him, and rumors were rife about the many Jews and heretics in his major colony. "There have been worse men than Philip II, but there have been hardly any who caused more blood to flow from the veins of their own people. His life is proof that a well-meaning bigot can do more harm than the most abandoned debauchee."[2] He once said that he would rather lose all his kingdom than permit freedom of religion. At another time he said to a heretic condemned by the Inquisition that he would carry the faggots to burn his own son if he were as perverse as the heretics.

Basing his action upon the bull of Sixtus IV of 1548 that granted leave to appoint inquisitors for ferreting out heretics, Philip decreed on January 25, 1569, the establishment of Inquisition Courts in the Indies. These Inquisition Courts were under the control of the king and the *Consejo de la Suprema*. The inquisitors were appointed by the king and were responsible to him. History has proven that the Holy Office came to be used more and more for political purposes, especially in its last 150 years, and that for the inquisitors in the New World it was a stepping-stone to episcopal offices. The Inquisition officials had *fueros,* rights, which included exemption from the jurisdiction of all secular courts, taxes, and military duty.

The Holy Office included in its aims the expurgation of all liberal ideas from Catholic minds. It controlled the *aduana,* customhouse, and placed a strict surveillance on the importation of books —not only books of a heretical nature but also, during the eighteenth century, books of political philosophy.

Moya de Contreras, the first Inquisitor General for the Tribunal in New Spain, arrived in Mexico in September, 1571. He waited until November for the official installation of the Holy Office. It was a magnificent show with all the pomp and ceremony worthy of the coronation of a king. Riva Palacio comments on its subsequent public acts by writing that the Inquisition of New Spain began to celebrate the autos-da-fé with a magnificence and incredible sumptuousness, and that the Holy Office spared nothing in order to show its power and wealth.[3]

A portentious event occurred in 1580—assumption of dominion by Spain over Portugal. The royal line of Portugal came to an end in 1579, and Philip II, without much opposition from weak Portuguese pretenders to the throne, became the ruler of the entire Iberian Peninsula. This event filled the Jews of Portugal with consternation. The Inquisition had existed in Portugal for many years, having had three principal Tribunals. From time to time it modified or curbed its persecution of Jews, many of whom had been sent to Brazil as a form of exile, a practice that was the reverse of the activities of the Spanish Inquisition both at home and abroad. Portuguese Jewry knew that the Spanish Inquisition was much more severe and that its first task on assuming jurisdiction would be to ferret out Jews and New Christians. Turberville wrote:

> In 1580, Philip II conquered Portugal and as a result this began a new phase in the history of the Spanish Inquisition and the Jews . . . [While] the two Inquisitions were not fused, the Portuguese Tribunal . . . was activated into greater zeal . . . Many emigrated to Spain where there was an Inquisition but it had not molested the Jews in recent times and besides, the new arrivals were less known in Spain than in the country they left.[4]

Pedro Moya de Contreras, first inquisitor in New Spain.
Taken from a painting in the Cathedral of Mexico

Julio Jiménez Rueda reported that the end of the sixteenth century witnessed a veritable exodus of Jews to New Spain and Peru.[5]
Others crossed the Spanish border and sought refuge in Seville, Madrid, and other cities in Spain, remaining there for several or many
years before emigrating to New Spain. Their rationale in going first
to Spain is easily understood. They reasoned that there would be a

concentration of effort by the Inquisition to apprehend those in Portugal; the hunt within Spain proper would consequently be less arduous and sanctuary could be more readily obtained. Their reasoning was correct. For a few years, Jews in Spain practiced their religion almost openly, and there were synagogues in Spain. The emigration to the New World at this time amounted to a stream compared to the trickle of the era prior to 1580. Where in earlier years they had come in tens, they now began to come in the hundreds. Campeche, on the peninsula of Yucatán, and coves on the shoreline of Honduras became important ports of entry for illegal immigration.

During the latter part of the sixteenth century, the slave trade with the New World grew to large proportions. The traffic was on behalf of the kings of Spain and Portugal and under their control. An agreement is said to have existed between the nations, or at least one of them and Holland, that they would not raid each other's slave ships when en route from Africa to the New World. A draft of an incomplete commercial treaty between Portugal and the States of Holland provides for cessation of war and refers to the slave trade.⁸

Jews were engaged in the slave trade as agents for both Iberian kingdoms prior to 1580 and thereafter continued as agents for Spain. There is reason to believe that the Catholic majesties knew that Jews were carrying on this traffic for them and also acting as brokers in the purchase and sale of slaves in New Spain. It has been said by a Mexican authority that as a form of emolument for importing slaves, Jews were to be given haven or the privilege of living in Yucatán unmolested by the Inquisition. In the absence of specific proof, some reliance or support for this assertion may be found in the combination of two circumstances.

Only one case was begun in Mérida, the capital of Yucatán, on the charge of judaizante in over 200 years. The charge was brought or instigated by Bishop Diego de Landa of Yucatán against Cristobal de Miranda, dean of the cathedral at Mérida. This case never reached final judgment, nor was there ever any judicial finding by the Inquisition that Miranda was a Jew or the descendant of Jews who were reconciled or burned at the stake in Spain. The original information against Miranda was filed in 1575, and by 1578 the dossier was full of letters attacking Bishop Landa by Miranda's friends and supporters. (It should be noted that Landa was a very controversial figure and a merciless religious zealot. He put 4,549 persons, men and women, to torture; of these, 157 died and 6,330 were whipped, fined, and their hair shorn.)[7]

As a result of personal interviews in Mérida and in Mexico City with leading Yucatecans, this writer has been informed that many of the leading families who have resided there for the past 250 years or more are descendants of Jews. Today most of them are Catholic, the conversions having taken place during the past 150 years. Among them is a branch of the Rivas family that attempted to block this author's research in Yucatán and Campeche. Some of the modern Yucatecans have requested that there be no disclosure of their family names in connection with Judaism; others have not hesitated to speak of their Jewish ancestry. There are some who still have Jewish family relics going back to the eighteenth century. Beyond that there is solely Oral Tradition, and oral statements have been accepted where there is some corroboration.

There are other facts which relate to the possible existence of a Jewish population in the Yucatán peninsula during the colonial period. The first is the birth of Francisco Rivas Puigcerver in Campeche about 1849. His great-great-grandfather fled the Inquisition in Spain and came to Yucatán. Francisco Rivas settled in Campeche. His grandfather moved to Tabasco. In 1889 he declared to the world that he was a Jew. He did this in the pages of a newspaper that he published, *El Sabado Secreto* (The Secret Sabbath). At that time, he was the chairman of the department of ancient languages at the preparatory school of the Mexican National University. He was a great linguist, could speak and write Hebrew, among many other languages, and was also a historian. In *El Sabado* on July 15, 1889 he wrote an article, "Singularidad de Merida," The Oddity of Merida, in which he stated, "Nothing, nor nobody in truth, has ever succeeded in uprooting the monotheistic people [Jews] from Spain as they adhered to that territory as (for example) the Yucatán peninsula." He then questions whether the word Yucatán may not have a Jewish source, "Could it be that the founders were Jews? To judge by the singularity of the Yucatán stereotype, no doubt remains about the truth of the last statement."

By coincidence, the first professor of Hebrew at the Mexican National University in 1933 was the late Pablo González Casanova, who was also born in Campeche of an old Yucatecan family, and who also headed the department of ancient languages. The Rivas and González families were old friends. González' sons deny that their father was a Jew, although almost everyone else who knew him states that he was a Sephardic Jew. He used to receive the Sunday edition of a Yiddish paper from New York and enjoyed going to all the concerts given by cantors who visited Mexico during the 1930's on concert tours.

In addition to the foregoing, there are certain foods indigenous to Yucatán that are not found in any other place in Mexico except where there are Jewish communities. They have been discussed in Chapter 4, "Customs in New Spain."

Professor Alfredo Barrera Vásquez, director of the Instituto de Antropología y Historia in Mérida, during an interview in 1965, repeated the same names of notable Yucatecan Catholic families with Jewish ancestry, as did several others. One of the most notable has letters written in Hebrew to ancestors in Yucatán in the seventeenth century. The Catholic daughter-in-law of the dean of the law school of the University of Merida traces her lineage back to colonial Jews in Yucatán.

In 1848, there began to appear in serial form in the leading paper of Mérida a novel called *La hija del Judío*, The Daughter of the Jew. It ran in weekly installments for a year and a half and was written by Justo Sierra O'Reilly. The novel was set in Mexico during the colonial period and involved the Inquisition. It would seem that reader interest could have been maintained without the injection of the Jewish theme and emphasis on the persecution of Jews. From an editor's point of view, one doubts that such a story would have run so long unless there was some special interest in the characters.

The establishment of the Tribunal of the Holy Office led to closer contacts among the various branches in Spain and in New Spain, Cartagena, Lima, Santiago, and, later, Rio de la Plata (now Buenos Aires). The five Tribunals in the New World cooperated in the search for Jews, Moors, and heretics; they were all branches of the Suprema in Seville. This coordination of effort was marked as early as 1578 by a document containing the names of individuals who were ineligible to be in New Spain because they were descendants of those burned at the stake, relaxed in effigy, or reconciled.[8] The document supplies many names and places of residence in New

Spain, ranging from Oaxaca to Zacatula. From this list, we find another illustration of a father, Juan Gómez, a reconciliado, who had put one son into a monastery and sent two other sons, Gonzalo Gómez and Melchor Gómez, to Mexico. This is a rare case of the sons bearing the names of their father, but, since no trace of the use of those names has been found in Mexico, the young men undoubtedly changed them on arrival in the New World. Rodrigo de Segura, the Cripple or One-legged, was in Mexico, as was the son of Alonzo Cardenel, but there is no record of any proceedings against these men.

Several of the people named in the document were arrested and ordered to return to Spain after disposing of their property. The people were imprisoned by the secular courts rather than by the Inquisition, and their fines were paid directly to the king's treasury. The Holy Office took no active part in these proceedings, and no reasons appear therefor. Each person had guarantors who filed bonds to insure their departure to Spain and their non-return to New Spain. It is doubtful if any of these people returned to Spain. It is probable that they remained, as did practically all others, or that they were dropped off at one of the West Indian islands, after bribing the ship captain, who then may have reported in Spain that they had drowned during a storm. The document ends with reference to Gonzalo de Morales and Diego de Morales. These names are the same as those mentioned in the auto-da-fé of 1528 in which Gonzalo was burned and Diego reconciled. It is unlikely that Diego was still alive in 1578. It is a coincidence in names and a further corroboration of the use of the same name by several individuals.

The character and morality of the Spanish population had not changed by 1571. Inquisitor Pedro Moya de Contreras and his fiscal spent their first years holding investigations and reconstructing the evidence which had led to sentencing people to wear the sanbenitos that hung on the cathedral walls. These were numerous cases of sodomy, concubinage, solicitation for sexual relations of women in the confessional by monks and priests, female bigamists, incest, adultery, and heretical statements against God, Mary, and the Inquisition.

Their first public auto-da-fé of this period was held on February 28, 1574, the first Sunday of Lent. There were seventy-four prisoners. Pedro Juarez, whose crime was heresy—the nature of which was undisclosed—had been sent to the Inquisitor General in Spain. The prisoners classified according to their crimes were: twenty-seven bigamists; five for having said that a sexual relationship between two unmarried people was not a sin; two for denying or blaspheming God; one for wearing prohibited garments since he was the grandson of a Jew burned at the stake; one for having spoken against the sacraments of confession and the Eucharist; one for having preached and uttered "not good Catholic doctrine" to Indians and mestizos and also because he was not a preacher; and one mestizo, who had a Jewish paternal grandfather, for having his wife confess to him instead of to the clergy. Also included in the auto were thirty Englishmen who were part of the Hawkins pirate armada that raided Spanish colonies. Their capture was due in part to Luis de Carvajal, who was named admiral and later was governor of the New Kingdom of León. There were also six Frenchmen in the 1574 auto.

In the next public auto-da-fé of March 6, 1575, there were thirty-one penitents, of whom twenty-five were bigamists or had made perjurious statements in applications for marriage licenses. Five were guilty of blasphemy or false visions. The last was Gonzalo Sánchez, a shoemaker, who was "of the generation of Jews" and who received 200 lashes and six years in the galleys for having secured his liberty from the Inquisition in Llerena, Spain, on the pretext that his wife and children had been captured by the Moors and that he wanted to ransom them and had come to the New World to raise the funds.

After the auto-da-fé of February 19, 1576, the number of Jews before the Inquisition increased. Prior to this auto, Pedro de San Lúcar (also Lucas) a descendant of Jews, was absolved because his crime consisted of not wanting to marry a young woman of an old Christian family for fear she might lose respect for him when she learned of his forebears. Pedro had studied in Russia, Bologna, and Salamanca and had a Bachillerato, a degree that was highly prized.

The first Jew who was tortured after 1574 was Hernando Alvarez Pliego. In the torture chamber he gave the names of many other Jews in New Spain. He was fined 500 pesos. There were other Jews, including children of those burned at the stake in Spain as Jews, but none were exiled. The first Jew who was burned alive after the establishment of the Holy Office in 1571 was García González Bermeguero, who had come to Mexico in 1559. This execution took place at the auto-da-fé of October 11, 1579. González' two brothers, their wives, and his uncle had been burned in Llerena, Spain. The inquisitors of Llerena informed the Inquisition in New Spain of González' presence. He was poor and the father of several children, one of whom was an Augustinian monk. There is no record of any proceedings against his children.

A casual reading of many of the procesos between 1574 and 1580 reveals the probability that many persons, such as Juan Franco, had had proceedings against them on other charges, as had often occurred prior to 1571, and during the hearings their real faith was ascertained. Franco had been charged with sorcery, but later it was learned that he was circumcised and prepared his food according to the Mosaic laws.

The laxity or ineptitude of Church officialdom vested with the responsibility of ferreting out Judaism and heresy prior to 1571 has deprived history of the developments in the early Jewish community in New Spain. Under inquisitors Pedro Moya de Contreras, Bonilla, and Alonso de Peralta and their associates, however, names, events, deeds, and indeed the record of a whole panorama of Jewish life have been preserved. The searching glare of the Inquisition's fury, the questioning of prisoners that concealed the fiendish game of entrapment, and the resort to torture exposed histories of lives that are revelatory of the changes and occurrences in Mexican history.

The Jewish participants are no longer seen as a series of individuals with tenuous connections between them. The actors were no longer solely Iberians, and the sex of those involved was no longer confined to the male. The characters were no longer prosaic men whose sole distinction from the masses surrounding them was the accident of birth of being born a Jew. Women appeared in the records, and many of them are richly deserving of Judaism's highest title, *ayshes chayil*, a woman of valor (Proverbs 31:10-31). Rabbis and their sons-in-law are easily identifiable. A panoply of Jewish holiday observances is unfolded, and beliefs and religious practices are disclosed. Some of the literary effusions of the first or second Jewish author in the New World have been preserved; these, together with other records, provide evidence that Judaism had taken root in the Americas and was thereafter never to be extirpated from the Hispanic New World.

Probably the most memorable person is Luis de Carvajal, *el Mozo* (the younger), a young man whose life was extinguished at the stake when he was twenty-nine years of age. It is around him that many of the events of the era unfolded. Although he never sired any children, his spirit pervaded Mexican Jewish history from 1590 to 1650, and his teachings echoed through the decades from the lips and through the lives of those who had known him. With this preface, the thread of Mexican Jewish history again goes back to Spain and the years 1579-1580.

LUIS DE CARVAJAL Y DE LA CUEVA

Two men, uncle and nephew, were named Luis de Carvajal. The uncle, Luis de Carvajal y de la Cueva, was a conquistador and became governor of the New Kingdom of León in New Spain; he was born in 1539 in Mogodorio of the kingdom of Portugal.[9] He was the son of New Christians, and there is no indication that they were not sincere converts to Christianity except that their daughter Francisca was betrothed when she was nine years of age to Francisco Rodríguez de Matos, a Jew who was then twelve years old. Francisca had been taken from her parents' home when she was three years old and had been reared by an aunt, who was a crypto-Jewess. The governor testified before the Inquisition in 1589 that he believed that his parents were old Christians and hidalgos. He left his parent's home at the age of eight when his father took him to the Abbot of Sahagún, a relative who educated him. Luis de Carvajal had been baptized, received communion, and religiously observed all Catholic rites. Alfonso Toro characterizes him as one who:

> belonged to the hidalgo class, brave, daring, high-spirited [men who] came to the Indies in search of honor and riches, masters of their fate and fortune and observing only the force of arms. They were half merchants and men-at-arms who conquered the Indians in order to despoil them of their goods and to enslave them, who developed mines and founded cattle ranches. They were a scheming people who built cities and burned with the fever of ambition and carved new roads in unknown territories across land and sea in search of fabulous kingdoms.[10]

While his ancestry included good Catholics and conversos, his maternal grandmother was Jewish. The governor's grandfather was Gutiérrez Vázquez de la Cueva. His maternal uncle, Francisco Jorge de Andrada, was a captain-general for the king of Portugal and later became an Augustinian monk. The governor had a brother, Domingo, who was a Jesuit monk.

Antonio Pérez was the secretary and alter ego of Philip II during the late 1570's. It was he who prepared the royal contracts. For several years he operated as if he had carte blanche to do as he pleased. He prepared the contract of May 31, 1579, for Luis de Carvajal that inaugurated a new era in Jewish life in New Spain. Pérez' biography reveals that he was a liberal, a descendant of Jews, and an agnostic if not anti-Catholic. There is no proof that he practiced Jewish rites, although the Spanish Inquisition charged him with that as well as crimes against the throne and heresy. Although Pérez escaped and died in freedom in northern Europe, there is no known writing by him to vindicate himself or to refute the Inquisition charges. Antonio Pérez probably was related to Marco Pérez of Antwerp. Marco Pérez was a marrano of Jewish ancestry, and his family, as that of Antonio's, came from Zaragossa, Spain.[11]

In the contract between the king and Governor Carvajal, Pérez failed to include the provision that the colonizers who were to accompany him had to provide certificates of limpieza de sangre. If Pérez were a Jew or were philo-Judaic, he might have seen the new governor's expedition as a means of aiding some of his coreligionists escape from Spain. The contract does not specify that those who accompanied Carvajal were to be Spanish subjects. Many were Portuguese.

Another explanation might be that Pérez' moral standards were those that prevailed at the court. If Pérez were neither a Jew nor inclined to be sympathetic to the cause of the oppressed, he might have yielded to a bribe to draw the contract as he did. While there is no ostensible link between Pérez and Carvajal, there may have been some connection between Pérez and one or two of those in Carvajal's company.

Henry C. Lea reports that in May, 1582, Philip II ordered an investigation into the various branches of the administration to find evidence against Pérez. Proof was thereby adduced that he had been selling royal favors. Several facts have been overlooked by many writers who stress the significance of the exemption from producing

certificates of limpieza for the colonizers. For one, Richard Konetzke has noted that in 1594 "the officials of Seville permitted the
passengers and their wives and children to go [to Rio de la Plata,
now Argentina] without requesting any information [about their
antecedents]."[12] The Rio de la Plata region required manual labor
for sustenance because of a lack of Indian and slave labor and had
no minerals. The area awarded to the governor had no proven
sources of quick wealth, and much work was required to colonize
the new province. By 1579, many Spaniards had heard discouraging
reports from New Spain, and Indian troubles had developed in the
north. As a result, royal grants tended to be more lax in their
requirements.

Another point to note is that practically all expeditions of exploration and conquest, including Carvajal's, were privately financed.
The king of Spain granted only the right to explore and promised
certain other rights to leaders of expeditions. Silvio Zavala states
that it was private capital that financed expeditions, "the Captains
and the soldiers bearing the expense of the enterprise."[13]

We must remember, too, that Spain itself was partially depopu-
lated by the earlier emigration, and King Philip II was having difficulty with England and the Netherlands. He needed money. If
Carvajal wanted to risk his fortune (not considerable), his life, and
the lives of those who would accompany him, the king had all to
gain and nothing to lose by encouraging the expedition.

Paragraph 8 of the royal contract with Carvajal reads:

> . . . on the confines of your territory of Panuco . . . are [certain]
> people (Indians) . . . these people were formerly Christianized,
> but for five years they have been in rebellion, destroying churches
> and doing other damage. The Viceroy has sent captains and sol-
> diers to subdue them. These captains have tried hard but have
> been unable to pacify the region. You are, therefore, obligated to
> bring these Indians to peace and Christianity within eight years
> from this date.[14]

All of these factors tended to cause Philip to encourage rather
than discourage the expedition. In addition, from 1550 on, Viceroy
Velasco realized that conversion and colonization were the only
means by which to pacify the Chichimecas, the Indians in this area.
By the 1570's, the situation had greatly deteriorated. No attempt

was made to deceive Carvajal about the conditions with which he was to be confronted. He had, furthermore, been in the Panuco area previously and had personal knowledge of the deplorable state of affairs.

His grant, the New Kingdom of León, extended from Tampico to what is now San Antonio, Texas, and westward 200 leagues (approximately 600 miles) from the Gulf of Mexico. It was one of the largest grants ever given—possibly the size was intended to compensate for the dangers. Carvajal received the title of governor general, which was to be hereditary.

The exact number of Jews who accompanied the governor is unknown, but they did not number 100 or more families, or 300 individuals, as has been erroneously stated by modern journalists. Among those Jews and Christians who accompanied the governor were his first cousins: Catalina de León and her husband; González Pérez Ferro and his illegitimate son; Doña Ginebra and Jorge de León; Diego Marquez; and Luis Pimentel. Others were Felipe Núñez, a relative of Doña Guiomar, wife of the governor; Diego Enríquez, the son of the viceroy, accompanied by two servants; Juan Salado; the pilot Pedro Sánchez; carpenters Juan de Saucedos Espinosa, Iñigo, and Vardales, all with wives and children; the tailor Juan de Nava and his wife; Ana Muñoz and her sister; Juan Izquierdo and his wife; Gaspar Delgado; Antonio Aguila, a scribe, and his wife Francisca Núñez Viciosa, the bastard sister of the governor's wife; two Galician laborers, Francisco Rodríguez and his wife and Antonio Rodríguez; Licenciado Antonio de Morales, a Portuguese doctor, and his family; Lucero, a mason and bricklayer; the ironmaker Ballesteros; Agustin Rodríguez; Domingo Martínez del Carreto and his son Pedro; Francisco López; Duarte Rodríguez, and others. (A descendant of Duarte Rodríguez with the same name appeared in the auto-da-fé of 1646 for observing Jewish rites.)

Also included among the passengers were the members of the family of Francisco Rodríguez de Matos, brother-in-law of the governor, who are discussed in detail in Chapter 8.

There were some learned Jews in the group that accompanied the governor in his search for gold and colonization, and there were other learned Jews already present in New Spain. Notable among these were Licenciado Manuel de Morales, Antonio Machado, Licenciado Antonio de Morales, and some women. One of these,

Beatriz Enríquez de la Payba, termed a dogmatizer by the Inquisition, was burned at the stake in 1596. Julio Jiménez Rueda considered her one of the greatest dogmatizers in the colony.

The Jewish women who accompanied their husbands on this expedition and who came to New Spain in the following years present an inspiring picture. They upheld the traditions of their faith and displayed fortitude and fervor as martyrs when such misfortune was forced upon them. One of the first questions asked of prisoners by the Inquisition was their civil (marital) status. Almost invariably, the answer of the women was *feliz casada,* happily married. Rabbi Dr. Hertz wrote that there was a period, centuries ago, in Jewish life when Jewish women lost their lives as martyrs with an unprecedented zeal and degree of happiness. The sixteenth and seventeenth centuries in Mexico saw a revival of this fervor among the females.

Jiménez Rueda wrote about Ana Váez, who suffered five turns of the cord on the torture rack and had six quarts of water forced into her without informing on her friends.[15] With only one exception (Isabel Clara, sister-in-law of Manuel de Morales), these women did not flee even when some of their husbands had fled. Among those who remained were Ana López, wife of Diego López Regalon, and Beatriz Enríquez, who was burned at the stake.[16] Antonio Machado's house was used as a synagogue, and he was called "gran rabino."[17] The most observant Jews congregated in his home to pray, sing psalms, and read the Bible and other pious works. They assembled in small groups so as not to attract attention. Machado practiced Catholicism publicly and was an intimate of several Carmelites and Jesuits.

Manuel de Morales' family included his wife, two young children, two brothers, and three sisters, one of whom was single. The spouses of the two married sisters had been in New Spain before they were betrothed. All escaped the clutches of the Inquisition. There also was another Dr. Morales, Antonio, who was a nephew of Manuel Morales. Antonio also succeeded in making his escape.

Manuel de Morales fled from New Spain before 1589. He feared the Inquisition since his father-in-law (a Grand Rabbi in Portugal) had been burned at the stake in Lisbon. Fleeing with Morales were his wife, his two children, and his brother Francisco's wife, Clara Núñez. His brothers, Francisco Hernandez and Pedro Hernandez, Pedro's family, and their sister Inés remained in Mexico. There is no record of a proceeding against Francisco Hernandez, which is additional evidence that a greater number of Jews were in New Spain than is revealed by the procesos.

Morales sailed first to Havana, then to Malaga, and from there he went to Seville. Two Carvajal brothers who fled in 1590 knew Morales' address in Spain and stayed with or near him after their arrival there. According to the testimony of a sailor, Juan de Micina, Morales had been seen in Venice by another sailor, a friend of the witness who had been a patient of Morales. He had been seen in the judería of Venice wearing the habit of a Jew, including a yellow hood or pointed cap.[18] Morales was also reported to have been in Pisa.

Manual de Morales had been in Mexico prior to the arrival of Governor Carvajal. When Antonio Machado became incurably ill and was in great pain, Morales translated Deuteronomy into Spanish so that Machado could read it more readily and be comforted by it. Morales also wrote many folk songs and much poetry in praise of the Mosaic laws. He knew or wrote prayers for Passover, Yom Kippur, and Shavuot, and taught additional prayers to other Jews.

It is likely that some of the works subsequently attributed to the governor's nephew Luis were those of Morales, who was known among the Jews as Abraham. Luis el Mozo had met a young Italian Jew, Francisco Rodríguez (not a relative), who was a descendant of a family that had been exiled from Spain in 1492. He had described the religious freedom whch Italian Jews were enjoying, and before he left New Spain for Salonica he gave Luis el Mozo a book of prayers. Hernando Rodrígues de Herrera testified on October 2, 1589, that Luis read from this book, written in Latin. Some of the liturgical poetry created either by Morales or Luis is included Poetas Novohispanos: 1521-1621[19] by Alfonso Méndez Plancarte and La Poesía Religiosa en México: siglis XVI a XIX by P. Jesus García Gutiérrez.[20]

The poems follow the traditional patterns of Jewish liturgy. They consist in the main of sentences and phrases taken from the Psalms and Scriptures. They evoke memories of the pleas of generations of Jews who humbled themselves before God and, through praise and tears, implored his intercession. Méndez Plancarte's included one poem beginning:

> *I raise my unworthy arms to Thee, my God*
> *And find myself without redeeming virtue, as the*
>   *impoverished earth;*
> *All my thoughts are vain*
> *And are eternally confused.*
> *Turn not Thy face from mortal man.*
> *If Thou dost not pardon those who sin*
> *Who will release them who are enmeshed in the trap*
> *And need someone to lift them?*

Another example cited by both Padre García Gutiérrez and Méndez Plancarte is:

> *Don't leave me, my Lord, in this moment of my anguish*
> *Nor abandon me, my Comforter;*
> *Who, if You leave me, will disturb You?*
> *Who will cool my fevered brow?*
> *Searching, my Love, I go from battle to battle,*
> *But I find myself without strength or vigor,*
> *Help me, O Lord, I am restless*
> *Do not leave my life and soul without fortitude.*

Governor Carvajal's sister, Francisca, wife of Rodríguez de Matos, testified in 1589 that her husband had been a Jew, that he had taught her and some of their children the tenets and practices of Judaism, and that prior to her marriage she had considered herself a Catholic. In 1558, her brother, the governor, married Doña Guiomar de Ribera, who was a Jewess but never revealed that fact to her husband. They had no children, and the governor, at his trial, denied that he ever had any illegitimate children. His marriage was unhappy because of his wife's refusal to accompany him on his first trip to the New World in 1566, where he gained fame as a naval captain, admiral, and fighter of Indians. The absence of heirs was another cause of marital unhappiness. His sister's marriage had produced nine living offspring. He likely found in his nieces and nephews substitutes for his own offspring.

Until 1587, when the governor began to suspect that his nephew Luis tended to Jewish practices, Luis was a favorite. Luis states in his autobiography written in 1594 that when he was lost one night in the territory of the barbarous Chichimecas, his uncle dispatched some soldiers to find him and when he was found and returned, "the happiness and joy of my uncle . . . was great."

After obtaining his contract from Philip II, the governor related the news to the Rodríguez de Matos family. In order to induce his brother-in-law to change his plans of emigrating to France, where Francisco had a brother, the newly-named governor promised to appoint his nephew Luis his heir and successor. The prospect of young Luis as a future governor with an assured career, and the thought that the New Kingdom of León would be far from the Inquisition (or, if worse came to worst, his son as governor would be protection against the Inquisition) undoubtedly contributed to Francisco's change of plans, and may also have been an inducement to other Jews to join the expedition. The governor needed colonizers since the royal contract provided that he establish a certain number of colonies within a specified time. The Jews may have also aided in supplying funds to outfit the expedition.

Toro states that the governor "had strong suspicions" that his brother-in-law was a Jew and that he wanted to save friends and members of his family from persecution,[21] but Toro and others elsewhere comment on the profound Catholic faith and belief of Governor Carvajal.[22]

Before they sailed, Doña Guiomar, who again refused to accompany her husband, asked her niece Isabel to attempt to convert the governor to Judaism after they arrived in the New World, whenever such a time might be propitious. The opportunity did not come until about 1586, when Isabel raised the subject with her uncle when he visited the family after a long absence. Upon hearing her words about the "old faith," he struck her so hard that she was thrown to the opposite wall and even threatened to kill her. Shortly thereafter, from a conversation with his nephew, he deduced that young Luis also had leanings toward Jewish beliefs and learned that his brother-in-law, who had died about two years previously, had been buried in accordance with Jewish rites.

The governor confessed his suspicions about his nephew to his personal priest, changed his will, and disinherited Luis. He later attributed his failure to report his suspicions concerning his relatives to the Inquisition in Mexico to his involvement in fighting the Chichimecas during 1586 and 1587 in an area distant from Mexico.

The Inquisition search for Jews had begun in earnest in 1589.

After the disclosure of Antonio Pérez' actions and his escape from the clutches of the Inquisition, an inquiry was initiated into all those who had profited from or had dealings with the secretary of King Phillip II. A study of the contract with Governor Carvajal may have been made and suspicions aroused by the absence of the requirements that all colonizers had to have certificates of limpieza de sangre. Concurrently, Governor Carvajal was in conflict with the viceroy in New Spain over lines of jurisdiction.

The governor's ancestry was reported to the viceroy by a monk, and the viceroy's soldiers arrested the governor. After he had been incarcerated in the royal prison, the inquisitors requested that he be turned over to them. The viceroy acceded to this request on April 14, 1589. The governor's testimony implicated a niece and a nephew; another niece had been jailed at an earlier date.

The governor's character and his devotion to Catholicism are revealed by his comment to his nephew Gaspar, the monk: "They tell me that my mother died in that [Jewish] belief. If that be so, then she is not my mother nor I her son." When asked if his mother were Jewish, he replied that if she were he hoped that her soul would roast in hell. He also built a church in La Cueva in the New Kingdom of León, the present state of Nuevo León. This town was founded by the governor and originally named Villa de San Luis. It was later changed to La Cueva. Its first mayor was Gaspar Castaño, alleged to be a son of Jewish converts, who came to New Spain with Don Luis.[23]

The trial of the governor presents an interesting aspect of inquisitorial proceedings. Dr. Lobo Guerrero, the prosecuting attorney, appended to the formal accusation (comparable to the modern criminal indictment) the following plea:

> And in the event that my contentions are deemed to be insufficiently proved, I ask that he be put to the question of torture and that the same be continued and persevered in until he confesses the whole truth, for all of which I invoke the justice of the Holy Office swearing that this accusation is made in proper legal form . . .

Although he had been originally accused of "observing the Law of Moses," the prosecutor, after several hearings, modified and reduced the charge to being "an aider and abetter and concealer of

Jewish apostates."[24] The ultimate verdict was that he was guilty of being "an aider, abetter, harborer, and concealer of apostates to the Holy Catholic Faith."[25] He had to abjure *de vehementi* and was sentenced to serve one year in jail and then to be exiled from the Indies for six years. The punishment meted out was not the result of unanimous decision. Some of the council of advisors who sat with the inquisitors voted for a milder sentence. There was no finding that he was a Jew or an apostate. He died in 1591 during the year of his incarceration. The abjuration was:

> I, Luis de Carvajal, born in the town of Mogodorio, in the Kingdom of Portugal, Governor of the New Kingdom of León, here present, of my free and spontaneous will, abjure and detest, renounce and abandon all and every species of heresy, especially of that of which I am accused, and confess out of my own mouth with a pure and true heart the Holy Catholic Church of Rome, and in which I desire to live and die, and I swear by the Lord God and the Saints, the Four Evangelists, and the sign of the Cross that I owe and will render obedience to the Successor of the glorious Peter, Prince of Apostles and Vicar of our Lord Jesus Christ, our Holy Father Sixtus V who today rules and governs the Church, and to his successors in their turn, and that I will always remain within the pale of the Holy Church and will support the Catholic Faith and prosecute all those who may be opposed thereto, presenting myself for the purpose of denouncing them, and engaging never to harbor or guide or visit or accompany them or give or send them presents or favor them; and if at any time I fail to keep these promises I agree to be treated as an incorrigible offender and cursed and excommunicated, and I ask the Secretary here present for a certified copy of this my confession, begging all present to bear testimony to what I say, and I sign with my name, the witnesses being the persons hereinbefore mentioned. (And the said abjuration having been made the accused was absolved in due form from greater excommunication).
>
> [Translated by A. J. Barker][26]

The abjuration was recited on Saturday, April 24, 1590, in the cathedral. The governor stood with a burning green candle in his hand on a high wooden platform in the presence of the viceroy, the inquisitors, the archbishop, and other notables of the colony. He began his imprisonment and died penniless within the year in the Royal Jail. He was never paid for his pacifications of the Indians, and the ship on which he had set sail from San Lucar de Barrameda with his colonizers in June, 1580, was lost. He died unmourned and unwept since he had accused his sister and her family of being his mortal enemies. Doña Guiomar had predeceased him in Spain.

The later history of the Carvajal family must be placed within the context of other events that occurred during the period from 1580 to 1596. The exodus from Portugal and Spain not only involved great numbers but also was marked by the quality of the Jewish immigrants. They brought learning and a revival of ritual observance to the existing colony.

Many of these Iberians disprove the contention that Jewish learning and the desire to learn had begun to decay and showed signs of attrition within 100 years of the Decree of Expulsion. Among the more learned were such persons as the doctors Manuel de Morales and his nephew Antonio de Morales; Manuel de Lucena; Dr. Miguel Franco, who was fined 1,000 pesos and had to do public penance but was not exiled and did not have to appear in a public auto-da-fé; and Isabel Carvajal and her brothers. These are but a few.

These people played a great role in the economic development of New Spain in the latter part of the sixteenth century. Robert Ricard wrote that they were:

> The leading merchants, both wholesale and retail, who carried on the traffic in trade between Mexico and the mining centers such as Sultepec [in eastern Mexico], Pachuca, Taxco, Tlalpujahua [eastern part of Michoacan], and Zacatecas. One passage of a proceso specified that Sebastian Rodríguez carried on trade between New Spain and China. It is notable that there were two doctors, Manuel and Antonio de Morales, uncle and nephew, and several artisans; three silversmiths, two manufacturers of soap, two tailors, one manufacturer of rope products, one knife or blade manufacturer. . . . They traveled incessantly in order to carry on their business or to flee from persecution or to find a safer residence. One merchant left for Macao, and about another, one does not know whether he returned to Spain or to Salonica.[27]

The names of the almost 200 Jews who appear in the Inquisition proceedings between 1589 and 1596 supply no real approximation of the number of members of the Jewish colony. Almost each proceso reveals names that were not the subject of further investigation. Not until 1609 did the Holy Office complete its labors with respect to some of those mentioned prior to 1596. The pardon granted in

1597 to all prisoners under trial or sentences in Murcia must have aided in ameliorating the activities of the inquisitors in searching out new Jewish heretics. Later a papal absolution for the New Christians who were suspect came to New Spain.

Juan de Castellanos had lived as a known Jew forty-eight years prior to 1590, when he was reconciled outside of an auto. He owned an *obrage*, a textile sweat shop. His age and infirmity saved him from the torture rack.[28] His religious practices were slight compared with those of his brother, Tomas de Fonseca, who came to Mexico about 1580. Tomas de Fonseca resided in Tlalpujagua, near the present town of El Oro, which had a second Jewish revival about 1870. Tomas de Fonseca was tried and acquitted in 1590 in spite of proof of strong Jewish practices. His acquittal resulted from the proof that the denunciation against him had been made by a "capital [mortal] enemy." The acquittal, however, merely postponed his conviction; he was subsequently rearrested for being a Jew and was burned alive in 1601.

The new immigrants created not only a great revival of learning and ritual observance but also the beginning of a definite Jewish community. Jews had begun to establish themselves in various parts of the New World during the sixteenth century. While there was communication between them and exchanges of visitors and leading figures, there was no pattern of common practices. Each community had its own local customs and each had indigenous communal developments.

Jewish males are traditionally classified into the three groups for religious observances: *Kohanim*, descendants of the priestly class of the days of the Temple in Jerusalem; *Leviim*, or Levites, the assistants to the priestly caste; and *Israeli*, all the other people. There is no mention of such divisions in New Spain.

The first detailed information concerning the knowledge of Jewish rites, ceremonies, or beliefs of the crypto-Jews in New Spain is found in the testimony of Luis de Carvajal, *el Mozo*, adduced on August 9, 1589, before the Inquisition. He narrated what his mother and older sister Isabel had been taught by his father.

Religious education was private and oral. There is no record of the teaching of Hebrew, although many could recite the Shema and a few prayers in Hebrew. Most prayers were recited in Spanish. Inspiration was derived from a few books and rare copies of the Scriptures. The literature stressed the tragedies of the past. It was at this time that *Shevet Yehudah*, the Scepter of Judah, was written in Hebrew by Shlomo Ibn Verga.[29] Translated into Spanish, it was titled *La Vara Judah* and was widely read in New Spain. The book recounts the tribulations of the Jews through the centuries and includes discourses about the coming of the Messiah. The title itself was taken from Genesis 49:10, which contains the prophecies which the patriarch Jacob related to his sons including Judah, "The scepter shall not depart from Judah—nor shall the ruler's staff from between his feet / until that which is his shall come; / and unto him shall the obedience of the peoples be."

Several of the Apocrypha, such as Tobit, were similar in content and were therefore widely read. In Tobit, the principal character is consumed by his Judaism and the sadness of being in exile. Luis *el Mozo* made several references in his last will and testament to Tobit, Esdras, and Judith. The Book of Judith is a worthy companion piece to Tobit, but the style of the former is more vivid. Judith has a strong religious orientation, serves as an inspiration for patriotism and piety, and proves that private fasts were frequent among Jews from the earliest times. In these writings, the ways in which Jews survived and ultimately were saved from persecution are described, and in some the Messianic theme is present. Tobit and others, written after the time of Christ, served as confirmation to the Jews that the true Messiah had not yet come.

Much of this literature also had a religious function. The widely read *Símbolo de Fé* contains excerpts from the Old Testament and the Prophets, especially Zechariah and Ezekiel. Among the phrases that heartened the readers were "There shall be no more than one flock and one Shepherd" (Christianity and Judaism each interpreted this in the context of its own creed); "The law shall be one"; and "Israel shall never again be captive."

Flos Sanctorum by Alonso de Villegas appeared first in Spain in 1593, made its way immediately to Mexico, and went into many editions. While meant for Christians, Jews gleaned from it passages referring to their Bible and biographical sketches of the prophets. The Psalms were a constant source of inspiration, and the Dominican *Day Book* and *Book of Hours* were used for over a century because of the inclusion of the Seven Penitential Psalms as well as others. The Book of Daniel was most important because of the apocalyptic revelation and the intensification of the messianic concept into the supernatural.[30] There are references to nonreligious poetry, some of which Rámon Menéndez Pidal has preserved in his "Romancero Judío-español."[31]

The *Espejo de Consolación* (Mirror of Consolation), another favorite, falls into the same category as the *Assumption of Moses* and the *Book of Wisdom of Solomon*. The last named is referred to in the Epistles of Paul. It was permissible for all these books to be owned and read publicly because they were considered good Christian works. A prohibited book was *La Clave de Salomon*, The Key of Solomon, of cabalistic origin. One of the prayers in this book was adapted for use in New Spain.

The amount of literature generally read by people of all faiths in the sixteenth century is much greater and more varied than is generally realized. Francisco Fernández del Castillo extracted from an unidentified *proceso* a Jewish prayer (in Spanish), which he contributed to Padre García Gutiérrez' anthology:

> *I was so deaf and without feeling*
> *So mute that I doubtlessly could be taken*
> *for a speechless man who dumbly beseeches,*
> *Buried in the dream of forgetfulness [of my sins]*
> *At a time when life has dwindled almost to naught.*
> *Because I wait, O Lord, for Thy greatness*
> *So that you may hear the humility of my complaints*
> *Hear, O Lord, my humble pleas*
> *Show satisfaction with my prayer*
> *So that I may know that you desire that I live rather than die*
> *And that I am not blotted out of Your tender love.*

From the 1596 *proceso* of Justa Méndez comes a prayer which she recited for the inquisitors without indicating the author or source. She remained a devout Jewess for the ensuing fifty-four years and reared a large family of children and grandchildren whose religious zeal equalled her own. The use of this prayer continued in her family and was recited until well toward the end of the seventeenth century:

> *Let us sing praises to the Lord.*
> *Those who trust in Him*
> *Will never lose His favor.*

Surely there is no count of the hundreds
And thousands among those, who people
The earth and seas, who rage
In faithlessness against His plan.
But those whose faith in the Omnipotent One is steadfast
Will sing His praises
And will never lose His favor.

Diego Díaz Nieto was born in Oporto, Portugal, and was twenty-one years of age when he testified before the Tribunal of the Holy Office of the Inquisition in 1596. Cataline Henríquez was born in Seville, although both of her parents had been born in Portugal; they had moved to Seville prior to 1560. Catalina was eighty years of age when she testified in 1643. Her husband was born in Osuna, Portugal, and she stated that he had indoctrinated her with Judaism.

The prayers of Diego and Catalina were transcribed by amanuenses of the Tribunal forty-seven years apart. Spelling in neither century was consistent. They are reproduced below exactly as they appear in the original records of the Inquisition. The "great sin" referred to in the prayers is, most likely, that of playing the role of a Catholic.

Año 1596
Prayer recited by
Diego Díaz Nieto
(From his proceso in the
Mexican National Archives,
vol. 159, Exp. 2)

Año 1643
Prayer recited by
Catalina Henríquez
(From her proceso, owned by
the Henry E. Huntington
Library)

Alto Dio de Abraan
Rey forte de Isrrael
tu que ouuiste a Ismael
ouue a minha orazón
tu que en las grandes alturas
te aposentas Señor
ouue a esta pecadora
que te chama das bas juras
pois tu que a todas criaturas
abres caminos e fontes
alzo meus ellos aos montes
donde vira minha ajuda
minha ajuda de con Adonay

Oh, Alto Dios de Abraham
Dios fuerte Dios de Israel
tú que oiste a Daniel
oye me oración
tú que en las grandes alturas
te pusiste mi Señor
eye a que esta pecadors
que te llama de las basuras
tú que a toda criatura
abres caminos y fuentes
alce mis ejos a los montes
donde vendrá mi ayuda,
ye bien sé que en mi se encierra

a que fez ho ceu e ha terra
libranos de tanta guerra
pues que somes os teuos seyes
de adorar ed Dioses alleihos
coissa en que tanto ho me
    encerra
eu confesso que en mi se
    encerra
gran pecado que en mi ay
minha a juda do con Adonay
Ee que fez eo ceu y aterra.

gran pecade que en mi hay
mi ayuda de Adonay
que hizo cielos y tierra
Santos Dios, fuerte Dies
misericordioso Dios
inmortal,
Habed misericordia de mi
    Señor.

High God of Abraham
Powerful King of Israel
Thou who hast listened to
    Ismael
A man of great piety
Thou who dwellest as Lord
In the heights,
Listen to this sinner,
Who calls Thee from the
    depths.
Since Thou openest roads and
    fountains
To all creatures, raise my eyes
    to the mountains
From whence shall come my
    help.
My help shall come from the
    Lord.
He who made heaven and
    earth.
Free us from so much war,
Though we are those who
    worshipped
Alien gods, in which I, too,
    have erred
And I confess to that great sin
    within me.
Help shall come from Adonay, .
Thou who made the heaven
    and earth.

Oh, high God of Abraham
Almighty God, God of Israel
You, who hearkened to Daniel
You, who dwell in high places
Listen to my prayers,
My Lord, You are able to help
    me,
Listen to this abject sinner
Who calls upon you from the
    depths.
Thou who openest roads and
    fountains
For all creatures
Lift up my eyes to the
    mountains
From whence shall come my
    aid
I well know that there is
    Within me a great sin.
But help for me is from God
Who made the heavens and the
    earth.
Holy God, Almighty God,
Merciful God and immortal,
Have mercy upon me, my
    Lord!

The following are translations and original prayers also recited
by Catalina Henríquez.

Have pity on me, Lord,	*Apiadame Señor*
Without my deserving it.	*Sin ayuda de mi* (Trans. - ti)
Transform my weeping	*trastorno mi lloro*
Into song for Thee.	*Por cantar a tí*
Open my heart;	*abre me corazón*
So that I may always praise	
Thee,	*para que siempre te lee*
Let my soul not be silent.	*mi alma no calle* (Trans. - caye)

[Translation by Dr. Richard A. Abraham]

Lord, our God,	*Señor, Dios Nuestro*
Don't subject us to perpetual,	
contemptuous ridicule.	*no traigas en escarnio perpetuo*
For the sake of Your holy	*per virtud de vuestro santo*
testament	*nombre*
Which you gave to Your	
people.	*a vuestro pueblo*
[Do this] for the love which	*ni distruvais vuestro santo*
you had	*testamente*
	por amor que tuvisteis
For Abraham, Isaac and Jacob,	*a Abraham, Isaac y Jacob*
Moses and Aaron,	*Moisen y Aaron*
For David and for Solomon.	*a David y a Salomon.*

During the Carvajal era, there were three Jews who were known by the name of Antonio López. One was Antonio López de Morales, a doctor and nephew of Manuel de Morales. The second Antonio López, who had been born in Celorico, Portugal, was burned in effigy, having also escaped. The third was born in Seville; he was a singer and a player of musical instruments in comedies. He was the son of Diego López Regalón (who had died prior to the auto and was burned in effigy). Luis testified against the young musical comedy star, who was condemned to perpetual prison in the auto-da-fé of March 25, 1601. In addition to his profession, the third Antonio López is noteworthy for his audacity. At a performance one evening, he conducted some Jews to seats in the first row (it appears that the actors or musicians also served as ushers). As a result of his giving the seats to known Jews, some "good Catholics" had to stand during the performance. At the conclusion of the performance, the brazen young man declined an invitation to late supper with the "good Catholics" who, in spite of their irritation, sought the company of a celebrity. Instead, Antonio went out, laughing, with the Jews.

A broad picture of life in the Jewish community can be gleaned only through studying records of many trials. Even for an understanding of a single individual the reading of his own proceso may not be adequate. For instance, the love interest and potential romance between Justa Méndez (known in the city as Justa la Hermosa, Justa the. Beautiful), and Luis *el Mozo* is understood only after reading the trial minutes of several of their associates. The romance never culminated in marriage because Luis' devotion to God had made him almost ascetic. It was, however, a platonic relationship of great depth.

Justa Méndez was reconciled in the auto of 1596 at the age of twenty and subsequently married Francisco Núñez. She merits a place in Jewish history with that of Hannah, whose seven sons were sacrificed for their faith. Seven or more of Justa's children and grandchildren felt the fury of the Holy Office. Justa's life reflects a full gamut of experiences. When she was to be married, she, as any beautiful maiden, desired to be adorned in fine raiment of silk and bedecked in jewelry, but since she was a reconciliada, these things were prohibited for her. The dauntless maid wrote to the inquisitors for permission to be wed in full bridal regalia. Within three months her request was not only granted but she received a full pardon and was released from all restrictions for the balance of her life.

In the 1630's she and her husband sued a man because he had called them "Jew dogs." The brazenness of this law suit may be gathered from the fact that she and her family were pious, secret Jews. The defendant in the suit might have been tempted to show not only that these plaintiffs were reconciliados (a matter of record), but, through bribery of their household servants, he might have been able to reveal the secrets of their true religious practices. In the discussion of the auto-da-fé of 1649 further details of this family are narrated.

8

The Carvajals and
Their Contemporaries

THE EVENTS at the close of the sixteenth century and some of the participants in that momentous drama represent the dark and somber color of tragedy. They reveal in stark reality the determination of the Jews to preserve their faith. They limn the characteristics and anachronisms of the Iberian Jew and the harsh, unrelenting struggle of the Holy Office to exterminate the vestiges of Judaic heresy. The Jews who persisted in their faith were truly a "stiff-necked people," but now their obstinacy was not an affront to God but rather devotion to Him.

This obstinacy, this obduracy, this attachment to their ancestral faith is an interesting phenomenon. There was no outside force compelling their adherence to Judaism. Their environment and their milieu militated against it. There were no social pressures exerted upon them to remain identified, as in modern times. Those who left the old lands sought only a new place where they could practice their faith freely and openly.

During the period from 1589 to 1605, the inquisitors persisted in a relentless search for Jews and probed for information from those apprehended. The men who ruled the Holy Office during those years were adroit, possessed little mercy, and were dedicated to their faith. The author of the relación of the 1596 auto-da-fé told of the valiant work of the Inquisition in preserving the Faith and said that "Alonso de. Peralta seemed to have been created by God to be an Inquisitor because of his perspicacity."[1] All their skills in ferreting out traitors to the Faith were necessary because Inquisition personnel were pitted not only against Jews but also against Christians who betrayed Inquisition secrets, carried messages among the prisoners, and aided them to escape. Some also stole from the Holy Office.[2] The Jews proved worthy and adroit foes.

On August 7 and 21, 1596, the king of Spain wrote letters concerning the activities of the Jews in the New World and their knowledge of Inquisition secrets.[3] In the second letter, addressed to the *Audiencia* in Santo Domingo, he refers to two statements received from Dr. Quesada de Figueroa in which he confirms that he had a witness, Tome Rodríguez, who stated that a group of Jews, all of whom he named, were going to England with their possessions. He added that all of the West Indian islands had many residents who lived according to the Jewish law and that those imprisoned were treated tenderly by the clergy. The Jews, he said, had knowledge of everything touching upon the affairs of the Tribunal in New Spain.

The inquisitors were insensible to the right of others to have honest differing convictions, and they were callous to the pleas of those whom they degraded. They dominated through coercion and fear. If they had not, young Luis de Carvajal would not later have been moved to utter, while on the way to the stake, "O this evil Tribunal of the Holy Office. If it had not existed in this kingdom, I could count the Christians here on these fingers."[4]

The accounts of the dramatic personality, Luis de Carvajal, *el Mozo*, his family, and some of his friends and associates provide insight into their lives and some impression of the Judaism of the times. Luis himself was learned in Latin and the Scriptures, had a phenomenal memory, and was God-intoxicated. His liturgical creations attest a Divine inspiration. He was a visionary and claimed to have dreams in which celestial beings appeared. His visions bear analogy to those related by the prophets of old. His dedication to the Almighty almost hypnotized two inquisitors—on separate occasions and years apart. He was a prophet in his own home and, given more years, he might well have illuminated the pages of Jewish history to a greater extent than he has. The facts of his life are revealed in the trials of his mother, sisters, friends, and his own two trials in 1589 and 1595-1596. They are also revealed in his autobiography written shortly before his second trial and in his last will and testament written in the Inquisition cell shortly before his execution.[5]

Young Luis was born about 1566 in Benavente, Portugal, the fifth child of his parents. Luis' father, Francisco Rodríguez de Matos, had been raised by the Count of Benavente. His mother, Francisca Núñez de Carvajal, was usually referred to as Francisca de Carvajal.

Facsimile of the signature of Mariana de Carvajal.
From México á través de los siglos, *Vol. 2*

Luis was one of nine living children. His elder brothers were Gaspar, a Dominican friar, and Baltasar; his elder sisters were Isabel, a childless widow, and Catalina. Luis' younger brother was Miguel or Miguelito, born about 1576, and his younger sisters were Leonor, born about 1574, Mariana, born about 1577, and Ana or Anica, born about 1581.

All of Luis' family traveled in Governor Carvajal's expedition to New Spain except for Gaspar, who had preceded them the year before. Luis' brother Baltasar was treasurer of the expedition. Luis was fourteen years old when they arrived in New Spain.

The Rodríguez de Matos family, except for Catalina, dropped their father's name after coming to New Spain and adopted Carvajal, the maiden name of their mother and that of the governor. Such an adoption of the name of an illustrious member of the family or of a *patrón* was a common Spanish practice at the time. Catalina was known as Catalina de la Cueva and also as Catalina de León de la Cueva, to differentiate herself from a contemporary of the same name.

The family members were then practicing Jews except for Luis, Gaspar, and the three youngest children, Mariana, Miguel, and Ana. Gaspar, the monk, eventually became aware of his family's true faith, but when he actually learned of it is unknown.

When Rodríguez de Matos informed Luis that he was a Jew and

was to follow the Mosaic tradition, he also told him that he could learn from Manuel de Morales. Luis' older brother, Baltasar, already knew that the Morales family as well as his own were Jews. The fathers of the young men followed the practice of not revealing the family faith to their children until they evidenced mental maturity and could be trusted to keep the secret. Miguel, the youngest son, probably learned that he was a Jew when he was taken on the flight from New Spain about 1590. Ana learned that she was a Jewess in 1589 when she was in the Inquisition cells.

Rodríguez de Matos died about 1585. During his last illness he instructed his older children to bury him according to Jewish rites, but he had never had his sons circumcised or told them about circumcision. Subsequently Luis circumcised himself when he was eighteen or nineteen years old, and Baltasar performed the rite upon himself when he was about twenty-five years of age. The narrations of these circumcisions are in Luis' *Memorias*.

The passing of Francisco Rodríguez de Matos and the estrangement between the governor and his niece and nephew caused the remaining members of the Carvajal family to fear that they would have no defenders in the area. Most of the other colonizers (including all of the Jews) had already left. A few had moved to the northern part of the province (the Monclova region) but among them there were no known practicing Jews.

Life in the Panuco area proved to be very hard. The soil was barren, grazing land was not good for the cattle, trade was nil, and there was the ever-present danger of barbarous Indians. In his autobiography, Luis called this area in the lands of the Panuco River "an uncomfortable and hot place full of mosquitoes where we lived in great poverty." The site is on the Gulf of Mexico, has steaming subtropical temperatures in the summer, and is harassed by hurricanes and by *nortes* (storms) in the winter. The area is now the site of vast Mexican oil fields. The poverty of the Rodríguez de Matos family was so great that they walked "barefoot constantly and dressed poorly." Leonor and Catalina married and lived in Mexico with their husbands. The sons-in-law had taken Doña Francisca, Isabel, and the two youngest children to live with them. Baltasar and Luis tried their hands at being traders and traveled to various parts of the southern and western populated areas of New Spain, and they finally also decided to move to Mexico.

ISABEL

The disclosure of the presence of many Jews in New Spain was attributable to Isabel, Luis' sister. In 1589 she was about thirty years of age and was regarded as a great beauty. A widow still in the full bloom of her womanhood, Isabel was a very devoted Jewess. She had learned about Judaism from her deceased father, her deceased husband, and, in New Spain, from Francisca Núñez Viciosa, the illegitimate sister of her Aunt Guiomar. Isabel was learned in Latin and her devotion to and knowledge of her faith was exceeded only by that of her brothers. Isabel's failure with her uncle did not deter her from attempting other proselytization.

After the family settled in Mexico, Isabel was wooed by Captain Felipe Núñez, a New Christian. We cannot be sure whether he was a devout Catholic or an *agent provocateur*. Captain Núñez had originally been on the staff of Governor Carvajal, who was suspicious of Isabel. Family ties would not have deterred him from reporting her to the Holy Office or using Captain Núñez as a spy.

Another possibility is that after the viceroy learned that the governor had a New Christian grandparent, he might have desired to secure further information that would strengthen any prosecution against the governor or his family in New Spain. He might have instigated the wooing of Isabel by Felipe. If this theory is correct, the viceroy's tactics proved successful. The attractive young widow must have thought her physical charms a bulwark against jeopardy resulting from her over-zealousness in bringing adherents to her faith. Captain Núñez, however, did report her to the Inquisition.

Isabel's arrest in 1589 and subsequent testimony implicated her mother, brothers, sisters, deceased father, husband, and aunt. Baltasar and Luis went to Veracruz to escape arrest and spoke of going to Campeche to take a boat owned by a Jew for Spain. Luis returned to Mexico, however, and Baltasar waited almost a year before departing with Miguel, taking passage on another Hebrew-owned boat. Luis, his mother, Leonor, and Catalina were arrested on May 9, 1589, after Isabel's confessions in the torture chamber. Anica and Mariana were held in protective custody.

Isabel recited the opening words of the Shema at the hearing of November 29, 1589. The transliteration of the Hebrew is given below as written by the Inquisition secretary:

Senis Israel, adonai alueno aga
Barosein quebo malento leo lambuiel
Oye Isrrael adoiai Judio

She added that the words of this prayer had been given by God to
Moses before He gave him the law.

FRANCISCA NÚÑEZ DE CARVAJAL

Luis' mother Francisca was a simple soul. Her feeble attempts to
hide her faith and to reveal nothing to the inquisitors arouse pity.
Before she was tortured she confessed that she knew some Jewish
prayers but could remember only two. The first began "We confess
to God because He is good and His mercy is eternal." The second
was a conglomeration of paens of praise of God. A few of the words
were apparently taken from the Shema, since she said that the Lord
must be loved "with all your heart." Although she was fifty years
of age when she was subjected to the first examination by the inquisitors, the secretary noted that she appeared to be younger. The following description of her trial is taken from records of her testimony
and from the account in Luis' memoirs.

One morning, through a small hole that Luis had dug under the
door of his cell, he saw his mother being taken to the torture room
by the warden, the executioner of the punishment, and two inquisitors. At eight o'clock in the morning, the court actuary started reading the sentence, invoking the name of Christ:

> *Christi Nomine Invocato,* We render verdict on the basis of the
> facts and merits of this trial and the evidence and suspicions, and
> the conclusions stemming from them are that we must and do con-
> demn Francisca Núñez de Carvajal to be put to torment, on the
> evidence and confessions, for as much time as we shall want.

"I have said," Doña Francisca answered, "that I have rightfully
believed in the Law of Moses and this is the truth. Sirs, have mercy
on me and on my orphan children for whom I grieve more than for
my life. For God's sake, do not disgrace me."

Doña Francisca was a woman who had known only hardships in
Panuco. At the age of nine, she had been promised in marriage to

Rodríguez de Matos. The marriage took place at the age of twelve. She had suffered the loss of her husband and for many years had been surrounded by dangers. In her later years her only comforts had been the pure love of her family and the practice of her religion. When her moment of trial arrived, she tried to defend herself and her loved ones. She refused to enter into details but proclaimed her faith. Upon her refusal to recant or to implicate others, the executioner was sent for. The executioner was instructed to undress her but she refused to let him do so.

"Kill me but do not undress or disgrace me, even if you give me a thousand deaths. You can see that I am a woman and an honest widow, to whom things like this cannot be done in this world; especially not where there is so much sanctity. I said that I believe in the Law of Moses and not in Christ, and there is nothing more, other than that. I am a forlorn, sad widow with children who shall clamor to God."

The executioner and his assistant undressed her while the notary admonished: "For reverence for God, tell the truth. Tell the truth if you do not wish to be in this danger."

"All is evil," cried the woman, "all is evil. Let this be for the forgiveness of my sins."

She was tied by force on the torture rack. They tied her arms and legs with rope, while the actuary chanted: "Tell the truth, tell the truth."

"Listen, I have told the truth; you are taking a mother away from her children. I never thought that such cruelty could be inflicted upon an old woman. I entrust my soul and offer this torture to Him, of whom I have read in the book *Mirror of Consolation* that the Maccabees adored Him."

The executioner turned the wheel once, and the ropes bit into her flesh. Groans issued from her while the cords cut into her. The twisting and howling in pain of the naked woman failed to move the men who sat in dignity on velvet chairs. "Oh, oh, such cruelty, so much of it. Oh, let me die."

At the second turn of the wheel, the clerk insisted: "Tell the truth, tell the truth."

"I have confessed all and nobody wishes to believe me. I die, I die. Kill me at once. Oh, they have crippled me and will put an end to my life. My God, I could not suffer more, and if I could, I would say so."

"Tell the truth, tell the truth."

"I said that I believe and adored the Law of Moses and not that of Jesus Christ. Have mercy on me, for I have told the whole truth. I die, oh, I die."

At the fourth turn, the woman was being torn apart physically and mentally. "Tell the truth, tell the truth."

"I cannot suffer more. My children have lost their poor mother."

"Tell the truth, tell the truth."

"Grieve, oh sirs, for this is my torture"—here the executioner turned the wheel for the fifth time—"because I die."

"We admonish you once again to tell the truth, putting a stop to this torture because you risk your life. You shall have much more to grieve for and you have only yourself to blame for the pains and tortures. For reverence to God, tell the truth, and have mercy on yourself."

She lost coherence and became delirious. "I have nothing to say but to repeat what I have already said. I have no further evidence . . . and those, God forbid that I utter them, I shall not tell, neither do I know it . . . Blessed be He, they treat me here with cruelty unheard of as being used on a woman."

"Tell the truth, tell the truth."

"I cannot say but that I was born sad from my mother's womb, and miserable was my luck and sad my old age."

The torment came to an end for the moment. Naked, covered with blood, defeated, she kneeled on the floor, and, sobbing, told the story of her life, managing, with the last of her strength, to hold back some things that might harm her children.

A short time before noon the trial was postponed; it was resumed at two o'clock in the afternoon. The prospect of new torture and pain destroyed her steadfast determination. Her maternal concern, the guarding of her religion, all that had been the marrow of her life was destroyed. Hopeless and helpless, she finally denounced her children, betraying her family and herself.

THE CARVAJALS RECONCILED

Luis changed his name to Joseph Lumbroso during this first imprisonment after he had a vision in which he saw and heard God command King Solomon to feed him some "sweet liquor of divine wisdom," which he drank. He adopted the name of Joseph after the biblical Joseph who was the dreamer and visionary, and added Lumbroso, the Spanish word meaning enlightened. His memoirs provide interesting details of this period. He prayed in jail four times a day, always wearing a head covering.

The monk Francisco Ruiz de Luna, who shared Luis' cell, had been brought to Judaism by Luis and had such a strong attachment to his new faith that he broke holy Christian images. Then, during a second trial, he refused to recant and proclaimed his adherence to Judaism, which he termed the "True Law." The clergy were usually spared from going to the stake, but Luis' convert had been defrocked and was sentenced to serve ten years in the galleys to Spain.

On February 24, 1590, Luis, his mother, and sisters abjured and were given certain spiritual penance, such as fasting on Fridays, reciting the short rosary on Sundays and holidays and in the three-day festivals. Luis was placed in the custody of Fray Matheo García, and the Hospital of the Convalescents served as his prison. Here he did whatever the hospital administrator ordered him to do; sweeping and cleaning were his principal duties. His mother and sisters were to have been imprisoned in a convent, but Jorge de Almeida suggested to the inquisitors that this might not be sound since the mother and daughters "are possessed of knowledge and have a very convincing manner. They could easily do the nuns a damage that would be difficult to repair." The inquisitor then changed the place of confinement of the women to a private home.

Luis later was transferred from the hospital to the monastery associated with the Colegio of Santiago Tlaltelolco, where he taught grammar and Latin to the Indians and acted as a secretary for the monastery. He had access to the library, and there he devoured the Scriptures and Oleaster's Commentaries on the Old Testament. He completed his memorization of the Psalms, Ezekiel, Isaiah, Job, and the books of the Apocrypha.

PARDON AND REARREST

On October 7, 1593, for reasons unknown, the Mexican inquisitors wrote to Spain stating that Luis, his mother, and his sisters Isabel, Leonor, and Catalina should receive a commutation of sentence upon payment of a fine of 1,300 ducats of Castile (later reduced to 850 pesos) in addition to the 200 which they had previously paid. In 1594, the entire family received a full pardon conditional upon the payment of the 850 pesos. It is difficult to translate this sum into modern values, but it was vast; there are reports that ship passage from Spain to New Spain could be purchased for nine pesos.

Luis had to raise the money for the fine within six months. The Vicar General of the Franciscans gave him fifty letters to various Franciscan monasteries in New Spain requesting their aid for Luis. The Provincial Abbott of the Augustinians gave him letters, and the viceroy himself gave him twenty-five letters. These and other acts of kindness described in Luis' memoirs indicate that the family were known throughout the city, were well liked, and that people did not regard the fact that they were reconciliados as a stigma. Luis' trip through the countryside in search of 850 pesos produced some cash and some pledges. A Christian neighbor advanced the final 430 pesos due and agreed to wait eight months for repayment.

Luis was a dogmatizer, and his friend Manuel de Lucena was his equal in fervor. One night while Luis was visiting Manuel de Lucena in Pachuca, Lucena tried to reconvert Domingo Gómez Navarro, who become a practicing Christian although his brother, Manuel Gómez Navarro, remained a Jew.

Domingo later denounced his brother Manuel and Lucena to the Inquisition, and both were arrested. At Lucena's fourth hearing he broke down and confessed, naming Luis as a great Jewish teacher.

First Luis and then his mother and five sisters were rearrested in February, 1595, and remained in jail until December 8, 1596. Mariana remained under arrest until 1601. A few weeks before the arrest, Luis wrote in his memoirs of plans for the family to leave New Spain, but this dream was never realized.

From the testimony of one of the Inquisition spies, given in the trial of Beatriz Enríquez de la Payba on December 19, 1594, we learn that Luis and Manuel de Lucena discussed the Mosaic Law. Lucena termed Luis "el gran maestro y sabio mucho mas que el y le enseñaría," the great teacher, and said that he knew very much more than Lucena, who had been taught by him. It was also inferred that Luis was either teaching others to circumcize themselves or was himself performing the operation for them.

On December 19, 1594, Gaspar de los Reyes, warden of the secret cells, testified that he overheard Lucena say that Abraham the prophet had broken idols. This statement is not found in the Bible, but is found in Midrashic literature and legends. Either Luis or Lucena had access to such sources or had learned it from Manuel de Morales or Antonio Machado. Luis was also familiar with the raison d'être for the sacrifices that had been offered in the days of the Temple. Another witness and defendant, Manuel Díaz, mentioned that Luis could play the harp, and that Luis and Lucena often sang together.

MANUEL LUCENA'S WIFE

The proceso of Catalina Enríquez (also Henríquez) presents some details that are of interest.[6] She was the daughter of Simon Payba and Beatriz Henríquez. Her husband, Manuel de Lucena, was one of the principal witnesses against her, although his actions were the result of the threat of torture. His explanation for having lied about her at prior hearings was that she was *amor de carne y sangre* (the love of his flesh and blood). He also said that the demon had misled him; innumerable Jews used this excuse when they changed their original denial. When he began to talk, he also involved his parents-in-law and others.

As a liar, Lucena was inept. He first claimed that he had learned that his wife was a Jewess only five years previously, whereas they had been married for fourteen years. Later he testified that she had observed Jewish customs ten years previously, and that Antonio López de Morales, upon discovering that Catalina and her mother were Jewesses, had given them lessons in the Law. Manuel discovered that his wife was a Jewess when he noticed that she habitually changed the bed sheets on Fridays and dressed immaculately on Saturdays. When she admitted to him that she did these things because of her religion, he declared himself to her, and *recibieron mucho contento ambos* (they shared this news with great happiness). She lit candles on Friday nights and let them burn themselves out. Before the onset of the Sabbath, she washed her feet and cut her nails.

She and Manuel observed Succot in October in commemoration of the forty year wanderings of the Jews in the desert before entering the Promised Land. Their observance included prayer and re-fraining from work. They did not build a *succa*, a temporary structure with only a partial covering made of branches for a roof, in which Orthodox Jews eat for the eight days of the festival to reenact the event, in accordance with Leviticus 23:42, "Ye shall dwell in booths . . ."

Catalina and Manuel observed Passover for eight days rather than seven. They observed Shavuot to celebrate the giving of the Law by God to Moses on Mount Sinai. Again, their observances included washing or bathing before sunset of the day prior to the holiday. Yom Kippur was observed as a day of fasting and praying. Penitential psalms were recited, accompanied by much crying. Not all the people fasted the full twenty-four hours. Some ate at 2:00 P.M. Although the fast was not to be broken until three stars appeared in the sky, one man went to the market at 5:00 P.M. to buy fruit for the group.

Many of the people who prayed together and were named by Lucena to the Inquisition were also among those named by Luis. Lucena's testimony indicates his humane concern when he said that he didn't want to involve "doubtful ones" and thereby expose them "to burning." He also hesitated to name women because among them was she "whom he loved more than his soul." He named some who had left New Spain. He reported that neither he nor several other men would engage in business on Saturdays, nor would they even mount a horse. Catalina and her mother swept and cleaned especially well on Friday afternoons and "adorned the house," presumably with flowers.

According to Spanish law, wine could be consumed only in the town where it was purchased. Lucena once violated this law by buying three *pipes*, barrels, of wine in Mexico and taking them to Pachuca. There is also the recital of a practice in a Jewish quarter of another country, presumed to be Italy, which consisted of fasting during the daylight hours for forty days, commencing in August and ending with the Great Day of Pardon, Yom Kippur.

Clara Enríquez, who was fifty-five years old when she testified, informed against Catalina, the wife of Lucena.[7] She had denied everything for several hearings, but ultimately she yielded to the pressures. Through the naming of people in Seville and Granada who had taught her about Judaism, we learn that the Jews in Spain still maintained active communities despite all decrees and prohibitions against their presence. Clara Enríquez had come to New Spain in 1587. Her teachers in Spain had been Simon Antuñez, Ines Fernández, and Martin de Miranda, a Castilian. (These names also appear fifty-five years later in New Spain but must have belonged to other Jews.) Jiménez Rueda wrote in his additional notes to Medina's *Historia* that the proceso of Clara Enríquez is one of the most interesting "of this generation of *judíos*."[8]

LUIS' BROTHERS-IN-LAW

Antonio Díaz de Cáceres was about forty-seven years of age when he married Catalina de León de la Cueva, a sister of Luis, as his second wife. This marriage was part of a double wedding, the other couple being Leonor de Andrada,[9] sister of Catalina, and Jorge de Almeida (also Almeyda). Díaz de Caceres had lived at the Portuguese royal court when young, had been a page for Count Vimiosa (*sic* - Viciosa?) and served the Infante don Duarte. He had relatives in the Philippines and friends in other parts of the East Indies. He was a ship captain, had two vessels of his own, and literally sailed the seven seas. His ships brought Jews illegally to New Spain.

After the double wedding ceremony, blessed by the brides' brother, Gaspar the monk, but which Luis did not attend, the two newly married couples took a trip to Spain where they remained for a short period. (The peregrinations of crypto-Jews during the sixteenth and seventeenth centuries are almost unbelievable. Ocean voyages were made with a facility and frequency that parallels modern traveling.) In 1589, when Catalina and others had first been arrested, Antonio Díaz fled to the Philippines and Macao for fear that he might also be implicated as a Jew before the Holy Office. Antonio returned to Mexico in 1592, after a prison break and other hair-raising episodes. Catalina and Antonio had one daughter born about 1588, Leonor de Cáceres, who was reconciled in the auto-da-fé of 1601.

About 1599, Díaz de Cáceres was arrested with several others. He and Rodrigo Franco Tavares were convicted of being believers in the Law of Moses. Both were subjected to incredible torture; twelve turns of the cords while on the *potro* (a wooden bed frame with

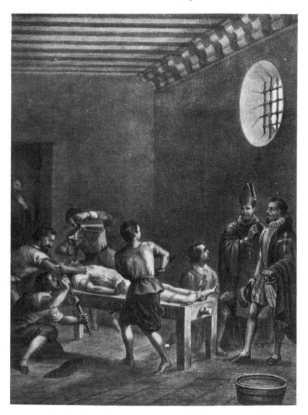

Administration of the water torture
to prisoner on potro

leather straps instead of a mattress and spring). Cords were tied
about their arms, wrists, thighs, and ankles, and six jars of water
were forced down their throats.[10] Rodrigo de Tavares was publicly
lashed as part of his penance, but Antonio Díaz was exempt because
"he was a man highly esteemed and had served his king on several
occasions." The other son-in-law of Francisco Rodríguez de Matos,
Jorge Almeida, was of medium stature, with a swarthy complexion
and a scar on his cheek. He was some thirty years old and had spots
on his head like scars of old ulcers, possibly from pox. He had lived
in Ferrara, Italy, with his mother Felipa de Fonseca and his brothers
Francisco Rodríguez (later called Hector de Fonseca) and Miguel

Hernández. At that time there were three Jewish communities in Ferrara: the Portuguese, the Italian, and the German. Jorge and his family left there in 1564 and moved to Spain where relatives of the Almeida family lived. While in Spain, Jorge became what is known in popular parlance as a "wheeler and dealer." The family emigrated to New Spain in the middle 1580's and were joined a little later by Jorge de León, an Italian cousin. Jorge's mother fasted every three days. The family quickly achieved an enviable reputation in the Jewish colony for their religious observances.

For the holy days, their table was lavishly set with silver service and fine tablecloths. The tables were laden with an abundance of well-seasoned foods. Roast hens were served in glazed earthenware casseroles and there were bowls of magnificent fruits. Candles burned for religious purposes were set aside so as not to be used for secular purposes, but there were many others used for illumination and set in elaborate candelabra. Open house was held for the Jewish notables of the city as well as for other numerous guests.

Jorge de Almeida owned and operated a silver mine in Taxco. About 1585 or 1586, he and Manuel de Morales were alleged to have strangled a Negress slave who had called a friend of theirs, Cristobal Gómez, a Jew. (Cristobal, a cousin of Licienciado Antonio López de Morales, had turned to Jorge and Manuel for advice about what to do with the Negress.) The incident was revealed by Manuel de Lucena during the course of his testimony to the Inquisition of 1595. In 1609, when Jorge de Almeida was burned in effigy in absentia by the Inquisition in New Spain (he had fled to Spain and there is no record of any arrest), the sole ground was "Jewish practices"—nothing was mentioned about murder. Almeida had fled through the back door of his house and escaped on horseback while the Inquisition official was at the front door with the order for his arrest and sequestration of his property.

In 1591, he had not yet been accused of observing Jewish rites. The inquisitors only wanted to question him about his wife's property and any dowry that she might have given him. Leonor was convicted of being a Jewess in 1589 and, although she was then reconciled, her property was confisicated by the Holy Office. The Inquisition therefore was attempting to exercise its prerogative of tracing any property that she had owned at any time. Leonor had not brought any dowry to Jorge. He did not know that the Inquisition interest at that time was limited to the confiscation of Leonor's property, past and present.

After hiding in Mexico for a while, Jorge and his brother Francisco Rodríguez went to Spain. Francisco subsequently abandoned his Christian wife in Spain and married a Jewess in Italy. Jorge established important connections in Spain. He later met Diego Díaz Nieto, the son of Ruy Díaz Nieto and Ines Núñez; this family is discussed in detail in Chapter 9.

BALTASAR AND MIGUEL

After leaving New Spain about 1590 the Caravajal brothers changed their family name to Lumbroso. Baltasar became Jacob Lumbroso and Miguel became David Lumbroso. This change was either agreed upon prior to the departure from Mexico or through correspondence. In the letters sent by Baltasar from Spain to Mexico, however, he used the name of Francisco Ramírez. This reflected a common practice of concealing the identity of the writer.

Upon arrival in Spain, Jacob and David contacted their brother-in-law, Jorge Almeida. He was in correspondence with his wife and her family in Mexico, and he was the one who secured their pardon in 1594. We know that Baltasar and Miguel were still in Spain in 1594 since Almeida introduced them to people there who were leaving for New Spain, among whom were Ruy Díaz Nieto and Diego Díaz Nieto.

After their arrival in Spain Manuel de Morales taught Baltasar some medicine and encouraged him to become a physician, and began to train Miguel in Hebraic studies. The Lumbroso brothers and the Morales family soon left Spain for Venice. Baltasar, or Jacob, studied medicine in Florence and Venice and became a famous surgeon. Miguel, or David, after studying intensively for the rabbinate, went to Salonica, possibly accompanied by Manuel de Morales. Subsequently David became one of the chief rabbis of Salonica, then one of the greatest Jewish communities of Europe.[11]

MANUEL GÓMEZ NAVARRO

Although he was not closely identified with the Carvajals, one of the most interesting characters of the last decade of the sixteenth century was Manuel Gómez Navarro. He was an unmarried merchant associated with the mines of Sichu not far from Pachuca, where Jews in that area assembled for the festivals. Although he never had any formal education, he knew how to read and write and recited perfectly the Peter Noster, Ave Maria, Salva Regina, the Ten Commandents, and the Articles of Faith. During his youth, he had served as a Spanish soldier in Cartegena and Guatemala. After his discharge, he came to Mexico. He denied any knowledge of the reason for his arrest when given his first admonition. He was told that "the Holy Office did not make a practice of arresting people unless it had sufficient information of something that had been done or said which was against our holy Catholic faith and evangelical law which was held, believed, preached, and taught by the Holy Mother Church of Rome" or "that [the arrested ones] observed the Law of Moses or some other prohibited sect . . ."

The charges against Manuel Gómez Navarro by the attorney for the Holy Office were many: that he awaited the Messiah promised in the Old Law and didn't believe that Jesus was the Messiah since the prophecies of the Old Law had not been fulfilled with the coming of Jesus and that Jesus had been hanged (*sic*) because he was a false prophet; that the true Messiah would save the Jews called the Chosen People; he denied the mysteries of the Holy Trinity, especially the Son and the Holy Ghost; he spat on images; he said that Christians adored idols, which contravened one of the Ten Commandments that said that there was to be no worship of idols or graven images and that Christians had substituted for this commandment another, "Thou shalt not fornicate";[12] he said that the Host was a piece of dough; he didn't believe in baptism but did believe that circumcision was necessary for salvation; he denied the Immaculate Conception and uttered blasphemies against it; he said that the Christians (Catholics) called others "Lutheran dogs" because they laughed at the miracles; that the pope could not dispense indulgences and remit sins and that he was only a man, at best inspired by God; that there were no saints and all the accounts concerning them were lies; that the Magdalena (*sic*) was a sinner and should be deprecated as a saint and that Christian faith was filthy and confused.

Prior to his arrest, Manuel had said he wanted to go to a place where he could observe the Jewish law freely and publicly and where he could be a good Jew and would not have to eat pork, lard, or any products of the pig, forbidden as food because the animal did not chew the cud. He taught the Mosaic law to other people because he regarded this as a grand service to God.

To all charges, he said that the truth was the best defense. Twelve witnesses confirmed his observance of the complete practice of Jewish rites. He had memorized many psalms and many portions of Isaiah. He fell on his knees when he spoke of God. Toward the end of his trial he promised to be a good Christian and to live and die as one. When requested to inform against others, however, he refused. Since his confessions were minimal and he recanted his desire to turn Christian, he was considered impenitent.

Ultimately, he convinced the inquisitors that he sought the evangelical law in good faith and with a contrite heart. In addition to the sentence of 200 lashes, he was to be carried through the public streets on a burro, stripped to the waist, with the town crier following him and proclaiming his crimes. He was also to serve six years in the galleys as an oarsmen without pay.

Of particular import in the charges was the reference to Luther and also the charges against the pope, usually made by Protestants, which were repeated by a Jew. Just as Russia today will not permit its Jews to leave for Israel or other places where they may observe freely, so the Church, in past centuries, would not permit Jews to leave the lands under its domination.

LUIS' SECOND IMPRISONMENT AND TRIAL

The minutes of Luis' second trial are replete with statements of his beliefs, his manner of religious observances, and his quotations from Maimonides' "Thirteen Principles of Faith," the Ten Commandments, and the Prophets. There is little question that his extreme religiosity, his awe-inspiring sincerity, and his all-consuming belief in the One God, Adonay, and the Scriptures almost hypnotized even the hard-hearted Alonso de Peralta.

One can almost read between the lines that occasionally Luis was treated with deference. Two doctors of theology, pursuant to the request of the inquisitors, debated with him in an attempt to have him alter his beliefs. He accepted the challenge because he hoped to be able to convince them of the error of their own beliefs.

His trial records reveal the Inquisition tactic of planting informers in cells with the prisoners in order to extract confessions and admissions which they would not make to the Tribunal. Eavesdropping at the cell doors on a twenty-four hour basis was also practiced by Inquisition employees. It also reveals that some jailers were amenable to bribes. Those loyal to the Tribunal carried messages for the prisoners, first exhibiting them to the judges. Luis sent several letters to his sisters. They are highly emotional and indicate a piety and determination that are deeply moving. Before he acquired paper and ink, he scratched messages on the nut of an avocado and on egg shells. One sister wrote to him on a banana skin.

Most of these physical exhibits were preserved with the minutes of the trial. Alfonso Toro, in the introduction to *La Familia Carvajal*, reported that a Brazilian Jew, on the pretext of doing research in the Mexican National Archives in 1932, stole these, among other things, and mailed them to a Mr. Lang in the United States. Some of the stolen material was recovered, but the physical exhibits were not among the recoveries. Fortunately, the messages and other documents had been copied about a decade earlier by either Luis González Obregón or Alfonso Toro, and these have been preserved.

The will of Luis de Carvajal is an ethical document since he had no property to bequeath. It is the declaration of his faith and follows the pattern of ethical wills which had been written for many centuries prior to his time by great rabbis and Jewish savants.

Luis' fear of physical pain was so great that he would be horror-stricken by the sight of inquisitor Alonso de Peralta. Luis said that his very flesh trembled at the sight of him. Equally strong was his spiritual awe of and gratitude to the Lord. Upon awakening in the morning, he recited, "Blessed be the name of the Lord forever, who brings the morning light . . ." On Yom Kippur, he and his family prayed on their knees. They recited "O Almighty, for the sake of Thy Holy name and for Thy Great Day which You have made so that we might fast and repent our sins, pardon us and have mercy on us." They wept bitterly and prayed all through the night. While in his cell during his first imprisonment, on January 26, 1590, Luis composed a 176-line poem which began, "Receive my penitential fast, O Lord, for all the sins which I have committed."

His hate of Christ was intense. In this respect Luis was unique.

Most other Jews never expressed odium of Christ, but Luis referred to him as swindler, imposter, and hanged (*sic*) man and claimed that the Host used by the priests was moldy. He and other Jews denied the virginity of Mary because she gave birth to a man.

Luis' fear of physical pain prompted his attempted suicide on February 16, 1596, after he had been in the torture chamber on February 10, 12, 14, and 15. Undressed except for his linen underpants, he jumped from a window in the Hall of the Inquisition but sustained only severe contusions and abrasions.

During his confession on the aforesaid days, he implicated over 120 other Jews, recited the Shema, and used the Hebrew name of God, Adonay, many times. He explained that the head must be bowed during the Shema, the left hand placed over the forehead, covering the eyes, and the right hand over the heart. During the four days in the chamber, words gushed forth from him in a veritable torrent. He sacrificed everyone to spare himself from torture. After the attempted suicide, he regretted his actions and declared that he had lied about some people. At this last hearing on November 7, he implicated Manuel Gil de la Guarda and used a derogatory expression about him. Of course his fate was doomed by Peralta, the senior inquisitor. His fifteen page sentence ended with the fixing of the date for the stake, December 8, 1596.

At the last hearing, he quoted, "Their idols are silver and gold, the work of men's hands. They have eyes but see not and feet but walk not and hands but handle not." He stated that he was not sure whether it was Psalm 111 or 112. (This was one of the rare instances that he was unsure. It is Psalm 115, according to the Hebrew edition. Luis had studied from the Vulgate, which runs one number lower than the Hebrew edition.)

Luis stated that Licenciado Feliciano de Valencia was related to him, but the Inquisition did nothing about this piece of information. The words of the psalms were the last recorded for him except those uttered on the way to the stake about the paucity of Christians there would be in New Spain if it were not for the coercion of the Inquisition.

THE AUTO-DA-FÉ OF 1596

The verdict against Leonor, wife of Jorge de Almeida, to be

burned at the stake was cast on May 29, 1596,[13] but neither she nor the others officially knew their sentences until the night before the burning. The mother, Francisca, had her fate determined on May 28 and reaffirmed on September 18. Catalina was the last to be sentenced. On October 2, 1596, the inquisitors and those who sat with them in judgment rendered the final verdict.

In the letters sent by Luis to his sisters while they were all incarcerated in 1595 and 1596, he referred to his sisters several times as martyrs and wrote of the glories of heaven that awaited them. It appears that he expected that the youngest, Anica, would also be martyred, because Luis gives a detailed picture of her wedding in heaven with the Almighty giving her away as the bride and King David playing his harp and the angels dancing and acting as a choir.

Whether Luis and his family knew of their sentences when the votes were taken is uncertain. Luis urged his sisters to think of the Paradise that awaited them in the next world, but, in his hearings, he never indicated to the inquisitors that he knew of the sentences. If he had definite knowledge, there surely would have been a plea for mercy on behalf of his mother and sisters. He never indicated any concern about Leonor, his niece, being made an orphan if her mother Catalina went to the stake.

There were two reasons for the time lapse between the date of the sentences of the Carvajals and their executions. The Holy Office preferred to celebrate Lent and the period before Christmas with "an act of faith." The date fixed for the 1596 auto-da-fé was the anniversary of the Immaculate Conception. In 1596, there was also the hope that Luis might break down and seek to be reembraced by the Church. This act would have been a triumph for the Church and, as he was considered a leader, his defection might inspire those not yet apprehended to defect also.

The place where the 1596 auto-da-fé was held is in dispute. The decree of the Inquisition fixed the chief plaza or Zocalo. This is the principal square in each city and village founded in New Spain during the colonial period. The relación also refers to the chief plaza. Henry Charles Lea wrote that the first real *quemadero*, stake, was erected in Mexico by the municipality in 1596 at a cost of 400 pesos. It was at the east end of the Alameda and remained there until 1771, by which time burning at the stake was growing obsolete. The Palacio de Bellas Artes now stands at the spot. Lea was correct about the cost, but the date of the establishment of the stake to which he referred was 1598.

The procession of the auto-da-fé was attended by a multitude of people. Many onlookers threw stones and fruit at the unfortunate ones. Some physically attacked the men and cut their beards.

Hubert H. Bancroft described the 1596 events as follows (all spelling and capitals as in original):

> Preparations on a grand scale were made to present to the authorities and people a spectacle worthy of the cause. To increase the solemnity of the occasion the day fixed upon was that of Immaculate Conception; and the place the chief plaza with its extensive appointments of railings arranged as in an amphiteatre, which was used after the celebration as a bull-ring.
>
> The time having arrived, the Viceroy Conde de Monterrey, accompanied by the justice and officers of the Audiencia, the royal treasury official, military officers, and other members of his suite repaired to the Inquisition building, where the Inquisitors Bartolomé Lobo Guerrero, an archbishop elect, and Alonso de Peralta, subsequently bishop of *Charcas*, awaited them. Sixty-seven penitents were then led forth from the dungeons, and the procession marched to the plaza. A great concourse of people, from far and near, followed the procession and occupied windows and squares to the very gate and houses of the holy office.
>
> The prisoners appeared, wearing ropes round their necks, and conical hats on which were painted hellish flames, and with green candles in their hands, each with a priest at his side exhorting him to Christian fortitude. They were marched under a guard of the holy office. Among those doomed to suffer were persons convicted of the following offenses: those who had become reconciled with the Church and afterwards relapsed into Judaism, in sanbenitos, and with familiars of the inquisition at their side; sorceresses, with white hats of the same kind, candles and ropes; blasphemers with gags to their tongues, marching together, and after the other, with heads covered and candles in their hands. First among them came those convicted of petty offenses followed in regular order of criminality by the rest, the last being the relapsed, the dogmatists, the teachers of the Mosaic law, who wore the tails of their sanbenitos rolled up and wrapped around their caps to signify the falsity of their doctrin. On arriving at their platform, the prisoners were made to sit down, the relapsed, the readers of the Mosaic law, the dogmatists occupying the higher seats; the others according to their offences, last being the statues of the dead and absent relapsed ones . . . On the right side of the holy office was a pulpit from which preached the Franciscan friar, Ig-

nacio de Santibañez, archbishop of the Philippines. Then followed the usual admonitions, opportunities to recant, and finally the fierce flames, the foretaste of eternal torments.[14]

Of the sixty penitents in the auto-da-fé, there were forty-five Jews, one of whom had only been suspected of Jewish practices. Nine were burned at the stake after receiving the garrote, ten were burned in effigy, and twenty-five were reconciled. Appendix A presents a digest of the Jewish participants as reported in the relación of the event.

Of those condemned to the stake, all except Luis de Carvajal were carrying crosses. Padre Alonso de Contreras was quietly and pleadingly urging Luis to kiss the cross which he held before him. The kiss would indicate that he had embraced Catholicism and thereby saved his soul from eternal damnation. This would entitle him to receive the garrote as an act of mercy before the pyre was lit. The padre also repeated many of the arguments advanced by the theologians who had spent Luis' last night with him attempting to show him the errors of his beliefs.

In a subsequent report to the Holy Office, Contreras described the last hours and minutes of the martyr. He wrote that Luis wanted to die with the title of "great zealot, grand teacher, and restorer of the forgotten Law." He attested that Luis never showed the slightest anxiety, repentance, or sorrow during the time of the procession. When he reached the cupola opposite the platform where the stakes had been erected, however, he saw the effigy of the Jewess to be burned—very likely that of Isabel Pérez, wife of Manuel (Abraham) de Morales—and looked at it tenderly and heaved a sigh.

As his sentence was being read aloud, the monk reported that "he stood like a column of marble." His mother and sisters, who had taken the cross a little earlier, added their pleas to that of the monk. The padre wrote that he finally converted after calling for one of the prophetical books and reading a sentence that seemed to confirm what he had been told the previous evening about the coming of Christ.[15]

There is a doubt of the legitimacy of the conversion. Two devout Catholic Mexican historians, Don Pablo Martínez del Rio[16] and Alberto María Carreño,[17] questioned it. Carreño wrote that if Luis did convert at the last moment it was only a stratagem to avoid the physical pain of the flames licking at his flesh. By accepting Christianity, he would secure the grace of dying by the garrote before his body would be burned at the stake.

In *Historia documental de México*, there is a document pertaining to Luis entitled "Ejecucion de la Sentencia," signed by Alonso Bernal, public scribe.[18] In it appears: ". . . y por el camino fue con demonstracion de haberse convertido y tomo en la mano un crucifjo y dijo alguno palabras por las cuales se entendio haberse convertido y arrepentido" (and on the road as a demonstration of having converted, he took a crucifix in his hands and said some words by which it was understood that he had converted and repented).

The finest epitaph for Luis, who died as Joseph Lumbroso, was written by Padre Contreras in his report:

> He was always such a good Jew and he reconciled his understanding, which was very profound and sensitive, with his highly inspired Divine determination to defend the Law of God—the Mosaic—and to fight for it. I have no doubt that if he had lived before the Incarnation of our Redeemer, he would have been a heroic Hebrew and his name would have been as famous in the Bible as are the names of those who died in defense of their law when it was necessary.

9

The Mass Immigration:

1596-1625

THE AUTO-DA-FÉ of December 8, 1596, added a new meaning to the word Portuguese. In the Spanish world, for the next century the word Portuguese was almost synonymous with Jew.

In his book, *The Dutch in Brazil: 1624-1654*, C. R. Boxer uses a Balzacian quote from J. Howell's *Epistolae Hoeliane, Familiar Letters, Domestic & Foreign* (London, 1645), "Above all, the Portuguese were closely associated with the Jews in the minds of contemporary Spaniards as exemplified by their coarse proverb, 'A Portuguese was born of a Jew's fart.' " For a person to be called Portuguese inferred to the colonists that such person was a Jew, or of Jewish descent, or a neuvo cristiano and a practitioner of Jewish ritual. This concept played a great role in the event of the 1640's. As may be readily seen from the places of birth of the victims of the 1596 auto-da-fé (Appendix A), practically all the Jewish participants came from Portugal. The same high percentage prevailed for the period from 1596 to 1660. In the autos-da-fé of the seventeenth century there were Italian, French, and German Jews, at least one Irish Jew, and many who were born in New Spain itself, but the majority were from Spain or were of Spanish or Portuguese descent.

The place of nativity is important for these who adhere to the traditional or Orthodox definition of "who is a Jew?" The consensus of historical opinion holds that the vast majority of Jews in Portugal between 1497 and 1507 was forced to the baptismal font or converted so as to remain with their children who had been converted. Julio Caro Baroja wrote that there were profound differences between the Castilian and Aragonese converts in the sixteenth century and the Portuguese, "or those who were so-called," who had fled from baptism in Spain and who received baptism in Portugal "by force and without any possible alternative."[1] He added that "the Portuguese converts adhered more stringently to the Old Law and so did the descendants of these baptized by force who, with great frequency in 1600, in 1650 or 1700 attached themselves to *Mosaísmo* as the special circumstances under which they lived permitted."

It has been previously noted that the Portuguese immigrants to New Spain at the close of the sixteenth century not only infused numbers and new blood into the existing Jewish communities but, predicated upon greater learning, they also were more devout adherents to Jewish observances. Luis de Carvajal, *el Mozo* had been trying to spread the tenets of Judaism and had engendered discussions about the messages of the Scriptures and the meanings and interpretations of many passages. The new arrivals, with their obeisance to the command to be devout or holy, as stated in Leviticus 19:2, stimulated the desire for knowledge.

The thirteen years after 1596 were significant for several reasons: the termination of the pending cases before the Tribunal or under investigation for several years, the papal pardon of Clement VIII in 1605 and its effect in New Spain, and the reign of Philip III of Spain. Philip II had died in 1598, and his son ruled until 1621. The new king was preoccupied with affairs in Europe. The Spanish Empire was in a marked and steady decline in the seventeenth century; each of her rulers during that period excelled his predecessor in malfeasance or misrule. The influx of Portuguese into New Spain at the beginning of the seventeenth century grew at a greater rate than previously. It is noted that there was even a synagogue located on the corner of Calle de Reloj and Puente de Acapulco that was not a part of an individual's home.

The events of 1590 and 1596 convinced the officials of the Holy Office that they needed their own prison for people sentenced to jail. The secret cells had been used for prisoners prior to sentencing. As had been done with the Carvajal women, many prisoners, after the rendition of the sentence, were committed to house confinement or were placed in a convent or monastery. In 1598 the Mexican Tribunal built its first prison. This adjoined the Casa de la Inquisición that faced the Plaza de Santo Domingo, now the Plaza de Corregidora. Neither the original secret cells nor the new prison cells were forboding underground cells. Mexico was built on a lake bed; and in the sixteenth and seventeenth centuries no building had a cellar that could be converted into prison cells. Some cells on the ground floor were dark because they were windowless.

The auto-da-fé of 1596 and the detention of some of the Jews did not deter continued immigration to New Spain. During the period from 1590 to 1640 the majority of the Iberian immigrants came from two main unrelated areas. One was the northern part of Portugal and the northwestern part of León. The second extensive area included Castelo Branco (also Castelobranco and Castelo Blanco), Covilha Escarigo, Fundão, Guarda, San Vicente Davera (also de la Vara), Sarzedas, Celorico, Serta, Belmonte, and Viseu. Of course, many people came from Seville and other parts of Andalusia but not in numbers to equal the first two groups. After fleeing from Portugal to Spain, they migrated to the New World. Descendants of the secret Jews still practiced vestiges of their faith in Belmonte until they were discovered in the twentieth century.

There were so many Jews in New Spain in 1602 that Friar Hernando de Ojea, a Dominican, was perturbed by their numbers. He published an apologetic work intended to convince Mexican Jews that they should convert.[2] The treatise was named *La venida de Cristo y su vida y milagros, en que se concerdan los dos Testamentos divinos Viejo y Nuevo* (The Coming of Christ and His Life and Miracles in which the Two Divine Testaments, Old and New, are in accord). In the introduction, Padre Ojea comments on the great number of judaizers in Mexico.

Evidence of the growth in Jewish population may be gleaned by noting that the autos-da-fé at the beginning of the seventeenth century included not only the prisoners of the previous decade but also their children.

This natural increase plus the legal immigration into New Spain in the early decades of the seventeenth century created a substantial Jewish population. Included in the auto-da-fé of 1601 were Leonor de Cáceres, the thirteen-year-old daughter of Catalina of the Carvajal family, and Anica Carvajal, then eighteen years old. In the auto-da-fé of 1603 there was Clara Enríquez, daughter of Manuel de Lucena, who already had been burned. In the auto of 1635, Simon Paredes, son of Manuel de Lucena, was sent to the stake. Martirology became almost a family inheritance, as witnessed by the Carvajal, Lucena, Enríquez, and Méndez families.

Antonio Machado, then deceased, was burned in effigy in 1596. His granddaughter, Antonia Machado, was penanced by the Holy Office in 1604 because she wore silk dresses with gold fringes. The sins of the fathers were visited unto the third and fourth generations according to the Inquisition. Gonzalo Molina, grandson of Machado and son of Gonzalo Rodríguez and Leonor Machado, however, was living in Chiauhtlan and was the official scribe of the town.[3] This post was equivalent to that of vice-mayor since he carried the "Wand of Royal Justice" in the absence of the mayor. Molina, who had been born in Taxco, was penanced because he wore silk and rode a horse. Although seven people in his town knew that he was the grandson of one burned at the stake, not one of them reported him to the Inquisition. The vagaries of Inquisition methods are illustrated by the failure to arrest Antonio Machado's daughter Leonor, not to mention the fact that Gonzalo Molina had no right to hold public office as the grandson of one who had been relaxed as a heretic.

Pedro de Espinosa was in the auto-da-fé of April 16, 1646, when he was forty-five years of age. He and his parents, Simon Rodríguez and Isabel Enríquez de Silva, were all observant Jews.[4] Isabel de Medina was thirty-eight years of age when she was sentenced on September 4, 1637. There was no public auto since she was the sole penitent. She was reprimanded and abjured *de vehementi*—significant is the absence of the order for exile. Alberto Marte Correa, who was seventy-two years old in 1647, was born in New Veracruz. In the autos-da-fé from 1646 to 1649 there were other Jews who had resided in Mexico for forty years or more. Notable were the children and grandchildren of Justa Mendez and Francisco Núñez, whose descendants by the second generation numbered almost fifty. One of their daughters, Isabel Núñez, wife of Duarte de León Jara-

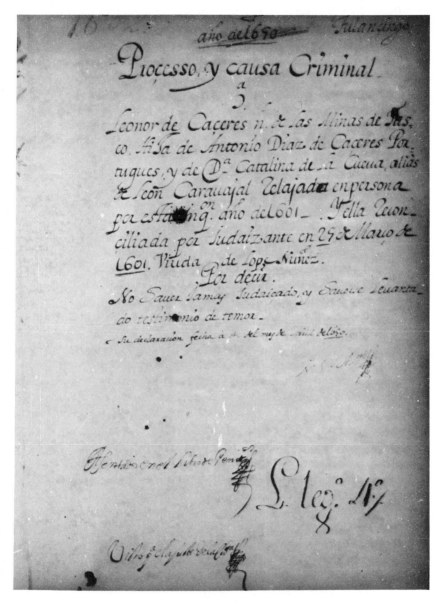

*Flyleaf of the proceso of Leonor de Cáceres. Courtesy
of the Henry E. Huntington Library*

millo, had seven children. She and all her children were born in Mexico.

These are but a few names of those who were born after 1600 and were reared as Jews in New Spain. For the colonial period our only Jewish population estimate is that which is based on the available Inquisition records. The inquisitors were not infallible in searching out Jews. If the United States Federal Bureau of Investigation (using modern techniques, including fingerprinting) estimates in 1968 that it and other law enforcement agencies are able to arrest only twenty percent of known criminals, how much smaller must be the percentage of the total Jewish population represented by Inquisition arrests.

In 1601 permission was granted by Philip III for irrevocable free immigration to the New World.[5] The king received 200,000 ducats for this grant, which endured for only nine years in spite of its "irrevocability." In 1610, the "irrevocable permission" was withdrawn.

The permission was a prelude to an even more important grant that followed in 1604-1605. The New Christians knew that they needed something else to insure their safety or that of their friends, families, and other crypto-Jews who sought new lives and fortunes in New Spain. After years of negotiations, the Portuguese Jews succeeded in making another contract with Philip III. (Portugal was then ruled by Spain.) In exchange for a large sum of money, they received special privileges which the Holy See confirmed in August 23, 1604, by a papal decree.[6] All reconciliados in Europe and those in the New World who confessed within two years needed to perform only spiritual penance. The papal brief was published on January 16, 1605. The Inquisition did not readily accede to the papal brief and threw obstacles in the way, but finally acceded to the directions. This arrangement lasted until 1630 or 1631. In 1632, the decadence of Portugal was imputed to the corrupting influence of the Jews "which in a singular manner was undermining the Spanish character and exercising pernicious influence" on the country.[7] The fanatics who brought about the termination of the papal bull believed that Jews were incorrigible, carried a hatred of Christianity in their blood, and as converts could not be sincere.

Julio Jiménez Rueda gives the date 1605 for Philip III's general pardon to all Jews descended from Portuguese who had been tried by the Holy Office, ordering them to be freed. Jimínez Rueda adds that only one Sevillano, Francisco López Enríques, gained such privilege.[8] But this number is in error because there are records of at least sixteen who made a request to go free in accordance with the grace extended them by Pope Clement VIII.[9] Padre Mariano Cuevas wrote that Clement VIII gave a full pardon to Portuguese Jews in New Spain if they converted. Apparently many did go through a conversion proceeding, which explains the appellation of "New Christians" to many of the Jews apprehended later in the seventeenth century. Padre Cuevas added that these Portuguese Jews who had converted "multiplied and spread over Mexico in the ensuing thirty-eight years and spread their hatred of Spain and the Catholic religion and Jesus."[10]

There is no question that the practice of bribing Spanish rulers continued for many years and won respite for the Jews from the Holy Office. These bribes ran as high as the 1,860,000 ducats paid to Philip II and the 50,000 ducats to "his whore Lerma." Henry C. Lea reports that the foregoing sums were exclusive of 40,000 and 30,000 ducats paid to two members of the council of the Suprema and an additional 30,000 ducats paid to its secretary. For this sum, a general pardon was given for past offenses, including cases still awaiting trial. Reconciliation was not to entail the stake in case of a relapse.

In 1606 an additional bribe was paid to Philip III to desist from molesting the Jews.[11] While these contracts, briefs, pardons, etc., were being received, Jews were populating other areas of the Caribbean. This colonizing effort ultimately reaped its reward as a place of haven for Jews in New Spain. In Cayenne, Guiana, a small French colony was settled in 1604; included among the colonizers were fifteen to twenty Jewish families.[12]

During the first three decades of the seventeenth century, Iberian Jews arrived in New Spain directly from the Iberian Peninsula as well as from Brazil and other parts of South America. In 1618, a zealous inquisitor was sent from Portugal to Brazil. His efforts caused many of the New Christians to seek refuge in other Spanish colonies. Many of these people traveled by boat from Brazil to what is now Uruguay, then by foot or horse into Argentina, and then across the pampas and over the Andean cordilleras into Chile. There were two classes of emigrants from Chile to New Spain. Those who had official licenses left from Valparaiso. Those who were leaving illegally and planning to land in New Spain without licenses left from Concepción. Some went to Lima, many remaining there, and many also went on to Acapulco and then to Mexico.

The exchange of aid and communication between the Jews in the Indies and the Spanish Jews in both Aleppo and Hamburg was very great in the seventeenth century. Kohut notes that the merchandise, supplies, etc., sent to Aleppo and Hamburg were "in turn forwarded to Holland and Zealand."[13] This statement explains why the Spanish-Portuguese archives of Amsterdam show only a few pieces of correspondence between the Jews of New Spain and those of Holland. In order to secrete their identity, this circuitous route was used. The Jews knew that Spain and Portugal maintained spies in Holland, London, and other areas to ascertain which persons from Spain and its colonies or from Portugal attended Hebrew religious services while abroad and which crypto-Jews were trading in the Low Countries.

In the seventeenth century, Simón de Cáceres, a Spanish Jew, aided the English in the conquest of Jamaica and acted as consultant concerning trade with Barbados. He was assisted in the Jamaica affair by Campoe Sabbatha and a man named Acosta. Acosta was a crypto-Jew, and Sabbatha was believed to be one also. Cáceres suggested raising a Jewish force which would fight under the English flag for the conquest of Chile.[14]

In the Public Records Office, Chancery Lane, London, may be found the "Calendar of State Papers: Colonial America and West Indies, 1661-1668." On page 436, #1368, is a description of Trinidad, and then follows:

> The chief town, St. Joseph, being settled by about 100 Spaniards, where in 1646, the English planted a colony . . . *Barbados*. Settled by the English in 1625 . . . in ten years it was brought to great perfection, as many tons of good are shipped from thence as from the two famous empires of Mexico and Peru.[15]

The report details the founding of colonies on various other islands between 1620 and 1650. There are references to the Dutch and French, but Spaniards predominated in St. Croix, Saba, St. Eustatia, and many other places. The majority of the Spaniards who inhabited and traded in these islands prior to 1655 were Jews. After 1655 all the Spaniards in the Caribbean area held by the English were Jews. It can be partially substantiated that many Jews who fled the jail sentences imposed in New Spain and which were to be served in the mother country escaped to the Caribbean islands, where Jews were engaged in the sugar and slave trade.[16] They brought slaves as agents for the crown from Angola and parts of Africa to New Spain, Peru, and to the Caribbean islands. Slaves were badly needed in the Caribbean area and were used as much, if not more, than they were used in New Spain. This was especially true in Yucatán and the Gulf of Mexico coastal area running south from Veracruz.

THE AUTOS-DA-FÉ OF 1601 TO 1609

Many of the details concerning the life of the people and their customs in the first decade of the seventeenth century must again be sought in the Inquisition proceedings. The testimony reveals many religious rites. In spite of the inherent dangers, several prisoners continued their practices even in the secret cells.

In 1597, the inquisitors had many prisoners on hand whose fate had not been determined prior to the auto-da-fé of December 8, 1596, and there were many matters which required further investigation. Some who had been reconciled in the 1596 auto-da-fé were soon rearrested for having relapsed. A case that presents many questions and has some interesting aspects will next be described.

DIEGO DÍAZ NIETO

Diego Díaz (also Diez) Nieto was the son of Ruy (Rui) Díaz Nieto against whom, as well as against many others, Manuel Gil de la Guarda testified. Diego was born either in Oporto, Portugal, or Ferrara, Italy,[17] and at thirteen had been taken to Lisbon. His genealogy on page 192 is typical of the unusual use of names which makes tracking relationships so difficult and confusing. His father, Ruy Díaz Nieto, had taken him to Italy where they lived for a protracted period in the ghettos or Jewish quarters. Diego's real name was Isaac Nieto and his father's, Jacobo Nieto.

Shortly before 1590, Ruy Díaz Nieto had secured a bull for a

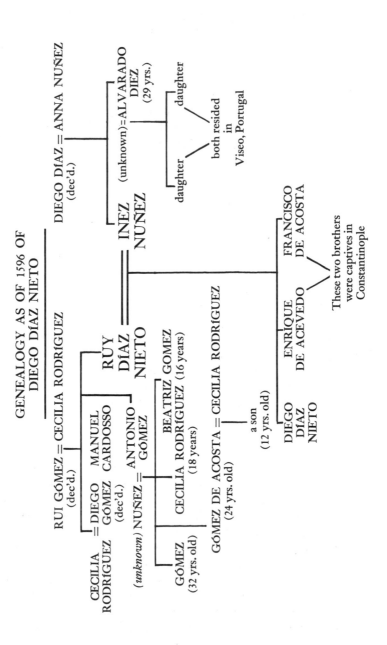

GENEALOGY AS OF 1596 OF
DIEGO DÍAZ NIETO

collection of funds for the redemption of the captives held by the Turks. In the absence of an examination of the bull, it is conjectured that the two sons who appear in the genealogy were among the fifteen to be ransomed. How they came to be prisoners and why they were held in Constantinople for ransom is inexplicable. At that time there was a large, thriving Jewish community in Constantinople on excellent terms with the Sultan. The Turkish Jews (descendants in the main of those expelled from Spain in 1492) felt a great kinship with Iberian Jewry and ransomed literally thousands from North Africa.

Ruy Díaz Nieto and his son went to Spain with the papal bull and there met Jorge de Almeida, who secured a license from Philip II for the father and his son to go to New Spain and seek funds for the release of captives. Ruy paid Jorge between 100 and 150 ducats for his services. Jorge's friend at court was Dr. Báez, personal physician of the king. (Báez, also Váez, was a name also borne by some Jews in the New World.)

Before leaving Madrid, Diego Díaz met Baltasar Carvajal (Jacob Lumbroso), who had married a woman by the name of Ana. Miguel Carvajal (David Lumbroso) was still a bachelor. Jorge de Almeida gave Ruy and Diego three letters to be delivered in Mexico: one was directed to Luis, and a second, a letter of pardon for Luis, his mother, and his three sisters, was directed to the Holy Office. This letter or document is dated June 7, 1594, and was delivered to the Tribunal in Mexico in November, 1594.

The Díaz Nieto family had some interesting relatives in Spain. A second cousin, Licenciado Jorge Cardosso, practiced law, and another cousin worked for a lawyer. Also among the relatives was a Franciscan monk. Ruy Díaz Nieto was termed a rabbi by the inquisitors and "the old saint" by many Mexican Jews. He was so orthodox that while he was in the Inquisition cells in 1601 he would not eat non-kosher foods, and he observed all Jewish rites to the best of his ability. His son, Diego, could recite the *Amidah* (the Eighteen Benedictions, which are part of the morning prayers) from memory. One can read the transliteration of the Hebrew made by the Inquisition amanuensis during his testimony after his arrest in Mexico. "Adonay, Adonay, shawfavsi tiftaw ufi yagid t'chelawsechaw," O Lord, open Thou my lips that my mouth may declare Thy praise.

Diego was twenty-one years old when he was reconciled in Mexico on December 8, 1596. His sentence was quite mild—confiscation of his property and one year in jail. On December 10, 1597, he was permitted to surrender his sanbenito. He was told that for the following year he was to recite a short rosary on Saturdays, fast on one Friday each month for twelve months in the Hospital of Our Lady in the Colegio de San Juan de Letran, and that he was to confess and have communion.

In Diego's first trial he did not implicate his father, nor was he asked any questions about his father's faith or religious practices. He claimed that Dr. Pedro Váez, a physician of the king (there is nothing to indicate that he was the same Báez who was Jorge de Almeida's friend but all circumstances would seem to confirm this), had taught him the Law of Moses while he was in Madrid in 1593. Diego had stayed in Antonio de Fonseca's home, which was across the street from the doctor's home. Fonseca had also acted as his tutor in Judaism.

Diego did not display much of his learning during his first trial. After his second arrest and his trial in 1601, he exhibited a knowledge of many traditional prayers, which he recited in Hebrew. He related to the inquisitors many of the customs that he had learned while living in the Jewish quarters of Italian cities. His testimony reveals, for the first time in New Spain, that Mosaic law required the washing and salting of meat and that only the forequarters, not the hindquarters, of some of the permitted animals could be eaten. Diego stated that the Messiah was to be a son of King David and not a son of God, and that the Messiah would redeem the entire world, that he would cause deceased Jews to arise from their graves, and that some Christians would incur eternal punishment. He further testified that he had been taught that Jesus was *un hombre docto* (a learned man) but not a son of God.

In spite of his learning and the religiosity of his father, Diego either planned poorly or was not concerned that he spent the Great Day of Pardon (which he referred to only as the tenth day of the September moon) in the Indian village of San Pedro, between Otucpa (the modern Actopan) and the mines of Pachuca. He added that his failure to eat on a fast day in an Indian village would occasion no disclosure of his religion.

Diego stated that Passover was observed for seven days beginning on the thirteenth day of the April moon. (This would be the Hebrew month of Nissan, but Passover begins on the night of the fourteenth day. The reference by one Italian who studied Judaism in Italy, to a seven- instead of an eight-day observance, is peculiar, since Jewry followed the diaspora custom of eight days.) In referring to the three-day Fast of Queen Esther, the Inquisition secretary spelled Mordecai "Mardocheo." This fast was concluded in Europe with dancing, singing, and banquets. This is the first reference in New Spain to the gaiety usually attendant upon Purim. In explaining this facet of the holiday, Diego did not state, nor was he asked, whether the festive aspect he described occurred in Spain, Italy, or New Spain. He related that he had been taught the necessity of washing one's hands and face upon arising in the morning. The hands were not to be put into the jar, but rather water was to be thrown directly from the jar over the hands and face since immersion of the hands would have dirtied the water. Washing was necessary because night dreams were under the aegis of demons.

To trace the places in which Diego observed the various holidays in New Spain requires a detailed map of a hundred-square-mile area with Mexico as the center. There is no explanation of why the young man traveled so much and so far and wide. The possibility exists that he was aiding his father to collect charity for the release of captives, but there may be a more cogent reason. The reading of the testimony against his father leads one to a confirmation of the Inquisition's claim that Ruy was a rabbi. This would be an explanation for Ruy's presence in New Spain. The son could have been sent around the countryside to inform the Jews of the presence of his father and to collect the farda from those who could not come to the viceregal seat to hear the elder Díaz and to learn from him. As a solicitor of funds, the title of rabbi would be helpful.

Admittedly, there is no mention of a collection by Díaz Nieto for the communities of Palestine. On the other hand, a collection for the release of fifteen captives might have served as a pretext to secure a bull and a license to go to New Spain. To believe that the alleged pretext was the actual reason strains credulity. With the thousands of Jews in the ghettos of Italy, the thousands of crypto-Jews in Spain and Portugal, and the thriving Jewish community of Holland composed of Iberian Jews, it would have been foolhardy and unnecessary to search out Jews in New Spain for contributions for the release of fifteen captives. The time spent in New Spain between the arrival of the father and son and the arrest of the son was much too long for a solicitation for charity for prisoners. On the other hand, the role of the solicitors for Palestine in that period required that the solicitors be learned Jews and that they spend time teaching and studying with each community from whom they sought support for the Jews of the Holy Land.

Diego testified about a book in Latin owned by Isabel de Carvajal. This book contained the psalms of David without the *Gloria Patri*, and parts of the book were in the vernacular. This may have been the book given to Luis *el Mozo* by the Italian Rodríguez. He also stated that men lit candles on the Sabbath.

When Diego Díaz Nieto testified in 1607 before the Inquisition in Mexico about some of the foregoing, he stated that he had never been baptized. The inquisitors had him take the oath of the Jews, as follows:

> Do you swear by the Creator, who made heaven and earth and the sea, and the sands, and wrote his name in four letters, *Job*, *He*, *Vav*, *He* [*sic*], and took the children of Israel out from the land of Egypt, and parted the sea, and gave them the manna, and gave the Law to Moses on Mt. Sinai, and brought the Children of Israel through the desert and afterwards took them to the Promised Land, to tell the truth in answer to the questions which may be propounded to you by this Holy Office—all other oaths which you may have taken to the contrary notwithstanding—whether the said questions refer to persons now living, and are either present or absent, or to persons who have departed this life?
>
> The prisoner answered "I do," and then the inquisitor continued.
>
> If you do so, may the Creator have mercy on you, and confer upon you all the promises made by the Prophets to the people of Israel. But if you fail to do so, may the Creator destroy you as he destroyed the people of the Flood in the time of Noah, and Sodom and Gomorrah in the time of Abraham, and may you be confounded like Korah and his companions Dathan and Abiram were confounded in the desert, and may all the curses set forth in the fifth book of the Law of Moses, and in the Psalms of David in the fifth book of Elohete and Lociategras [*sic*], fall upon you; and may no son who inherits your name be born in your house. You must state the truth, without adding to it or taking from it anything at all, and must not fail to do so either because of love or kinship, or for the sake of peace, or because of gifts given to you or interest of any kind. All that you may say must be said and ex-

plained in such a way as to permit its being put down in writing and understood, and confirmed and ratified at all times as the expression of the truth. And you must not pay any attention to any threat or any consideration of fear, because our Lord will deliver you from all evil if you say the truth and nothing but the truth *baruthic sinc aruthic*.

And the said Diego Díaz said then "Amen."[18]

Domingo, brother of Manuel Gomez Navarro,[19] was the catalyst who brought the downfall of those in the auto-da-fé of 1596, in which there were forty-five Jews and possibly two more; one was involved in each of the autos-da-fé of 1601 and 1602; one (from Cartagena) in that of 1603; and one, Diego Díaz Nieto, a second offender, in 1605.

One of the witnesses against Diego and his father was Gómez de Acosta. Ruy had a brother by that name, but Diego had testified that he had resided in Lisbon and was deceased. Diego was rearrested in 1601. During his second trial in 1601 Diego was compelled to debate with several learned Catholics. They admired his mental nimbleness and he bested them several times. He sought forgiveness and permission to return to Italy. This was denied, and he then was sentenced in 1605 to two years as a recluse in a monastery and then to life imprisonment.

One of the persons included in the 1601 auto-da-fé known to Luis de Carvajal and Diego was Manuel Rodríguez, nicknamed *El Chiquito*, the Little One; he had come to New Spain from China. Diego López Regalon, alias Felipe López, had come to New Spain from Peru where he had been a prisoner in Lima. The individuals passing through the House of the Inquisition at the close of the sixteenth and the beginning of the seventeenth centuries included Juan Nuñez de León, an official of the royal mint who was suspected of being a Jew and an alumbrado, and Martinez de Briones of Puebla, who was arrested for calling an official of the Inquisition "Jew dog." Juan Nuñez de León was burned at the stake in the auto of April 20, 1603, according to Medina.[20] He refused to eat pork and he washed his hands before and after eating. The sixteen year old slave, María de la Cruz, was imprisoned for being a Jewess although her master Carlos Samano was not. María was a friend of some of the servants who worked for Jews.

The auto-da-fé of March 25, 1601, included forty-six Jews and one person suspected of being Jewish. Eight hundred priests marched in the processional (see Appendix B).

After the 1596 auto, the remaining members of the Carvajal family in New Spain were Gaspar the monk, Anica, Mariana, and Leonor de Cáceres, the daughter of Catalina. In the auto-da-fé of March 25, 1601, Anica and Leonor, eighteen and thirteen years old respectively, were reconciled. The aunt and niece were forced to watch Mariana de Carvajal, sister of Anica and aunt of Leonor, garroted and then burned at the stake. Leonor's father was reconciled.

From 1596 to 1601, Leonor had been boarded with two families under the direction of the Inquisition. (Leonor had taken a great dislike to her aunt Anica and her uncle Gaspar, for reasons unknown.) The second family had been invested with the responsibility of inculcating Leonor with good Catholic doctrine. She was called to the Inquisition in November, 1600, and lived in the quarters of the warden until March 25, 1601. She was interrogated at great length in the intervening period. In her testimony there are preserved additional facets of the life of her uncle, Luis, and her parents. Included also are liturgy and couplets which the child remembered after the lapse of five years. Leonor de Cáceres was to outlive all the members of her mother's family. Her story and that of her descendants has been traced to the eighteenth century, and these are recounted in later chapters.

Among other interesting people were Manuel Gil de la Guarda and Marco Antonio. Marco Antonio was a dueling master; Manuel Gil de la Guarda was the first Jew to inform the Inquisition about occurrences in the secret cells and about the activities of some of the freed reconciliados.[21] He had been arrested in the Philippines.

Manuel Gil, reconciled in the auto-da-fé of March 25, 1601, was thirty-nine years of age in 1603. He had been spying on Ruy Díaz and Hector de Fonseca from the time that they had left the Inquisition cells in 1601. During Ruy's incarceration he would not eat any food except cheese and fruit unless Hector, his cell-mate, examined the meat or fowl carefully to insure that it had been ritually slaughtered and prepared. Ruy washed his hands upon arising, then seated himself upon a chest and faced the east, covered his head with a turban-like cloth, crossed his hands over his chest without a rosary in his hands, and recited his prayers. Manuel Gil stated that he could

Mariana de Carvajal at the stake, 1601. El Libro Rojo

not understand the prayers. (They undoubtedly were recited in Hebrew, which Gil did not understand.) Ruy prayed for an hour in the morning and again in the evening before supper.

When Ruy took sick a second time in 1603 he ate only raisins, nuts, and some preserves except for some fowl brought to him by Isabel Rodríguez. She and her husband, Sebastian de la Peña, had been reconciled in 1596. Manuel Gil knew that Isabel prepared the hen according to Jewish law. Isabel referred to Ruy as "the old saint." He always cleaned his candlesticks on Friday afternoons, lit candles before dusk, and then recited his prayers. When he was well, Ruy Díaz did his own cooking and used only oil to prepare fish, chick-peas, eggs, and vegetables. He refused even to use the jar of other people to take liquid refreshments.

Manuel Gil also intercepted written communications between the Jews of the city. The messages were often secreted in the food that was sent from one to another. When Diego Díaz Nieto was also confined in the secret cells, the father and son constantly wrote to each other with an ink *de ceniza de selucuestle y agua,* a form of disappearing ink. Manuel could not read many of the notes because they were written in what he described "an occult manner." The notes were written in Hebrew, which both father and son knew.

Antonio Méndez was another against whom Manuel delated. He told the inquisitors that one day Méndez had prayed all day and that parts of the prayers were understandable and others were incomprehensible. The ones that Gil understood were the psalms. One prayer began, "The Heavens recount the glory of God, etc." Antonio Méndez had memorized, in Spanish, more than sixty Davidic psalms. He also prayed with his head covered and a cape, probably a Jewish prayer shawl, over his shoulders. Once Antonio told Gil that Jews fasted for eight days after the death of a parent. Méndez also termed Ruy Díaz "the old saint." As further proof that Ruy possessed great learning and probably the status of a rabbi, we learn that he used to deliver sermons based upon excerpts from the Old Testament.

Meetings were often held in the back room of Sebastian de la Peña's store. Among those who assembled there, besides those already mentioned, were Ruy Díaz de Lemos, Francisco López Enríquez, Antonio Díaz Marquez, and Ana López; all had been participants in earlier autos-da-fé and had been reconciled. The continuance of Jewish practices would have branded them as second offenders if not for the papal pardon. Their meetings were religious services. The *Espejo de Consolación* (the Mirror of Consolation) was used as teaching material.

Every now and then small differences in personal practices are revealed. Ruy Díaz Nieto cut the hair under his armpits as well as washing that area and his feet in preparing for the Sabbath. Antonio Méndez would disrobe for his Sabbath bath and his newly imported Negro slave, Juan Angola, washed him, pared the callouses of his feet with a knife, cut his nails, and shaved the hair under the armpits and from the area of the genitals. Méndez and Ruy Díaz Nieto walked through the streets with rosaries in their hands.

Ruy Díaz never extinguished his candles on Friday nights and never hawked his wares on the public streets on Saturdays, as he observed that day as the Sabbath day of rest. Ruy refused invitations to dine at the homes of several people named by Manuel Gil and another Inquisition spy, Captain Esteban de Lemos. Manuel Gil was assaulted by Marco Antonio early in 1604. This was the result of a conspiracy among the Jews to do away with Gil after learning that he had turned informant. Marco Antonio was never punished for this attack, nor were any of the others in the conspiracy, although the Inquisition knew who were involved.

The testimony of Esteban de Lemos corrobates in great part that of Gil. However, he implicated many other people not named by Gil and cited additional incidents. An interesting feature of the 1603 events was the disclosure of a partnership between Juan de León Plaza, warden of the secret cells, and Antonio Méndez. The warden, who was sixty years old and had been in Mexico for many years, swore that he had not known that Méndez was a reconciliado and that he was barred from being in business with him.

Captain Esteban de Lemos, a cousin of Pedro Fonseca, the notary of the Holy Office, was not a Jew but played the role in order to secure information. He was able to deceive the Jews because he could speak Portuguese and knew Antonio Díaz de Cáceres from Spain. (Díaz de Cáceres had returned to Spain, where he lived as a good Christian. His daughter Leonor testified in 1600 that her father liked pork and used to throw pieces of it into the stew when her mother Catalina was not looking.)

On December 2, 1602, Captain de Lemos advised the inquisitors that the following letter, dated August 10, no year, from Spain had been received by a Jew:

God knows how much I desire to give you and your group of people good news. It is certain that the King has given a general pardon and that he has given it to the unfaithful [*sic*] for a million and a half, which is a tremendous sum of money. An important friend told me today that he was going to Rome to confirm this and that there are many letters talking about this. . . . Trust in God that all prayers will be answered in the month of August. I am coming and everything is well with me. They have given me all that I require because I have complied with all in my power and I owe nobody. Buy whatever de Peña has in his store and also from Antonio Méndez, who are close friends, and from Francisco Núñez . . . I sent you some money, fruit, cheese, preserves, and butter with all my good will that God will leave you in peace and that He gives you all that you desire. Amen. Patience until the fleet arrives. There is some news that it will leave Spain at the beginning of June.

Captain Lemos did not know who wrote the letter. It took two more years for the king to effectuate the general pardon and the pope to confirm it by a bull. The knowledge of the contents of this letter may have caused the inquisitors to desist from persecuting Jews for a considerable period.

In the auto-da-fé of April 20, 1603, were Francisco Rodríguez de Ledesma, who had come from Cartagena, Clara Enríquez, and Rodrigo del Campo, a scribe. The three were reconciled. Rodríguez was supposed to have gone to the stake in the auto of 1601. The testimony against him concerned an incident of 1592 when he was ten years old and had ridiculed Christian rites. Shortly before the auto of 1601 he confessed to some Jewish practices, but his sentence was commuted and he was returned to his cell. Clara Enríquez, the daughter of Manuel de Lucena, was accused of expressing herself in shameless terms on the subject of Mary's virginity.[22] Francisco Rodríguez de Ledesma, born in Toledo, was returned to his cell at the last moment. He became gravely ill and died in the hospital after having been tortured. He was reconciled in effigy.

Captain Esteban de Lemos translated many letters from Portuguese into Spanish for the inquisitors. He also testified as a handwriting expert and identified the script of several Jews. In 1602, Ruy Díaz Nieto sent his son Diego a message rolled up and inserted in a cheese. The message was intercepted and the captain identified the handwriting as that of the father.

Manuel Gil knew of the conspiracy to kill him and informed the inquisitors of the plot and those involved. He said that fifty pesos were to be paid to the assassins. He did not know that Marco Antonio was involved. Manuel Gil had petitioned the Tribunal for the liberation of Marco. The actual price to be paid for the assassination was 200 pesos; it cost 100 pesos for knifing a face. One of the details of the complicated plot was that six young men from Holland (whose religion was not specified) were available in Mexico for work of this nature.

Aspects of economic life are revealed in the testimony of Juan de León Plaza, the warden. When he testified on December 16, 1603, he told the story of his business relationships with Antonio Méndez, which had begun in 1601, shortly after the auto of March 25 of that year. He had sought Méndez because he needed funds, and Méndez was recommended to him as a good merchant and an honorable man. Since his salary as warden for the Holy Office was insufficient to sustain himself, Juan invested 1,500 pesos with Méndez in a joint enterprise. The investment was very profitable, and Juan gave one-half of his profits to Antonio as a bonus because Juan had done nothing to help in the enterprise. Many of their deals and agreements were oral. When Juan wanted to buy a house, Antonio loaned him 5,000 pesos, which was more than Juan's interest in their joint business. The rate of interest of the loan was ten percent, considered a nominal rate at that time. It may be surmised that more existed between the warden of the secret cells and a reconciled Jew than Juan de León Plaza revealed.

The Abecedario discloses the names of several monks, priests, and employees of the Tribunal who revealed secrets of the Inquisition during the seventeenth century. During the years from 1600 to 1605 seven such cases are reported. As a class, the Jews were the ones who would be most interested in learning as much as possible about the internal operations of the institution. Their activities along this line was revealed in letters sent by the king of Spain.

Sebastian de la Peña was also involved in the business affairs of the warden. The ineffectiveness of the Inquisition in attempting to confiscate all the property of the Jews who were reconciled, or the successful attempts of these same Jews to salvage and preserve their property, is attested by the ability of Méndez and de la Peña to be able to trade and deal within weeks after their release from the Inquisition. These illustrations can be multiplied many times. Juan de

León stated that Antonio Méndez had been freed with little more than the shirt on his back, but within a little less than three years Méndez' bed linens alone were worth more than 400 pesos.

Evidence of fraternization between Jews and Christians in the cells is unfolded by witnesses. The camaraderie continued after the people of both faiths were released from the cells: Jews and Christians made minor loans of money to each other and difference of faith was not a barrier to socialization, especially among the criollos. The Christians despised Manuel Gil as much as did the Jews.

Maria Enríquez, the daughter of Isabel Rodríguez by her first marriage, married Pedro Jorge in 1605. Isabel was scrupulous in her observances of Jewish dietary laws and was highly regarded by Ruy Díaz Nieto, whom she revered. However, this did not deter Pedro Jorge from informing against Ruy Díaz. The testimony of Pedro Jorge was almost a repetition of that of Manuel Gil. His additions included the information that Ruy refused to eat from anyone else's tablecloth, take bread from another, or even use their cups. Ruy's Indian slave brought him raw food and eggs, clean linens, and a tablecloth for the Sabbath. Presented here is a picture of the Inquisition cells that is different from that usually conjured by the words "secret cells." They were fairly large, and each prisoner was permitted to furnish his cell as he pleased. Chests, beds, and tables were brought, and some of the cells could lodge three prisoners comfortably. The use of the word "secret" is amusing because songs could be heard from different parts of the cell-blocks, wall-tapping was resorted to, and holes were bored in the walls. Prisoners were not incommunicado.

Pedro Jorge denied being a Jew although he was accepted as one by other Jews. He sought to implicate Rodrigo del Campo and Ruy Díaz de Lemos of Cartagena, a brother of Luis Díaz and brother-in-law of Francisco López Enríquez, all of whom were reconciliados. Pedro mentioned many other names. He told how he eavesdropped and searched the garbage of Jews for incriminating evidence against them. One of the things that he found was a poem belonging to Luis Fernandez Tristan of Cartagena. It read:

> *Clara, who brightens the world*
> *And in whose radiance I find myself joyful,*
> *To enjoy the sight of you*
> *Gives rare contentment to my soul.*[23]

The addressee, Clara, the daughter of Francisco López Enríquez, was very beautiful and ready to be wed. Luis Ferdinand Tristan had brought from Cartegena a small book which contained prayers. The auto-da-fé of March 25, 1605, was more sumptuous and costly and the total number of penitents was larger than that of the 1603 auto-da-fé. Of the thirty-five penitents, the only Jew was Diego Díaz Nieto. In 1606, sixteen Jews were pardoned, but they had had to file a petition to go free. The inquisitors were loath to release them and waited until the prisoners themselves found out about the papal bull pardoning them. In New Spain, the pardon came from the king, not by or through the pope, because of the *patronato real*.

No Jews appeared in the autos of 1607 and 1608. In that of 1609, Jorge de Almeida was burned in effigy and Diego Hernández was convicted of bigamy after being acquitted of the suspicion of being a Jew. He had come from the Isle of Tenerife near Chalco, where there were many crypto-Jews. The bribes brought the Jews many years of surcease from molestation. No Jew appeared in any auto-da-fé until 1620, when Domingo de Sosa was reconciled in effigy after dying in jail under suspicious circumstances. He had been born in Lisbon, was a Franciscan monk, and had been accused of Jewish practices. Monks were never burned in person or effigy.

Although the inquisitors knew, as early as 1607, that Jews were entering the country, they did nothing about it until 1620 except to prepare dossiers and lists. Jews lived in all parts of New Spain, and many were tenants in Christian-owned houses. The Jewish community had grown to such an extent that Jews were unknown to each other. Cliques had come into being. These cliques were centered about business affairs. Common places of origin or nativity played a minor role in cementing relationships. Within each group mutual confidence was unlimited. Fernández Tristan gave Luis Díaz merchandise worth more than 7,000 pesos on credit. Luis Díaz traded in China, and others traded in Cartagena, the port for New Granada, and places farther south. The incidents of Gil and Jorge made all Jews distrustful. The groups were distrustful of each other, although there were some individual friendships bridging the groups. With the cessation of Inquisition activities the divisiveness disappeared. Intermarriage between members of the different groups and intermingling became common. By 1620 there was a single community in Mexico. Veracruz was organized,

*Denunciation of Jorge de Almeida. From Publications of the
American Jewish Historical Society, Vol. 4*

and communities were growing in Guadalajara and in the area between Pachuca and Ixmiquilpan.

Jews were coming from Europe and South America. There was little emigration from New Spain to Peru or other parts of South America, but the reverse did take place in great numbers. Many established themselves in Tlaxcala. Tlaxcalans were very industrious, and the Spaniards, Christians, and Jews, with the help of the vicious obraje system, developed the area into an important textile center and the source of exportable merchandise.

Puebla became another important center. Two of the villages that abutted on the Royal Highway from Veracruz to Mexico were Tepeaca and Amozoc. Jews held municipal offices in Tepeaca as late as the eighteenth century. It was an important Indian center prior to the Conquest. In Amozoc there is a large church with a sky-blue tile dome that is octagonal in shape. The dome is visible for miles as one approaches from Veracruz on the Royal Highway. There are four crosses and four six-pointed stars alternating on the facets of the dome.

The cross and the six-pointed star, called the Star of David by Jews, were religious symbols in Mesoamerica for centuries before the arrival of Cortés. Such symbols were almost nonexistent, however, in the valleys of Puebla, Mexico, and surrounding areas. They were common in Chiapas, Yucatán, and northern Guatemala. It has been impossible to trace the reason for the use of the cross and star on the dome of the Amozoc church. Doubtless there were Jews who were prominent in these villages. They must have played a part in the erection of the church as part of their duplicity in attempting to conceal their true faith. They may have desired to place some discernable sign to Jews coming up from Veracruz that the Amozoc-Tepeaca area had Jewish inhabitants. The new arrivals were probably told the names of Jews who would serve as their hosts en route to Mexico and with whom they could spend the Sabbath or observe any other Jewish holiday that might occur while they were traveling.

Investigation of the period subsequent to 1605 reveals that Jews were porging their meat in Puebla and were observing other Jewish rites. Jews had begun to infiltrate Guatemala and active *comisaries* there were sending reports in 1609 and 1610 about Jewish burials. Reports came from Manila in 1613 about Jews there. One Juan Méndez de Esporan, also known as Juan de Lemus, a soldier, forty-eight years old, who had been born in Viseo, Portugal, denounced himself and his mother, Mencia Gómez. He swore that he was a Jew and narrated Jewish customs observed in his mother's house, such as decapitating the fowl and draining the blood and the examination of the internal parts of slaughtered animals to insure that they were healthy. He also told of religious fasts. The soldier said that his was a voluntary confession induced by his conscience. No proceedings against him or his mother have been located.

The 1614 trial of Cristobal de Herrera of Zacatecas has been previously mentioned. One of the witnesses had his deposition taken by Licenciado Juan de Ortega, canon of the cathedral at Guadalajara. The witness, Juan Roze, had been born in Genoa, Italy, and was a friend of Antonio de Lemos de Gama of the Knights of Christ. De Ortega related the conversation about the eight Portuguese in Oaxaca who were teaching the Mosaic laws to the Indians. Christobal de Herrera said that the eight were Jews, but not Portuguese. Lemos de Gama contradicted this and insisted that they were Portuguese. When Herrera asked him why he believed so, the reply was, "The Portuguese are very intelligent and the Law of Moses was attractive, and it was for that reason they were drawn to it."

This case dragged on for over a year before Herrera himself was called as a witness. He was never arrested nor his property sequestered, and no action was ever taken against him by the Holy Office. The case indicates the provincial concept held of the Portuguese and of the Jews, and of the existence of many non-Spaniards in various parts of the country. While the proceedings state that eight Portuguese Jews had been arrested by the Inquisition in Oaxaca, no record pertaining thereto has been found. There have been two known incidents of the burning of archival and municipal records in Oaxaca within the past century, and it may be that the missing records were among those destroyed.

During the course of investigation, this writer found references to a street in the city of Oaxaca in the seventeenth century called "Calle del Judío," and to an Italian Jewish family, Fenochio. All attempts to secure data about the street and the family proved futile. The Director of the Biblioteca Nacional (part of the Universidad Benito Juarez de Oaxaca), Dr. Jorge Fernando Iturribarria, wrote on January 6, 1962, that there had been a street in Oaxaca, "El Judío, but nothing further than that is known about it or about

Jews, neo-cristianos, or hebreo-cristianos, or about the Fenochio family." We do know that Jews did reside in Oaxaca in the seventeenth century. Robert Ricard wrote that during the colonial period there was an important current of Judaism which endangered Catholicism in New Spain. This "is abundantly acknowledged by the various acts and publications such as the complaints of the municipal council of Oaxaca."[24]

During the first quarter of the seventeenth century, events took place in the northern part of Europe that affected the Jewish communities of New Spain. Between 1593 and 1600 Iberian Jews had settled in Holland, which had won its independence from Spain. The Jews were permitted to establish their first synagogue in Amsterdam in 1596. Rabbis were trained and Jewish schools founded. By 1618, the Jewish population had grown to such an extent that three congregations were in existence. Scholars came from Constaninople and northern Italy, and the renown of the learning, scholarship, and commercial success of these Jews spread over the Western world.

An innocuous but revealing statement was made to the Inquisition in Lisbon in 1639. ". . . whatever they [Christians] might do in Spain, they could not prevent them from being Jews, because *all the New Christians in Spain were Christians by violence,* and every year there went certain Jews from Holland to the capital of Madrid and *to many other parts of the realm of Spain to circumcize the New Christians*"[25] (italics mine).

The Dutch Jewish community was the stronghold of Sephardic Jewry during the seventeenth century. Spanish and Portuguese were used not only in the synagogue in addition to Hebrew but were also the languages of the home and street and of the books published in these languages. Spanish and Portuguese Jews were islands of Iberian culture although they were integrated into the life of Holland. Their concern for their coreligionists was great. They so detested Spain that Salvador de Madariaga has imputed to them Machiavellian plans to overthrow the Spanish Empire. Dutch Jewry donated considerable amounts of wealth to aid those of the Iberian Peninsula who wished to flee. They raised funds for bribes for inquisitors, other prelates, and officials of the Church to halt the persecutions of Jews.

The proceso of Manuel Díaz Enríquez (also Henrriquez) revealed that he had letters from Holland at the time that he was apprehended by the Inquisition comisario in Guatemala in 1621. Although he was charged with being a Jew, there never was a formal proceeding or the production of any evidence to prove the charge. The Inquisition did not confine him to their secret cells when he arrived from Guatemala. He traveled alone but was under a financial bond. He was permitted to remain at large in Mexico, again under bond, but was restricted from leaving the city except by permission of the Holy Office.

Bail bonds were most unusual for the release of Inquisition prisoners. For no trial or proceeding to have taken place after so much effort to arrest Manuel Díaz Enríquez is also unusual. The *vita* of Manuel is contained in a letter he wrote to the Tribunal. He denied that he was a judaizante. He was born in Portugal, and his uncle, a broker or dealer in Negro slaves, took him to Angola and then back to Lisbon. He left for Brazil in 1617, then went on to Paraiba with a sugar dealer. In 1620 he came to Campeche and Guatemala.

His three bondsmen and all the people with whom he dealt in Puebla, Campeche, and Guatemala were men who subsequently (1635-1649) were proven to be Jews. Despite his bond, he disappeared from Mexico about 1624. He later appeared in Amsterdam and went through the procedure necessary to be accepted as a full Jew in the synagogue there.

I. S. Revah of the Colege de France, in his article on the genealogy of Ishack de Matatya Aboab,[26] shows that a Miguel Díaz had traveled three hundred leagues to Spain in ten days in an attempt to save his brothers Manuel and Simón from the Inquisition in Mexico. Miguel was a descendant of the last *Gaon*, the head of a Talmudical academy of learning, of Castile. The Aboab family used the alias of Díaz. Miguel died as a result of the exertions of his journey. Cecil Roth has confirmed that Manuel Díaz Enríquez made his way to Holland, where he used his real family name and was known as Matatia Aboab.[27] He was the son or grandson of Rabbi Isaac Aboab II and was a contemporary of Rabbi Aboab de Fonseca, who went to Brazil in 1642. Manuel died in Hamburg.

Whether there is any connection between the fact that the Inquisition never prosecuted Manuel Díaz Enríquez, alias Matatia Aboab, and the influence of the Aboab family in Holland is conjectural. The connection between the Jewish communities of Holland and New Spain is important. The association of Manuel with many Jews in New Spain is a link in the chain of communication and mutual help.

Holland had grown. Its ships were traveling to the New World, and its merchantmen were equaling the English in acts of piracy and in raids on Spanish colonies in the Western Hemisphere. Holland coveted Brazil and ultimately succeeded in capturing it. Many Jews resided in Brazil.

The flight of Jews from Portugal to Holland and the New World was very great in the years between 1619 and 1640. Including the Tribunals of Lisbon, Evora, and Coimbra, 230 Jews were relaxed in person, 161 in effigy, and 4,995 were penanced. Lea states, "Notwithstanding these superhuman exertions, the Inquisitors complained that their labors were unavailing; Judaism was still increasing."[28] As a note to this he added that the Bishop of Faro appealed for aid in 1622 because the New Christians "were all secret Jews . . . and that they were very numerous . . . There was no city in which they were not powerful." In 1628, the prelates wanted to extend limpieza de sangre to the tenth degree instead of the prevailing fourth.

Anti-Semitic literature was being produced in Lisbon and was being shipped to the New World. Vicente de Costa Mattes wrote *Breve Discurso contra le Perfidia de Judaismo* in 1623. This book reveals the antagonism to Jews and Judaism and that while Bishop Jóão Soares of Coimbra had been in Cyprus he met some Spanish and Portuguese refugees who discreetly revealed the presence of Jews in Llerena, Extremadura, and other places. The bishop transmitted this information to the Inquisition when he returned home.

In the article "A Contemporary Memorial Relating to Damages to Spanish Interests in America done by Jews of Holland (1634)," Cyrus Adler states that the Dutch Jews were active against both Spain and Portugal and tells of their interests on the American continent.[29] The body of this article consists of a translation of a document written by Esteban de Ares Fonseca in Madrid on April 23, 1634, and which was included in the Council of the Inquisition Book 49, f. 45 at the archives at Simancas. Fonseca reported the depradations of the Dutch which finally led to their capture of Brazil. The article quotes Henry C. Lea's comments on the discoveries made by the New World Tribunals that "many Judaizing Portuguese in the colonies had correspondence with the synagogues in Holland and

the Levant and [upon opening mail to the Portuguese in Spain] a
cypher [secret code or language] was used in correspondence with
the synagogues of Holland and, further, that a million and a half had
been pledged from Spain" (undoubtedly either for the Braganza
rebellion or to succor Jews from the Inquisition about 1640). A
Dutch colony with many Jews had been established about 1625 in
South America in a place known today as Surinam. There was much
surreptitious trading between the Jews there and those of New
Spain.

During the seventeenth century, the Spanish and Portugese royal
courts used their ambassadors and other diplomatic personnel as
spies. They, in turn, hired local people as informers. The information which they were expected to supply included lists of those who
attended synagogues and associated with known Jews. They also
bribed ship captains to gain access to packages of letters brought
from Spanish New World possessions to England or Holland. These
letters frequently revealed the identity of Jews or those who corre-
spond or traded with Jews. These diplomats and hirelings turned
over all information to the Inquisition in Spain and Portugal.

The information garnered sometimes revealed the names of relatives in the Iberian Peninsula who were secret Jews. Sometimes
these secret Jews acted as commercial agents of the Dutch and English Jews who were barred from trading in the Spanish Empire.

The following letters and data illustrate the results of the investigations. They were translated by Elken A. Adler from original
state papers that were in his possession.[30]

King Philip IV to the Council of the Inquisition
Sir,—By the decree of the 30th December 1655, your Majesty
deigned to forward to the Bishop Inquisitor General and this
Council the Memorandum which Dn. Esteban de Gemarra, your
Ambassador to the Estates General of Holland, sent by letter of
the 16th October last, saying that it was from the Consul of Spain
residing in Amsterdam, with the names of the Jews of that City
who have relations with these Realms and those of their correspondents, adding the different aliases which they use in their correspondence so as not to be recognized or suspected of being in-
fected with the same errors, and you commanded that it should be
seen into so as to take note thereof.

It, having been examined in the Council, we give your Majesty
thanks with all sincerity for the grace and favor which have been
and are being shown to the Holy Office, so genial to your Catholic

zeal and faith, and the augmentation of our sacred Catholic Faith, so that your realms may retain its purity and the unity of Religion and preserve them from the heresies which others practice, for similar notices are always of much import (give more hold) for the greater assurance of the cases and matters of Faith dealt with in the Inquisitions.

We, the Bishop Inquisitor General and the Council, beg your Majesty that, touching the matter in question, he should command to write to the said Ambassador and Consul of Spain residing in Amsterdam to continue the information he can give in this matter in conformity with those he has already written, which we judge to be of much importance and service to God and your Majesty.

Madrid, 20th January 1656

There then appears a list of the names of Jews in Amsterdam, with their aliases (David Ossoria, alias Bento Ossorio; Jacob del Monte, alias Jacobus Bandemberg; Abraam Isac Perera, alias Francisco de Guerre; Antonio de Guerra, alias Gerard Carlos Bangardel; etc.) and the names of their agents and correspondents in Madrid, Cadiz, Santander, Bilbao, San Sebastian, Seville, and Cáceres.

In the Manuscripts Division of the British Museum (Additional 29, 868, Jewish Inscriptions) are notes written in 1677 and 1678 by E. Mendes da Costa. These biographical notes, written in Portuguese, contain the types of cipher writing used by the writer's forebears for correspondence with Jews in various parts of the world. These codes are reproduced as they appear in the original manuscript.

	1	2	3	
I.	A K T	B L U	C M W	
	4 D N X	E O Y 5	F P Z 6	
	7 G Z	H R 8	I S 9	

	1	2	3	
II.	E N O	D P Y	C Q P	
	4 S T B	I K L 5	M X Z 6	
	7 F W	G U 8	A H L 9	

III.

e m a n u e l

⌐ ⌐ ⌐ ⌐ ⌐ ⌐ ⌐ = Emanuel

This illustrates a use of Code 2. Code 1 or Code 2 could be used by writing the number of the space followed by one, two, or three dots which would indicate the letter within the space. I have been unable to verify whether any of the foregoing codes were used or known by the Jews of New Spain, but it is known that their correspondence to Salonica and Constantinople was rewritten in cipher form before being relayed to their destinations in London, Amsterdam, or Antwerp.

The Thirty Years' War started in 1618. Spain sided with the Habsburg Emperor Ferdinand for family as well as religious reasons. For Spain, the war really lasted from 1620 to 1659 and occupied the attention of Philip IV, who reigned from 1621 to 1665. Philip was "of a frivolous and dissolute nature," and his favorite, the Count-Duke of Olivares, served as the general factotum.[31] Spain forcibly expelled the Moors in 1606. The Treaty of Granada of 1492 had guaranteed them religious liberty. Philip III, however, secured a papal bull absolving him from upholding his grandfather's treaty. Charles Chapman wrote that "murder, robbery, and outrages against women went unpunished." In many places, children under seven had to remain in Spain even when their parents left. This was similar to the fate of the Jews in Portugal in 1497. Another similarity with the prior exodus of the Jews occurred. Many returned and converted to Catholicism "for, after all, the Moriscos had in many respects become Spaniards."[32]

It had been estimated that the non-Indian population of New Spain in the early seventeenth century was approximately 10,000 to 15,000 persons. As contrasted with this figure, in the viceroyalty of Peru—which at that time included all of Spanish South America except part of the northern coast on the Caribbean—there were 10,000 Spaniards and 10,000 mulattos and other castes exclusive of the Indians.[33]

Included in the closing years of the era discussed in this chapter is the charge against Baltazar del Valle of Zamora of being a Jew (1624),[34] and the same charge against Domingo Díaz, alias Domingo Rodríguez, a Portuguese residing in Puebla (1622). Domingo was the son of Constanza Rodríguez and Sebastian Rodríguez, who were in the auto-da-fé of 1596. His mother did not remain in jail for life as sentenced. Her son, Domingo, had been born in Mexico but was

King Philip IV; painting by Velasquez. Courtesy of Museo del Prado

termed a Portuguese. (Other facts concerning him are in the account of the auto-da-fé of June 15, 1625, Appendix A.)

Baltazar del Valle was tortured but did not confess, and his case was suspended. He was rearrested in 1634 when the Inquisition had firm proof that he and his wife, Isabel Cardado, practiced Jewish rites. He confessed after his wife was tortured. She died two months after beginning to serve her sentence of life imprisonment.

The case of Díaz Enríquez and Pedro de Silva Sauceda can be compared to a game of "cops and robbers." It portrays the ludicrous difficulties of the Holy Office when it operated away from large urban areas, the penuriousness in providing adequate funds to its "branch" officials in the distant provinces (in this case Guatemala), and the extent of the sentence of "town" imprisonment. It reveals that the Jews traded in slaves, rented out mule trains, owned haciendas in various places in the southern part of present-day Mexico, Honduras, and northern Guatemala, and communicated with each other in much less time than the Holy Office could transmit its letters to local comisarios. The Jews blazed trails and traveled over them and through forests with apparent ease and fearlessness. Those who lived in Honduras were wealthy. It was those who were carrying on trade with Holland and who knew the location of all the ports on the Gulf of Mexico where illegal shipments could be made and the onerous Spanish taxes avoided.

In 1622, the Holy Office was informed of the location of a synagogue in Mexico on Calle de Santo Domingo, just a few streets away from the House of the Inquisition. Jews congregated there on Saturday mornings and a passer-by could hear them praying. The inquisitors did nothing. At least the records fail to reveal even an attempt to verify the facts. The 1622 denunciation also states that there were about 500 Jews in the city.[35]

The most famous immigrant of the 1596-1625 era was Tomas (also spelled Thomas) Treviño de Sobremonte. His trial of 1624-1625 marked more than a turning point in his own life. It marked the beginning of a new epoch which, although brief, was perhaps the most sanguinary in the history of the Jews in New Spain. Treviño was a leader of his people and died an example of religious devotion—al kiddush ha-Shem—for the santification of the holy name of the Lord. His story is among the most dramatic of the ensuing era.

10

The Drama of 1625-1650

EVENTS occurring during the second quarter of the seventeenth century cumulatively contributed to the tragedy that beset Mexican Jewry in the last decade of that period. Among these events were internal strife in Spain; war between Spain and other European countries; the increase of raids on Spanish shipping and on the Spanish colonies in the New World; and the rising dissatisfaction by the Spaniards with some of their institutions. The revolts by the province of Catalonia and the regained independence of Portugal shook the throne and the Church.[1]

Jewish and Christian mystics were making prophetic announcements of the coming of the Messiah. The Church warned again that the Jewish Messiah would be anti-Christ. Christian mystics believed that the second coming of Christ would take place in 1666. Jewish cabalists predicted that the date of advent of the one whom they would regard as the true Messiah would be 1648.[2] Jews in New Spain ardently believed in the coming of the Messiah, and they also believed that he would be born of one in their midst. Europe generally was seething with movements spiritual, secular, and intellectual that perturbed the wearers of crowns.

In 1625 the two decades of freedom from molestation of Jews in the Spanish New World colonies came to an end with the auto-da-fé of June 15, 1625. The ensuing period, 1625-1650, witnessed more autos-da-fé in New Spain in which Jews were the principal penitents than any other era in the colonial period and in any other viceroyalty. The confiscation of the Jews' wealth by three inquisitors, ran into millions of pesos, and the inquisitors' moral depravity was rarely, if ever, exceeded during the entire history of the Inquisition. Lea wrote that the three inquisitors became a terror to the innocent as well as to the guilty.

During this time, Mexican Jewry attained its greatest degree of importance both to the colony and as a religious community. The Jewish community waxed in numbers and wealth. As so often occurred in Jewish history, schisms developed that caused the community to split into three groups. Each of these groups had a titular head who towered above the masses. There were other impressive figures, male and female, in this period, but their great statures were diminished by comparison with two dramatic contemporaries—Treviño de Sobremonte and the influential Simón Váez de Sevilla.

From 1625 to 1635 inclusive, there were six autos-da-fé. Some of the Jewish dramatis personnae of the epoch were involved in these acts of faith. The two autos of 1635 were portents of the storm that was to follow. Just as Nebuchadnezzer could not understand the meaning of "*Mene, mene, tekel, upharsin,*" which had to be read for him by Daniel, Mexican Jewry failed to interpret the significance of the forces that had begun to close in upon them. This unfortunate blindness is ironic, since these people revered Daniel above many other prophets. All that can be said in extenuation of their failure to feel apprehension is that they had become inured to searches for heretics, as had their ancestors. They believed that this too, would pass and that there was more smoke than fire.

Francisco Gómez Medina and Simón Montero were two among many who felt that they could live as Jews securely in New·Spain. Montero held this belief even though he had been before the inquisitors in 1635, his case being suspended on July 29. He requested and received permission to leave New Spain. He went to Italy and studied in the various Jewish communities there, was circumcised, and was ordained as a rabbi in the Jewish community in Rome. He then returned to Mexico about 1639 and joined his family and that of his brother, Duarte de León Jaramillo. Gómez de Medina, as had many others, first left New Spain and other Spanish dominions but later returned to Mexico.

The feeling of security was not greatly disturbed by the 1636 abortive revolt for independence by Portugal or the Spanish discovery of mail exchange and commercial trading between Jews of New Spain and Holland. Margarita Morera testified that in 1636 and 1637 as many as 200 Jews gathered together to pray in Mexico.[3] Consideration was not given to the possibility that Spain might seek retribution against Portuguese Jews in New Spain because of the revolt in Portugal or because of the raiding of Spanish galleons and colonial ports by the Dutch. The great auto-da-fé of January 23, 1639, in Lima, which burned or penanced sixty-one Jews, spread no inquietude in any of the Jewish communities in New Spain. This harassing of Peruvian Jews was the result of a plot called "Complicidad de 1635," alleged to have been aimed at the liberation of Peru from Spain. The trial proceedings in Lima contain information about the extensive connections between the Jewish communities of New Spain and Peru. Many escaped from Lima but ultimately were apprehended in various parts of New Spain.

Many Limeño Jews had relatives in Mexico. According to Salvador de Madariaga, branches of the family of the fabulously wealthy Manuel Bautista Pérez of Lima, called the "Great Captain" and "vicario de Moysen," were in Mexico.[4] His former home is now the La Casa de Jarava o de Pilatos near the Cardinal's Palace in Lima. The brother-in-law of Bautista Pérez was García Váez Enríquez, born in Seville of Portuguese parents. The similarity of name, birthplace, and origin of parents to Simón Váez might indicate a relationship, although the possibility of mere coincidence in name must not be excluded.[5] Luis Pérez Roldan, who left Peru for New Spain, was distantly related to Manuel Bautista Pérez. Rodrigo Váez Pereira, burned at the stake in Lima in El Gran Auto-da-fé of January 23, 1639, was a first cousin of Duarte Rodríguez of Veracruz, reconciled in New Spain on January 23, 1647, after escaping from Lima.[6] Duarte's wife, Clare Texoso, had been born in Lima.

The years 1626 to 1635 also saw activities of the Tribunal's representatives in the provinces, e.g., Michoacan, Sinaloa, Zacatecas, Truxillo, Guadiana, and Taxco, and reports emanating from the Holy Office in Cartagena. Manuel Xuárez was apprehended in Mexico because of testimony that had been forwarded from Cartagena. Antonio Prieto de Villegas of Guatemala was imprisoned in Cartagena. Isabel de Carrion of Tepeaca and Rufina González of Campeche were arrested because they were porging meat. Diego Gómez

Pereira of Zacatecas was apprehended because he was circumcized.[7] These are only a few examples of renewed Inquisition activity in the rural areas.

No attempt will be made to discuss all the cases of Jews arrested during the years 1625 to 1639, many of which never proceeded to a final judgment. There were at least eight other Jews who were incriminated prior to 1642 because of testimony from Lima. One of the Inquisition practices that became common was that of creating a dossier on an individual. The inquisitors frequently would do nothing about denunciations or testimony from other Tribunals until ten or twelve years later; then they would apprehend the person and use the accumulated data in the file to convict him.

With hardly an exception, from 1635 to 1649 every Jew was charged with being "a Jew, observer of the Law of Moses." It was the rare exception for inquisitors to be concerned about the baptism of the prisoner, but questions were asked about communion and confession. Those who denied that they had been baptized, denied being Catholics, or denied or had no recollection of communion fared no differently from those who admitted having had the sacraments administered to them. The questions were concerned primarily with whether the prisoner observed Jewish ritual and with the identity of other Jews who did.

At the first audience, all prisoners were requested to recite the Lord's Prayer, Hail Mary, Salve Regina, the Ten Commandments, the Sacraments, the Articles of Faith, and the General Confession. Almost invariably, the comment that appears after the response is "recited badly." This contrasts with the comments made prior to 1605 when almost every Jew was able to recite the foregoing with ease. Those who admitted that they had gone to confession rarely could recall the name of their confessor and the place was usually said to be a distant village.

Cyrus Adler wrote that the 1635 drive against the Jews came in retaliation for what the Jews of Holland were doing against Spain and that the drive also resulted from the interception of mail between the New World and the Iberian Peninsula.[8] The facts, however, do not corroborate any such drive in New Spain, although there was an intensive drive in Cartagena between 1625 and 1635 and in Peru between 1635 and 1639.

Manuel Alvarez Prieto was tried by the Tribunal in Cartagena in

1625.[9] During the course of his testimony, he referred to *la Cofradia de los Judíos de Holanda*, the Brotherhood of the Jews of Holland. He mentioned this brotherhood several more times in answer to the interrogation of the inquisitors but shortened the title to *"la Cofradia de Olanda" (sic)*. (Or the amanuensis may have abbreviated the title.) If this is not the first, it is at least one of the earliest references to this brotherhood.

The purpose of this organization was to raise funds for three ends: for military aid to Holland in the capture of Spanish and Portuguese New World possessions; for the use of the Jewish community in Amsterdam to purchase the release of Jews from slavery, since many Jews were being captured by North African pirates; and for the benefit of the contributors, to be turned over to them at such time as they settled in Amsterdam or demanded the funds standing to their credit.

The revelation of the existence of the brotherhood must have struck the warning note for all the Tribunals in the New World and thereby precipitated the activity against Jews in all the viceroyalties. While no mention of the name of the Cofradia is found in connection with the *Complicidad Grande* in Peru, the Lima *El Gran Auto-da Fé* of 1639, and the conspiracy in New Spain and its *El Gran Auto-da-Fé* of 1649, it must have been a factor in all inquisitorial actions from 1625 to 1649. Don Simón Osario, also known as Simón Rodríguez, was one of those in the Lima "El Gran" auto. He and his brother had 8,000 ducats in *Compañia de los Olandes* to be used against Spain.

The auto-da-fé of 1635 in Mexico included twenty-two Jews, but the majority were members of a single large family. The Del Valle brothers were married to two sisters, Violante Méndez Cardado and Isabel López Cardado. Both women were daughters of Ana Fernández and Manuel Juárez. The mother was the sister of Antonio Fernández Cardado. Ana Gómez and María Gómez were half-sisters; their mother was Leonor Núñez, and the father of Ana was Diego Fernández Cardado. The father of María was Pedro López, also known as Simón Fernández. The genealogy of María Gómez on p. 222 illustrates the relationships and also serves to present many of the important figures from 1635 to 1649.

There have been two general theories for the causes of the wave of arrests of Jews in the 1640's. While it cannot be denied that there

GENEALOGY OF MARÍA GÓMEZ - WIFE OF
TOMAS TREVIÑO DE SOBREMONTE

Key:
b. = born
d. = deceased
dog. = dogmatist
Fsco. = Francisco

r = reside
rec. = reconciled
rel eff. = burned in effigy
rel. pers. = burned in person

Rios = Rodriguez
= or || = married
All capital letters refer to
explanatory notes on facing page.

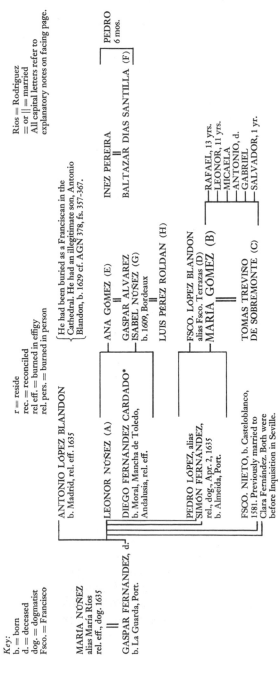

MARÍA NÚÑEZ
alias María Ríos
rel. eff., dog. 1635
=
GASPAR FERNÁNDEZ, d.
b. La Guarda, Port.

ANTONIO LÓPEZ BLANDON
b. Madrid, rel. eff. 1635

{ He had been buried as a Franciscan in the
Cathedral. He had an illegitimate son, Antonio
Blandon, b. 1629 cf. AGN 378, fs. 357-367.

LEONOR NÚÑEZ (A)
=
DIEGO FERNÁNDEZ CARDADO*
b. Moral, Mancha de Toledo,
Andalusia, rel. eff.

ANA GÓMEZ (E)
=
GASPAR ALVAREZ
ISABEL NÚÑEZ (G)
b. 1609, Bordeaux
=
LUIS PÉREZ ROLDAN (H)

INEZ PEREIRA
=
BALTAZAR DIAS SANTILLA (F)

PEDRO LOPEZ, alias
SIMÓN FERNÁNDEZ,
rel., dog., Apr. 2, 1635
b. Almeida, Port.

FSCO. LÓPEZ BLANDON
alias Fsco. Terrazas (D)
MARÍA GÓMEZ (B)
=
TOMAS TREVIÑO
DE SOBREMONTE (C)

PEDRO
6 mos.

RAFAEL, 13 yrs.
LEONOR, 11 yrs.
MICAELA
ANTONIO, d.
GABRIEL
SALVADOR, 1 yr.

FSCO. NIETO, b. Casteloblanco,
1581. Previously married to
Clara Fernández. Both were
before Inquisition in Seville.

* Diego Fernández Cardado was the uncle, by marriage, of Tomas Treviño
de Sobremonte and the natural uncle of Francisco Botello, who was burned
at the stake, alive, in the auto of 1659.

is validity to each of these theories, it may be that they were effects rather than causes. Three added theories are advanced by this author as possibilities, but the renewed vigor of Holy Office action against the Jews was the result of a combination of the reasons mentioned in all these theories.

The first theory is based upon the premise that Portuguese Jews were plotting to capture New Spain for Portugal.[10] Josephine

---

EXPLANATORY NOTES TO GENEALOGY OF MARÍA GÓMEZ, WIFE OF TOMAS TREVIÑO DE SOBREMONTE

(A) Leonor Núñez was born in Madrid in 1585. She had lived in San Juan de la Luz and Bordeaux, France, and in Pachuca and Ixmiquilpan, New Spain. She came to Mexico between 1609 and 1613. Her daughter María (B) was born in Mexico in 1613. She had two daughters by her first husband; Ana Gomez (E) was born in Madrid in 1606 and Isabel Núñez was born in Bordeaux in 1609. Leonor Núñez was reconciled in 1635. She, her daughters Ana and María, her son Francisco López Blandon, and her son-in-law Thomas (C) were burned in person.

(B) María Gómez, daughter of Leonor, above, and Pedro López, alias Simón Fernández, was born in Mexico in 1613. She was the wife of Tomas Treviño de Sobremonte (C) and mother of five living children in 1649. She had been reconciled in the auto-da-fé of April 2, 1635 and was burned after being garrotted in the April 11, 1649, auto-da-fé.

(C) Tomas Treviño de Sobremonte is described in detail in the text. Of the thirteen Jews burned at the stake in the 1649 auto, four were related to Leonor Núñez, above.

(D) Francisco López Blandon, alias Francisco Terrazas, was born in Mexico in 1618. He was a relapso in the 1649 auto-da-fé.

(E) Ana Gómez was born in Madrid in 1606, was reconciled in 1635, and was burned at the stake in 1649.

(F) Inez Pereira and Baltazar Dias Santillan were both reconciled in 1649 and sentenced to exile and life imprisonment in Spain. She was born in Mexico in 1628 and had lived in Ixmiquilpan. Her husband's store was used as a synagogue. They both greatly revered their parents as outstanding Jews.

(G) Isabel Núñez was reconciled in 1635. She was noted for her observance of a great number of fasts. She prayed thrice daily with her head covered and a handkerchief over her interlocked hands, facing the east. She prayed upon arising, at 10:00 A.M., and at sunset. She acted as secretary for Duarte de León Jaramillo and held discussions with him and his brother, Rabbi Simón Montero, about Mosaic laws.

(H) Luis Pérez Roldan was born in Mexico in 1599. His sister was married to Duarte de León Jaramillo, and she bore the same name as his wife, Isabel Núñez. Duarte, who was burned in person in 1649, was one of the most pious Jews in the colony. Luis Pérez Roldan was circumcised. His mother was Justa Mendez; his parents were in the auto of 1596. During incarceration from 1644 to 1649 in the secret cells, he was called the Friar. He escaped the pyre, was reconciled, and was ordered to Spain to serve life imprisonment. He never left the country, however, and appears again in the auto-da-fé of 1659.

Yocum McClaskey used the term "Great Conspiracy of 1642" to describe this alleged plot.[11] This term referred to a conversation overheard by a servant (other versions stated that they were two servants of a priest) in which three (some say four) Portuguese (Jews) stated that with other men of equal courage, the Inquisition building could be destroyed and New Spain captured and made a colony of Portugal, which had regained its independence in 1640. Miss McClaskey also includes political and economic motives for the Inquisition activity against the Jews. Medina wrote that the Portuguese Jews planned to overthrow Spanish dominion in 1642 but offers no corroboration.

The second theory involves the desire of the inquisitors to acquire the property of the Jews. Clarence Haring and Henry C. Lea stress the economic jealousies and greed.[12] The Jews had increased in numbers and had prospered. The Spaniards, and particularly the criollos, were turning to trade and commerce. The Jews had practically preempted the field until the middle of the seventeenth century. The days of exploration were waning. W. Roscher theorized that the stranger (the Portuguese Jew in New Spain) "acts as the merchant for the less cultured group, which finally emancipates itself from the foreign merchant as it develops its own commercial organization."[13] This theory aptly describes and applies to the trend of events in New Spain.

As for the opportunity to sate the inquisitors' desires of greed and avarice, Medina and Lea give some figures on the confiscations made from the Jews.[14] These figures reveal the economic status of some of the wealthy Jews in New Spain. Legajo 1737, Expediente 5 of the Archivo Historico Nacional de Madrid contains the reports on the auction sales between 1643 and 1647 in New Spain of the property of forty-two Jews imprisoned by the Inquisition. The sums realized total millions of pesos and reveal the nature of the possessions of these prisoners (see also the report on Simón Váez in the following pages). In the auto of 1646, 38,732 pesos were confiscated, and in 1649 over 3 million pesos. Between November 20, 1646, and April 24, 1648, the inquisitors remitted to Spain 234,000 pesos in bills of exchange. Medina wrote that between 1640 and 1646 the sequestrations realized 429,389 pesos. The inquisitors themselves pocketed a considerable part of the sequestrations. Since much of the property was sold at auction and there is a repetition of the names of the same buyers, one doubts the legitimacy of these public sales.

Another theory involves the conjecture that the era of Messianism and the belief in the advent of a Messiah must have disturbed the Church. The rumor that Gaspar Váez was believed to be the Jewish Messiah and that Jews would worship him when he revealed himself must have been a motivation for the drive to suppress the "anti-Christ" and any incipient revolt against Christian authority.

Jorge Antuñez may have informed on his coreligionists or blundered in his mission and given the inquisitors enough reason to renew arrests. A cryptic remark was made by Treviño to Luis Pérez Roldan while they were incarcerated in the secret cells.[15] He said that "Antuñez going to Spain" was the cause of their trouble. Unfortunately, the reason that Antuñez went to Spain was never clarified or amplified.

Last, but definitely not least, the testimony of Gaspar de Robles gave information which ultimately involved about four hundred Jews.[16] Gaspar was the nephew of Vincente Enríquez, alias Francisco Ome (also Home), of Veracruz. Gaspar lived in California prior to 1641. Whether he had been near death or otherwise "in danger of his life" is not clear. However, he had gone to a priest, Naba, and had related the story of his life, including his Jewish ancestry and the Jewish practices of his family. The priest gave him absolution but directed that he report to the Inquisition and repeat all the details. He followed the command of the priest and came to Mexico. He again confessed in the Church of Santo Domingo and began his testimony to the inquisitors on March 26, 1641.

He had been born in San Vicente de la Vera, Portugal; orphaned as a boy, he was reared by his aunt and uncle. When he was about fourteen, his uncles, Vicente Enríquez and Gaspar Méndez, took him to Angola, from where they brought Negroes and transported them to Brazil, Jamaica, and New Spain While in Angola, his uncles taught him about Judaism and persuaded him to leave the Christian faith. His uncles taught him about the fasts, the washing of meat two or three times in warm water in order to drain off the blood, some prayers, and many details of how to live as a Jew. His testimony revealed the use of separate dishes for meat and dairy dishes and that new pots were bought for certain (unnamed) holy days. When they lived in Mexico, his uncles sent him to school, but he had to be absent on fast days so that his friends would not observe that he fasted.

Between his first hearing and the second on April 11, 1641, Gaspar wrote seven pages of his recollections of things he had learned and the names of Jews whom he had met in New Spain. He spared no one. He listed his grandparents, parents, his sister Blanca Méndez, and relatives who had befriended him. His loyalty to Catholicism was stronger than family loyalties.

Among those whom he implicated were the families of Treviño de Sobremonte and the saintly mother-in-law of Simón Váez. By August, 1641, the inquisitors advised him not to appear before them in the House of the Inquisition but to go surreptitiously to the house of their secretary and there continue his confessions. In his later testimony he involved some who lived in Queretaro and other places in New Spain. His testimony reveals that many Jews were trading in China, Havana, South America, and other parts of the world.

His uncle Francisco Home, formerly known as Vicente Enríquez, was arrested in 1641. Gaspar's testimony put into motion or reactivated the hunt for Jews, which gained momentum as each new prisoner informed against others. The delations were not immediate, but as time went on and the expected release from Spain promised by each leader to his adherents did not materialize, personal confessions were made. Ultimately the threat of torture *in caput alienum* caused the revelation of the names of others. The early arrests and the testimony of Gaspar de Robles weakens the theories of a plot and other motivations as causes for the inquisitors' actions.

By 1640, the Jews of Mexico were mainly divided into three groups, but there were some who were not identified with any one group. Their independence gave some of them an anonymity which aided them to escape notice of the Tribunal. The leaders of the three groups were Tomas Treviño de Sobremonte, Simón Váez Sevilla, and Sebastian Vaz (or Báez) Acevedo. The first named of these leaders is a classic figure, and a later chapter will deal with his life in detail. His individual stature and life story capture the imagination.[17] His group as an entity was the most orthodox in its religious practices and piety.

Simón Váez led a larger group. His position was undoubtedly due to his great business acumen and wealth; the personality of his wife Juana Enríquez; his political influence in the viceregal court and with some of the provincial governors, particularly the governor of Nueva Viscaya; and his connections in Spain. He had relatives in Italy and Holland.[18] He also had an uncle in Seville.[19]

Simón Váez was an international merchant, reputed to have owned seven ocean-sailing vessels. The inventory of his assets in the Inquisition files in the Archivo Historico Nacional de Madrid is almost book length. His ships carried wares ranging from the coarsest burlap to the finest damask. In addition to his friends in the viceregal court, he had influence in the court of King Philip IV. His brother-in-law, Francisco López Sevilla, was on the verge of bankruptcy in 1644 because of advancing funds to aid Simón. Francisco's wife was Beatriz Cid. Her sister Clara Cid was married to the attorney for the crown. We may assume that much of the funds advanced by Francisco went to the king's counsellor, either to line his own pocket or to dispense the funds to others.

Simón's father's patronymic was Soburro. He had been a butcher and had also served as a hangman. His mother was Leonor Váez. Before migrating to New Spain Simón had sired a "natural" daughter whom he raised and named Leonor Váez. Juana, his second wife, testified that the mother of Leonor was Simón's first wife. Leonor Váez, the daughter, lived with Simón's sister, María Aeres, in Pisa, Italy. Simón's second daughter, born to Juana, was also named Leonor Váez. She was reconciled in effigy in the auto-da-fé of 1649, having died prior to 1642. His sister María, married to Francisco Lopez Sevilla, had a daughter also named Leonor Váez. María lived in Pisa, but her daughter Leonor lived in Mexico. Leonor married Agustin de Roxas, who committed suicide by hanging himself in his cell shortly after being imprisoned in 1642 by the Inquisition. This Leonor Váez was reconciled on April 21, 1649, received 200 lashes, and was sentenced to life imprisonment in Spain. This was in lieu of going to the stake, since she and Isabel Núñez, wife of Duarte de León, had made complete confessions at the final moment (3:00 A.M.) before going out in the auto-da-fé of April 11. They were sent back to their cells for ten days and then received identical sentences. During her seven years in the secret cells, Leonor was called "The Baker." She feigned insanity and raised a great hue and cry with shouts which were really coded messages for other Jewish prisoners. She exhorted them to pray and fast and to persevere in the Mosaic laws so that they would be worthy, eventually, to leave as Jews and go to lands where there were synagogues and open juderías without chains or gates. Simón's other child was Gaspar, who proved not to be the anxiously awaited Messiah and who was reconciled in the auto-da-fé of April 10, 1646.

Among the documents in the Archivo Historico Nacional de Madrid pertaining to the property of Simón Báez de Sevilla is a report dated 1660 rendered by Pedro de Medina Rico, visitador of the Holy Office. This report is the judicial determination of conflicting and questionable claims filed before the bankruptcy commission. It records the creditors' meeting concerning the disposition of the property of Simón Váez that had been taken over by the inquisitors at the time of his arrest in 1643. This document reveals many aspects of the economic life of the colony and the role of Simón Váez as merchant and banker. The Franciscan Convent of Texcoco had entrusted 1,645 pesos to Simón, who was acting as their banker and was making investments for them.

Andrés de Urrutia, the tax collector, filed a claim for funds deposited with Váez between 1632 and 1646. Váez informed the royal attorney that he had been jailed in 1642 and therefore could not have received any funds after 1642. He also claimed that Urrutia was not the tax collector between 1632 and 1639 so that he had no government funds to deposit. A reading of this report leads to the belief that Simón Váez might have been in Mexico during the late 1650's in spite of his sentence of exile.

The mayor of Acatlán also filed a claim. The heirs of Don Juan de Pareja Rivera, canon of the cathedral, contended that their testator claimed that Simón Váez owed 9,300 pesos for money left in trust. There were claims for jewelry, grains, mules, cocoa, cloth, damasks, and other merchandise. Goods were shipped on consignment to Váez from various parts of the world.

The attorney for the royal treasury filed a claim for 6,000 pesos, which represented the dowry that the parents of Juana Enríquez, Simón's wife, had given him. This vast sum reveals how wealthy Juana's parents were. The attorney also claimed one-half of all Simón's holdings on the theory that his profits had resulted from the investment of the dowry.

The accountant of the artillery squadrons of the royal navy claimed 12,595 pesos as assignee of Francisco López, Váez' brother-in-law. López had originally received the sum from the accountant who was acting for royal officers. López was unable to reimburse the officers because of Simón's failure to repay his indebtedness to Francisco.

There were many creditors from Seville and members of the nobility who were all involved in Váez' affairs. The total amount of the claims is in excess of a million pesos.

An undated instrument in the Inquisition files is entitled a "Report of the criminals who have been advised of their sentences in order that they go to Spain pursuant to the judgment of exile." Since some of the prisoners were sentenced as late as April 21, 1649, the document[20] must have been prepared subsequent to that date. Since fingerprinting was then unknown, physical descriptions were given so that the prisoners could be identified when they appeared in Spain before the Suprema to be assigned to a jail. Seventy-three people are described. Some of them had been sentenced in the autos-da-fé of previous years but had not yet been sent to Spain. Among those listed were Gaspar Váez and his parents. His mother, Juana Enríquez, was described as "the wife of Captain Simón Báez Sevilla, born in Seville, somewhat dark complexioned, round face, black eyes, of good appearance, and no infirmities, of a good body [*buen cuerpo*], forty years old, little more or less." Simón Váez was "more than fifty years old, tall, thin, expressionless face, blue eyes, and receding hair line at the temples."

The leader of the third faction was Captain Sebastian Báez (also Vaz) de Acevedo. He had been born in Lisbon, where his father had been penanced, was fifty-eight years old, and married to Doña Lorenza de Esquivel, of a renowned Catholic family. His wife was related to a minister of the Holy Office. He was sentenced on April 11, 1649, to 200 lashes, exile, and a fine of 2,000 Castilian ducats "for the extraordinary costs of the Holy Office." There is no mention, however, of confiscation of all of his property. His imprisonment was to be determined by the Inquisitor General in Spain, to whom he was to present himself thirty days after arriving in Spain. He was to leave New Spain with the first fleet leaving from Veracruz, but he was not listed on the document of those scheduled to leave.

He usually spent fast days in bed, pleading illness. His home in Mexico was a meeting place for his adherents. Why the suspicions of his wife were not aroused by his duplicity, which ranged over a period of years, is inexplicable. She may have been sympathetic to

his faith, she may have been a devoted wife, or she may have detested the Tribunal, thus pretending to be unaware of his real religious affiliation. The Jesuit historian of El Gran Auto-da-fé of April
11, 1649 wrote of Sebastian ". . . he kept Saturdays and did not wish
to be paid on that day, overcoming his great greediness in order to
keep the lapsed law, so observing was he of Saturday."

He played the dual role of being a Jew and being an intimate of
personages in social circles and the Church. For sixteen years he attended the Convent of the Barefoot Franciscans of Saint Isabel on
Holy Thursday and carried the royal standard in the religious procession. The Catholics, upon learning that he was a Jew, contended
that he had celebrated Holy Thursday, accompanied by his Jewish
friends, because Jesus was imprisoned on that day. They said that he
rarely attended the procession on Holy Saturday since that was the
anniversary of the Resurrection. When the mass arrests began in
1642, he went to Veracruz with another Jew to help the latter to
escape but did not himself attempt to flee.

The Jewish communities were quite large. In the proceso of Micaela Enríquez there are several reports and conversations indicating
both a lack of knowledge of other Jews and lack of contact or communication among the various groups.[21] Each group, however,
knew that there were others.

Prior to 1640, it was generally believed that Juana Enríquez
would bear the long-awaited Messiah. The belief was predicated
upon her many virtues, the importance of her husband Simón Váez,
and the fact that he was a descendant of the tribe of Levi, one of the
original Twelve Tribes of Israel. When their son Gaspar failed to
prove that he was the Messiah, the hopes of the communities shifted
to Ines Pereira, a niece by marriage to Treviño de Sobremonte.

There is nothing to indicate the existence of any social relationships among the three men who were the leaders of the groups, nor
are there any records of any commercial transactions among them.
There is some support to the theory that there was little or no socialization between the families of Treviño and Simón Váez. Juan
Pacheco de León lived with Váez for three years, from 1639 to
1641. During his trial he named almost seventy families as practicing
Jews, but he did not mention Treviño or any of his close followers.

We do learn of ad hominen animosities. The family of Blanca de
Rivera, unaffiliated with any group, were mortal enemies of Tre-

viño, and he had little use for some members of the Rivera family. He claimed that Manuel de Mella, a leader of one of the two Guadalajara Jewish groups and a son-in-law of Blanca de Rivera, was a confirmed gambler who lost his wife's dowry and defrauded several people. The reason for the animosity between the families may have been engendered by Margarita de Rivera, one of Blanca's five daughters. She was the most venomous in denouncing Treviño to the inquisitors.

Prior to 1629, Margarita had had sexual relations with Treviño as well as with Captain Antonio Váez Casteloblanco, an older brother of Simón Váez. She informed the Holy Office during her trial in 1644-1645 that both men had been circumcised. There is little question that Treviño's marriage to María Gómez had embittered Margarita. She also testified against Treviño's brother-in-law, Luis Pérez Roldan. He, in his defense, characterized her as his "enemy, a woman of evil tongue and bad judgment in whom no trust could be placed."

In 1624, Captain Antonio Váez and Treviño had shared an Inquisition cell. The captain was much older. He was born about 1570 and Treviño was born about 1592. They were fast friends until at least 1635; subsequently, a coolness developed. Antonio Váez was "a lone wolf" and not actively associated with the group of his younger brother. Although the captain said a little about Treviño, and that primarily at about the time of the first trial of 1625, his son (called *El Cachopo*, zealous observer), did implicate Treviño. He narrated some of Treviño's Jewish practices which showed his association, if not affiliation, with the more orthodox community. Further proof of such association is his testimony of conversations with Ana Gómez, sister-in-law of Treviño. His nickname further evidences his religiosity. His father is referred to as a religious officiant and we know of his father's great Jewish learning.

A reported conversation between El Cachopo and Ana Gómez is interesting. He told her that a Jew, recently arrived from China, had said that "in China there are many Jews who met together secretly for religious purposes."[22] The Jewish traveler must have alluded to groups of Iberian crypto-Jews in the Philippines and on the coast of China where agents of the Inquisition were functioning since both colonies were then under Spanish dominion.

Not all witnesses who informed against other Jews were hostile, but many, under duress, testified against members of their own families. Rafael de Sobremonte, son of Tomas Treviño, implicated his father on several occasions. The youngster, then about thirteen years old, recited a Jewish prayer which his father had taught him to say upon arising:

> *Blessed be the light of day,*
> *And the Lord who gives it to us.*
> *All peoples praise the Lord and*
> *The Lord is praised by all peoples*
> *Because he has confirmed His truth which supports us*
> *And His truth shall remain forever.*

The Rivera family was closer to the Váez group, yet they revealed the Jewish practices of Juana Enríquez. However, this was done without malice and in an attempt to mitigate the sentences of the Holy Office against themselves.

Gregorio M. De Guijo, an observer of the 1649 auto-da-fé, wrote in his *Diario* that the judges of the *Audiencia* (Supreme Court) and their wives had given presents to Simón Váez and his wife and respected them "as if they were the highest nobles of the kingdom." Juana was the most charitable woman in New Spain. Her mother, Blanca Enríquez, was the matriarch of the Simón Váez faction until 1639. Her learning was considered great and she reared her daughters to be observant Jews. However, despite this training, Juana made "seven stations to Saint Moses" during her pregnancy—acculturation from Christianity took many forms.

Juana Enríquez was tortured twice by the Tribunal. The first time was on Saturday, July 7, 1644. Before being put on the torture bed, she gave thirty-nine *fojas* (seventy-eight pages) of testimony. Upon the second turn of the cords on her left leg, she began to scream, and the names of those against whom she testified gushed forth in an uncontrolled torrent. She also incriminated her husband and son. Nothing was withheld, but later she revoked some of her statements and withdrew some of the names of people against whom she testified.

At 9:15 A.M. of October 15, 1648, she was again disrobed, put on the rack, the cords were tightened, and she began to scream, "I am a Jewess, Jesus be with me! ay! ay!" Then with further tightening, she cried out, "I have said all that you gentlemen want me to

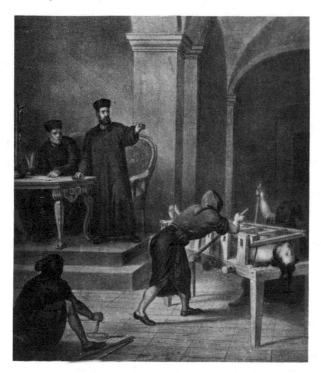

The potro *in the Inquisition chamber*

say, *I say that all those who are in Mexico are Jews*, ay! My God of my life for the love of God, I have confessed the truth."

Then follow ten pages of frantic imprecations of a woman in pain and anguish who alternately shrieked for relief, made more damaging admissions, mentioned names in high circles, and prayed for death as a release from the agony of the cords on her limbs. She cursed the souls of the inquisitors, but they remained unperturbed. Among those whom she implicated as Jews was the Marques de Serralbo y Cadereita.

In each community, the members ran the gamut of all types and personalities—from the very pious to non-observers, from the saintly to high-priced women of pleasure. Some were learned and could recite prayers in Hebrew. Women were taught as well as the men; in education, there was equality of the sexes. Prior to 1642, there were synagogues and meeting places and the Jews prayed almost publicly.[23]

The National University, which had been established by royal decree in 1551, was not open to Indians nor any of the eighteen strains[24] that resulted from mixing of Indian, white, and Negro bloods.[25] Proof "of Christian ancestry without a trace of Judaism or heresy" and purity of blood made it dangerous for Jewish youths to apply. However, there were a few crypto-Jews who did receive degrees from the school. Even the Colegio de San Juan de Letran (a primary school intended only for mestizos) was closed to all non-whites because criollos filled the classes. Private teachers instructed the young Jews. European Jewry knew that Jews in New Spain needed teachers, primarily spiritual, for their children. During the 1630's, several teachers claiming to have the title of rabbi came to Mexico. They capitalized on their smattering of learning and many, being single, used their status to obtain rich brides. Some were fortune hunters and believed that New Spain offered opportunities to acquire wealth easily.

A distinguishing characteristic of the mothers and grandmothers of this period was their insistence on children marrying within the faith. Rafaela Enríquez caused her daughter, Ana Juárez, to divorce her husband, Juan Méndez de Villaviciosa, a Jew, so that she could marry Francisco López de Fonseca. The latter's claim to greater fame as a Jew was based on the fact that his father, Enrique López Martínez, had been burned at the stake in Coimbra and his mother, Isabel de Oliverares (or Olivera), had escaped the clutches of the Inquisition. She was an observant Jewess who lived in San Juan de Ruz, France. Mention is made of the "impediment" (impotency) possessed by Ana's first husband which provided the excuse for a divorce, which he, according to Jewish law, had to give to her.

The early summer of 1642 held no augury of unusual activity in the House of the Inquisition or among its officials. Without notice or warning on July 9, 1642, the Holy Office issued an order to Veracruz prohibiting the embarkation of any Portuguese who did not have a special permit from the Tribunal authorizing departure. This action alarmed them but also prevented many Jews from escaping. Others remained out of loyalty to their families. The leaders looked for aid from their friends and relatives in Spain. Concern was felt and fears mounted but, as yet, there was no feeling of impending doom. Slowly but inexorably the number of arrests continued, and the number of imprisoned was so great that by 1644 there was a shortage of cells. The Holy Office rented houses numbered 8, 9, and 9½ of the Calle de la Encarnacion, owned by nuns of the Order of Encarnación. Additional cells were built in the Calle de Perpetus, and finally some private homes were also rented.

Communication between the prisoners was not too difficult. Holes were made in the walls and messages passed through them to the outside. Slaves brought meals and carried instructions. Between 1642 and 1644, many meetings were held by each of the communities during which each member was assigned a name which was to serve as a password in the secret cells. Some of these were Big Dove, Great Hat, Pilgrim, Big Parrot, and Little Dove. Many of the men used the Nauhautl, Zapotec, and other Indian languages, which most Inquisition officials did not know.

Among those imprisoned was Ana de León, the youngest and last of the Carvajal children. She was sixty-six years of age when she was burned at the stake on April 11, 1649. She had been regarded as a saint by all the Jewish communities. Medina and Bocanegra wrote that the devil and celestial figures visited her while she was in the cells. She had a cancer of the chest so deep that it consumed her outer flesh and one "could see her entrails, and the stench emanating therefrom" was appalling. There is no record of medical attention for her.[26]

11

Tomas Treviño de Sobremonte, His Family, and Friends

TREVIÑO DE SOBREMONTE was a *rara avis*.
The span of the years from 1624 to 1649 found him in many places
in New Spain, and marked the evolution of an adventurer into a
devoutly religious figure. He was one of the most dramatic figures
of seventeenth century Mexico. His name was also spelled Thomas
Trebiño and Tremiño de Sobremonte. A. J. Barker wrote at the
outset of his translation of the procesos of Treviño de Sobremonte:[1]

> The proceedings in the trials of Tomas Treviño de Sobremonte
> ... are the most important relating to Jews in the 17th century ...
> The documents appear to me to be of considerable importance ...
> but they require careful editing by Jewish scholars.[2]

Barker's evaluation of the man and the documents pertaining to
him are correct. Treviño was an epic figure whose biography runs
the gamut of adventure and human emotions. He feared no man,
and although his amatory escapades would not rival in number those
of Don Juan, he knew the straw palettes of Indian women in the
mountains of Oaxaxa and the fine linens and silk sheets of such
women as the wife of a marquis in the city. He played the role of a
lone wolf until he married, and then he became a devoted father and
husband and an extremely pious Jew. He was a leader of one of the
Jewish communities of his era.

His contemporary, Gregorio M. De Guijo, who might be called the Samuel Pepys of his day, wrote in his *Diario* that even during the march to the stake there were "no words of condemnation of Treviño." In fact, he commented that the onlookers of the parade to the stake on April 11, 1649, were left with admiration when he refused to kiss the cross.[3] His refusal denied him the privilege of the garrote, and he was burned alive. In the prologue to the *Diario* (p. viii) Manuel Romero de Terreros wrote that Treviño exclaimed as the flames licked at his body, "Throw on more wood, this [fire] is costing me enough money." He turned the moment of tableau and tragedy into an unforgettable, vivid legend.

The *Diario* is at variance with the report to the Holy Office made by Licenciado Francisco Corchero Correno, who was employed by the inquisitors. His report, appended to the trial proceedings, covered Treviño's last hours and the unsuccessful attempts of the Dominican theologians to convince the prisoner to relent and convert. A different version is rendered by Correro, who claimed that the populace lining the path of the Procession of the Green Cross were angered by Treviño and threatened him with mayhem. The Director of the Mexican National Museum, José de J. Nuñez y Dominguez, quoted a long poem written in the nineteenth century about the martyr.[4] The free-verse poem speaks for itself.

> *Old parchments narrate*
> *that the excommunicated criminal*
> *caused terror by his blasphemous aspect.*
> *As he was going to his torture,*
> *the mule on which he rode and which*
> *had been selected to carry his body,*
> *reared several times*
> *and caused him to fall to the ground.*
> *Through fear that he might not be alive*
> *by the time he reached the stake,*
> *it was ordered that a Negro*
> *should climb up on the mule*
> *in order to hold him with his arms*
> *throughout most of the way.*
> *The populace, which was looking at such*
> *awesome events, was muttering,*
> *not knowing the case:*
> *"This heretic has the devil so deep*
> *inside his body that not even the*
> *mule will tolerate him*

in order not to offend heaven."
Thus more than one hundred excommunicated men
arrived with slow steps at the place of torture
(all being firm and having confessed).
The Jew's turn came, he was the first
to be burned alive on account of his
sacrilegious acts.
It is said that when he was tied
to the rough steel pole
and when the red flames of the fire
were all around him, he shouted
to his executioners with a mad voice:
"Throw more wood on, you wretched
ones, because I am paying for it."
Two centuries have passed and
the place where the unfortunate criminal
lived is still standing
His name was Tomas Treviño;
he was neither old nor young when he died;
he had a strong character and was intelligent.
His name is still present in the people's memory,
because misfortune of Christian and Jews alike
cause good hearts to palpitate and cry.

[Translated by Dr. Enrique Rivas]

Actually, there were 109 Jews, male and female, dead and alive, in El Gran Auto-da-Fé of April 11, 1649. Fifty-seven had died in the secret cells or prior to arrest, and the bones of others were disinterred so as to be burned at the stake. Of the total 109, thirty-four were females. The house referred to in the poem, once a Mexico City landmark, was demolished about 1910.

Great oppobrium was evidenced by the Jesuit historian of the 1649 auto-da-fé and the theologians who accompanied Treviño to the pyre, but this was exceeded by the venom of Licenciado Corchero, the attorney for the Inquisition. Following are a few of the descriptive names and phrases he applied to Treviño during the course of the second trial: perfidious Jew; rabbi; great Jew; perverse Jew; a Jew of the highest rank; a false priest and rabbi; a cursed prisoner; a backsliding Jew; a teacher and zealous dogmatizer in his false law; an indomitable and rebellious Jew; an ignorant criminal; an audacious criminal; a depraved and astute Jew; dog who returns to his vomit in order to lick up that which apostasy has ejected from his stomach.

The first Inquisition order for Treviño's arrest was issued on

House of Tomas Treviño de Sobremonte in Mexico.
Historia y Leyendas de Las Calles de México

October 15, 1624, and directed that Tomas Treviño de Sobremonte and his brother, Francisco Treviño, both of Old Castile, be apprehended, separated, and not permitted to speak to each other. The order was forwarded to Antequera in the Valley of Oaxaca where it was received by Licienciado Barroso. Francisco had left the area about ten years earlier and was thought to be in Peru. The sequestration of Treviño's property at the time of his arrest attracted a great deal of attention because Antequera was a small town where Treviño had lived for eleven years and was a person of importance. He was born in 1592 in Medina de Rioseco, Spain, where his father had been a *mayordomo* of the Church of Santa María. His mother, Leonor Martínez de Villagómez, was a Jewess, as were all her ancestors.

Treviño de Sobremonte had escaped from Spain in 1611 under the name of Geronimo de Reprensa when the Inquisition had begun to ferret out the Jews. His mother was ultimately arrested and died at the stake in Spain in 1623. His brother, Jeronimo Treviño, also imprisoned by the Holy Office in Valladolid, gave the testimony in 1619 in the torture chamber that led to Treviño's arrest.

Treviño arrived in the New World through the port of Veracruz and made his way to San Luis Potosí. It was his plan to go south, overland, to Peru accompanied by a Senor Sefuente. However, at

Oaxaca, Sr. Sefuente turned back to Mexico City and Treviño remained in Oaxaca as a shepherd. Later he began bartering and eventually opened a store. Within a few years he was considered the wealthiest man in town. The proceso notes that he also had a reputation for paying too much attention to women, which was "a common weakness in these times." He was also known for his charitable contributions and for attending mass regularly.

When the inquisitors in Mexico asked him the pro forma question, "Do you know, presume, or suspect the reason that you have been arrested and brought to this Holy Office?" he began a series of possible reasons, some of which confirmed his weakness for women. He first replied that about two years previously he had slept with an Indian in the mountains and months later heard that she had given birth to twins, crediting him with their paternity. He also admitted that he had been intimate with Doña Luisa de Bilona, the wife of Marquis Alonso de Canaga. At the time that she was six months pregnant and all efforts to have her abort had proven unsuccessful. He then recalled that when he was a lad, he had killed a page to Don Rodrigo Enríquez, uncle of the Admiral of Castile, for calling him a Jew. None of these answers satisfied the inquisitors, and he finally admitted that his arrest may have been due to the fact that some of his relatives went to the stake in 1623 in Spain.

He had no hesitancy in stating that his mother had taught him about Judaism and about the Law of Moses, which he followed until he came to live in Oaxaca. But, he said, he desired to continue to live as a good Catholic, which he had been in recent times. It was in the first trial that he recited some of the Jewish prayers that he had been taught. One of those that he recited daily was "Holy, Holy, Holy is the Lord of Hosts, the whole earth is full of His Glory" (Isaiah 6:3). He recited the foregoing and several others in Hebrew. He knew the Shema and the several names of God which appear in the Bible and prophetical writings. His mother had taught him a prayer in Spanish to be recited at washing before eating. "Blessed be the Almighty God who in His lessons has taught me the washing of the hands, mouth, and eyes, in order to bless, serve, praise, and honor Thee, O, God, according to the Law of Moses."

He also recited in Hebrew the last verse of Psalm 90, "And let the graciousness of the Lord our God be upon us; / Establish Thou also upon us the work of our hands; / Yea, the work of our hands

establish Thou it." (The transliteration of the Hebrew into Spanish
by the secretary of the Inquisition does not facilitate the identification of some of the prayers, the sources of which Treviño did not
seem to know.)

While the Jews ridiculed Church dogma, beat crucifixes and
images, and derided Christian beliefs, their antagonism was not directed to Christians as people. There is no evidence, for instance, of
maledictions against Christians or of prayers invoking God's curse
or retribution toward Christians. Their prayers were filled with hu-
mility, penitence, and requests for absolution and earthly salvation.

The longest prayer of Treviño de Sobremonte recited in Spanish
was:

> *To you, great ineffable God,*
> *To Your essence beyond the knowledge of man,*
> *To You, everlasting glory,*
> *To You, unchangeable Lord,*
> *Forgiveness and mercy.*
> *If you consider that I have offended you*
> *By my bearing and insolent acts,*
> *You will have no forgiveness for me;*
> *but do not consider me*
> *and my iniquities and vices,*
> *Great God; consider only Yourself,*
> *and do not judge me who have offended You.*
> *I have sinned more than anyone else,*
> *He, the Devil, knew how to lure me into the world,*
> *I tasted so much of his pleasures*
> *that I thought of him much more than I thought of You.*
> *Seeing now Your sovereign and clear light,*
> *I find that he was my enemy,*
> *And I see that my guilt requires Your punishment.*
> *But if You trust that I will remember*
> *What my obligations are towards You*
> *I will come out triumphant and victorious*
> *Over the world, the flesh and sin.*
> [Translated by Dr. Enrique Rivas]

While in the secret cells in 1624 Treviño asked for a companion,
and Antonio Báez, about fifty years old, was placed in the cell with
him. Antonio was also known as Antonio Váez Casteloblanco, Captain Tirado, and Captain Casteloblanco and was also suspected of
Jewish practices. They became good friends and Antonio, very

learned in Jewish lore, taught Tomas, circumcized him, and gave him a Hebrew name, Isaac, from the Old Testament. In the proceso of Antonio Caravallo,[5] Antonio Váez Casteloblanco is referred to as a *munidor*, beadle or sexton, but in the proceedings of Antonio Váez himself, the inquisitors and their attorney referred to him as rabbi and dogmatizer.

No physical examination for the mark of circumcision was made of Treviño de Sobremonte during his first trial, and his 1625 sentence was mild. This benevolence of the inquisitors was undoubtedly due to Treviño's uninhibited confession of past Jewish practices. The inquisitors noted in their judgment that he showed signs of contribution and repentance. He was sentenced to be confined to a cell for one year and wear a sanbenito of yellow cloth with a diagonal cross of St. Andrew on the front and back. His property was to be confiscated. He was also to attend mass and sermons on Sundays and to recite with great devotion, five times on Saturdays, the Pater Noster, Ave Maria, Credo, and Salve Regina, and to confess and receive the Holy Sacrament on all three-day festivals. He abjured on June 15, 1625, in the Church of Santo Domingo.

The year in Treviño's life subsequent to this date might be termed the "Great Deception." He cajoled, wheedled, and lied to gain his ends. Within a month after being sentenced he wrote to the inquisitors complaining of illness since "the cell in which I am, being so damp and full of water, is making me grow deaf and my strength is failing, which prevents me from doing anything to earn my food." His request to be transferred to a hospital for from four to six months was granted on July 14, 1625, and he was taken to the Hospital de los Desamparados (the Hospital of the Friendless) with leave to go out to earn his living during the day but to return at night to sleep. This permission was to expire within four months. On September 22, 1625, he requested the return of some of his clothes that had been originally sequestered, so that he could "realize a little money for my wants." The inquisitors acceded to his request.

On November 6, 1625, he asked for and received a four-month extension of his stay in the hospital because he was not cured. He curried the favor of the Tribunal on November 13, 1625, by reporting that he had forgotten to tell them that in Spain, the other Jewish members of his family used to read *Flos Santorum* by Villegas because it contained the lives of the patriarchs and the prophets and the marvels and miracles "which God had worked through the saints of the Old Testament."

On July 16, 1626, his petition to remove the sanbenito was granted and he was freed. The Inquisition dossier shows an accumulation of denunciations against him commencing in 1629. He was seen riding a horse, bearing arms, and wearing silk and fine cloth, all of which were prohibited to him as one reconciled. One of the denouncers was López de Erenchum, the receiver and notary of the Holy Office, who reported seeing Treviño de Sobremonte in Calle de Santo Domingo in Mexico, in the shop of Gaspar Suarez "dressed in a doublet and hose and short cloak of fine cloth and wearing a belted sword." Such denunciations accumulated in the Inquisition files without any action being taken.

Finally, in 1633, he was requested to report to the inquisitors because the Inquisition prosecutor, who had been directed to investigate, stated that Treviño rode up to his office on a horse and was attired in all the prohibited clothing. Treviño wrote a letter to the inquisitors in which he blithely stated that he had received a pardon or letter of rehabilitation, dated May 6, 1631, from Cardinal Antonio Zapata, the Inquisitor General for all of Spain. Treviño de Sobremonte had this letter in his possession for over a year and explained that he had "overlooked" delivering it to the Holy Office. He added that "as a fine for my failure to present the rehabilitation until today and having belted on my sword, I venture to offer 100 pesos toward the expenses of this Holy Tribunal." The 100 pesos was accepted and the letters filed.

During the years 1633 to 1644, more correspondence accumulated in his file. Most of them were from people who declared that they had not heard him say "Gloria Patri" after the name of the Trinity had been invoked although he was known in Mexico, Guadalajara, and Zacatecas as a reconciliado. About 1638, in Mexico, he saw a Spanish captain abusing a civilian, a Jew known to Treviño de Sobremonte. Treviño stepped between the two and ordered the captain not only to cease the abuse but also to apologize. Upon the captain's refusal, Tomas picked him up by the scruff of the neck (or the collar of his uniform) and held him aloft until he apologized. This presents a picture of Treviño's physical strength and audacity.

His role as husband and father are as noteworthy as his role as a

Jew. After his release in 1626, Tomas remained in Mexico rather than returning to Oaxaca. We do not know if the marquesa finally aborted or bore his child, but illegitimate births were not uncommon among Spanish Catholics or Jews. Treviño's brother Francisco, who had gone to Peru, had sired an illegitimate child in Cartagena who bore the name of Antonio Treviño. Other Jews seemed to have left such "by-blows" on the paths of their peregrinations, but most of these affairs preceded the entry of the male into matrimony.

Tomas married María Gómez in 1629. He must have been a knowledgeable Jew by then because his mother-in-law, Leonor Núñez, would otherwise not have permitted the marriage. Leonor Núñez had trained and reared her daughter in all the minutiae of Jewish wifehood. In minutes of the trials of her two daughters, stepsisters Isabel Núñez and María Gómez, we read of some Jewish marital customs which have been and are practiced by some of the most orthodox Jews.

On the marital night of María and Tomas, "they knew each other," but thereafter he waited seven days before again having sexual relations with her "in order not to make her impure." This custom or law is alleged to have stemmed from the desire to permit a virginal wife to recover from the first act of intercourse and to permit the healing of any laceration.

Another marital custom is revealed in the proceedings of Tomas' brother-in-law. Luis Pérez Roldan required his wife, Isabel Núñez, to have relations with him on Friday evenings, according to an old Jewish custom which directed cohabitation on that night unless the wife was "unclean." This commandment was fulfilled even on the occasion when Isabel had not been asleep the previous night due to having maintained a vigil with the corpse of her mother-in-law. Such a vigil is mandatory because of the possibility that actual death may not have occurred.

The wedding meal preceding the marital night of María and Tomas was prepared in accordance with strict Jewish law. Leonor Núñez, the bride's mother, recited the prayer, "Blessed be He who created thee for my sustenance" when she had, personally, slaughtered the fowl which served as the main course. Before decapitating the fowl she had inspected the knife for nicks, tested it on her fingernails, and then plunged it into the ground three times while facing east.

The men ate with their heads covered. The first course was a honey cake. The explanation for this custom given to the inquisitors was that honey cakes "were eaten in memory of the honeycomb which the angel gave to Asenath, the oldest daughter of Potiphar, when she married Joseph." This interesting custom reminds Jews of Asenath, who bore Joseph two sons, Ephraim and Manasseh. On Friday evenings Jewish fathers bless their sons by placing hands on the head and saying "May you be as Ephraim and Manasseh." The honey cake is eaten at weddings in anticipation of the birth of sons with the qualities of Joseph's sons. After the meal, blessings were recited and cold water was thrown on each hand prior to praying. The hands were dried "with a towel in a peculiar way." Then Tomas and María went to church where they were wed according to the Catholic rites.

Treviño de Sobremonte prospered greatly. After the Great Flood of 1629 in Mexico he moved his family to Guadalajara and lived there until 1644, except for one short period in Mexico. He was a traveling merchant and also a manufacturer of cochineal dye for export. He went to Acapulco or Veracruz when the fleets arrived to buy the wares that came from China or Spain. Among the merchandise he once bought were "housecoats." They were of finest material and cost 100 pesos each (approximately $500 in modern coin.) At one time, he had seven of them in his bedroom but, following a visit of Blanca de Rivera and her grown daughters, one was missing. This loss caused a rift between the two families since Treviño did not hesitate to accuse them of the theft.

María called her husband a saint and had once objected to moving from a certain house because it was "an abode of felicity." Six children were born of the union; one child, Antonio, died when he was about four years old. Rafael, the oldest, born about 1631, was circumcized by his father when he was about ten years old. Tomas used a special knife and remained in his son's room for the week that it took him to convalesce. At the outset of his son's Jewish training he required that the boy fast on Thursdays. Once when the boy was caught eating a piece of bread on Thursday, his father upbraided him and threatened to bury him alive. Rafael's grandmother, mother, and his Aunt Isabel impressed upon him the importance and truth of all his father taught him. Fast was broken with boiled eggs and fish prepared with oil and vinegar.

When María was reconciled by the Inquisition in 1635, she and Treviño schemed that he should pretend to refuse to take her back until the Holy Office ordered him to do so because of his reconciliation in 1625. They wanted to avoid any suspicion that he was still a practicing Jew. "He kept up the farce of reluctance before complying." They were an ideal married couple. She reared her children to adore their father and to abide by their faith. Her mother lived with them and was accorded the greatest respect by her son-in-law. About 1639, when they were dining in their house on Calle San Francisco, Mexico (now Avenida Madero), Leonor Núñez had a premonition of impending danger. She insisted that they abandon their afternoon meal and leave the house. They complied and half an hour later, the roof caved in. The following day, they all fasted in thankfulness.

When Tomas had his store in Guadalajara, he placed a cross under the threshold. Those who stepped on it when entering received a discount if they were Jewish. In order to fool his servants about the reason for his fasts, he complained of his liver and said that from time to time that he had to abstain from food.

He prayed four times every day: about one hour upon arising, a half hour in the afternoon, a similar time shortly after Angelus, and for about an hour at midnight. In order not to violate the Sabbath by extinguishing the candles lit for religious reasons and in order not to arouse the suspicions of his servants, he did not blow out the candles on week nights in the upstairs room that he used for his midnight prayers.

Treviño believed, as did Jacob ben Asher[6] in *Arb'a Turim*, that it is especially meritorious to arise during the night and pray to God to redeem the people of Israel from their fearful exiles and to restore Jerusalem and the Holy Sanctuary (cf. Psalm 119:12). Nahum N. Glatzer refers to this custom and quotes the verses from Job (13:15) which would be most meaningful to the Jews in New Spain.[7]

Sometimes Tomas prayed standing and at other times on his knees. His head was always covered, usually by a skull cap. From the numerous references to a cloth which covered him, it is presumed that it was a prayer shawl. There is a single reference that indicates that he used phylacteries. A dispute once arose between him and Antonio Váez Casteloblanco as to the date of the Great Day (Yom Kippur). Treviño claimed that the Jewish calendar sometimes had twelve, and other times, thirteen months in the year. (There are seven leap years of thirteen months in each cycle of nineteen years.) Because of doubt as to the exact day of Yom Kippur, Treviño fasted two days. He tried to educate other Jews and performed circumcision on many of them.

While only vegetable oil was used for cooking in his home and his family didn't eat pork, pieces of pork were put into the stew when non-Jewish guests were present. Bread was always cut before the Sabbath to avoid the act of slicing or tearing on the Sabbath. His faith was shared to such an extent by María that when she was incarcerated in the cells in 1645 and knew what her fate as a relapso was to be, she said, "this Tribunal may condemn our bodies but cannot condemn our souls."

The women of Treviño's family, his wife, mother-in-law, and sister-in-law, went to confession in the church. Before going, they washed completely, donned their clean and best linen, and then returned home to "kneel with hands turned down, and their bodies bent so low as to almost touch the ground and ask the Almighty for pardon" for resorting to the Catholic practice.

Leonor Martínez, daughter of Treviño and María, was the apple of the family eye. She bore the name of Treviño's martyred mother. She and her brothers performed Jewish rites "in a manner which compared favorably with the performance of grown people and was a joy to behold," as stated by Francisco López, el Chato (the snub-nosed) in his testimony in the second trial of Treviño. Of Leonor, Genaro García commented that at fourteen years of age she was taken for a little saint, and her sentence of exile and the wearing of a sanbenito in Spain was a cruelty to a child accustomed to the graceful, affectionate kindness of her mother and grandmother and the copious richness of emotion of her father.[8] She was sentenced in the auto of March 30, 1648, so she was spared having to watch her parents go to the stake in 1649.

Leonor had been taught her prayers when eight or nine years of age and practiced her religion devoutly. She sang religious duets with her grandmother and recited a blessing when seeing the first star at dusk or a falling star. She fasted and had new shoes for all holy days and did not eat dairy products with meat. She accompanied her grandmother, who used to shout in a loud voice for the benefit of their Christian neighbors, "Get ready, we must go to mass."

However, they would only walk by the church, and the child never heard a mass. Before leaving New Spain, she was placed in the home of an official of the Holy Office for the purpose of being taught Catholicism.

Treviño denied all the charges against him at his second trial. He even denied that he had circumcized his son, knowing or surmizing that his son had testified about this. His knowledge of Latin is revealed by his discussion of the Latin sources of *circuncido* and his general knowledge by his references to Ptolemy and others. His denial of having performed or been subjected to the Jewish rite of circumcision was predicated on the fact that the scars that he and his son bore were longitudinal. One of the slips in his testimony was a denial of any knowledge of the custom of farda and then following the denial by describing the history of the custom. He asserted that this custom was not a question of faith or contributing to oppressed Jews in the Holy Land, but that it was a campaign begun during the reign of Philip III to raise funds for the release of Portuguese of Jewish descent who were thrown into prison in Spain, and that the funds were paid to the Duke of Lerma for their release.

He explained why Blanca Rivera and her daughters, particularly Margarita, were permitted to come to his home even though he regarded Margarita as a mortal enemy. He said that his wife permitted their visits because "they might think we despised them for being poor and it might be that they came on account of being hungry." Margarita was the proverbial woman scorned. Her animosity to Treviño was brought fully to flame by the marriage of Baltazar Díaz Santillan to María's niece Ines. Margarita, having lost Treviño, had set her cap for Baltazar. The double loss probably caused her to focus blame on Tomas.

At one hearing Treviño became angry with the attorney for the Tribunal and did not hesitate to attack him. While in jail denying all charges, he invented hundreds of excuses to maintain all dietary laws. He prayed and his religious fasts ran into many days, causing the inquisitors to send doctors to examine him. At the time he went to the stake, he had fasted for seventy-two hours.

Being a proud Spaniard, he ridiculed those who testified against him, saying that they were Portuguese, to whom "it comes natural to their black souls to cry 'Death to the Spaniard' and they are a crowd of lunatics." His words, "I have been a source of profit to the

Holy Inquisition" preceded a detailed list of its confiscations of his parents' property in Medina de Rioseco (which would have been his as heir of his parents); of his own property in Oaxaca, including 500 pesos; and the dowry which he had received from his wife and which he had had to surrender when she was arrested in 1635.

For several years prior to 1642, he had planned to take his family to the Low Countries where he knew that he could practice Judaism openly and freely. However, he wanted first to retrieve 3,000 pesos from his wife's uncle, who had either stolen or defrauded this large sum from him. This uncle had fallen in love with a mulatto, taught her the Mosaic laws, and then married her. The high degree of emotion behind Treviño's attempt to retrieve his loss was not due to avarice, but rather to the blow to his ego at having been tricked. His procrastination in leaving cost him his life as well as the lives of his wife, her mother, his sister-in-law, and his brother-in-law Francisco López Blandon.

Treviño was convinced that his persecution by the Inquisition could have been halted if he had given information concerning the location of fourteen ingots of silver which he had secreted some time prior to his arrest. However, he did not believe that he would end at the stake since he knew people in Spain were working for his release. His written answers to the thirty-two charges in the fiscal's accusation against him reveal a high degree of legal talent. His acute mind and his piercing, penetrating logic used words as rapiers that tore away the tissue of lies, weaknesses, inconsistencies, and ignorance in the case against him. But all this availed him naught. The Holy Office stood adamant.

Not until he was told his fate did he avow his true beliefs. Then, and for the ensuing twenty-four hours, he reiterated that he had lived and wanted to die as a Jew. Three theologians were assigned to him, but they were unsuccessful in converting him. His constant cry that there was but One God and He was the God of all people. He went to the stake firm in his belief.

POSTSCRIPT

About the year 1660, Daniel Levi (Miguel) de Barrios wrote a poem in Spanish which was intended to be in the nature of an elegy for Tomas Treviño de Sobremonte. About that time de Barrios resided in the Caribbean area, either in Tobago or Cayenne. The poem confuses Treviño and Francisco Maldonado de Silva, the great Peruvian martyr. The first line reads, "Fourteen years of rigorous jail," which was the time served by Maldonado before he was burned in the 1639 auto-da-fé in Lima, but the main theme is the story of Treviño. What is important is that within eleven years of El Gran Auto-da-Fé of Mexico, the story of Treviño had spread, becoming so powerful and appealing a legend that his fame and devotion to his faith inspired even non-Mexican Jews to write of him as a folk hero.

12

Autos-da-fé, 1642-1649

THERE WAS no act of faith between 1637 and 1646. In the auto-da-fé of 1637, there was only one Jew, Isabel de Medina, thirty-eight years old, who was Portuguese. She was sentenced in the courtroom of the Tribunal. She abjured *de levi* and was reprimanded —the lightest possible sentence.

Despite the great number of Jews arrested between 1641 and 1644, there was no auto until 1646. Jails were overcrowded and the inquisitors overworked. It is true that their many activities accrued more to their own benefit than to that of the Faith, but they were endlessly active. The secretaries were bedeviled by the demands of the prosecuting attorney for the minutes of the various hearings. Copies had to be made of the record of each hearing for transmittal to the Suprema. It is these copies which have aided in supplying data from the originals which have been lost, stolen, or destroyed.

Although Appendix A contains a list of the penitents in the autos-da-fé between 1646 and 1649, some account of these events and a few of the individuals who were participants in the spectacles are noteworthy. Many published statistics on the operations of the Holy Office do not include the many *autillos*, small autos-da-fé, and the very frequent private, non-public sentencings.

With respect to the relaciónes, errors of two kinds exist. First, they are not always complete. Second, ages as reported may vary by as much as five or six years. The latter errors may be due to the fact that sometimes the age at the time of arrest is used and at others the age at the time of the auto-da-fé. The mills of the Tribunal did grind very slowly in this decade. Prisoners were in the cells for as long as eight years before they were sentenced, and when a jail term less than life imprisonment was imposed, the time of prior incarceration was not credited.

The relación of the April 16, 1646, auto was written by Dr. Pedro de Estrada y Escovedo, then prebendary of the Mexican Cathedral and one of the counselors whose services were offered to prisoners. He was later elevated to the post of inquisitor. According to Genaro García's copy of this relación, there were forty-eight people in this auto-da-fé. They included two priests who had married, four bigamists, one who posed as an Inquisition official, and one monk who performed sacraments beyond his powers. The remainder were forty Jews—twenty-four men and sixteen women. Joaquin García Icazbalceta gives a total of thirty-one in this auto-da-fé.[1] The Abcedario supplies the names of five others for the year 1646, but they were sentenced at different times during the year. The case of two of the five were suspended and they were freed.

All of the Jewish males who were examined during this period bore the mark of circumcision. Not all the Jews were exiled from New Spain. Notable among these few exceptions was Gaspar de Robles, who had been an informer. Some received brief jail sentences and then were to be exiled from all of the New World and from Madrid and Seville. These people were free to go wherever else they desired.

One of the conclusions that must be drawn from reading the brief notes on many of the individuals is that they not only lived as Jews in the fullest sense of the word, but they were accepted as Jews in other lands where Judaism was openly professed and practiced.

Among those in the 1646 auto was Margarita de Morera, thirty-six years old and born in Mexico. She was associated with the Treviño de Sobremonte group and had reconverted many to Judaism. She related the manner in which the Jews in Mexico were called to religious services or special meetings. A Negro was dressed in a red suit and went through the streets playing a tambourine. This was the signal to congregate for a special community meeting or for prayer. Margarita was one of those who escaped exile.

According to Elkan N. Adler, Francisca Tejoso was a thirty-year old single woman who had had "criminal connexion" *(sic)* with the celebrated Irishman, Azuzena, as she had with many others.[2] Medina fails to mention her amorous affairs, but he does state that she was a baker and that "in order to make the bread more tasty and whiter, she and her sisters used water for the dough which they had first used to wash their private parts."[3] According to the relación, she was fifty-four years of age and had contended that she "had consecrated her virginity to the Virgin Mary." However, she confessed to being a Jewess. The relación reports the same curious story of the preparation of the dough.

Another interesting person in the same auto was Juana Tinoco, wife of Simón Suarez de Espinosa. She was sixteen years of age and he twenty-four. Both were born in Mexico and were to be exiled. He was sentenced to serve a six-month jail sentence while she was to serve a year. She was the daughter of Diego Tinoco and Catalina de Silva Enríquez. She was one of thirteen children and a granddaughter of Antonio Rodríguez Arias and Blanca Enríquez, both of whom were called "rabinos dogmatistas" by the inquisitors.

When Simón Suarez proposed marriage to Juana, she took him to the cathedral and showed him the tabilla of her grandfather hanging on the cathedral wall and asked him if he were willing to marry into that kind of family. The young gallant did not have a Jewish background, although he was a descendant of converts. Juana, a gifted, comely maiden, meant more to him than life itself. He therefore converted to Judaism, following which they were wed.

Tomas López de Monforte came to New Spain in 1637, when he was twenty-five years old. He had been born in Monforte, Portugal, but his parents had moved to Seville when he was young. He related to the inquisitors that he had been accorded hospitality in the home of a rich Jew in Mexico, that of Simón Váez. This home was the hospitality center for many Jews who were newcomers from Spain and Portugal, and meetings were held there "as in a synagogue." There were communications between Fernando Rodríguez in Veracruz and the rich Jew in Mexico, both of whose homes accommodated the Jewish immigrants.

THE AUTO-DA-FÉ OF JANUARY 23, 1647

The author of the relación of the auto-da-fé of January 23, 1647, is not named on the flyleaf or elsewhere. G. García lists only the penitents. There is no copy of the sermon or a description of the parade.

Four who were suspected of Jewish practices were acquitted. Twenty others (eighteen men and two women) were found guilty. Eleven of the men had been circumcized. Six of the men and one woman are especially interesting.

Fernando Rodríguez was fifty-eight years old and was the leader of the Veracruz Jewish community. For thirty-eight years he had practiced Judaism, and his home had served as a guest house for all Jews arriving in New Spain. He was a broker and trader of Negro slaves. His four sons, who studied medicine, were also penanced. He frequently cried when reading of the lives and virtues of the patriarchs and prophets of old. He fasted frequently and abstained from the midday meal so as to avoid eating with Catholics and being offered non-kosher foods.

Duarte Rodríguez, unrelated to Fernando, was fifty-two years old. He had migrated to Peru when a lad. His wife, Clara Texoso, was born in Lima and fled the Inquisition there. He was considered a great scholar whose fame had preceded him to Veracruz. His home was used as a synagogue and study center.

Although Duarte de Torres had a wife in Spain, he married a mestiza from Patzcuaro; her father was Spanish and her mother an Indian. They had one child, a daughter. When he heard that his family in Portugal were inquisition prisoners, Torres voluntarily confessed to the inquisitors in Mexco. In his testimony, however, he gave false names for other Jewish practitioners and while in prison ridiculed Catholic practices and Holy Week. The latter earned him 200 lashes.

Francisco de Acosta had lived in Guatemala and owned a store in Cartagena, another illustration of the diffusion of Jews all through New Spain. He had been taught Judaism in Mazagan, Africa, by members of the Jewish community. He was known among the Jews in the secret cells by the name "Orange." They communicated with each other by a code transmitted by blows on the walls, shouts, songs, and even the use of a cat which carried messages.

Tomas Méndez had lived in Loanda in Angola, and in Pernambuco and other places in Brazil before coming to New Spain. Juan Cardoso, alias Gabriel Peregrino, was fifty-seven, had been born in

Simide, Portugal, and resided in Orizaba, New Spain. He had lived in Amsterdam and there was circumcized and given the name of Gabriel Peregrino. He attended the synagogues, owned a *talid (sic)*, prayer shawl, and could recite Hebrew prayers. He bowed when the "parchment written in Hebrew letters" was taken from the Ark in the synagogues and desisted from eating the flesh of any animals or fish listed in the Bible as prohibited. Neither would he on Saturdays collect monies due him, even if this meant risking a loss.

Juan Méndez Villaviciosa was born in Viciosa, Portugal, in 1605. He was tall and dark complexioned, with good features set off by a black mustache. He had proclaimed that the Mosaic law was universal and should be followed by the entire world. He advocated red clothes for all disciples of the Mosaic laws as a sign of happiness. When and if the world should eventually adopt these laws, he thought there should be celebration in the form of a great feast. Although he feigned insanity in the secret cells, as had many other prisoners, he admitted that he had been a Jew ever since he had the ability to reason.

He had served as a spy for the Jewish community in 1642 in order to note the Jews who were being taken to the House of the Inquisition. He also aided Jews in secreting personal property and helped Simón Váez Sevilla burn some of his incriminating papers and documents. After abandoning the pose of insanity as a defense, he cited his many acts of charity for the Church. He stated that he had been an observant Jew because he was afraid that the Jews would kill him if he failed to continue his observance, since his parents had been dedicated Jews. He was sentenced to 200 lashes and five years in the galleys as an oarsman without pay. At the termination of that part of the sentence he was to report to the Tribunal in Seville to begin life imprisonment.

AUTO-DA-FÉ OF MARCH 30, 1648

The relación of the March 30, 1648 auto-da-fé lists twenty-three Jewish penitents out of a total of twenty-nine who appeared. The Abecedario lists a total of thirty-one penitents, but one died in jail before sentence and the other was in a private auto. Included were fifteen men and ten women of the Jewish faith; eight of the men had been circumcized, and each led a colorful life in which various facets of Jewish communal activities are disclosed.

Juan Méndez, a Portuguese, was a tailor and resided in Orizaba. His father was a notary of the ecclesiastical vicar and his mother was a New Christian. In spite of his denial, he was convicted of being an observer of the Law of Moses. He did state, however, that the blood of his maternal ancestors inclined him to doubt the Catholic faith and that if he had known what the Law of Moses was, he doubtlessly would have followed it. His conviction was one of the few that may be attributed to the fact that he had been circumcized. His effrontery was also unique.

Beatriz Enríquez, born in Mexico, was the daughter of *los famosos judíos rabinos*, Antonio Rodríguez y Arias and Blanca Enríquez. When Blanca's grandmother, also named Blanca, died, it is noted that the funeral services were attended by people "greater in number than one would be able to see in a public synagogue."[4] The title of Beatriz' grandparents as famous Jewish rabbis appears over 300 times in the Inquisition records for the years 1642 to 1650. Beatriz Enríquez was married to Tomas Nuñez de Peralta, who appeared in the 1646 auto-da-fé. The description of Beatriz given in the receipt of the captain of the ship which was to take her to Spain reads, "a beautiful white face, blue-green eyes, blond hair, and good body." She died aboard the ship taking her to Spain. In the secret cells, her name was *Rubia*, the blond.

Her rhapsodic description of her married life would satisfy the most romantic, and her observance of Jewish rites would please the most pious. The author of the 1648 relación charged her with witchcraft because of her ministrations to the dead. She prayed each morning after washing and would not even drink her chocolate until she had completed her prayers, some of which she recited in Hebrew. This same rite was also observed by her sister, Micaela Enríquez, wife of Sebastian Cardoso.

Ana Núñez, thirteen years old, and her sister Antonia, fifteen years old, were the children of Duarte de León Jaramillo and Isabel Núñez. Antonia, her father's favorite child, prayed on the eve of the Sabbath, with a covering on her hair, for an hour to an hour and a half.

Blanca Juarez, the wife of Jorge Jacinto Bazan, was called "Little Dove" in the secret cells. She was so pious that she was called saintly and some believed that she would give birth to the Messiah.

Melchor Rodríguez López had come from the Isle of Tenerife and had friends in Angola and Amsterdam.

In the relación of this auto, the unnamed author three times asserts that Jews and Jewesses "had money and riches." In addition to the Jews in this auto, there was Sebastian Domingo, alias Munguia. He was a Negro slave born in the Congo and was convicted of bigamy. He was a slave of Thomas Nuñez de Peralta, and prior to his arrest he carried messages and money from the outside to his mistress and master. He was faithful to them because they had purchased him from a textile sweatshop where the slaves and Indians were chained to the chairs and tables and worked eighteen hours a day, seven days a week.

THE AUTO-DA-FÉ OF APRIL 11, 1649

The "Great Auto-da-Fé of 1649"[5] introduced some new names into the history of colonial Jewry in the middle of the seventeenth century. One figure stands out from the others because he was the secretary of Bishop Juan de Palafox y Mendoza, one of the most notable churchmen in Mexico. Bishop Palafox had been feuding with the Jesuits and vice versa. His secretary, Melchor Juarez, may have been chosen as a target by the Jesuits for the purpose of undermining the illustrious clergyman.

Melchor Juarez played no role in the communal life of the Jewish communities of Puebla and Mexico. He did live in a house with several Jewish families but denied that he knew their faith. He was accused of bigamy and Jewish practices. His case never reached final determination, although he was exonerated on the first charge. His first wife had remained in Spain when he left for the New World. Fortuitously for Melchor, she had died shortly prior to the request for information about her which had been made by the Tribunal in Mexico. Technically he had been a bigamist, because he had contracted marriage in Mexico while his first wife was alive. However, since she had passed away while the charge was pending, the Holy Office ceased its interests in this phase in the case. The Jewish aspect seems to have been forgotten in view of the position he held and because of behind-the-scenes support from his employer.

The statistics for the auto qualify it to be called the Jewish Auto-da-Fé. There were 109 Jews involved, of whom fifty-seven were already dead. Ten had died in the secret cells and eight had escaped. The bones of forty-seven were disinterred. Two were reconciled in effigy; they had requested to be taken back into the bosom of the Church and their wish was granted post mortem.

Of the living, thirteen were burned at the stake; seven were men and six were women. Twelve were first garroted; Treviño was the only one burned alive. Of the twenty-nine who abjured, twenty-two were males and seven females. Two of the women had their abjuration postponed to April 21 due to confessions and statements that they made at 3:00 A.M. of April 11, as previously noted.

Among those at the stake was Ana de León de Carvajal of the illustrious family of martyrs. Her reputation in the Jewish communities was great. She was greatly revered and was requested to pray for newly deceased in order to save their souls from purgatory. Her fasts were more numerous than any other Jew in Mexico. The omission of any mention of her name by De Guijo in his *Diario* is unusual. De Guijo wrote of several people in the auto and he knew details of their lives, even of the women whose appearance was postponed. Bocanegra in his official *relación* mentions that Ana was the niece of Governor Luis de Carvajal. She chewed on paper on fast days to deceive her Christian neighbors. For congregational praying, she attended services conducted in the store of Duarte de León Jaramillo. She also attended meetings of Jews at the Royal Hospital for Indians, where many of the reconciled were incarcerated prior to 1649.

Her daughter, Maria de León,[6] had married another Jew, Diego Nuñez Pacheco, in 1629. They moved to Cretano, near Queretaro, early in 1642. Diego died in the secret cells on March 14, 1643, and was one of those burned in effigy in the auto-da-fé. Prior to his marriage, he sired a daughter born to a mulatto, Catalina, who was a slave of Catalina Enríquez in Veracruz. With María de León he had four children. There is no record of any proceedings against any of his children, and there is no record of any arrest of María or any proceedings against her.

Francisco López Blandon, an unmarried gilder, was thirty-one years of age in 1649. He was the son of Leonor Núñez and Pedro López, formerly known as Simón Fernández, who had been burned in effigy as a *dogmatista judaizante* in the 1635 auto. His parents had been denounced from Peru. Francisco appeared in the 1635 auto-da-fé and was reconciled.[7] Data concerning his relatives are found in the genealogy of María Gomez (p. 222).

His 1635 arrest was *por judío;* in 1649 he was arrested *por judío observante de la ley de Moysen,* for being a Jew observer of the Law of Moses. He had circumcized an infant born to him and a mulatto. The circumcision was intended as an act of contrition for the statement made to the inquisitors when he told them in 1635 that he would believe only in the law of Christ. He and the other members of his family intended to instruct his "natural" son in Judaism when he attained mental maturity. This never came to pass because the boy was only seven years old when Francisco and others related to him were jailed for a second time.

López Blandon was a worthy brother-in-law of Treviño de Sobremonte. His Jewish-Spanish ancestry could be traced back to the fifteenth century. His mother, Leonor Núñez, had taught him some prayers that her mother had taught her. Her mother, María Rodríguez, had been an Inquisition prisoner in Toledo and never told her daughter how she had been freed. The following is one of the prayers taught him:

> *Look at me O Lord with eyes filled*
> *With pity and mercy. Keep me in the*
> *grace which Thou hast bestowed upon*
> *me, guide my soul, keep me in Thy*
> *paths, test my deeds. Fulfill Thy*
> *promises and let my heart be consumed*
> *with holy thoughts; forgive me my past*
> *sins and help me correct the present*
> *ones and protect me from those that*
> *will assail me in the future.*
> *Hold me worthy to receive Thy blessings*
> *from heaven, Thou who art my God and in*
> *whom I trust.*[8]

Neither Leonor Núñez nor her children, including Francisco López Blandon, recited any prayers in Hebrew, but the Shema (without the opening two lines) was recited in Spanish, in a literal translation of the Hebrew. While it was recited, a hand was placed over the eyes. Reference is made to a little book containing this prayer and others, including those used for the Fast of Queen Esther. One of the prayers recited by this family was among the best known among Mexican Jewry; the first four lines are from Psalm 121 verses 1, 2:

> *I raise my eyes to heaven*
> *From whence will come my succor,*
> *My comfort is from the Lord*
> *Who created the heaven and the earth.*
> *I confess, my Lord, that I am without*
> *moral strength and though I have sinned*
> *before Thee, look kindly upon me my Lord.*

Francisco had begun to observe fasts when he was eight years old. The first year that he was made to fast, he could not complete the twenty-five hours, and he surreptitiously ate a little bit of *alfajor* (also *alaju*), which is a sweet made of almonds, walnuts, honey, etc.

The entire Rivera family had testified against López Blandon, as they had against all the other members of his family because of their antagonism toward Treviño de Sobremonte. While Francisco and his brother-in-law were in the cells, they spoke in Nahautl. He fasted every Monday and Thursday while in jail from 1643 to 1649. He prayed on his knees asking the God of Israel, as the God of justice, to free him and his family as He had freed the Hebrew people from the oppression of Pharaoh. His prayer was, "Great God of Israel, receive from your servant this sacrifice which I make and the prayer from my heart which I offer, on behalf of my mother, sisters, nephews, and nieces; free them from misery and suffering." Then he recited, "Great God of Israel, why don't You heed me, O Great God of Abraham, Almighty King!" At other times he referred to Susanna, he would cry, beat himself, and plead in the name of the innocent sheep of Israel. He testified only against those who had testified against him. He had a Negro slave who brought him food and messages from the outside. This slave also eavesdropped in the office of the head jailor and reported all that he heard. Francisco threatened to kill those who testified against him. He was placed in solitary confinement because of these threats. During 1648 and early 1649, he fasted for two or three days without even imbibing liquids, but this did not appear to affect him physically.

Catalina Enríquez, one of those reconciled in effigy, mistress of the slave who bore a child to Diego Núñez Pacheco, was eighty years old. She had twenty-two brothers. She had practiced Judaism ever since she had been twelve years old. She and her husband had lived in Havana, Mexico, and Veracruz. Six months before she died in the secret cells she had begun her full confessions because "Christ Crucified surrounded by lights and in all His resplendent glory appeared to her and brought her to her senses." She was buried in a Christian cemetery.

Justa Méndez, who had been a disciple and friend of Luis de Carvajal, was burned in effigy. Luis had told Manuel de Lucena that he had had a dream in which he saw Justa Méndez and Antonio Díaz Marquez as two perfect observers of the Law of Moses.[9] Every one of her children and grandchildren were observant Jews. The Jesuit Bocanegra wrote that she was not merely "content to teach her children but in her depraved zeal she also injected them with the Law of Moses many times."

Justa's daughter Isabel Núñez had married Duarte de León Jaramillo, and they had six children. In the "Epitome Sumario" of the relación of the April 11, 1649, Duarte was "*convicto de su relapso y de Dogmatista Rabino*," convicted of being a second offender and a dogmatizing rabbi. Isabel prayed thrice daily facing the east. Duarte was burned in person. His last words, unknown in English until now, are more vibrant than those of Treviño. Duarte cried out as he was about to be garrotted, "Look, Mother of the Maccabees, how you are being revived to be the mother of so many who are going to the stake [for their faith]."

Other children of Justa Méndez were Luis Pérez Roldan, who married the daughter of Leonor Núñez and was a brother-in-law of Treviño de Sobremonte and assumed the name "Friar" while in the secret cells; and Francisca Núñez, burned in effigy in the 1649 auto and who had been married to Julio de Rojoso, also known as Juan de Roxas. Thirty members of the family of Justa Méndez and her husband Francisco Núñez, alias Rodríguez, were penanced at one time or another by the Holy Office.

The Rivera family were represented in this auto by María and Catalina. Not only had Treviño and Simón Váez termed the family their enemies, but Beatriz and Juana Enríquez stated that they were the cause of the arrest of Tomás Núñez de Peralta. Blanca Rivera, the mother, and some of her daughters habitually beat images of Christ. There is little doubt that Blanca was slightly deranged. María, one of the daughters, a widow and mother of Gabriel and

Raphael de Granada, starved herself to death in the secret cells. This was indeed one of the most unhappy families in Mexico.

The punishment meted out to the members of the Rivera family was asserted to be of "help as an example to the newly converted Indians and in terrorizing Hebrews."[10] This admission by the inquisitors Juan Saenz de Monozca, Francisco Estrada y Escobedo, Licenciado Domingo Velez de Assas y Argos, and Licenciado Bernabe de la Higuera y Amartilla in a letter to the Suprema dated November 27, 1643, was found by Medina in the Archivo de Simancas. It points up the tenuous relationship between the Indians and Christianity and the problem of controlling the Jews, whose numbers were increasing in spite of the efforts of the Inquisition.

The trial record of Gabriel de Granada includes the names of several Jews against whom no proceedings were ever brought. Gabriel was thirteen years old at the time of his arrest in 1642; he was kept in the cells for over five years. He is one of the few who had been circumcised in infancy by a "famous rabbi." He named over 100 Jews and gave proof of their Jewish observances. His arrest came just weeks after his mother had told him that he was a Jew, as was his father, who died in China. The records of the Holy Office do not disclose why the inquisitors brought no proceedings against some of those named by Gabriel. It may be that they needed to empty the cells before continuing their arrests.

Rafaela Enríquez was a participant in the 1648 auto-da-fé. She is described as "born in Seville, forty-four years old more or less, somewhat dark complexioned, a beauty-mark or birth-mark on her throat, brown eyes, and the widow of Gaspar Suarez." (This name appears elsewhere as Xuarez and Juarez.) The notary of the Inquisition is alleged to have had "a sexual affair" with her. One hundred and eighty-seven people (an unusual number) testified against her to prove her adherence to Jewish rites. She made careful marital matches for her daughters to be sure that they married within the faith. Her name in the Inquisition cells was Rafa, or gypsy.

Micaela, sister of Rafaela, and her husband, Sebastian Cardoso were friends of the inquisitor Estrada and the Inquisition secretary Eugenio de Saravia. Before Micaela and Sebastian were imprisoned, they were permitted to go to Saravia's house and make their confessions and file the inventory of their property that was to be sequestered. Their statements were, of course, filled with deceit, and the inventory was only a partial one. The visitador stated that the excuse given for this unusual clemency was the alleged pregnancy of Micaela, but he noted that there were many pregnant Jewish women in the secret cells who did not receive such consideration. After they were finally imprisoned, Micaela and Sebastian shared the same cell.

A minor incident may reveal something of the character of Simón Váez. He caused Pedro Fernández de Castro, his son-in-law, to come to New Spain in order to collect his dowry. Pedro had married Simón's bastard (she is so termed in Pedro's proceso) daughter, Leonor Váez, who had remained behind in Pisa.[11] Pedro is reported to have gambled and drank; Simón even accused him of stealing some things from his house. There appears no justification, however, for Pedro to have been kept waiting in New Spain for almost three years for the dowry promised to him. All this time his wife was waiting in Pisa with their two small children. Pedro probably never saw his wife again, unless he managed to escape, because in the auto of January 23, 1647, he was sentenced to serve in the galleys for five years as an oarsman without pay.

On April 4, 1644, Francisco López de Sevilla wrote a letter to Simón Váez, who was already imprisoned by the Inquisition.[12] It is clear that Francisco López was attempting to secure Simón Váez' release by giving money to certain influential people in Seville, some of whom are named. López' brother-in-law, the attorney-general for the throne, is not named. Although there is no doubt that Simón and Francisco were brothers-in-law (some say brothers), the language of the letter is not that of one relative to another, but rather of a confidential employee (Francisco) to his master (Simón). There is a fervent plea for money since Francisco's creditors were pressing him for the payment of his debts and he was virtually bankrupt. Reference is made to monetary advances made by him in 1634, 1635, 1638, and 1641.

Francisco was also known as Francisco Rodríguez and Simón Rodríguez. He had two children in New Spain, but his letter makes no mention of them. His son, Gonzalo Flores, formerly known as Gonzalo Váez Méndez and known among the Jews as Samuel, lived in New Spain and claimed that Manuel de Mella and his wife Violante Suarez were his mortal enemies.[13] He was burned at the stake in 1649. His sister was Leonor Váez, the widow of Agustin Roxas who had committed suicide in the Inquisition cells. During the years 1646 to 1649 Leonor exhorted other prisoners to adhere to Jewish law and "to go out of jail as Jews." She believed in the ability of her uncle to extricate them ultimately from their difficulties. She was reconciled and sentenced to life imprisonment in Spain. This comparative leniency resulted from her disclosure to the inquisitors that the insanity of her brother had been feigned for three years.

In 1649, there were three Jews burned at the stake in Manila. This is one of the very rare instances of sentences being executed away from Mexico.

13

A Forgotten People:

1650-1699

✡ THE EVENTS that characterized the latter half of the seventeenth century included a conclusion of the cases not adjudicated prior to the 1649 auto-da-fé, the visitation of Pedro de Medina Rico, the failure of a Messiah to appear, the open legal return of Jews to England, the changing attitude of the inquisitors, and the planting of the seeds of revolution in Mexico.

One of those whose case was not terminated until 1650 was Juan Pacheco de León, also known as Juan de León and, among Jews, as Salomon Macharro.[1] He and his father, David Macharro, alias Antonio Farfán de Narváes, had set sail from Italy for New Spain in 1639. Stories were rife in the Jewish communities of Italy concerning the riches and adventure to be found in the Philippines and the New World. Many were enticed to seek fortunes and new lives in these areas. Others followed the same routes for different purposes. People such as Juan Pacheco and his father were learned Jews who were going to serve as teacher and spiritual leader, respectively, in the outpost of the New World.

Juan was probably born in Leghorn, Italy, in 1619. He was his father's assistant when they left Italy for New Spain and was to serve as instructor to Gaspar Váez who, it had been predicted, would be the Messiah. The elder Macharro died at sea while enroute to Mexico. Juan proposed to take his father's place. Prior to

1639, Blanca Enríquez, mother-in-law of Simón Váez, and "*la famosa rabina dogmatista*"[2] had been the spiritual leader of the Váez community. She was a descendant of a family of illustrious learned Jews. She tested Juan upon his arrival, found him to be learned and qualified, and relinquished in his favor her position as arbiter of disputes among the Jews and as the authority in matters of ritual.

Blanca had been tortured by the Inquisition in Seville before coming to New Spain. She had admitted nothing and had involved no one. Her arms and legs still bore the marks of the torture. She had ruled her group prior to 1639 as a veritable matriarch. She died on January 1, 1642, and was buried in the Church of the Barefoot Carmelites, dressed in a shroud in accordance with Jewish rites. One of the oddities noted at her burial is that "her teeth were thrown into the coffin." This appears to be one of the earliest references to false teeth in New Spain.

Juan Pacheco, during the time he lived in the home of Simón Váez, became the inseparable companion of Gaspar. In 1641, he was set up as a merchant in Queretaro. This enterprise was a source of income while he served the community as teacher and rabbi. The old Jewish custom that a rabbi had to have his own trade or occupation to earn his livelihood still existed. He was not expected to accept payment for performing religious duties.

Juan was arrested on May 22, 1642. His first audience took place on July 2 of that year. His testimony about his life in Italy and his schooling gives interesting information pertaining to Italian Jewish history. He was educated in a Hebrew Academy, where he learned to read and write Hebrew by the time he was six or seven. In his narration to the Mexican inquisitors of his early years, he said he used a tallit when he recited *tfilas* (prayers). He was a regular synagogue attendant. When he compared a part of the synagogue service with the Catholic mass, the inquisitors listened in a frigid silence of such hostility that it seems to pulsate through the intervening centuries from the pages of the proceso. After having observed his bar mitzvah he had been sent to Izmir, Turkey, and other places abroad to continue higher education. He had been a captive of the Turks for four years in the island of Jú (Argel) where there was a synagogue.

In the indictment against him, there were 104 charges. He was termed "a famous rabbi" by the Inquisition's attorney. As a single

Juan Saénz de Mañozca, Archbishop of Mexico and inquisitor

man, he lit candles on the eve of all holy days. He admitted that he wore the same clothing in Mexico which Jews wore who lived in lands where freedom of religion existed, and he spoke of games which were played at the end of Purim. (Inquisitor Manozca persisted in calling him a Portuguese. Juan had originally stated that he was born in Antequera, Spain, but later changed this to Italy, on advice of other Jews who thought that Italian birth would save him from severe punishment.) No proof that he had been baptized was ever adduced.

He once went to Pedro Tinoco to ask him to desist from studying and attending classes at the university on Yom Kippur. The inquisitors thought this request was contrary to Jewish law since Jews were accustomed to studying on holy days. Juan explained to them that on those days study was restricted to holy texts. He recited the candle-lighting prayer of his hostess, Juana Enríquez, "O, Almighty God of Israel, who gives health to all Your children, give health to my husband, my children, and to me." Juana said she repeated this prayer seven times together with a petition for good fortune.

The record of the trial also reveals that the prayers of Luis, *el Mozo*, and those of Manuel de Morales were still being recited sixty years after they had composed them. A great favorite for Yom Kippur was the one which began, "Pequé, Señor, mas no porque he pecado . . ."[3] Juan was one of several Jews who went to the *baños de los japoneses*" (Japanese bath house) for ablutions prior to Yom Kippur. These bath houses were not described, and consultation with three noted Mexican historians revealed that they had not known of the existence of such baths. Juan stated that Blanca Enríquez blessed her grandson, Gaspar, on Fridays before dusk by placing her hands on his head, bowing her head, and saying, "May the Lord bestow upon you and your children the blessings of Jacob and Israel."

Juan Pacheco had a Hebrew prayer book in his cell and prayed four times daily, at 5:00 and 10:00 A.M. and 3:00 and 6:00 P.M. He repeated the prayer recited by women on slaughtering fowl, "Blessed be He who has created you to sustain me." He used the words Kippur for the Great Day and Tisha B'Ab, and referred to observances during the three weeks prior to the ninth day of the Hebrew month of Ab, which marks the anniversary of the destruction of both Temples in Jerusalem. (The Inquisition secretary spelled the day of mourning as *Thesabes*.) During the three weeks prior to Tisha B'Ab, the Jews ate no meat. They dined on lentils and eggs and ate on a tablecloth spread on the floor. On the day, they fasted all day in the synagogue.

He revealed that there were Jews in Ferrara, Italy, who denounced to the local bishop Spanish and Portuguese Jews who visited their synagogues. The bishop then established the identity of such visiting Jews and reported them to the Tribunals in Spain and Portugal.

Juan deprecated those Jews who beat or reviled statues of Christ. He displayed little sympathy for those who could migrate to Holland or Italy but did not and continued to live as Catholics. This attitude toward crypto-Jews is typical of the lack of sympathy which was growing among non-Iberian Jewish communities that had begun to ignore the Iberians who lived as secret Jews. This feeling was expressed in a statement during a conversation between Juan and Francisco Botello, another Jew, in the Inquisition cells. It came in answer to Botello's question as to why the Jews in New Spain were held in little regard by non-Iberian Jews.

Juan used the words Pesach instead of *Pascua de Cordera* and Succot instead of *Cabañacitas*. He explained the differences in religious practices between Italian and New World Jewry. One difference in the slaughtering of animals seemed to intrigue the inquisitors. In Italy, but not in New Spain, lambs and cattle after being slaughtered were opened at the chest, and the lungs and liver were examined to see that they had no imperfections. If none existed, the meat was fit for Jewish consumption since it was *caser*, meaning clean. If there were blemishes, the meat was sold to the Catholics since it was *treph*, unclean.

When Juan prayed, he put his feet together and covered his body and hands with a cape. He also referred to the tallit as a *sábana*. Normally a sábana is a sheet, but it is also defined as an altar cloth. A *capa* (the word used by Juan Pacheco and, almost fifty years earlier, by Manuel Gil de la Guarda) is defined as anything laid over another garment. A *capa magna* is a pontifical vestment worn by bishops while officiating at the altar. Toward the conclusion of his prayers, Juan stepped back and then forward, and sometimes he bent forward. These steps and genuflections are part of the ritual accompanying the recital of the *Amidah* or Eighteen Benedictions. Even during his period of incarceration, he discoursed about "the law which was on the parchment," the scroll of the Law, or Old Testament.

On December 17, 1648, he was put to torture but supplied no new names or data. He had earlier implicated almost seventy Mexican Jews. One of his companions in jail was Guillermo Lombardo, also called Guillen de Lamport, termed one of the putative fathers

of the Mexican War of Independence of 1810.[4] There was a great
exchange of ideas and plans of strategy between Juan and Don
Guillen. Guillen made suggestions to Juan on the question of
baptism.

No reason appears for Juan Pacheco not being sentenced prior to
April 11, 1649. He was sentenced on July 8, 1650, to 300 lashes and
eight years as an oarsman in the galleys, to be followed by life imprisonment. Gregorio M. de Guijo, in reporting the 1650 auto-da-fé
in the Convent of Santo Domingo, doesn't mention his name, but the
identification is unmistakable since he wrote that ". . . from the age
of two, his parents had taught him the old Law of Moses. In his confessions also he declared that he had not been baptized, that he had
been a prisoner since 1642 . . . and had resided with Simón Váez
Sevilla."[5] The other prisoner in the auto was a Negro slave who had
declared that "the Jews were accustomed to have good fortune."
Guijo reports Juan's term in the galleys to be ten years, instead of
eight as it appears in the minutes of the trial.

We do not know what happened to Juan nor what happened to
many other Jews who had been sentenced to exile. We do know
that many, in spite of this sentence, did not leave New Spain. Luis
Pérez Roldan was in the auto-da-fé of 1659, having been apprehended for not leaving the kingdom as directed in 1649. There were
190 Jewish penitents in the four autos-da-fé between 1646 and 1649.
In the auto of March 30, 1648, Simón de León, son of Duarte de
León Jaramillo, was sentenced to one year in prison, to wear the
sanbenito publicly over all his clothes, to certain spiritual penance,
and to be exiled from all the Indies. However, the AGN volume
contains his petition of April 26, 1649, for a release and notes that
on April 27, 1649, the sanbenito was removed and "the prisoner is
set free." On June 20, 1650, a certificate was prepared for transmittal to the Suprema about those directed to go to Spain, but nothing was ever done to enforce the exile.

Henry Charles Lea wrote that the Jews roamed New Spain because the Inquisition took their money and property. "They wan-
dered through the land, throwing off their sanbenitos and infecting
the population with their errors." The ship captains would not trans-
port them to Spain without payment, and the inquisitors would not
part with any of their ill-gotten gains.[6] Many Jews had successfully
concealed part of their money, however. Eight of them were

caught one evening in Puebla in 1650. The men were attired in evening clothes, and the women were elegantly dressed, wearing mantillas.[7]

If human lives had not been at stake, one could be amused by the exchange of correspondence between the Tribunal in New Spain and the Suprema. On May 24, 1649, the three inquisitors, Estrada, Mañozca, and Higuera, wrote about the penitents "who boast of their wickedness" and only two of whom presented themselves to the Tribunal in Spain.[8]

In the letter of August 24, 1965, Dra. Pilar León Tello, senior archivist of the Archivo Historico Nacional, Madrid, stated that Legajo 1729, No. 9, contained a list of twenty-nine Jewish penitents who had been ordered to leave New Spain and report to the Holy Office in Madrid where they would be assigned the place in which to serve their life imprisonment, but that they had never appeared. The Mexican inquisitors explained to the Suprema that some of the penitents had to remain in New Spain because of sickness or because they were related to other prisoners. She continues, "At the end there is a notation dated in Madrid, January 16, 1649, that a number of those sentenced in Mexico on May 28, 1647, had arrived in Sevilla toward the end of 1648, but only two had presented themselves to the Council of the Inquisition in Madrid." There is no other record of any other Jewish penitents returning to Spain.

Of the almost 200 Jews directed to return to the mother country between 1646 and 1649, twenty-nine made the voyage, but only two reported to the Spanish inquisitors. The names of these two are not disclosed in the Mexican or the Spanish archives. The twenty-seven could have found refuge with the many crypto-Jews of Spain or other parts of the Spanish Empire. Richard B. Morris wrote that the English playwright, Richard Cumberland, was sent as an intermediary by King George III to the Spanish Court in 1779 and "He made contacts with numerous Marranos, or crypto-Jews . . ."[9] Many abandoned ships or were permitted to leave ships when they stopped for water and supplies at West Indies islands.

There were 150 or more Jews who never left New Spain, and untold numbers who were never apprehended by the Inquisition. Groups of these Jews banded together and began to disperse over the viceroyalty. These groups did not constitute all of the Jews in New Spain. The notable exception to those who remained in Mexico and the twenty-nine who wended their way to Spain in 1648 were the few who were condemned to serve in the galleys. These men were herded to San Juan de Ullua, the prison fortress in the water facing Veracruz; from this point they were taken aboard the galleons.

In 1656, Simón Suárez de Espinosa and his wife Juana Tinoco were still in New Spain. Many others went to Monterrey and adjacent areas in northern Mexico. There they founded the Jewish community which spawned many great industrialists and leaders of Mexico in the nineteenth and twentieth centuries. Others went to Yucatán. There they found refuge among the Frenchmen and pirates who used the small inlets and coves along the coast line. Many of these sailors were Lutherans and were glad to aid the Jews.

Guatemala and parts of Oaxaca were also islands of safety from inquisitorial detection. Many Catholics also were glad to aid in the defeat of the Tribunal. Chapman wrote of the seventeenth century, "few periods of history more clearly illustrate the distinction between Catholicism as a religious faith and the Catholic [Spanish] Church as an institution, a difference which the people of the United States do not readily grasp."[10]

The Carvajal family did not end with the martyrdom of Ana in 1649. In 1652, Leonor de Cáceres was alive and was again arrested. She was the daughter of Catalina, one of the Carvajal daughters burned in 1596. Leonor had been reconciled in 1601. Her father Antonio had gone to Spain, but she lived in Tulancingo, eighty-eight miles from Mexico, where she was arrested in 1652. She had told her confessor that she had followed some Jewish practices between 1596 and 1598 but had not informed the inquisitors of this at her hearings in 1600. He had instructed her to convey this information to the Holy Office. She complied and her arrest followed. In June, 1653, she was ordered to be released and her property returned. Pedro de Medina Rico stated that this was done without notification to the senior fiscal and implied that a bribe was paid. A reading of her testimony in 1652 and 1653 clearly indicates that she was a devout Catholic and slightly senile.

The prelates of the Church were increasing their efforts to inflame the people against the Jews and other heretics, but the power of the Church to do so was on the wane. Francisco Corchero Carreno, who accompanied Treviño de Sobremonte to the pyre in an effort to have him kiss the cross, was chaplain of the royal prison. He wrote a book in 1649, *Desagravios de Cristo en el Triunfo de Su Cruz contra el Judaismo*, Christ's Satisfaction in the Triumph of His Cross against Judaism.[11] This book paled into insignificance in comparison with *Centinela contra Judios* by Fray de Torrejoncillos. The latter book was originally published in 1673 and was reprinted in 1728 and 1731. Its style is infantile and the literary quality is deplorable. As Lea commented, "in this popular exposition of Christian rancor, no story is too wild and unnatural to be worthy of credence." The book also states that 124,000 Jewish families left Spain in 1492 due to the Decree of Expulsion and quotes Dr. Velazquez for the figure of 420,000 people, of whom 20,000 families went to Portugal. Only a few were affected by these books, however, because the writings of the new thinkers in Europe were being read in New Spain.

Clement Motten wrote that many are not aware that in the seventeenth and eighteenth centuries Mexico was a metropolis with a high degree of culture which must be measured "not on a per capita basis but on its quality, and Europe failed to do this . . . Mexican intellectual leaders had occasion to cry out against European preoccupation with New World barbarism rather than its cultural achievements."[12] A people known as Mexican had begun to emerge in the viceroyalty. They had begun to develop resentments against the mother country, which was more of a stepmother than a fond parent. The Mexican equated Spain with the Church. While foreigners in the country legally were few, there were many who came illegally to trade.

Spain was growing weaker and weaker. In 1665 and 1667, it made treaties with England that abolished Spain's right to inspect English boats in Spanish ports or to search the houses of British subjects. In 1680, the French ambassador estimated that there were about 120,000 foreigners working in Spain.[13] Some of these foreigners traveled to New Spain and Peru.

Some of the Jews sentenced to exile made their way to the West Indies, especially those islands under British dominion. There were persons named Francisco López Díaz in Jamaica and Barbados respectively in 1670.[14] Cyrus Adler, in his article, "Jews in the American Plantations Between 1600 and 1700," gives a list of "persons of quality; emigrants; religious exiles, etc.," who were in Barbados about 1680.[15] Though mindful of the criticism leveled against those who hang theories on the similarities of patronymics, it must be noted that the names of Núñez, Díaz, Rodríguez, Sousa, Medina, López, Valurede, Mercado, Serrano, Gómez, Antunes, Navarro, and Pacheco appear in the West Indies list, and that there were people in New Spain with identical family names. The people in Barbados bearing these names were all Jews. Adler's article reports that those named in his list were immigrants to the thirteen colonies in North America. Some of these people were escapees from the Inquisition, so that they or their descendants were among the early Jewish settlers of the United States. Those who were not escapees were related to and had dealings with the Jews in New Spain. Evidence exists of trade and commerce between the Jews of New Spain and the Jews of the Dutch and English Caribbean colonies.

The article, "A Review of the Jewish Colonists in Barbados"[16] supplies additional presumptive proof of a relationship and communication or an identification of the Jews of New Spain with those of the Caribbean area. Daniel Bueno Henríques of Jamaica came from Seville but is also referred to as a Portuguese; he was one of the four sons of Pedro Henríques of Medina del Rio Seco of Castile. Many Jews in New Spain also came from Medina del Rio Seco. In the sixteenth and seventeenth centuries it was rare to find Jews who came from the same place and were not kinsmen. In his report of June 11, 1681, Governor Sir Richard Dutton wrote from Barbados, "There are about 260 Jews, men, women and children, either born on the Island or made denizens by royal letters patent." Many of these either immigrated or were children of immigrants from either Brazil or New Spain.

Others who fled New Spain made their way to Cayenne or Curaçao where relatives lived and haven could be found. In Curaçao, we find that Joseph Núñez de Fonseca was burned in 1652 and Abraham Haim López in 1671.[17] Gaspar Rodríguez fled to Curaçao and then to Amsterdam. Gonzalo Pérez Ferro and Antonio Machado found their way to Martinique from New Spain.

In 1656, as a result of the efforts of Menasseh ben Israel, a Dutch rabbi, England, under Cromwell, "connived" at the settlement and return of the Jews. The crypto-Jews of the Iberian Peninsula began to move north into Holland and England because in those lands merchants and financiers could practice their trades free of the Inquisition and the Spanish Church, and these two nations had assumed supremacy in international trade. This movement contributed to the approaching isolation of New World Jewry from the world stream of Jewish life.

Many Mexican Jews had abandoned the viceregal seat and other places where they had congregated in large numbers. Many established themselves in the interior provinces. Their contacts with the foreigners who visited the capital became more infrequent. Having left Veracruz, they ceased being a factor in international trade. They were content to live inconspicuously and unostentatiously in areas remote from the active interest of the Holy Office or its agents.

Sabbatai Zevi, who had proclaimed himself the Messiah in 1648, had created a great turmoil in European Jewish life. Tens of thousands believed in him. Manasseh ben Israel mentioned him in his correspondence with Cromwell and advanced the Messiah's arrival as one of the reasons that England should open the doors to the return of the Jews. Many Jews began to sell their businesses and liquidate their affairs so as to join Zevi's entourage and accompany him on his expected triumphal return to the Holy Land. When the Sultan offered him the choice of death or conversion to Islam in 1660, he chose the latter, thereby disillusioning the majority of his followers and exposing the falsity of his messianic pretensions.

Dr. Jacob Petuchowski, in quoting from Nahum Sokolow's book *Spinoza and His Time*,[18] wrote that Sokolow did well "in stressing the fact that the pivotal point of Marrano resistance to full conversion to Christianity was their belief that the Messiah had not yet come . . . If the Messiah had come, all their suffering would be in vain. On the other hand, if He were still expected, there would be purpose in their suffering." As a result of the great disillusionment with Sabbatai Zevi, many left Judaism. Others concentrated on their own financial affairs and sought free lands and new opportunities.

The Italian city-states were losing their places of primacy in commerce and as banking centers. At the same time eastern European Jewish communities, as well as those of the German states, were attaining importance as centers of learning and religion. Many of their leaders had scoffed at Sabbatai Zevi's claims. As a result of these and other factors, there was an exodus from southern Europe to Holland and the British Isles. It also marked the onset of the supplanting in numbers and importance of Sephardic Jewry by Ashkenazi Jewry.

The almost imperceptible signs of a rift between these two groups appeared. There was no bond between Ashkenazi Jewry of eastern Europe and the Sephardic crypto-Jews of the New World. The European and Turkish Sephardic Jews, noted for their Iberian trait of individualism, thought less and less of their overseas brethren and became preoccupied with their own problems and interests. Spain was the enemy of England and Holland. Nationalism was sweeping the civilized world, and citizens of nations began to experience the new emotion of patriotism. The Jew, like all other people, became a citizen of his new nation. He developed political loyalties which transcended religious ties. The Arabs have an adage, "The friend of my friend is my friend and the enemy of my friend is my enemy." Likewise, Jews who became citizens of Holland and England viewed Spaniards in general with distrust. The Jews in New Spain began to be a forgotten people.

THE VISITATION OF PEDRO DE MEDINA RICO

Prior to April 11, 1649, the inquisitors had received a letter from Spain advising them that the families of Simón Váez Sevilla, Tomas Treviño de Sobremonte, and Tomas Núñez Peralta were considered to be friends of those at the royal court. It is obvious that the inquisitors were being told discretely that their judgments against these people should be tempered with an unusual amount of mercy. The letter was conveniently misplaced. This act and the punishments administered to members of the three families supplied additional incentive to the Suprema's desire to thoroughly investigate the New World branch, which had begun to act as if it were autonomous.

A few years before 1649, the Suprema had decided to review the actions of the inquisitors of New Spain, beginning with the administration of Alonso de Peralta. In 1645 they appointed Archbishop Juan de Manozca as a visitador with complete powers. He was a first cousin of the inquisitor Saenz de Manozca, one of the three in the Tribunal at that time. In spite of his desire to be loyal to his cousin, the archbishop could not refrain from reporting that Edicts of Faith had not been read in many places for over twenty years and that everything was in the control of the Jews. One illustration of the relationship between the Holy Office personnel and Jews was the con-

siderate treatment accorded to relatives of Simón Váez by the notary of the Holy Office as a result of special friendship or bribery.

The proceedings against many employees of the Tribunal ultimately revealed that they were selling the secrets of the Holy Office, carrying messages to and from the secret cells, and completely
ignoring any pretense of prison discipline. It was the obvious disregard of instructions from Spain which gave impetus to the Suprema
on May 9, 1651, to order Pedro de Medina Rico (then in Cartagena
on another investigation), to go to New Spain.

He started his work in Mexico in 1654 and uncovered so much
incriminating data that he feared for his life. He accused three inquisitors, Pedro Saenz y Manozca, Bernabe de la Higuera y Amarilla, Francisco de Estrada y Escobedo, and their attorneys and notaries of thousands of crimes, including misfeasance, malfeasance,
stealing, subornation of perjury, incontinency, rigging the auction
sales of prisoners' property so that they could acquire it for themselves, borrowing and not repaying loans, living ostentatiously, bribery, and last, but not least, almost 100 charges against the inquisitors
in matters of faith. Bernabe de la Higuera had lived with two female
slaves, a Negro and a mulatto. He had lived openly with the mulatto
for over twenty years, during which time she had borne him eight
children.[19]

Among the charges was that of permitting Catalina de Campos,
an eighty-five year old Jewess, to die in her cell and her body to be
eaten by rats. She had asked for medical aid and had requested to be
reconciled. The inquisitors had ignored her pleas. They had likewise ignored many other canons of the Holy Office. They had never
permitted prisoners to prove their defenses. No witness was ever
called for a defendant nor was a deposition taken of anyone who
could corroborate any defense. In 1654, 1,200 legal suits were pending by creditors of Jews against the Tribunal arising from confiscations. The punishments meted out by the Suprema to the inquisitors
do not compare with what they had meted out to others. For example, Juan Saenz de Manozca was fined 1,300 pesos and suspended for
nine years but within two years was named Bishop of Cuba; Estrade
y Escobedo was fined 100 pesos, suspended for two years, and
barred from ever again serving the Inquisition. Higuera y Amarilla
was directed to cease living with his mistresses, was fined 100 pesos,
and suspended as an inquisitor for two years.

Although Pedro de Medina Rico was unsparing in his accusations against the officials of the Holy Office of Mexico, this should not imply that he himself was above reproach. His assignment to investigate and judge did not expire until May 17, 1662, when he pronounced his verdict. During that time, an elaborate auto-da-fé was held on October 8, 1659, in which one of those burned was Don Guillen de Lamport. The Suprema had expressly ordered that he was not to be relaxed. De Medina Rico was present at the auto and saw those sentenced to be burned. He could have prevented the "wild Irishman" from going to the stake, but he did not. When the Suprema learned of Don Guillen's execution, they wanted to know the reason for this action. A year later, a noncommittal reply was sent. Not until 1667 were transcripts of his proceso sent to the Suprema.

The book-length report of de Medina Rico reveals that in hundreds of cases involving Jews the testimony of many witnesses could not be found. Many names of Jews, otherwise not known, are learned through this source, and additional facets of Jewish life are disclosed.

THE AUTO-DA-FÉ OF 1659

From 1651 to 1659, no Jews appeared in any auto-da-fé except Jorge de Espinosa, who had been reconciled in Lima on January 23, 1639. He escaped from his captors while being transported to Spain, and found haven in one of the English Caribbean colonies. Despite his safety there, he came to New Spain, dropped his old name of Jorge Serrano, and eventually became the vicemayor of Cuatzaculco. His proceso is missing from the Mexican National Archives; his name does not appear in the Abecedario, and his ultimate fate is unknown.

In the auto-da-fé of 1659, four Jews were penanced—one woman and three men, two of whom were burned alive. One of the men was Luis Pérez Roldan, who was a fencing master. (To indicate the deficiencies of the Abecedario, his name does not appear among those penanced in 1649 or 1659.) In 1649 he had been condemned to 200 lashes, perpetual wearing of the sanbenito, and life imprisonment in Spain. He was known to the Inquisition as one of the most audacious and learned Jews. He was a brother-in-law of Treviño de Sobremonte and related to Duarte de León Jaramillo. Despite being ordered to do so, he had not left New Spain after the auto-da-fé of 1649.

After his rearrest about 1656, he admitted that he had discarded the sanbenito but explained that if he wore it he could not earn a livelihood selling thread made from the agave plant or giving dueling lessons. He received 100 lashes and was sentenced again to life imprisonment and placed in jail, from which place he was to be exiled on the first possible occasion. Again there is no record of his arrival in Spain. More interesting than his punishment is his brazenness in engaging in occupations in New Spain which were public and which would bring him into contact with important people. Seventeenth century mestizos, slaves, and ordinary people were not engaging fencing instructors, and a fencing instructor could not peddle thread surreptitiously. Since he did not leave New Spain, several members of his family also remained.

María de Zarate lived in Tacubaya, a town adjacent to Mexico, with her husband Francisco Botello, who had been reconciled in El Gran Auto, lashed, and sentenced to exile. He was another who did not leave. For seven years, 1642 to 1649, he had been in the secret cells and was grilled and tortured, but he had consistently denied being a Jew or knowing any Jews. Both his parents had been imprisoned by the Inquisition in Cordoba but released under the general pardon of 1605. Francisco's uncles, aunts, and cousins had been convicted of being Jews in autos of 1635, 1646, 1647, and 1648. In fact, over thirty of his relatives in Mexico were admitted Jews. His cousin, Isabel Núñez (burned in 1649), testified concerning him that "if he lost all the Judaism he had, he would still remain a Jew," because he was so fine a Jew and Judaism was so inbred in him. He had been known as Pilar during his first incarceration. He was overheard by an Inquisition spy stating that he felt neither weakness nor hunger when he fasted but rather great strength, consolation, and happiness, which he interpreted as acceptance by the God of Israel. He prayed three times daily, standing erect, with a cap on his head and his arms at his sides. He had also stressed the fact to María that their children had to be taught Judaism lest they fall into error.

Botello's defense for not leaving New Spain was that he was penniless and, besides, he denied all the charges and statements against him. He was sixty-five years old when he was burned on November 19, 1659, with his wife being forced to watch the execution. (There is a discrepancy between the proceso and the relación by Rodríguez Ruis de Zepeda Martínez as to whether he received the garrote. The proceso indicates that he did, but Ruiz de Zepeda and Medina fail to mention it.)

María de Zarate was in the same auto and was fined 1,000 pesos and sentenced to serve four years as a nurse in a hospital. María had been tortured, the cords having been turned twice on her legs and four times on her arms. She endured this torture for an hour. Her difficulties had been caused by her half-brother, José de Sanchez, who had appeared voluntarily to denounce her and one of her slaves. He was the illegitimate son of her father and a servant. María, who was well versed in the Bible and Jewish law, had raised him, but he was more Catholic than Jewish. The slave whom he denounced was Luis de la Cruz, who had carried messages from María to her husband, Francisco, while he was in jail prior to 1649. Her proceso refers to a curious practice that existed in New Spain. Stockings were manufactured on which a representation of Christ was placed on the sole, making the normal use of the stockings a desecration of Christ. Handkerchiefs also were so made, and the manufacture and use of both had been condemned by the Church. It may be deduced from María's proceso that Jews had been engaged in the manufacture and sale of these forbidden items.

Diego Díaz also resided in Tacubaya. His wife, Ana Gómez, was burned in the 1649 auto-da-fé. He had been in the same auto but only had to abjure and was sentenced to exile. He was apprehended in 1652 and burned alive in 1659 when he was eighty years old. During his second trial, he also denied being a Jew. At the stake, one of the functionaries began to apply the garrote but was stopped because Díaz refused to kiss the cross. When one of padres pleaded with him to kiss it, because it was the instrument of his salvation, he replied, "Stop, Padre, that stick can't save anybody." Díaz was only half-dead from the partial application of the garrote when they set him afire.

This auto had another impenitent heretic, who, although non-Jewish, rebuffed the cross and said, "Friend, if there is a hell, there we will have friends with whom we can spend our time." The relación states that 40,000 spectators lined the streets to watch the procession to the stake. Included in this vast, motley crowd were Negro, Oriental, and Indian slaves.

The investigations of visitador Pedro de Medina Rico had a deterring effect on later inquisitors since it seemed better to do nothing than to risk censure. Autos-da-fé became infrequent and the few held ceased to be as spectacular as those of the past.

There were also several acquittals. One of the most famous personages accused of *judaísmo* in the seventeenth century was Bernardo López de Mendizabal, governor of the province of what is now the state of New Mexico.[20] He was a descendant of Juan Núñez de León, who had been convicted of Judaism, but Mendizabal was not a Jew.[21] There is no question but that the Inquisition was used by the clergy of New Mexico with whom the governor had been quarreling in order to harass him.

In 1667, Baltazar Pereyra, a fifty year old Portuguese, abjured and was fined 2,000 pesos "applied to expenses of the Holy Office."[22] It was his second arrest on the suspicion of being a Jew.

Diego de Alvarado, alias Muñoz, was a traveling salesman. Born in Peru in 1625, he resided in Puebla for many years and was an observer of the Law of Moses. He died in the secret cells in 1688.

Jorge Jacinto Bazan's name appears in 1667. The royal treasury sought to recover from him the dowry which he had received from his wife, Blanca Juárez. Jacinto had been ordered to be exiled in 1647.

In 1678, the Portuguese Antonio Lorenzo, also known as Francisco de Medina, was sent from Manila to the Holy Office in Mexico because he was a Jew. The letter of transmittal states that there were several other Jews in Manila. The prisoner was fifty-eight years old and had been punished for judaizante at San Benitado, Portugal. His uncle, Manuel Suarez Olivera, a Jew, had died in the Philippines.

Pedro Serrano, alias Pedro Antonio Serrano (known as Isaac Jacobo among the Jews), was born and circumcized in France. He had been reconciled by the Inquisition in Llerena, Spain, for Judaism. Although he was a second offender, he was only fined one-fourth of his property, plus payment of his debts and the cost of food and expenses while in jail. He was banished to Spain.

The case of Pedro Carretero, in 1696, involved six others. Carretero, alias Pedro de la Vega, was a tailor born in Tlaxcala. He received 200 lashes and was sentenced to serve six years in the Philippine galleys without pay, followed by a jail sentence in New Spain.

The last person to be burned alive in the seventeenth century was Fernando de Medina, alias Fernando de Medina y Merida, alias Alberto Moises Gomes, a Jew. Born in Bordeaux, France, he was thirty-five years old when he was arrested in 1691 for "Jewish practices and for being an observer of the Law of Moses." He had spent twelve years in Spain before coming to Mexico in 1687.[23] He was an observant Jew. Eight years of incarceration did not break him down or cause him to testify against others. There were several other Jews before the Tribunal during the last decade of the seventeenth century. Two of them were in the same auto-da-fé with Fernando de Medina, but they escaped the pyre.

Simón Luis de Herrera y Enríquez, alias Luis de Herrera, was born in Seville and had been reconciled by the Sevillano Tribunal. When he was fifty years old he was apprehended in New Spain for continuing Jewish practices and admitted the truth of the charges. He had to abjure, pay a fine of one-fourth of the property plus his debts and jail expenses, and return to Spain for life imprisonment. At this time the Inquisition rarely resorted to torture *in caput alienum* and displayed no great interest in ascertaining the identity or existence of other Jews in New Spain.

Whether it was due to coincidence or other causes, at the close of the seventeenth century many Jews owned stores in Mexico on the Calle de los Plateros (now Avenida de Francisco I. Madero); in Palma, Majorca, there was also a Calle de los Plateros where crypto-Jews (there called *Chuetas*) owned many shops.

The Inquisition in New Spain by now had lost its initiative in the prosecution of Jews or its power had been reduced by the Suprema. Support for the foregoing is found in the denunciation made on July 21, 1694, by Antonio Silbera y Cardoso against the baker, Manuel de Sossa y Prado.[24] Silbera y Cardoso was a friend of the baker; both were Portuguese. The grounds for the charge that Sossa y Prado was a Jew were substantial, detailed, and not based on hearsay or suppositions, but the Inquisition did nothing. It did not even call corroborating witnesses. The next entry in the file of the accused is a copy of a letter dated May 19, 1696, almost two years later, written by the inquisitors Don Juan Gómez de Mier and Don Juan de Armejo y Ron to the Suprema in Spain stating that they enclosed the lengthy denunciation and requesting advice on what steps to take.

The new century brought the Bourbon dynasty to the Spanish throne, and the Bourbons were to regard the Inquisition more as a political than a religious office.

14

From Faith to Superstition:
1700-1821

AT THE Sephardi Leadership Conference at Yeshiva University, New York City, on February 21, 1965, Haham Dr. Solomon Gaon, Chief Sephardi Rabbi of the British Commonwealth, stated: "The tragic quality of independence and disunity among Sephardic Jews resulted in not only the weakening of Sephardic influence on world Jewry, but also the gradual and consistent decline of spiritual and religious standards." These words succinctly describe the transformation of colonial Jewry in the last century of New Spain's existence.

In 1700, the last Spanish monarch of the Habsburg dynasty died without heirs. This precipitated the War of Spanish Succession waged among the nations supporting the various contenders to the throne. Finally, Louis XIV of France succeeded in placing his grandson on the Spanish throne. This inaugurated the Bourbon dynasty, which endured beyond the era with which this book is concerned.

The new King, Philip V (1700-1746), "cared only for hunting and praying . . . and was born to be ruled by someone else."[1] He was seventeen years of age when he ascended to the throne and spent the ensuing years in debauchery and immorality, which induced a melancholia and neuroticism that bordered on insanity. He was greatly influenced by his French advisors.

Under the Treaty of Utrecht of 1713, Spain ceded Gibraltar and the island of Minorca and other territories in the Mediterranean to England. Spain also relinquished the monopoly of importing Negro slaves into her American colonies. Furthermore, Philip's reign was marked by constant warfare that bankrupted his nation's treasury and further whittled away her empire. During the War of Jenkin's Ear (1739-1746) the English attacked even the Spanish colonies, raiding Acapulco and other Pacific Coast settlements of New Spain. Spain's entry into the American Revolutionary War on the side of the colonies resulted in a fiasco for Spain. Although the Americans gained their independence and their Spanish allies regained Minorca and Florida under the treaty signed at Versailles on September 3, 1783, the United States acquired most of Spain's possessions within a few decades thereafter.

Philip's attitude toward the Inquisition may be surmised by his refusal to attend an auto-da-fé upon his accession.[2] Although he considered the Inquisition necessary, he decided to terminate it as an *imperium in imperio*. His successors, Ferdinand VI and Charles III, had a similar policy. The eighteenth century inquisitors became wary and more lenient in order to retain what power and authority they still had.[3]

During the eighteenth century, the criollos and mestizos of New Spain enjoyed economic prosperity. The Mexicans began to throw off the remaining vestiges of loyalty to the mother country. Not only were new political concepts acquired, but new, liberal, and nonreligious attitudes toward the Church also were adopted. The Church became institutionalized and its hold remained strong only on the people in the rural areas. There was a direct relationship between ignorance or lack of education and religious fervor or blind acceptance. In the urban areas, atheism, Freemasonry, Protestantism, and agnosticism took firm root.

The Church had grown lax and its clergy even more venal than formerly. The actions of Catholic women of that era attest to these facts. The numbers of women who dared to report to the Inquisition the solicitation for sexual purposes during confession by friars and clergy during the eighteenth century run into the hundreds. Just as it has been noted previously that the number of Jews unearthed by the Holy Office constituted only an insignificant percentage of the total number present in New Spain, so can it be said that the recorded number of Inquisition cases *por solicitante de sus hijas espirituales* (for solicitation of his spiritual daughters) is only a fraction of the total number.[4] Obviously, it took a woman of extraordinary courage to accuse her confessor of such a violation of clerical conduct. That so many did is indicative of the low state to which the spiritual leaders had fallen. Many priests married or lived in concubinage. Although belief in the Church and its spiritual efficacy continued, awe and respect for the spiritual officiants were lost.

The laxity and diminishing activities of the Inquisition may be judged by the fact that the reading of the Edict of Faith in Puebla in 1713 was the first such event since 1656. In 1715, Philip V decreed that a *visita* was to be made again of the Inquisition in New Spain, and Don Francisco Gazzaron was appointed as visitador. His signature appears on the new forms of the edict, which were a compendium rather than a detailed listing of the religious practices of the various heretical groups, including Jews. There was only one sentence pertaining to Judaism; it read:

> Especially if you know or have heard said that some one or more persons has observed or is observing the Law of Moses or has performed any ceremonies as an observance of it or have said that the Law is good.

Besides being a greatly decreased description, the last few words were a significant innovation. Many had begun to evidence an intellectual interest in Judaism. These people were not necessarily Jews nor were they thinking of converting to Judaism, but they ceased to look upon it as "the dead Law of Moses." They also did not regard Jews as pariahs.

Don Francisco Gazzaron served as an inquisitor as well as visitador, but even he did not seem to investigate all denunciations. In 1721, a denunciation was sent directly to him from Puebla. It involved an Irishman, Juan Guillermo, accused of heresy and Jewish practices. The practices were nonreligious, the principal act consisted of putting a cross in the heel of a shoe. There is no record of any action being taken by inquisitor Gazzaron.

According to Hubert Howe Bancroft, the total population of Mexico in 1695 was about 140,000, "of whom the Spaniards and the mixed races formed but a small proportion."[5] The Jews could not have exceeded five percent of the Spaniards as against an estimate of twenty to twenty-five percent fifty years earlier. The decline in the Jewish population in the regal seat was due to the establishment of the Jews in the northern part of New Spain, in Yucatán, and in the Guadalajara area. Some had departed to settle in the Caribbean islands or Curaçao and Surinam.

By 1680, Judaism in Spain seems to have resolved itself into keeping the Sabbath, occasional fasting, hoping to be saved through the Law of Moses, and denying Christ and Christian doctrine.[6] In the Lisbon auto-da-fé of September 6, 1705, the Archbishop of Crangnon, noting the lack of learning among many Jews, started his sermon to the Jews to be penanced with these words:

> Miserable relics of Judaism! Unhappy fragments of the synagogue; Last remnants of Judea! Scandal of the Catholics and detestable objects of scorn to the Jews, for you are so ignorant that you cannot observe the very law under which you live.[7]

Henry C. Lea's comment on the foregoing was that the "hammer was gradually wearing away the anvil." Blind faith alone was not sufficient to keep Judaism alive, except in individual cases. The study of their religion by the Jews of New Spain was almost nonexistent. Some of the Jews in the eighteenth century who had the financial means went to Jamaica or Barbados for synagogue or holy day observance, a custom similar to the Moslem *haj*. What the Holy Office had been unable to accomplish by torture and flame, they began to achieve by two other methods.

The first was a prohibition of the Talmud and other books of learning. The prohibition was not new but a more rigid enforcement was. For forty-six years (1690-1736) there had been no search for prohibited books in the ships coming from Manila.[8] Many heretical books had entered the viceroyalty from the Philippines. As late as 1740, Bibles in Spanish, Portuguese, Dutch, German, and Persian were exported from Manila to Mexico.[9] One shipment being caught would not mean that others did not get through. This was one of the underlying weaknesses in Spanish colonial administration—the chasm between rules and the enforcement of rules, between theory and practice.

In 1707, there was issued the "Reglas, Mandatos y Advertencias Generales del *Novissimus Librorum et Expurgandorum Index;* Pro Catholicis Hispanorum Regnis, Philip V, Reg. Cath." Rule XIV pertained to the Talmud and other books of the rabbis and Hebrews. All books were excluded: every class of commentary and any books of Jews which taught Jewish law *(la ley Judaica)* or its ceremonies. Writings pertaining to Islam were also excluded, but that did not appear in the headnote. The last paragraph repeated the general prohibition, then mentioned specifically:

> Histories or grammars, the Massorite and the *Masora Magna,* y *Parva* . . . printed by Juan Buxtorsio; the Hebrew concordance of Rabbi Mordecai Nathan and such works as philosophy, etc., translated in Latin by Sebastiano Munstero de Elias Levita, Rabbi Salomon, R. David Kinhi [*sic* - correct name is Kimchi], et al; the Book of the Origins [Raizes] of R. David; el *Ductor Dubitantium* [Guide to Perplexed] by R. Moses Egypt [*sic.* - the author was Moses ben Maimon, known as Maimonides] and all such books even though they do not treat with religion nor of the Jewish sect nor of its ceremonies.

Dra. Perez-Marchand's book in which the foregoing is quoted in Spanish is based on the Inquisition documents in the Mexican National Archives. She wrote of the eighteenth century forces which fought the Inquisition in New Spain and the tremendous irregularities in its administration. During that century, Judaism had fallen to the state of being a minor concern of the inquisitors. Their two primary problems were the inroads of several Protestant sects and the importation of prohibited books. Then came the immorality of the various monastic orders and the difficulties of the Holy Office with monastic orders. The Bethlemites had become the enemy of the Inquisition toward the end of the previous century. The Inquisition as a political arm of the throne was concerned with the Jesuits, who were finally expelled from all the Spanish dominions in 1767.

With respect to problems of research in Inquisition records Dra. Perez-Marchand wrote, "Everything confirms our suspicions about the loss of volumes from the Archivo General de la Nación or the irregularities in handling them or in greater defects in the functioning of the Holy Office . . ."[10]

The incompetency of the Inquisition officials in the areas distant from Mexico further impeded the effectiveness of the Holy Office. This explains in part why the Jews of Nuevo León and its capital, Monterrey, lived free of molestation. This was a second partial cause of the undoing of their attachment to their faith. This freedom lasted for over 100 years and contributed to Jewish assimilation. Many of the leading families that are now Catholic or Protestant are descended from the crypto-Jews who came to Monterrey, Linares, and other towns beginning about 1640. These Jews aided in making Nuevo León the leading, most progressive of the twenty-nine states of modern Mexico. One of the most illustrious members of the Garza family of Monterrey made a generous donation to the Jewish community center when it was erected in this century because his ancestors had been practicing Jews in Monterrey. One of the former governors of Campeche, Licenciado Luis MacGregor, stated that his great-grandparents were Jews in that state.

Dr. Frank Brandenburg, in *The Making of Modern Mexico*,[11] wrote of "Catholic Jews," "Jewish Catholics," and "Sephardic Jews who kept coming to New Spain and independent Mexico, 'Catholicized' or not." He (and this author) have been shown source material and proof of Jewish ancestry, dating from the pre-Independence era, of modern Christian families who wish to remain anonymous.

There are legends about Neuvo León. The words mean "new lion," and one story has it that it represented the Lion of Judah as a symbol of Governor Luis de Carvajal. This may be far-fetched, because the governor was not a Jew. Moreover, since many other Mexican provinces were named for provinces in Spain: Nueva Viscaya, Nueva Granada, Galicia, etc., it is more likely that the name came from Spain. Another legend is that the town of Jujutla in Nuevo León means Jehudah or Juda. There is a legend among people of the state that when the crypto-Jews went to mass or participated in a Christian service they had a unique method of secretly crossing their fingers.

An American consul in February, 1960, in his "Post Report" from Monterrey to Washington, D.C., named fifteen of the prominent families who had Jewish ancestors and stated that the Monterrey inhabitants were called "the Jews of the North" even though their families had been Christians for over a hundred years. The people from Monterrey had not found baptism any more effective in secreting their ancestry than the Jewish converts of the thirteenth and fourteenth centuries had found the holy chrism.

Among the "Jews of the North" could be added the ancestor of President (1910-1911) Francisco I. Madero. His family came to New Spain in the eighteenth century, reputedly from the Madeira Islands, and settled in the state of Coahuila, which is adjacent to Nuevo León. According to Howard F. Cline, "Some of the Apostle's ancestors were of Portuguese-Jewish stock who prospered in the State of Coahuila."[12]

An illustration of the difficulty of forgetting one's forebears is found in an epilogue to the Carvajal story. Leonor de Cáceres was the daughter of Catalina, niece of Luis, and granddaughter of Francisca Núñez Carvajal. In 1688, one of her grandsons was in a minor order of the clergy. He went to the Inquisition to secure a copy of his grandmother's testimony because he felt that he could not be elevated to the post of presbyter without proof of his own purity of Catholic lineage. His petition was denied.

In 1706, a great-grandson went to the Holy Office because his neighbor in Tulancingo was accusing him of having bad blood— namely, accusing him of being a descendant of Jews. The inquisitors directed that he submit proof of his great-grandmother's good Catholic conduct. José de la Rosa, the great-grandson, submitted seven affidavits of clergy and prominent laymen who had known Leonor. All of them attested to her devotion to the Church. In addition, she had studied a medical book by a Dr. Farfan, memorized prescriptions, and ministered to the poor.

The inquisitors ordered that a certificate be issued stating that Leonor de Cáceres had been reconciled in 1601 and that no evidence had been found against her or her husband, López Núñez. Two of her grandchildren had become Franciscan monks, a daughter had entered a monastery after becoming a widow, and one grandchild and one great grandson had become presbyters. But gossipy neighbors would not let the descendants forget that once upon a time they had Jewish antecedents.

In 1965, this author went to Tulancingo armed with the family names of four generations of descendants of Leonor de Cáceres. No living kin could be located. No record except that of the cemetery exists of Carvajal descendants.

Freedom from religious persecution existed in the extreme south, especially in Guatemala and Yucatán. About 1750, Ricardo Ossado lived in Valladolid, Yucatán. He wrote an outstanding book and several monographs on Mayan herbs and diseases, with a translation into Spanish of the Mayan terms. His book was called *El Libro del Judío*. It is said that he was an Italian and his original name was Juan Francisco Mayali. Some claim that the term "judío" did not necessarily indicate his faith. Howard Cline contends that the natives and others used the term judío for anyone who knew herbs, medicines, and illnesses. If no Jews lived among them, however, judío would have been a meaningless term as it still is today in much of the hinterlands of Mexico and even within parts of the Federal District. Some say that Ossado fled Yucatán because he feared the Inquisition. José Ignacio Rubio Mañé, a Yucatecan and director of Archivo General, subscribes to this theory. Others say that Ossado died in Yucatán on May 27, 1770. One person inferred "that he was called Jew, not because he had ceased to be a Catholic (no proof exists that he was) but because the common people had the bad habit of so calling all strangers . . ." This person did not know that many Jews lived on the peninsula before, during, and after the eighteenth century.

The freedom from religious persecution, lack of learning and proper spiritual guidance, and divorce or isolation from Jewish centers of population in other lands made it inevitable that this minority ethnic or religious group would dissolve or assimilate into the majority.

On May 27, 1783, the Suprema ordered the Holy Office in New Spain not to imprison Jews or to sequester their property, seemingly without direct cause.[13] The Suprema's retraction of its order years later was meaningless. Dom José I of Portugal in 1773 had abolished all differences of treatment between his subjects regardless of faith. The inquisitors wrote the Suprema earlier than 1783 that they were overworked, that they could not find people to work for them, that many positions in the provinces were vacant, and that they were understaffed in their own offices. They beseeched an increase in their emoluments. In 1767 a rumor swept through Mexico that the Inquisition was to be abolished.[14]

Jews were coming into New Spain as soldiers and as merchants. G. Baez Camargo wrote that at the end of the eighteenth century,

Charles III, an enlightened monarch, authorized the merchants of Cartagena to import foreign merchandise. This brought into the Spanish colonies an influx of Danish and Dutch non-Catholic merchants, Protestants from other countries, and many Jews.[15] The faith of some of the French soldiers was revealed at their trials by their having been circumcised. There were a few who had escaped from the Inquisition at Lima and thought that they could find safety in New Spain.

The cases at the beginning of the century were concerned with residents of Puebla, Guadalajara, Veracruz, Guanajato, Oaxaca, and other areas.[16] There was one former Bethlemite who had been expelled from his order for being a Jew. He was reconciled but was caught thereafter and burned in 1712 because he had relapsed. Among those accused of Jewish practices were the mayor of Panuco and Tampico; the mayor of Tecali, Don Jose de Cardenas; an army scout; various gachupines; the attorney for the royal court; a surgeon, and army officers.[17] One of the cases was that of a merchant, Don Agustin de Espinola, who went to Kingston, Jamaica, and while there attended the synagogue. Unfortunately for him, he was seen by a Mexican who denounced him to the Holy Office. His punishment was light.

There is a denunciation by Don Antonio Deonicio Garrote of New Veracruz.[18] Don Antonio reported that Captain Don Andres Verdejo told him that there were Jews in the city who were mocking the Catholic religion although they were living as Catholics to dissimulate their real beliefs. No investigation was made of this denunciation, which was based on hearsay. Since hearsay evidence had always been acceptable to the Tribunal and since other names appear in the denunciation, the lack of effort or attempt to verify the statement is indicative of the flagging interest in Jews by the Holy Office.

The final case of a Mexican Jew prior to independence in 1821 was that of a circumcised Franciscan monk, Rafael Cristano Gil Rodríguez, who was serving his order in Guatemala. He was sixty-six years old and had been born in Antigua, Guatemala. He was arrested in 1788 and subsequently convicted of being a circumcised practitioner of Jewish rites and an aider and concealer of heretics.[19] He was to be burned at the stake in 1795, but, minutes before the event, he begged for mercy and promised to repent. He was re-

Plaza de Santo Domingo where autos-da-fé were held for over 100 years. Now called the Plaza de Corregidora. House of the Inquisition on the right (arrow)

manded to the secret cells. The Inquisition was abolished in 1813 and reestablished in 1814, but Gil Rodríguez was not released in the intervening period. He was finally freed in 1821 by Captain Llop, when Mexico attained its independence and terminated the Mexican Tribunal forever. He was the last person found in the secret cells.

Although Gil Rodríguez was the last Jew to be tried, the last person to have the charge of judaizante leveled against him was Padre José María Hidalgo y Costilla, the "George Washington of Mexico." The curate began the revolt against the representatives of Spain who had placed Joseph Bonaparte on the throne in place of the rightful monarch, Ferdinand VII. Padre Hidalgo was accused by the Inquisition of Lutheranism, atheism, libertinism (he did have children), Judaism, and of attacking the story of the Immaculate Conception, as well as several other crimes. The Church defrocked him after his capture in 1811 and then let the army shoot him. The absurdities uttered by what was then termed (by Rafael López, historian of the Mexican National Archives) the "Unholy Office," in accusing Hidalgo of Jewish practices, may have been based on the idea current after 1700 that liberalism and democratic concepts were equated with Judaism. It was believed that these concepts had their roots in Judaism. Another fairly prevalent belief was that the laws of Judaism were better than those of the Spanish crown or the Spanish Church. The last words of the compendium of the Edict of Faith read in the eighteenth century shows that such belief was held. In 1795, a man was denounced by his wife for saying that the best law was that of the Jews.[20]

Rabbi Alan D. Corré of the University of Wisconsin, in reviewing a book on Jews in Barbados, wrote that the Jewish community in Barbados had become entirely extinct because:

> Jewish communities cannot live in isolation. *Habruta o mituta* (fellowship or death) applies to them as to individuals. When Barbados was prominent on the commercial map and Jews maintained their ties with their co-religionists, they prospered. When these ties were out, they withered. Secondly, the community apparently developed no tradition of Jewish culture and learning . . . Added to assimilation, emigration and lack of cultural increase, these factors spelled the death of the community.[21]

This fairly describes what happened to the Jewish communities in New Spain at the turn of the nineteenth century. There were Jews in various parts of the colony and there still existed substantial groups in the north and in the south, but the practice of Judaism had degenerated to a few rites and superstitious beliefs. The undoing of Gil Rodríguez, the monk, was his wish to be buried in accordance with Jewish rites. He had put in writing final instructions for the care of his cadaver. This paper was found and served as the basis for the charges.

One of the tantalizing references which should motivate further research is found in the diary of the First Lord of Egmont. On page 116 there appears under the entry of "Feb. 20-Mar. 1" the following:

> The proposal of a Jew was delivered to go over and make cochineal provided he had suitable encouragement. He had been bred to the business in Mexico, but his religion being discovered, he was obliged to flee. His proposal was reasonable till we came to the latter part, where he demanded a reward of £2000, upon showing a quantity made by him and his partner. We desired he might come to us next Wednesday.

According to the journal of the Earl of Egmont, which is contained in the *Colonial Records of Georgia,* V, page 317, we know that the year was 1740. Tomas Treviño de Sobremonte was engaged in the manufacture of cochineal 100 years earlier, and it became a principal export of New Spain. One of the articles secreted by Sebastian Cardoso in an attempt to salvage some of his small fortune from sequestration by the Inquisition was cochineal. Many Mexican Jews were engaged in manufacturing and selling this valuable dye. The diary states that the Mexican Jew did not appear on Wednesday, February 27.

In the same *Colonial Records* on page 44, there appears this entry, "9. Certain Jews appl'd for encouragement to propogate cochineal in Georgia, but their proposal was so unreasonable that we unanimously rejected it." The entry of June 2, 1738, page 252, reveals the names of the Jews: Balanger and Núñez. Mexican Jews had traveled from New Spain to Georgia, one of the thirteen colonies, and then to England. We presume that Balanger and Núñez were the same Jews who were in Georgia in 1738 and in England in 1740.

15

Conclusion

IN 1922, Rabbi Martin Zelonka wrote, "If the story of the Inquisition is to be accepted as a test of their loyalty to Judaism, then these early immigrants to Mexico were Princes of Israel." These "Princes of Israel" fought for the survival of their religion for almost 300 years. Threats and torture could not prevent their passing on the principles of their belief to their children and grandchildren. Flames could not eradicate their faith. How, then, did they lose in forty-odd years what they had previously guarded for centuries?

The character of the Ibero-Sephardic ethos of the colonial era is an important factor in the search for an answer to the question. A Sephard wrote of the fundamental sociological attitudes which mark the Sephardic Jew, "Hermeticism to all influences that in the long run would disrupt the quintessence of Judaism; and porousness to all new forms and ideas that possibly could modernize and revitalize the venerable tradition."[1]

The very ambivalence in the foregoing statement confirms the characteristic noted in an early chapter of this book, but the statement can be accepted only in part. The new forms and ideas that permeated New Spain in the eighteenth and early nineteenth centuries were absorbed by the Mexican Jews, and they diluted and then dissolved the venerable tradition of which they had been so proud. The Jew in New Spain also had lost his hermeticism and the bulwark of his tradition—learning.

Yitzhak (Fritz) Baer wrote of the tribulations to which the religio-ethnic existence of the Jews in thirteenth and fourteenth century Spain was subjected. He stated that the external forces of political and religious oppression "assisted from within by a rationalism and scepticism which undermined tradition . . ." ultimately resulted in bringing the Jewish community to a tragic end.[2] The Jew of eastern Europe was also exposed to the rationalism and scepticism of the era of Enlightenment. Many thousands in Europe became agnostics and early socialists and abandoned their ancestral religious practices. They comprised a large percentage of the *haskala* (secularist) movement. However, in eastern Europe there coexisted schools of learning, devout spiritual leaders, and committed lay leaders who valued the ethics, morality, and traditions of their faith. Although the learning of the Enlightenment and the heady wine of liberalism and secularism attracted many, the erudition of Judaism held many within its discipline. Some found a modus vivendi between the two learnings, and so there arose men such as Leopold Zunz, Franz Rosenzweig, Moses Mendelsohn, and historians and philosophers who sought for and found accommodation between the two schools of learning. Mexican Jewry, being outside the intellectual stream, had no philosophic defenses, and thus walls upholding empty, blind tradition crumbled.

Those who came to Mexico in the eighteenth century from South America were products of the same empty ritualism. Some, from what is now Colombia and Peru, brought religious objects such as a menorah, a small scroll of the Torah, and a vial for tears. These family heirlooms remained as revered treasures even after the families had abandoned Judaism. They were passed from eldest daughter to eldest daughter. The chain of inheritance was not broken although the chain of tradition had long since ceased to exist. In 1962, a leading Mexican Christian cardiologist informed this author that he knew two nuns who are descended from old Mexican families who light candles in their convent each Friday night and know no reason for their actions other than that their mothers had done so and had told them that they must carry on the family tradition.

We believe that before the Jewish traditions passed from the Jewish communities certain of their concepts were implanted in the

Mexican. For instance, the unsuccessful efforts of Guillen Lamport to start a revolution against the crown in the 1640's did not mean that the seed bore no fruit. Luis González Obregón and a few others credit him with planting ideas of independence. Henry Brenner, in his master's thesis at the University of Texas (1955) wrote that Mexican chauvinism has prevented Don Guillen from receiving his deserved accolades. Just as Guillen Lamport acquired some of his concepts through years of sharing an Inquisition cell with learned Jews, there were others who were inculcated with liberal concepts, ideas on the dignity of man, the universality of One God, and the brotherhood of man by association and intermarriage with Mexican Jews.

Decade after decade, the interest of Mexican Christians in Jews and Judaism was piqued by the narration and reports of the Jews who were participants in autos-da-fé. While in 1646, it was slanderous per se to call anyone a Jew, ultimately some people came to believe that the Jew may have had insight into a worthy faith and that the Inquisition was not infallible. The case before the Inquisition of the man who called another a "Jew dog" could not have arisen a century later when people began to say that perhaps the Jewish law was the best.

There were other contributions made by the Jews to Mexico's growth and development, as indicated by the following statistics based on approximately 300 cases involving males. Of this number there were twenty-one merchants; seventeen government officials and holders of public office; sixteen brokers including dealers in slaves; four exporters and importers; twenty-four owners of retail shops in the nature of general stores; three tailors and textile makers; five doctors; two carpenters; two tavern keepers; six soldiers; five silver- and goldsmiths; two soap and candle manufacturers; four musicians and actors; four dealers in foodstuffs; two pharmacists; three shoemakers; six miners and mine owners; two barbers; one dueling master; one swordcutter; twenty priests and monks; four peddlers; two university students; and one manufacturer of dyes. The cases from which the foregoing statistics were gleaned were selected at random over the 300 year colonial period, and exclude six who were rabbis.

The American reader usually envisions a community as numbering inhabitants at least in the thousands, each of whom is primarily and basically identified as American. To this day, however, people in modern Spain feel a greater allegiance to their town or province than to the state. The rural Mexican speaks with reverence, even after becoming urbanized, of his *tierra*, the town where he was born. His nation is a vague concept, taking second place in feelings of pride or patriotism.

Although the Jews of New Spain felt a common interest in repelling the inroads of Catholicism into their faith, this bond was too tenuous to cause the formation of large communities. To the Jew, a large group presented the danger of betrayal. Julio Caro Baroja stated that "the plague of the informers was a constant danger to the crypto-Jewish community".[3] A large community was an unknown sociological development during the colonial period except for seats of royalty and viceroyalty in the colonies.

The membership of each of the three Jewish communities in Mexico during the seventeenth century was comprised of people whose origins were in the same geographic area of Spain. The groups might be compared, in a loose fashion, to the modern sects in Judaism: Orthodox, Conservative, and Reform. These groups in modern times have theological differences which are discussed by their intellectual leaders and theologians. The vast majority of the modern affiliated laity identify themselves with the respective sects on the basis of their acceptance of the differences in ritual and other religious observances. The community headed by Tomas Treviño de Sobremonte may be compared to the Orthodox group. Religious observance among his adherents was traditional and as punctilious as possible. Form, as dictated by the rabbis, was the criterion and modification of form was not tolerated. In the relación of the 1649 auto-da-fé, Padre Bocanegra termed Luis Pérez Roldan as one of the "most important Jews that the Inquisition ever apprehended and he could not be less because of the group [Treviño's] to which he belonged."

The modern Conservatives preach unity in diversity. The points of view represented range from those on the right who are almost Orthodox but have insisted on some modifications, to the liberals on the left who are but a hair's breath from the Reform group. All find a place in the house of conservatism. Simón Váez Sevilla's community is analagous to conservatism. Some members of this group worked on the Sabbath if they found it necessary; some used pork products in their stews when they had Christian guests and were not criticized for it. Others deviated only in minor ways from orthodox practices.

The third community under Sebastian Vaz Acevedo might be compared to the Reform movement. They believed in associating freely with their Catholic neighbors. Sebastian himself had a Christian wife, which would not have been countenanced by the other two communities. Sebastian's group was what might be termed "integrationist." If freedom of religion had been declared during their lifetime, they would have been leaders in interfaith activities. This group had the lowest number of children per family.

Not all the Jews in Mexico City belonged to one of the three communities. When reading the lists of the witnesses whose testimony was used in the various trials, one can begin to identify the members of each group. There were two lists in each proceso—one naming those whose testimony was used against the accused and the other the names of those against whom he deposed, together with a description of the acts and rites of Judaism which they practiced. However, in the proceedings of the unaffiliated, the two lists of names are miniscule. Francisco Franco de Morera[4] was considered by the inquisitors to be an "astute Jew" who had managed to conceal his identity by not being intimately involved with any of the three communities and by living "very decently." The last words meant that he practiced Jewish ritual in a solitary fashion.

Two explanations have thus far been advanced for the dissolution and ultimate disappearance of these three communities in the eighteenth century, and what had happened to them: the decline of Jewish learning with the degeneration of religion to mere ritual, and the isolation from all other Jewish communities.

Cecil Roth wrote: "Judaism is based upon understanding: and it is obviously impossible for an integral Judaism of any sort to flourish under conditions of stealth, uninstructed and isolated, cut off from the outside world and minutely divided even within itself."[5]

There is an additional sociological factor: the absorption of a minority by a preponderant majority, especially when the minority is not reinforced by the infusion of new vigor and blood. In several interviews with modern Christians who are descendants of colonial Jews, the question was asked, "do you know why your ancestor converted or abandoned Judaism?" In each instance where an answer was proffered, it was invariably the same, "My ancestor, as the family tells it, married a Catholic [or a Protestant] and since it seems that religion was more important to the non-Jewish spouse than to my Jewish ancestor, an accommodation was made for the sake of love."

Not all were formally converted. Some just abandoned Judaism —merely dropping it without adopting another faith. Some continued as Jews until the latter part of the nineteenth century. In interviews with a few Mexican-born Jews over the age of eighty, each reported that during his youth he knew of other Jewish families in Mexico, but that Judaism was a reference of identification without religious significance. There were at least two Jewish generals in the Mexican army in the 1870's, but their families ceased being Jews over eighty years ago.

Rabbi Harry Halpern wrote many years ago: "No event of any significance happens to us without leaving some trace behind. For some the tracings are clear while with others the impressions are dim. The letters of the Hebrew word meaning 'to forget,' if rearranged slightly, spell the word meaning 'to darken.' Forgetfulness means plunging a past experience into darkness while memory means to see it in a clear light."

Mexican colonial Jews forgot their past. They blotted it out of their minds and from their hearts. The Mexican says "No vale la pena," it isn't worthwhile. *Vale* also means value, and when Judaism ceased to have intrinsic value, it dissipated and vanished. This forgetfulness on the part of the descendants of colonial Jews contributed to the darkness that served to obscure the history of the early Mexican Jews, keeping unrevealed the lives and activities of those who deserve an honored place in the annals of Mexico and Judaism.

Appendix A

Digests and Translations of Official Accounts of Autos-da-fé

The material translated here has been condensed or paraphrased in the attempt to furnish as clearly as possible all of the personal data, the nature of the crimes, and the sentences and punishment for the prisoners involved. In addition, explanatory notes and cross references are sometimes included. Names are given in the order of their appearance in the original documents.

Note that all reconciliados abjured *de vehementi*. Where no particular charge is set forth in the official account it meant that the penitent had been charged with being a descendant of Jews and an observer of the Law of Moses.

THE AUTO-DA-FÉ OF DECEMBER 8, 1596

Reconciled

Ana Báez: born in Fondon, Portugal; wife of Jorge Alvarez (p. 307).
[Genaro García wrote that the Relación states that she was born in Seville and received the return of all of her property although she abjured *de vehementi*. In the *Libro Primero de Votos* her birthplace is given as Fondon as per the original records. Return of property to a reconciliado who abjured *de vehementi* was exceedingly rare.]
Reconciliation.
Violante Rodríguez: born in Salceda, Portugal; widow of Simón González. She observed the Law of Moses, its rites and ceremonies, and hid heretics.
Perpetual jail.
Leonor Díaz: born in Seville; wife of Francisco Rodríguez Deza; daughter of Diego López Regalon and Ana López, who were born in Fondon, Portugal. She awaited the Messiah according to the Mosaic law, did

not eat fat or pork, and fasted on the Great Day that the Jews called Penitence.

Jail for six years and confiscation of property.

Isabel Rodríguez: born in Salceda, Portugal; daughter of Violante Rodríguez, above; wife of Manuel Díaz, who was burned in person. She was a descendant of Jews, awaited the Messiah, and made bad confessions.

Life imprisonment and confiscation of all property.

Ana López: born in Seville; wife of Diego López Regalon.

Same crime and punishment as Isabel Rodríguez, above.

Constanza Rodríguèz: born in Seville; wife of Sebastian Rodríguez. She was a descendant of Jews, awaited the Messiah, made bad confessions, fasted on all fast days, and did not believe that Jesus Christ was the Redeemer.

Life imprisonment and confiscation of all property.

Sebastian Rodríguez: born in San Vicente Davera [or de la Vera]; a merchant; husband of Constanza Rodríguez, above.

Life imprisonment, orders to wear a sanbenito, and confiscation of all property.

Clara Enríquez: born in Fondon, Portugal; widow of Francisco Méndez. She celebrated the Passover of the Lamb and fasted on Mondays, Thursdays, and other fast days such as the Great Day of Penitence.

Life imprisonment and confiscation of all property.

Justa Méndez: born in Seville; daughter of Clara Enríquez, above. She observed the Sabbath; prayed in accordance with the dead Law of Moses; did not eat bacon, fat, or pork; and perpetrated the other things of which her mother was convicted.

Life imprisonment and confiscation of all property.

Catalina Enríquez: born in Seville; daughter of Simón la Payba, deceased, and Beatrix Enríquez, who was relaxed in person in this auto; wife of Manuel de Lucena; resident of the mines of Pachuca. Same crimes as Justa Méndez, above, with the addition of fasting on the Fast of Queen Esther.

Life imprisonment and confiscation of all property.

Sebastian de la Peña, also known as Sebastian Cardoso: single; born in San Juan de Pesquera in the Bishopric of Guarda, Portugal, of the caste and generation of Jews. He observed the Law of Moses and believed its rites and ceremonies.

Life imprisonment, the first two years of which were to be spent in a monastery where he was to be instructed in the Catholic faith.

Diego Díaz Nieto: born in Oporto, Portugal; single. [He appears again in the auto of 1605. He was circumcized in the Jewish quarter of Ferrara, Italy, and had never been baptized.]

Jail for one year and confiscation of property.

Pedro Rodríguez: born in Fondon, Bishopric of La Guarda, Portugal, of the caste of New Christians, descendant of Jews. He observed rites and ceremonies of the dead law of Moses and made bad confessions.

Four years in the galleys an an oarsman without pay and perpetual jail in Seville.

Marco Antonio: born in Casteloblanco, Portugal; single, resident of the town of Trinidad, Guatemala [then part of New Spain]; a dueling master.

Perpetual jail and confiscation of all possessions.

Domingo Cuello: born in Almofala, Bishopric of Amago, Portugal; a cattle dealer. Heretical Jewish practices.

Perpetual jail and confiscation of property.

Jorge Lais: born in San Vicente, Davera, Portugal; resident of Puebla; a merchant and trader.

Jail for four years and confiscation of property.

Manuel Rodríguez: born in Fondon, Portugal, in the village of Cubillana; single.

Six years in prison and confiscation of property.

Pedro Enríquez: single; son of Simón la Payba and Beatriz Enríquez de la Payba. Observed the Sabbath and various fast days; prayed in accordance with the dead Law of Moses; did not eat bacon, fat. or pork; wore clean clothes and placed clean sheets on the bed on Fridays; observed the Law of Moses while in jail after saying that he had converted; and bored a hole in the wall of his cell and communicated with other prisoners.

Five years in the galleys as an oarsman without pay and thereafter, life imprisonment in Seville.

Manuel Francisco de Belmonte: born in Cubillana, Portugal; a merchant in the mines of Cultepeque.

Confiscation of property, 100 lashes, and life imprisonment.

Diego López: born in San Vicente Davera; single. He prayed with his face turned toward the east and communicated with other prisoners in the secret cells.

Confiscation of property, 100 lashes, and jail for three years.

Manuel Gómez Navarro: born in San Martin de Trebajos, Portugal; single; a trader and merchant in the mines of Sichu. He used clean bedding on Fridays, prayed facing the east, and declared that Jesus Christ was crucified because he was a false prophet; he denied the Holy Trinity and contended that it was a multitude of things without order; he said that the Holy Sacrament was just a piece of dough and uttered other blasphemies which he taught to other persons. He falsely declared to the Holy Office that he was converted. He knew prayers and psalms and observed fast days while in the secret cells for four years.

Two hundred lashes, six years as a galley slave without pay, and orders to wear a sanbenito for life in jail in Seville.

Jorge Alvarez: born in Fondon, Portugal; son of Manuel Alvarez; a merchant and trader in New Spain. Made an incomplete and unsatisfactory confession.

Confiscation of property, 100 lashes, and life imprisonment.

Duarte Rodríguez: born in Cubillana, Bishopric of La Guarda, Portugal; single; a merchant and trader in Texcoco. Communicated with other prisoners.

Confiscation of all property, 100 lashes, and life imprisonment.

Andres Rodríguez: born in Fondon, Portugal; single; a merchant and trader in Texcoco. Same crimes as Pedro Enríquez (above) and also observed Mosaic laws in jail after confessing and asking for mercy, made incomplete and false confessions, and communicated with other prisoners.

Two hundred lashes, five years in the galleys, and life imprisonment in Seville.

Daniel Benítez: born in Hamburg, Germany; a tailor and a soldier at the Fort of San Juan de Ullua [in the bay across from Veracruz]. He was first a member of the sect of Martin Luther and then, after being taught the Law of Moses, observed it and all its rites and ceremonies.

Confiscation of all property; 200 lashes "in the form of justice" for having communicated with other prisoners; and life imprisonment, the first two years of which was to be spent in a monastery where he was to be instructed in Catholicism.

Burned at the Stake

Manuel Díaz: born in Fondon, Portugal. Many persons testified against him.

Beatriz Enríquez de la Payba: born in Fondon, Portugal; widow of Simón la Payba. She was impenitent and refused to confess.

Diego Enríquez: single; son of Beatriz Enríquez, above. He had been found guilty previously of Jewish practices.

Manuel de Lucena: born in San Vicente Davera, Portugal; a merchant in the area known as the mines of Pachuca; the son-in-law of Beatriz Enríquez, above. Found guilty of observing all Jewish practices plus teaching and dogmatizing the Laws of Moses, impugning the purity and cleanliness of the Virgin, and making false confessions.

Francisca de Carvajal: born in Benavente in Castille; widow of Francisco Rodríguez de Matos. She had been found guilty previously of Jewish practices.

Isabel Rodríguez de Andrade: daughter of Francisca de Carvajal, above; widow of Gabriel de Herrera. Also a second offender.

Catalina de León y de la Cueva: daughter of Francisca de Carvajal; wife of Antonio Díaz de Cáceres. Also a second offender.

Leonor de Carvajal: daughter of Francisca de Carvajal; wife of Jorge Almeida. Also a second offender.

Luis de Carvajal: son of Francisca de Carvajal, above, and brother of Isabel, Catalina, and Leonor, above. A second offender and also guilty of writing books and prayers, of being impenitent, and of being an obstinate Jewish proselyte.

Burned in Effigy

Francisco Baez: single; resided in Pachuca. Escapee.

Fabian Granados: born in Lamego, Portugal; resident of Taxco. Escapee.

Francisco Jorge: born in Benevente, Castile. Escapee.

Antonio López: born in Orico, Portugal. Escapee.

Antonio López de Morales. Escapee.

Isabel Pérez: wife of Manuel de Morales. Escapee.

Antonio Rodríguez: Portuguese. Died prior to auto.

Domingo Rodríguez: Portuguese. Died prior to auto.

Juan Rodríguez de Silva: Portuguese. Escapee.

Manuel [Miguel] Rodríguez de Matos: son of Francisco Rodríguez de Matos and Francisca de Carvajal. Escapee.

Abjured "de levi"

Francisco Rodríguez: born in SanVicente Davera, Portugal. Was convicted of having concealed Jews and suspected of being an observer of Jewish rites.
    One hundred lashes and exile from Mexico [City] for two years.
Geronimo Rodríguez: born in San Vicente Davera, Portugal; resided in Puebla de los Ángeles. Convicted of concealing Jews.
    Abjuration.

RELACIÓN OF THE AUTO-DA-FÉ OF MARCH 25, 1601

Ana de Carvajal: born in New Spain; daughter of those relaxed by this Holy Office for burning at the stake.
    Two years imprisonment.
Andres Núñez: born in Mogodoro, Portugal; a servant.
    Burned in effigy, having escaped.
Antonio Machado: born in Lisbon.
    Burned in effigy as a dogmatizing Jew and as a master and teacher of the Law of Moses.
Alvaro de Carrion: born in Castille; resident of Tilquatla near Pachuca; of Portuguese descent. He had been tortured.
    One hundred lashes and life imprisonment.
Antonio Gómez: born in Fondon, Portugal; a merchant. It is noted that the charge was not well proven.
    Five years in the galleys and permanent exile from the Indies.
Antonio Díaz de Cáceres: born in Villa de Sancta, Bishopric of Coimbra, Portugal; the husband of Catalina de la Cueva of the Carvajal family.
    Abjuration *de vehementi* and a fine of 1,000 duros of Castille.
Antonio Méndez: born in Portugal; resided in Pachuca; a servant. He had been tortured.
    Abjuration *de vehementi* and 200 lashes.
Antonio López: born in Seville; son of Diego López Regalon and Arenas López.
    Reconciliation.
Antonio López: from Portugal; son of Ana López; singer in theatrical comedies. A Jew and concealer of those reconciled.
    Sentenced to wear a sanbenito and to perpetual jail.
Antonio Díaz Marquez: born in Alvala near Lisbon; a merchant. A supporter and concealer of Jews.
    Reconciliation.
Alvaro González: born in Fondon, Portugal.
    Burned in effigy in absentia as a fugitive.
Alvaro Rodríguez Achocada: born in Portugal.
    Burned in effigy in absentia as a fugitive.
Alvaro Zambrano: born in Villa de Parras, Extremadula. Burned and broke holy images. [His religion is not stated; he has been included to indicate, if he were not a Jew, that Christians also desecrated holy images.]
    A fine and penance outside of the auto-da-fé.

Bernardo de Luna: born in Lisbon. A Jew and concealer of those sentenced.
Reconciliation, 200 lashes, and perpetual jail.
Blanca de Morales: wife of Pedro Hernández; sister-in-law of Manuel de
Morales.
Burned in effigy in absentia as a fugitive.
Cristobal Gómez: born in Escarego, Portugal.
Burned in absentia as a fugitive.
Mariana Carvajal: born in Benavente, Castille; of the Carvajal family. "She
died as a Christian with sorrow for her sin."
Burned alive.
Hector de Fonesca: born in Visseo [also Viseo], Portugal; resided in Taxco.
Reconciliation, 100 lashes, and perpetual jail.
Ruy Díaz Nieto: born in Oporto, Portugal. He has been reconciled previ-
ously. During the trial he was called a Pharisee and a concealer of
Jews. ["Pharisee," as used here, meant a traitor to his faith because he
had been baptized as a Catholic. He had married a woman called Esther
and after her death he married a woman named Raquel. He had a "nat-
ural" son, Salomon.]
Confiscation of all property for the king's treasury, 100 lashes, and
perpetual jail.
Jorge Rodríguez: born in Seville. Previously reconciled.
Two hundred lashes and, as a relapso, ten years in the galleys.
Diego López Regalon: born in Fondon, Portugal. Deceased.
Burned in effigy.
[Hernando de Carvajal was also in his auto. He was a Catholic and unrelated
to the Carvajal family traced in the text. Convicted as a bigamist.]
Diego Flores: resident of Guadalajara; a wealthy encomendero. He was un-
der suspicion.
Case suspended.
Francisco Rodríguez, alias Francisco Rodríguez de Seas: born in Portugal; a
silversmith.
Burned in effigy as a fugitive.
Francisco Rodríguez: born in Portugal; a shoemaker.
Reconciliation and 200 lashes.
Gonzalo Pérez Ferro: born in Villa Flor, Portugal.
Reconciled. [A person with the identical name was in the auto of
February 24, 1590, was given 200 lashes, and was ordered to be exiled
but never left the country. There is no explanation as to why he, if the
same person, was not treated as a second offender in this auto.]
Hernando Rodríguez de Herrera: born in Cavilla, Portugal. Previously rec-
onciled in 1590.
He was tortured and died in the secret cells.
Isabel Clara: wife of Francisco Hernández; sister-in-law of Manuel de
Morales.
Burned in effigy as a fugitive.
Isabel Machado: single daughter of Antonio Machado.
Reconciliation and life imprisonment.
Inez Hernández: wife of Francisco Alvarez; sister of Manuel de Morales.
Burned in effigy. [In the Genero García papers at the University of
Texas, p. 17, she is termed the deceased daughter of Lic. Morales. Her
bones were disinterred and burned.]

Jorge Fernández: born in Villa de Clazada, Portugal.
>Reconciliation and 200 lashes.

Jorge Alvarez: born in Fondon; a merchant. Previously reconciled in 1596.
>Two hundred lashes, galleys for ten years as a second offender, and exile from New Spain and the Indies.

Jorge Díaz: born in Portugal; a silversmith.
>Burned in absentia as a fugitive.

Juan Rodríguez: born in Portugal; a bondsman.
>Burned in absentia as a fugitive.

Leonor Rodríguez: born in Fondon, Portugal; wife of Manuel Alvarez.
>Abjuration *de vehementi* and a fine.

Luis Díaz: born in Portugal; a silversmith.
>Burned in absentia as a fugitive.

Leonor de Cáceres: born in Taxco and resided in Tulancingo; daughter of Catalina of the Carvajal family and Antonio Díaz de Cáceres; about 14 years of age at this time.
>Reconciliation.

Manuel de Bases: from Portugal. A Jew, a descendant of Jews, and a practitioner of Jewish rites.
>Two hundred lashes, eight years in the galleys, and perpetual jail.

Miguel Hernández: born in Portugal; single.
>Burned in absentia as a fugitive.

Manuel Gil de la Guarda: born in la Guarda, Portugal; a resident of Manila.
>Reconciliation.

Manuel de Tavares: born in Cubillana, Portugal. A Jew, practitioner of Jewish rites, and a supporter and concealer of Jews.
>Two hundred lashes, eight years in the galleys, and life imprisonment.

Manuel Alvarez: born in Fondon near the village of Cubillana; 41 years of age; a merchant.
>Life imprisonment.

Manuel Gómez Silvera: born in Castille but Portuguese; resided near the mines of Zultepec.
>Five years in the galleys and life imprisonment.

Pelayo Alvarez: born in Freyre, Portugal; resided in Taxco; a commercial dealer. He died in the secret cells.
>Reconciliation in effigy.

Rodrigo Tabares: born in Fondon adjacent to Cubillana.
>Abjuration *de vehementi* and 200 lashes.

Simón Payba: born in Portugal; resided in Pachuca. Deceased.
>Burned in effigy.

Simón Rodríguez: born in Portugal; a merchant; a descendant of Jews. His mother had worn a sanbenito. He was a supporter and concealer of Jews and had been sentenced previously.
>Reconciliation.

Thomas de Fonesca: born in Viseo, Portugal; resided in Castellano. Previously charged in 1590 and then acquitted; resided in Taxco. He was a supporter and concealer of Jews. "He died well."
>Burned alive.

Thomas de Fonesca: resided in mines of Talpujahua, Michoacan.
>Reconciliation, orders to wear a sanbenito, and life imprisonment.

AUTO-DA-FÉ OF JUNE 15, 1625

Antonio Báez, alias Antonio Tirado, alias Captain Casteloblanco: born in Portugal. Sentenced outside of auto.
Prison for two years.
Tomas Treviño de Sobremonte: born in Medina in Old Castille; resided in Antequera in the Valley of Oaxaca.
One year imprisonment.
Diego de Lozado: born in Lemos, Portugal; resided in Guadalajara. Suspected of Jewish practices.
Case suspended.
Domingo Díaz, alias Domingo Rodríguez: son of Constanza and Sebastian Rodríguez of the 1596 auto-da-fé; a resident of Puebla. An "observer of the Law of Moses," he was convicted of being a Jew after three years incarceration.
Service as a galley oarsman for five years and life imprisonment in Spain.

AUTO-DA-FÉ OF MARCH 3, 1626

Baltazar del Valle. Tortured but did not confess.
Case suspended.
Marcos del Valle, alias Simón López: born in Quintala, Portugal. Suspected of being a Jew, but he failed to confess while being tortured.
Case suspended.
Simón Davila: born in Troncoso, Portugal. Suspected of being a Jew. Torture produced no confession.
Case suspended.

1628 (NO AUTO)

Duarte de León, later known as Duarte de León Jaramillo: born in Casteloblanco, Portugal. Suspected of Jewish practices.
Case suspended. [He was rearrested in 1634 and again in the 1640's. He and his entire family were apprehended, and he was burned at the stake in 1649.]

MARCH 17, 1630 (NO AUTO)

There was no public auto in 1630 although there were five penitents for that year.

Antonio de Medina: born in Portugal; resided in the mines of Tora (see below) near Guadalajara. [The word "Tora" will interest Jewish readers because it is the Hebrew name for the five books of Moses. In Spanish, however, it also refers to "the figure of a bull in artificial fireworks," according to Appleton's 1891 edition of the Spanish dictionary based on Neuman and Baretti.]

Abjuration *de vehementi*, 100 lashes, a twenty-one peso fine, and penance outside of a public auto.
Diego Pérez Alburquerque: born in Bordeaux, France; resided in Puebla; described as Portuguese. He had been arrested in 1624.
    Two hundred lashes, six years in the galleys, and life imprisonment in Spain.

AUTO-DA-FÉ OF APRIL 2, 1635

Antonio Fernández Cardado: born in Moral, Holland; resided in Pachuca, where his parents had been reconciled.
    Two hundred lashes, five years in the galleys as an oarsman without pay, and life imprisonment in Spain.
Baltazar del Valle, alias Baltasar Díaz; husband of Isabel López Cardado (below). Second arrest.
    Reconciliation.
Ana Gómez Botello: born in Villa de Riego; resided in Pachuca; wife of Simón de Burgos; the daughter of parents reconciled in Portugal.
    Reconciliation and one year of imprisonment.
Ana Gómez: born in Madrid; wife of Gaspar Alvarez, a Portuguese; resided in Ixmiquilpan about 35 miles north of Pachuca. Her parents and grandparents had been reconciled as observers of the Law of Moses.
    One year of jail.
Ana Fernández: had been married to Manuel Juarez, deceased: they had lived in Veracruz; was the aunt of Ana Gómez Botello. Deceased.
    Burned in effigy with her husband.
Antonio López Blandon: born in Madrid; had resided in Guadalajara; deceased. He was the son and grandson of observers of Judaism who had been burned at the stake.
    Burned in effigy as a Jew.
Duarte de León: He is the same person listed in the 1628 auto.
    Abjuration *de vehementi* and a fine of twenty pesos.
Dominga Fernández: born in Torre de Orloncarbo, Portugal. She died in jail. Her sentence was read in the Church of Santo Domingo on July 2, 1635.
    Reconciliation in effigy.
Francisco López Blandon: brother of Antonio López Blandon, above.
    Reconciliation.
Isabel Núñez: born in Bordeaux, France [another source states Madrid]; 26 years old; wife of Luis Pérez Roldan.
    Reconciliation and life imprisonment.
José Báez y de la Torre: single.
    Reconciliation.
Manuel Juárez: born in Portugal; resided in Veracruz; the husband of Ana Fernández, deceased. He was also deceased.
    Burned in effigy with his wife.
María Gomez: born in Mexico; wife of Tomas Treviño de Sobremonte.
    Reconciliation.
María Rodríguez: born in Portugal. Died in her cell.
    Burned in effigy.
Pedro López, also known as Simón Fernández: a Portuguese; husband of

Leonor Núñez, who had been reconciled by the Holy Office in Mexico; had lived in Ixmiquilpan. He was a dogmatist. Deceased.
Burned in effigy.
Simón Paredes: son of Manuel de Lucena, previously listed.
Burned alive.
Simón Montero: born in Casteloblanco; had lived in Seville. He requested permission to go to Spain and this was granted. He went to Italy and studied in rabbinical schools in Pisa, Leghorn, and finally in Rome. He was circumcized and ordained as a rabbi, and then returned to New Spain.
Case suspended because of failure to confirm the suspicion that he was a Jew.
Violante Méndez Cardado: daughter and descendant of New Christians; wife of Marcos del Valle, alias Simón López.
Reconciliation and prison for two years.

AUTO-DA-FÉ OF APRIL 10, 1646

The following names are taken from the Relación as contained in Genaro García, *Documentos inéditos o muy raros para la historia de México*, Vol. 28, pp. 40-94.

Diego Méndez de Silva: born in Alburquerque, Extremadura; emigrated from Seville to Mexico in 1640; the son of Manuel Gómez and Blanca de Silva, both born in Viseo, Portugal and both of whom had died in Cuidad Rodrigo; married to Luisa de Mercado in Ciudad Rodrigo. She had been born in La Guarda, Portugal. He was 46 years old and originally was only suspected of observing. He was convicted in observing and had to abjure *de vehementi*.
Two hundred lashes, a fine of 2,000 ducats of Castile "for extraordinary costs of the Holy Office," exile, and to be sentenced to jail by the Tribunal in Seville.
Luis Burgos: born in Villanueva, Archbishopric of Toledo; the son of Simón Rodríguez de Burgos and María Díaz, "Hebrews and New Christians"; circumcized; 66 years of age; a merchant. There was no prison sentence or requirement to report to the Holy Office in Spain.
A fine of 3,000 pesos of "pieces of eight" and exile.
Antonio López de Orduna: born in Seville; a merchant and vice-mayor of the town of Chichicapa, New Spain; circumcized and 27 years of age; unmarried and the son of Fernando Váez de Torres of Casteloblanco, Portugal, deceased; distantly related to Simon Váez.
Reconciliation, jail for one year, and exile, but was to report his presence to the Suprema in Seville so they could punish him further if he ever reverted to judaizing.
Blanca Méndez (her name recognized in Spain), also Blanca de Rivera (New Spain): born in Seville; the widow of Diego López Rivero, a merchant born in Casteloblanco; the daughter of Enrique Rodríguez Obregon of the city of Llerena, Extremadura, who had been a broker of slaves between Angola and New Spain, and Margareta López of Seville. She was a Jewess, had feigned insanity, had been contumacious, and was

filled with hate, rancor, and enmity—which suffused the hearts of the Jews and their descendants—against the Holy Office.

Reconciliation, one year in jail, and exile.

Clara Antúñez, also known as Clara Enríquez and Clara Duarte: born in Mexico and 19 years old [the AGN file shows her to be 15 years old]; the daughter of Isabel Duarte of Seville, reconciled in Mexico, and Diego Antúñez, who had died in Mexico. She had tried to marry Manuel Carrasco a few days before being imprisoned; they had desired to observe the Law of Moses together. She confessed to being a Jewess.

Reconciliation, one year in jail, and exile.

Clara Texoso: born in Lima, Peru; 38 years old; a resident of New Veracruz of New Spain; the wife of Duarte Rodríguez "of the Hebrew nation," a merchant imprisoned for Jewish practices; the daughter of Pedro Gómez Texoso, a Sevillano who had died in Lima where he was a market broker, and of Violante Rodríguez of Lisbon, Portugal, who had died in New Veracruz. She had feigned illness while in the cells in order to transmit and carry messages to and between other persons; she had been negative in her confessions although she had admitted being a Jewess and a practitioner of Jewish rites.

Reconciliation, 200 lashes, and perpetual jail.

Esperanza Rodríguez: born in Seville; 64 years old; a mulatto, but with white skin; the widow of Juan Baptista del Bosque, a German sculptor and carpenter who had died in Guadalajara, New Galicia; the daughter of Isabel, a Negress of Guinea who had died in Seville, and Francisco Rodríguez, a "Hebrew New Christian." Esperanza was a seamstress; she had been freed by her former mistress Catalina Enríquez, who was then in the Inquisition cells imprisoned as a Jewess. Esperanza feigned insanity while in prison, but ultimately confessed.

Reconciliation and life imprisonment in Spain.

Francisco Núñez Navarro: born in Chazin, Portugal; resided in New Galicia [the middle-western part of present Mexico]; 43 years of age; a peddler; son of Francisco Núñez, who was born and had died in Chazin, and Catalina Enríquez, born in Torre de Moncorbo, Portugal.

Reconciliation and permanent jail in Spain.

Francisco Díaz de Montoya, also known as Francisco Díaz Yelba: born in Casteloblanco, Portugal; 46 years old and circumcised; had married and resided in Manila, Philippines, with Nicolasa de Bañuelos, who had been born in Manila; the son of Diego Méndez de Elbas [or Yelbes in Castilian] and Isabel Enríquez of Casteloblanco; both parents were dead. His father had mailed him proof that he was a descendant of Old Christian families such as the Acevedes and Vasconcelos, who were among the greatest Portuguese family names.

Reconciliation, six months imprisonment, and exile.

Francisca Texoso: born in Seville; single; 54 years old; the sister of Clara Texoso and Captain Francisco Gómez Texoso.

Captain Francisco Gómez Texoso: born in Valencia del Cid; single; 58 years old and circumcised; a merchant and resident of New Veracruz, where he was also a captain of the infantry; his father was Pedro Gómez Texoso, a Sevillano who had died in Lima where he was a market broker, and of Violante Rodríguez. He was a brother of Clara and Francisca Texoso who appeared in this auto with him. When he was baptized, his grandmother gave him the name of Tristan [Sad] Manuel because he would have a life of sorrow due to the incidents at his baptism.

Reconciliation and life imprisonment in Spain.

Gaspar Váez Sevilla: 22 years old; single; the son of Simón Váez Soburro, also known as Simón Váez Sevilla, born in Casteloblanco, Portugal, and Juana Enríquez, born in Seville. All of their ancestors had been burned at the stake in person or in effigy or had been reconciled by various Inquisitions in Castille and Portugal.

Reconciliation and perpetual jail in Spain.

Gabriel de Granada: born in Mexico; 18 years of age and circumcized; son of Manuel de Granada, who died in the Philippines, and María de Rivera, born in Seville. The "famous rabbi" who circumcized him was related to his father. His mother had hoped that he would grow to be as great a Jew as the rabbi.

Reconciliation, jail for one year, and exile.

Geronimo Núñez, also known as Rojas: born in La Guarda, Portugal; son of Rodrígo Núñez and Isabel Fernández, both of whom had been born and died in Linares, Portugal; 33 years old, circumcized, and single; a servant in the mines at Zacatecas. He was a half-brother of Agustin de Rojas and inserted the wrong date in a promissory note representing an alleged indebtedness from Agustin to himself.

Reconciliation, jail for one year, and exile.

Juana Tinoco: the daughter of Diego Tinoco, who had died in Guatemala, and Catalina de Silva or Enríquez, then in an Inquisition cell. Her husband, Simón Juarez de Espinosa, reconciled in this auto, had a dry goods store.

Reconciliation, jail for one year, and exile.

Juana del Bosque: born in Cartagena; a mulatto, 29 years of age; the wife of Blas López, a Portuguese who had fled; the daughter of Esperanza Rodríguez, reconciled in this auto, and Juan Baptista del Bosque. She confessed to being a Jewess and observing Jewish rites. She had conferred prior to imprisonment with certain Jews and her mother and sisters about plans not to reveal any information about other Jews in the cells. While she was in a cell, she communicated with other Jewish prisoners in order to ascertain who had testified contrary to the plan.

Reconciliation, 100 lashes, six months imprisonment, and exile.

Isabel del Bosque: born in Mexico; 24 years old; the sister of Juana, above. She had begged her mother to teach her about the Law of Moses because she learned that a famous deceased Jewess had bequeathed money to her sister so that she would make fasts for the soul of the departed Jewess.

Reconciliation, 100 lashes, six months imprisonment, and exile.

Isabel de Rivera: born in Seville; 25 years old; the daughter of Blanca Méndez, also known as Blanca de Rivera, who was reconciled in this same auto. She made hoop skirts and headpieces of feathers and ribbons for women. At the death of her father she tried to prevent the administration of Catholic last rites. She believed, as did many other Jews, that concubinage between a Jew and a Christian would bring the Jew to the Devil. She believed it to be a sin to confess, receive communion, to hear mass, and to recite the rosary. She testified about many other Jewish beliefs.

Reconciliation, 200 lashes, and exile.

Isabel Duarte, alias She of Antúñez: born in Seville; daughter of Marcos Rodríguez Tristan, deceased, and Ana Enríquez, deceased, also of Seville, where she had been reconciled by the Holy Office; the widow of Diego Antúñez, a circumcized Jew and a merchant who died in Mexico; 41 years old. Isabel was a gambler and an outstanding "faster"—the fee for a fast was a "piece of eight"—for which she received much charity.

Reconciliation and jail in Spain.

Isabel Texoso: born in Seville; a resident of New Veracruz; single; over 60 years old; a baker; sister of Captain Francisco Gómez Texoso and Francisca Texoso. She had been a practicing Jewess since she was 12 years old when she had lived in Montilla, Spain. She accused other Jews of having taught her Judaism after she came to Peru when she saw a painting of St. Peter. She also paraphrased Catholic prayers by deleting the names of Jesus and Mary so that Jews could recite them.

Reconciliation, 200 lashes, and life imprisonment in Spain.

Luis Núñez Pérez: born in Samamede, about six miles from Lisbon; son of Manuel Rodríguez Acuña, of Samamede, and Barbola Díaz de Silva, of Lisbon; 30 years old; single; circumcized; a vendor of cocoa beans and peanuts. Found in his pockets were some papers which contained an agreement between Portugal and Holland. While in prison he communicated with some other Jews in the secret cells to map a plan by which a Portuguese armada could come to New Spain and free them.

Reconciliation and life imprisonment in Spain.

Luis de Mezquita, also known as Amézquita Sarmiento: born in Segovia, Castille; the son of Lope de Mezquita, alias Amezquita, and Isabel Gómez, both of Segovia; 50 years of age; single; a merchant in Mexico.

Reconciliation and life imprisonment in Spain.

Leonor Núñez: a Sevillano; more than 70 years old; widow of Manuel Coronel, a broker who died in New Veracruz; the illegitimate daughter of Gaspar de Agurto of Oñate, Spain, and María Núñez, a Hebrew, New Christian, who was born and died in Cadíz. Leonor did not know the four prayers or anything of Christian doctrine although she claimed to be a good Christian. She ultimately confessed. After completion of her jail sentence in Mexico she was to serve in a hospital to be designated.

Reconciliation, prison for two years, and exile from New Veracruz and the area twenty leagues around.

Margarita de Rivera: a Sevillano; the daughter of Blanca Méndez (p. 314); 33 years of age; engaged in making hoop skirts and headpieces of feathers and ribbon. She had been married "in accordance with Jewish rites" to her cousin Miguel Núñez de Huerta, then in the Inquisition cells. She was noted among the Jews for her numerous fasts and her hope and prayers, especially in 1642 and 1643 [the years of the massive hunt for Jews] for the coming of the Messiah. She was one of the important people who prepared the dead for burial. She washed the bodies of Jewish men and women in accordance with Mosaic laws and prepared their shrouds. She constantly searched for the wisest Jews in the communities and herself was learned in the patriarchs and prophets of the "Old Law." When she had bad dreams, she went to confession "in order to throw the evil omen upon her confessor." She even reproved another Jew for cleaning his teeth on the Sabbath and told him that the Mosaic law forbade even scratching one's head on that day.

She denied that there was eternal damnation for Jews except for those who mixed with Old Christians and refrained from marrying young Jewish girls. She conceded that there was some temporal punishment in this life for those who were not "such good Jews." She urged Jews to do penance regularly; to fast on Thursday and on the occasion of the carrying the banner of Virgin of Carmen in order to deceive the Christians; to eat hard-boiled eggs with salt; to wear a hair shirt in the evening; to permit a group to administer thirty lashes with a whip and recite Jewish prayers and psalms. She also made love potions to be used by women to make men fall in love with them.

Reconciliation and perpetual jail in Spain.

Margareta de Morera: born in Mexico; 36 years old; daughter of Pascual Morera of Camina, Portugal, a capmaker, and Catalina Díaz of Seville; the wife of Amaro Díaz Martaraña of Camina, a merchant who died there. Her second husband was Pedro de Castro, a Sevillano, who was a New Christian on his mother's side. She confessed. One day she had been with some Catholics and they saw a man being lashed by order of the Holy Office; she exhibited great compassion for him as well as the others imprisoned for observing Jewish rites. The Catholics were amazed when she said, in answer to their questions, that she would practice Judaism if her husband commanded her to do so. She testified about the manner in which Jews were called together for meetings for religious purposes.

Reconciliation and perpetual jail in Mexico.

Manuel Antúñez: single; 22 years old; without occupation; the son of the circumcized Jew, Diego Antúñez, a Portuguese merchant who was born and died in Mexico, and Isabel Duarte of Antúñez (p. 317). She was constantly searching for the despicable mob (*ruin canallas*) of Jews and Jewesses in the city.

Reconcilation, jail for one year, and exile.

Manuel Carrasco: born in Villaflor, Portugal; 22 years old; the superintendent of a sugar mill in the Valley of Amilpas; the son of Francisco Rodríguez Carrasco and Felipa López, Hebrew New Christians, both born and died in Villaflor. He had tried to marry Clara Antúñez before he was imprisoned; she was reconciled in this auto and labeled a Jewess. He carried matzot in a bag suspended from his neck and used them to place on the head to cure headaches.

Reconcilation, jail for six months, and exile.

Manuel Rodríguez Núñez; in New Spain known as Manuel Núñez Caravallo: born in Casteloblanco, Portugal; 34 years old; no occupation; the son of Francisco Rodríguez, who died in the secret cells of the Inquisition in Seville and was burned in effigy for Judaism, and of Beatriz Núñez, who was born and died in La Guarda and had been a Hebrew New Christian. When he and other Jews saw so many of their coreligionists being jailed by the Holy Office, they plotted to change their names to avoid detection. His was changed to Manuel Méndez or Díaz; the name Méndez was to be used if he claimed to have come from Perote, 40 leagues from Mexico, and Díaz if he claimed to have come from Cuernavaca, 12 leagues away. He was among the disputants in 1640 over the date of the Great Day or Day of Pardon according to the Hebrew calendar. In Guadalajara, the disciples of the groups differing over the date resorted to acrimonious debate and fights.

Reconciliation, jail for two years, and exile.

Manuel Díaz de Castilla: born in Cuidad Rodrigo; 41 years old; circumcized; single; a drygoods peddler; the son of Enrique Rodríguez de Castilla, a Portuguese, and Felipa de Maqueda, of Villarreal, Portugal.
Reconcilation, jail for two years, and exile.

Manuel Tinoco: born in Mexico, 23 years old; single; apprenticed to a silversmith; the son of Diego Tinoco, a Portuguese circumcized Jew who died in Guatemala, and Catalina Enríquez, a Sevillano, then in Inquisition cells. He was a sexton, sacristan, for the Jews; every year, three days before the annual commoration of the Resurrection, he distributed among his family matzot and the dough prepared by his grandmother, the great Jewess Blanca Enríquez, so that all could celebrate the Passover of the Lamb.
Reconcilation, jail for two years, and exile.

María del Bosque: born in Guadalajara, New Galicia; mulatto; 19 years old; single; a seamstress; the daughter of Esperanza Rodríguez (p. 315). She also had made her mother teach her about Judaism. She was very friendly with some noted Jewesses who used to sneer and made snide remarks about the Catholic processions, cursing them.
Reconciliation, 100 lashes, jail for six months, and exile.

Nuño de Figueroa, alias Nuño Pereira or Peredo: born in Lisbon; circumcized; 39 years old; a merchant in Guadalajara, New Galicia; the son of Antonio de Tabera, born in Lisbon, and Isabel de Figueroa, born in Hielbes [*sic*], Portugal; both parents had died in Lisbon. He admitted that he had observed the fasts and other rites of the Jews, but said he had not intended to be a Jew. He kept to this tale for three years in jail. He was, however, the greatest enemy of the saints of the New Testament. He even had composed indecent poems against San Felipe de Jesus [the great Mexican-born saint who was martyred in Japan about 1619]. He had desired to marry a certain Jewess whose mother insisted that her daughter marry only a Jew.·
Reconciliation, 200 lashes, and life imprisonment in Spain.

Pedro de Espinosa: born in Mexico; 50 years old; circumcized; a functionary of the courts of Mexico as well as in charge of the meat market of Sayula, Province of Avalos, New Spain; married to Isabel de Silva or Enríquez, a Sevillano, then also in Inquisition cells; the son of the Portuguese Simon Rodríguez, reconciled by this Tribunal, and Bernardina de Espinoso, born in Burgos, Castile, who had died there. He and other Jews used to read *The Mirror of Consolation*. He contended while in jail that the Inquisition did not want poor Jews, only the rich. Although he had joined the ranks [of the Jews] late, he succeeded in becoming one of the leaders of religious ceremonies. He threw Blanca Enríquez' teeth into her tomb when she was being buried.
Reconciliation and life imprisonment in Spain.

Rafael de Granada: born in Mexico; 19 years of age; circumcized; single; a student of rhetoric; the son of Manuel de Granada, who died in the Philippines, and María de Rivera, Sevillano a brother of Gabriel de Granada (p. 316). He had also been circumcized, when he had been in New Spain, by the famous rabbi who was a member of the family.
Reconciliation, jail for one year, and perpetual exile.

Simón Juarez de Espinosa: born in Mexico; 28 years old; circumcized; a dry goods peddler; married to Juana Tinoco, reconciled in the same auto-da-fé; the son of Juan Juarez de Figueroa, of Lisbon, a New Christian, and Ana de Espinosa, born in Mexico; grandson on the maternal side of Simón Rodríguez, Portuguese; also reconciled for Jewish practices by this Tribunal. It was because of his love for his wife that he consented to convert to Judaism in accordance with the condition imposed by his mother-in-law. Several Jews in addition to his beloved and her mother had shown him the sanbenito of her grandfather in the cathedral.

Reconciliation, jail for six months, and exile.

Simón Fernández de Torres: born in Govea, Portugal; 36 years old; circumcized; a merchant; single; a resident of Guadalajara; the son of Diego Antúñez de Torres, deceased, and Isabel Núñez of Santa Maria, Portugal, both Hebrew New Christians.

Reconciliation, jail for two years, and exile.

Tomas Núñez de Peralta: born in Cubillana, Portugal; 46 years of age; a merchant; the son of Jorge Váez Alcacería, leather tanner, and Isabel Rodríguez, both of Cubillana and deceased; married to Beatriz Enríquez, then in the Inquisition cells. He supplied employees for Zacatecas and and other parts of the interior of the country. Because he was renowned Jew, his mother-in-law, Blanca Enríquez, had arranged his marriage to her daughter. He was termed one of the most malicious, sly, and astute Jews ever seen in the Tribunals of the Inquisition. Once while he was eating in the home of a rich Jew, they put roast ham on the table. He knew that his host was a Jew and was mollified when he was informed that the ham had been put on the table to deceive any Catholics who might arrive while they ate dinner. He never ate ham or used lard. He observed the most minute rites of the "dead law." When the roundup of the Jews involved in this conspiracy by the Holy Office began, he took all of his property to Zacatecas and Parral and delivered it to certain people for them to sell and remit the proceeds to Mexico. He then tried to flee to Spain with his wife. His family used to write to him in prison informing him of the events which he should know. He communicated with other prisoners by blows on the walls and united them by telling them what to confess and what to deny. He had assumed the role of the commander. He gave the war-whoop of the ancient Spaniards. He cursed the ministers of the Holy Office and wished them every evil on their bodies and souls. He deceived the other prisoners for a long time and induced them not to confess by telling them that the Holy Pontiff and the king would send a general pardon by the first flotilla, because they would neither want nor permit such large and important families as his and that of Simón Váez Sevilla to go out in autos, and that they had contributed great sums of money to the Jews of Seville for such purposes.

Reconciliation, 200 lashes, and life imprisonment in Spain.

Tomás López de Monforte: 39 years old; no occupation; the son of Francisco González, a merchant, and Constanza López, both born in Monforte and both died in Sevilla.

Reconciliation and imprisonment in Spain.

Tomé Gómez: born in Casteloblanco, Portugal; 45 years old; a merchant; married to Catalina de Samaniego, who had been born in the town of Ahuacatlan, New Galicia, where they lived; the son of Manuel Rodríguez and Beatriz Gómez, both of Casteloblanco. His father died in Seville and his mother still lived there. She had been reconciled by the

Inquisition in Seville. He used to investigate and seek out the Jews in the province of Michoacan.

Reconciliation, 200 lashes, and life imprisonment in Spain.

Violante Texoso: born in Lima, 23 years old; resided in New Veracruz; single; a dressmaker; the illegitimate daughter of Rafael Gómez Texoso and a certain neighbor of his in Lima. Her father had died in Lima. She exhorted other Jews not to confess, and they used false names or numbers; some of the names were Valonas [a kind of trouser] and Vanilla, and for money they used the name George.

Reconciliation and exile in Spain.

Clara de Rivera: a Sevillano; 25 years old; married to Felipe López de Norona; the daughter of Diego López Rivero, of Casteloblanco, Portugal, and Blanca Méndez, alias Blanca de Rivera (p. 314). She made hoop skirts and headpieces of feathers and ribbons. She refused to enter churches so as not to bend her knees to the saints, which she believed was one of the greatest sins that a Jew could commit. She confessed to having made more than 300 fasts before she was married. She died in her cell, but was absolved because she confessed and received communion.

Reconciled in effigy.

The following people were also penanced in 1646, and they appear in the Abecedario and the records of the AGN.

Antonio Baez de Acevedo: born in Lisbon. [This is the only note in the Abecedario. No other information was found elsewhere.]

Agustina de la Cruz: born in Azcapotzalco; a mulatto; 30 years old; daughter of Andres de la Cruz, a Negro, and María de Guzman. She had been accused of Jewish practices.

Case suspended.

Gaspar Robles: 32 years old. He was not exiled in the auto of April 23, 1646.

Confiscation of property.

Melchor de Acosta: born in Portugal; 64 years old; resident of New Veracruz; a horseshoer; married to María de Bustos, of noble descent. He was suspected of Judaism.

Case suspended on August 30, 1646.

Violante Rodríguez: wife of Pedro Gómez Tejoso [Texoso]; resided in New Veracruz. She died in her cell.

Bones burned in effigy.

THE AUTO-DA-FÉ OF JANUARY 23, 1647

Antonio Méndez Chilón: born in Lisbon; 54 years old; circumcized; single; a merchant; resident of New Veracruz; the son of Francisco Méndez of Tomar, Portugal, and Beatriz López of Lisbon, both New Christians. He confessed at this first hearing and cried. He had observed Judaism since he was seventeen.

To return to Spain on the first flotilla and report his presence to the Tribunal in Seville.

Beatriz Enríquez: born in New Veracruz; 34 years old; the daughter of Fernando Rodríguez of Haveiro, Portugal, who was reconciled in this auto, and Blanca Enríquez of Lisbon, a prisoner of this Inquisition; married to Tomas Méndez of Camina, Portugal, a merchant, also reconciled in this auto. She had practiced Jewish rites since she was thirteen. She had first tried to convince the inquisitors that she fasted many times as a form of reverence for the law of Jesus Christ.

Reconciliation, 200 lashes, and life imprisonment in Spain.

Diego Juarez de Figueroa: born in Lisbon; 52 years old; circumcized; a merchant; resident of Patzcuaro; the son of Nuño Alvarez of Badajoz, Extremadura, and Inez Juarez de Figueroa of Lisbon. His first marriage was to Clara de Silva, a Sevillano and a famous Jewess, who died in Seville; his second wife was Teresa de Alarcon of Patzcuaro. He stated at his second hearing that his twenty-three year observance of Jewish rites and fasts was to please his first wife. He said that he never came to the Holy Office to voluntarily confess because he did not want to dishonor her. He said that there were 662 precepts which Jews must observe [there are 613 positive and negative precepts], that Jews were not permitted to mention Jesus Christ or the Holy Mother, and that when they say "the Virgin of Carmen" to deceive the Catholics who hear them, they mean to invoke Elias and not the Holy Mother. On the day of the New Moon, there is certain worship but no fasting. Blood must be drained from all meat and the forequarters may be eaten, but from that part of the hindquarters which may be eaten the thigh vein must be removed. Animals that chew the cud and have a cloven hoof may be eaten. On the Sabbath the head must be covered; although the covering may be raised as a courtesy, one could not even pick up a match from the floor. The soul of a Jewish adulteress would be tried by God with her head covered by a filthy rag. Those who believe that the souls of the dead are transformed into birds that drink and bathe put a jar of water together with a washcloth next to the body of the deceased and vases of water all over the house of the day of the funeral.

Reconciliation, jail for two years, and exile.

Duarte Rodríguez: born in Alpendrina near Guarda, Portugal; 52 years old; resident of New Veracruz; a merchant; the son of Baltazar Rodríguez and Mencia Rodríguez, both of Alpedrina and New Christians; married to Clara Texoso, of Lima, who was reconciled in the auto of 1646. He was a first cousin of Rodrigo Váez Pereira, who had been burned at the stake in the Lima auto of January 23, 1639. Duarte testified about Jewish practices of his cousin and wife, with whom he had resided before coming to New Spain. In addition to reading *Flos Sanctorum*, he was an avid reader of the books of Judith and Esther while in the cells; he cautioned the other Jews to confess to Jewish rites for only a two-year period. He finally confessed to having judaized since 1619.

Reconciliation, 200 lashes, and life imprisonment in Spain.

Duarte de Torres: born in Casteloblanco, Portugal; 37 years old; circumcized, a peddler; the son of Geronimo Rodríguez and María Enríquez, both of Casteloblanco and New Christians; married to Josefa Ruiz, born in Patzcuaro, a mestiza, the daughter of a Spaniard and an Indian woman. He confessed that he had judaized for at least sixteen years.

Reconciliation, 200 lashes, and life imprisonment in Spain.

Fernando Rodríguez: born in Haveiro, Portugal, 58 years old; circumcized; a merchant; previously a broker in Negroes [a slave trader]; resided in New Veracruz; the son of Fernando Lanzarote and Beatriz de Herrera and the husband of Blanca Enríquez of Lisbon, who was in the Inquisition cells. He confessed to having lived as a Jew since his youth. He had indoctrinated his four children with Judaism "when they had hardly attained their reason." They were taught to be doctors. They used to cry when they read Scriptures and performed Jewish rites. His home was a synagogue.

Reconciliation, 200 lashes, and life imprisonment in Spain.

Francisco López Correra: born in New Veracruz; 27 years old; single; no occupation; the son of Fernando Rodríguez, above, and Blanca Enríquez.

Reconciliation, jail for one year, and exile.

Francisco de León Jaramillo: born in Mexico; 21 years old; circumcized; single, an apprentice merchant; the son of Duarte de León Jaramillo of Casteloblanco, a reconciliado, and Isabel Núñez, born in Mexico, then an Inquisition prisoner. He was the descendant of grandparents (one of whom was Justa Méndez) who had been reconciled by this Holy Office. He had helped his father bury bars of silver prior to imprisonment. His father's warehouse was used as a synagogue. His father instructed him to buy fowl with either all black or all brown feathers and to be sure there were no white feathers. During Holy Week and on every Friday and Sabbath, Jews gathered and prayed "with great shouts and noise."

Reconciliation, jail for two years, and exile.

Francisco Franco de Morera: born in Camina, Portugal; 46 years old; single; a merchant; circumcized; the son of Hernando Franco, a barber from Cobas 2 leagues from Camiña, and Ana Fernández of Camiña. He had kept aloof from the Jewish communities and was a very learned Jew.

Reconciliation and life imprisonment in Spain.

Francisco de Acosta: born in Lisbon; 33 years old; resident of Guatemala; a merchant, and he also had a store in Cartagena; the son of Juan Váez Mesignana and Isabel de Acosta, both of Lisbon. He had been brought to Judaism in Mazagán in Africa, and he maintained contact with the Jewish community there. He was known as *El de Naranja*, He of the Orange, in the cells. He used to pull his beard and put his fingers over his nose in front of figures of Jesus.

Reconciliation, in jail for one year, and exile.

Gerónimo Fernández Correa: born in New Veracruz; 37 years old; single; a merchant; resident of Campeche, Yucatán, where he had been a captain of the infantry; the son of Fernando Rodríguez, above. He had judaized since he was eight years of age. He had a written collection of prayers when he and his two brothers were in Campeche. His parents used to write to give them the dates for fasts and particular prayers.

Reconciliation, jail for six months, and exile.

Isabel Enríquez, alias Isabel de la Huerta: born in Malaga, Spain; 40 years old; resided in Puebla; the daughter of Juan Méndez de Escobar of San Vicente Davera, Portugal, who had died in Texcoco and had been imprisoned by the Inquisition in Granada on suspicion of judaizing, and Ana López de Chavez, of Osma, Galicia, who had died in Puebla, also a judaizer. Her first husband was Miguel Rodríguez de Orta or de Huerta, a Jew who had died in Puebla; her second husband was Pedro Gutiérrez de Peralta. Isabel began to practice Judaism when she was fifteen years of age. She was called *La Rosa* in the cells. She used a cat to carry messages to other prisoners.

Reconciliation, 100 lashes, and life imprisonment in Spain.

Juan Méndez de Villaviciosa: born in Villaviciosa, Portugal; 43 years old; a merchant; the son of Pablo Núñez de Franca and Isabel Méndez de Sequera, both Hebrew New Christians; married to Ana Juarez, daughter of Gaspar Juarez and Rafaela Enríquez, both in Inquisition cells. He had been a Jew ever since he had the ability to reason. He had admitted to being sexually impotent so that he and his wife could be divorced. He was a professional mourner and was considered "a grand and fine Jew"; some people wouldn't fast unless he was with them. He was known as *Zurron* (husk) in the cells.

Reconciliation, 200 lashes, and life imprisonment.

Juan Rodríguez Juarez: born in Lisbon; 42 years old; circumcized; a merchant; the son of Juan Rodríguez Juarez of Leira, Portugal, and Luisa Castro of Lisbon. He was a great entertainer *(gran regalador)* on the days that they used to fast. He married his cousin according to Jewish law.

Perpetual jail in Spain.

Juan Cardoso alias Gabriel Peregrino: born in Simide, Portugal; 57 years old; circumcized; resided in Orizaba; the son of Francisco Cardoso and María Duarte, both New Christians of Simide. He had never crossed himself or acknowledged Christianity, and went to Amsterdam from Portugal for fear of the Inquisition. He was circumcized in Flanders and his name was changed to Gabriel Peregrino. He used to pray in the synagogue with his talid and the *pergamino* would be held aloft. [The parchment for the Torah scroll is known as *pergamino* in Spanish and derives from "skin dressed for writing."] In addition to refraining from eating the animals and fish prohibited in the Bible, he also refrained from eating the permitted animals unless they had been ritually slaughtered by the rabbis. His affairs to celebrate the important holidays were formal, with written invitations. On the Sabbath, his pockets were empty and he carried nothing.

Reconciliation, jail for six months, and exile.

Manuel Alvarez de Arellano: born in Jelvez (or Jelbes), Portugal; 43 years old; circumcized; a skipper or carrier of merchandise from Spain to the New World; the son of Luis Méndez of Jelvez, an apothecary, and Isabel López of Lisbon. He had been arrested in Havana after he had been rescued in 1642 from the loss (not clarified) of his fleet. During his visits to Mexico, he was in communication with many Jews of the city. He aided the Jewish needy and attended funerals and other sad events. He used to send dinners to families who were in mourning. He investigated the priple who wanted to marry members of the family of Simón Váez because the family did not want to violate the Jewish precept against marrying a non-Jew. On fast days, he used to take Jews in his carriage out of the city so that they would not be observed fasting.

Reconciliation, jail for one year, and exile.

Pedro López de Morales: born in Ciudad Rodrigo, Castile; 49 years old; a miner in Ixtlan, Guadalajara; the son of Juan Morales of Mercado, Troncoso, Portugal, a silk merchant, and Blanca Enríquez of Travazos,

Portugal. His father had been a collector of rents for the king in Cuidad Rodrigo before becoming a merchant. Pedro married his second cousin in the Jewish manner in Madrid and celebrated the wedding with a solemn fast. He practiced Judaism in the mines of Amaxaque, New Galicia. He told another practitioner of Judaism that he regretted that he was not able to live openly and freely as a Jew because of the fear of the Holy Office. He had sired a daughter with a mestiza and he wanted to bring the child to Spain so that his family there could teach her the Mosaic laws.

Reconciliation, 200 lashes, and life imprisonment in Spain.

Pedro Fernández de Castro, alias Juan Fernández de Castro: born in Valladolid, Castile; 34 years old; circumcised; an itinerant merchant; lived in Santiago de los Valles, outside of Mexico; the son of Ignacio Aguado of Valladolia, who was a descendant of New Christians and was an attorney in the Royal Chancellery, and Mariana del Castro, of Palencia; both parents were deceased. He was married to Leonor Váez, who was born in Casteloblanco and resided in Pisa, living freely as a Jewess. She was the "natural" daughter of Simon Váez Seville. Pedro was known as Sombrero, the hat, in the cells. He admitted that he had committed some Jewish acts in Ferrara but denied that he had ever been an observer or that he ever knew the Law of Moses. He stated that he had been circumcized to please a Jewess, Esther, so that he could have an affair with her. Ultimately he admitted that he used to go to synagogue in Ferrara where the men wore white robes, the rabbi read from a Torah scroll, and all the congregants bowed low when it was raised aloft. Jews from Spain, Peru, the Philippines, and other places used to stay at the home of his father-in-law in Mexico. While in the cells, the prisoners used to report to each other what they told the inquisitors so that there would be no inconsistencies and so they would agree on what things could be withheld.

Reconciliation, 200 lashes, service in the galleys for five years, and life imprisonment in Spain.

Rodrigo Fernández Correa: born in New Veracruz; 23 years old; holder of a bachelor's degree; a doctor; single; the son of Fernando Rodríguez and Blanca Enríquez. He had judaized from the age of ten.

Reconciliation, prohibition from using his title of Bachelor of Arts and Medicine, and exile.

Tomás Méndez: born in Camiña, Portugal 43 years old; a merchant; resided in New Veracruz; the son of Francisco Rodríguez of Camiña, penanced by the Lisbon Inquisition for judaizing, and Leonor Méndez of Oporto, Portugal; both parents died and were "fine Hebrew New Christians." He was the brother of Pedro Méndez, reconciled by this Inquisition for Judaism, and was married to Beatriz Enríquez (p. 321). He had lied and perjured himself during his hearings. He began judaizing at the age of twelve when he was in Pernambuco, Brazil, and in Loanda, Angola.

Reconciliation, 200 lashes, and life imprisonment in Spain.

OTHER CASES OF 1647

The following people were sentenced during 1647 but did not appear in the auto-da-fé of January 23 or in any public auto.

Alberto Marte Correa: born in New Veracruz; 72 years old. He had been suspected of Judaism. He was tortured on August 21, 1647, but never confessed. [His proceso is lost and there is only the above notation in the Abecedario.]

Antonio González Jamaica: born in Sujara, Portugal; 40 years old. He was arrested on suspicion and was tortured on June 6, 1647. He never confessed.

Acquitted July 6, 1647.

Diego López Coronel, alias Diego López Núñez: born in Seville; 33 years old; resided in Campeche. He was suspected of Judaism.

Case suspended.

Diego Méndez: born in Tangier, Africa; resided in New Veracruz; 50 years old; a Portuguese; married to Juana de Alvardado of New Granada [now Colombia]. He was a mariner and a broker. He was arrested as a Jew and an observer of the Law of Moses; he was tortured but never confessed.

Case was suspended on September 2, 1647, and his property returned.

Manuel Franco de Barrios: born in Lisbon; 50 years old; a resident of New Veracruz; married to Catalina de Arco. He was arrested on suspicion of Judaism.

Acquitted on August 19.

Roque Díaz Calleteros: born in Mexico; 36 years old; a resident of Guadalajara; married to Augustina Pinto de Villasana.

Absolved on November 6.

THE AUTO-DA-FÉ OF MARCH 30, 1648

Francisco de León Jaramillo: born in Mexico; 22 years old; circumcized. He was resentenced because he had not made complete disclosure prior to being in the auto of 1646. He had imparted to others many events that had taken place in the house of the Inquisition. He had also reverted to judaizing after 1646. He had bribed one of the Negro slaves who worked for the warden of the Inquisition and had sent messages concealed in peaches to his mother.

First sentence: 200 lashes and two years in jail; resentence: life imprisonment in Spain.

Juan Méndez: born in Sossel near Ebora, Portugal; 35 years old; circumcized; a tailor in Orizaba.

Exile in Spain.

Jorge Ramírez de Montilla: born in Montilla, Andalusia; 31 years old; circumcized; a resident of Queretaro; the son of Diego Enríquez de Montilla, a Portuguese and a merchant, and Isabel Ramírez of Carmona. Both parents had died in Seville. They were Hebrew New Christians. His mother was the sister of Duarte de León Jaramillo and Simón Montero, and she was related to many others who were imprisoned for judaizing. Simón Montero was married to Elena Ramírez, who was a sister of Jorge Ramírez de Montilla. Reference is made to the lavish fortunes of the Jews which they had concealed so that the Inquisition could not find the property. There is the disclosure that Jewish merchants kept two sets of inventories to deceive the Inquisition.

Reconciliation, perpetual exile from the Indies, Madrid, and Seville, and a fine of 2,000 ducats of Castile for extraordinary costs of the Holy Office.

Melchor Rodríguez López: born in Cubillana, Portugal; 40 years old; a grower of cocoa beans in Zacatula; resident of Mexico; the son of Juan López of Guimares, Portugal, a merchant, and Ana Rodríguez of Cubillana, both deceased and Hebrew New Christians. He had lived in Angola and in the city of Laguna on the island of Tenerife, with three compatriots who had been in Flanders and Absterdam [Amsterdam]. Many members of his family had been penanced by the Inquisition in Portugal.

Adjuration *de vehementi*, exile, and a fine of 3,000 ducats of Castile for extraordinary costs of the Holy Office.

Ana Juarez: born in Janay, near Mexico; 25 years old; the daughter of the merchant Gaspar Juarez of Lamego, Portugal, then in Inquisition cells, and Rafaela Enríquez of Seville, reconciled by the Tribunal. Her first husband had been Juan Méndez de Villaviciosa (p. 324). Her second husband was Francisco López de Fonseca, alias Francisco Méndes, of Botan, Portugal, also in Inquisition cells. She had judaized from the age of 14 and had been taught by her grandmother, Juana Enríquez. Her second husband was held in high esteem because his father had been burned at the stake in Portugal. She was known as *Paloma Grande*, the Great Dove, in the cells.

Reconciliation and life imprisonment in Spain.

Ana Núñez: born in Mexico; single; 13 years of age; the daughter of Duarte de León Jaramillo and Isabel Núñez. She was taught about Judaism when she was 7 years of age. She believed that the Messiah had not yet come, that he would be born in Mexico to Inés Pereira, and she adored and believed in Moses. He was to be greeted with these words, "Our father, our father, God save you, amen, amen." She was prohibited from playing with and visiting her Catholic friend. Once her father tied her to a ladder and lashed her with a whip because she recited a rosary. She had the flesh cut off her left shoulder by her father after her mother had been jailed.

Reconciliation; she was not to leave for Spain at once but was to be put into the home of one of the ministers of the Inquisition to be kept busy in the affairs of Catholicism and ultimately, exile.

Antonia Núñez: born in Mexico; 15 years of age; sister of Ana Núñez, above. She was the perfect little Jewess and followed everything that her parents taught her. She prepared the meals of fish and salads. She feigned headaches on fast days. On Friday nights after dinner, she used to wear a red dress of dimity with a hood, face the wall, and recite Jewish prayers for a half hour—sometimes one hour. She also had a piece of flesh removed from her left shoulder.

Reconciliation, jail for two years, and exile to Spain.

Beatriz Enríquez: born in Mexico; 29 years old; the daughter of Antonio Rodríguez Arias and Blanca Enríquez, previously listed, who had had edicts concerning them read and published in Seville; married to Tomas Núñez Peralta of the 1646 auto. He had received an additional 200 lashes on March 21, 1648, because he had not complied with his sentence, had doffed his sanbenito, left the city, and traveled to various parts of New Spain without the permission of the Tribunal. She observed the custom of bringing a hard-boiled or fried egg to mourners, to be eaten without salt; this custom was called *aveluz* [a distortion of the Hebrew word *avelut*]. She revealed the custom of throwing out the water from all the jars in the house of the recently deceased because the soul of the deceased had bathed and washed away their sins in this water. Jews were prohibited not only from marrying Christians but also from having carnal relations with them. The latter was considered the greatest sin for which there was no forgiveness. Teaching the law to children was a firm precept for Jews all over the world. Living in concubinage was not a sin if both parties were Jews and no one was present to perform the marriage. Beatriz assisted her mother in preparing the dough for making matzot, and prayed with her on the nights of Yom Kippur and other fasts. She recited the Jewish prayers on these occasions and prayed in stocking feet. There is a lengthy recital of a dream and also descriptions of funeral rites and shrouds. She was noted for her witchcraft. Her husband had received a dowry of 7,000 pesos.

Reconciliation and life imprisonment in Spain.

Blanca Juárez: born in Mexico; 22 years old; the daughter of Gaspar Juarez and Rafaela Enríquez; the wife of Jorge Jacinto Bazan or Baca, born in Malaga, Castile, and reconciled in this auto. Her grandmother taught her Judaism when she was 10 years of age. Her mother, Rafaela, had been trained by a great dogmatizer who had come from Spain. She was considered a contrite and saintly Jewess. On the eve of the Great Day of Pardon she and all her sisters, aunts, and cousins went to her grandmother's house and each, on her knees, was given "the blessing of Abraham, Isaac, and Jacob, 'our fathers, cause us to survive.'" She used to light candles. She gave a detailed account of her observances of various Jewish holidays. The matzot for Passover which Rafaela and her grandmother baked were distributed by messenger to all the members of the extended family throughout the city. Many members of the family thought that Rafaela might give birth to the Messiah because she exceeded all others in her observance of the Mosaic laws. She was also noted for her great beauty. Once, in an odd ceremony, she was seated on the floor with a silver candle, nude except for a tunic, and all the family were seated about her; they then prayed that she give birth to the Messiah. At the conclusion of the praying her grandmother imagined that an angel had revealed to her that their prayers would be granted. A great party was then held, preceded by a fast and bathing; Blanca was dressed in new fine white silk. The midday meal consisted of fish, with sweets of all kinds including licorice, and lasted until after 10:00 p.m. Blanca's principal entertainment and desire was to study the Law of Moses with people who were knowledgeable and observant. She was known as the Little Dove in the Inquisition cells. She was able to speak an African language that was used by the Negro slaves. Her sentence was due to her having deceived the inquisitors about her repentance, false reconciliation, and because she communicated with other prisoners and advised them of all events.

Reconciliation and life imprisonment in Spain.

Clara Núñez: born in Mexico; 23 years old; single; the daughter of Duarte de

León Jaramillo and Isabel Núñez. She was not permitted to associate with Christians. She liked to eat ham. Christians who despised Jews called them "Jew dogs." She used to twist the neck of hens instead of cutting the necks with a sharp knife and draining the blood. [She appears to be a rebel against the strict observances forced upon her by her father and by Rabbi Simón Montero, her uncle.] She had to pray on her knees and observe the New Moon. She couldn't even wash her hair on the Sabbath. On the night her mother was imprisoned by the Inquisition her father and brother, Francisco de León, hid the family silver, money and bars of silver. After the imprisonment of her father she changed her name to Josefa de Alzate, saying that she was a Moor and had been born in New Veracruz. She had been called Clara *la Judia,* Clara the Jewess. The jewelry which had been hidden for her and for her sister Antonia Núñez and that they might need in the case of imprisonment had been dissipated.

Reconciliation, jail for six months, and exile.

Diego Rodríguez Arias: born in Seville; 45 years old; single; circumcized; the son of Antonio Rodríguez Arias and Blanca Enríquez. He was the despair of his parents. He had had a brother who had apparently lived and died among Christians, and over whose death his mother cried endlessly. Diego's name in jail was *Gigote,* minced meat or hash.

Reconciliation and life imprisonment in Spain.

Francisco López Díaz, called *El Chato* (Flat Nose): born in Casteloblanco, Portugal; resident of Zacatecas, New Galicia; 41 years old; single; the son of Pedro Diaz Santillan, collector of royal rents, and Juana Estevez, also of Casteloblanco, who had been reconciled by the Inquisition in Seville. His whole family had fled the Inquisition at Lisbon and hid in a house in Seville for one year. They changed their names and were befriended by other Jews in Seville. On the "Fast of the Great Day or of Pardon," one of the family acted as rabbi and read from the book in Hebrew. They sat, stood, and bowed their heads many times while praying. All the men wore head coverings and the women large hoods, and many candles were lit. El Chato came to Mexico in 1637 and stayed in the home of a famous Jewess, whose house served as a reception center in Mexico for all newly arrived Jewish immigrants. He joined the community of Simón Váez because he wanted to marry Váez' niece. Jews outside of the city sent money and gifts as charity for the Jewish poor in Mexico. There were committees to visit the sick Jews in the hospitals. The Jews had secret signs to identify themselves to each other. The Jews used to say that the Holy Office was not persecuting the Jews because they had converted to Judaism but because the Holy Office wanted the wealth and property of the Jews. El Chato was respected as a saint among the other Jews. He had served as a spy for his community when the arrests of the Jews commenced, observing who was being taken prisoner. He told of an emergency meeting in the home of Simón Váez and how they planned strategy for the testimony they should give and what should be concealed. He was called Tobacco in the cells.

Reconciliation, five years in the galleys, and life imprisonment in Spain.

Jorge Jacinto Bazan, or Baca: born in Malaga, Spain; 38 years old; circumcized; a merchant; the son of Diego Núñez Baca of Rambla, near Córdoba, a merchant, and Elena Rodríguez of Malaga, both deceased in Marseille, France; married to Blanca Juarez. He had been trained in Judaism since he was 13 years old, and had been circumcized by a Florentine Jewish surgeon. He came to New Spain in 1637 with a letter of recommendation to Simón Váez from a Spanish contractor of military supplies. A famous rabbi (Juan Pacheco de León) lived in Simón Váez' house; Jorge knew him from when he had attended a Hebrew school for children. Jorge had been in Pisa and Leghorn, where there were public synagogues; he had a letter of recommendation to the rabbi from someone who had gone to Salonica. Jorge's parents lived openly as Jews in Marseille and wore "the clothing and habits of Jews."

Reconciliation, 200 lashes, and life imprisonment in Spain.

Leonor Martínez: 14 years old; born in Mexico; the daughter of Tomas Treviño de Sobremonte of Rio Seco, Old Castile, and María Gómez, born in Mexico, a reconciliada. Leonor had begun judaizing at the age of 8 or 9 years. When she had new shoes she would first wear them for the Sabbath. She was not permitted to eat any pork products or anything cooked in lard; she could eat only things fried in butter or oil. Meat that was slaughtered had to be in complete health *(con entera salud)*. She attended weddings of Jewish couples; these were first performed "in the Jewish manner" without a priest; later the couple would be married in Church. When her father left on a trip, she and her brothers would stand before him while he blessed them with Jewish prayers and Davidic psalms.

Reconciliation, exemption from wearing a sanbenito, and orders to place her in a house of the Holy Office and instructed in Catholicism before being sent to Spain for life imprisonment.

Manuel de Acosta, alias Francisco de Torres: born in Lisbon, Portugal; 29 years old; a merchant; the son of Antonio de Acosta of Orense, Galicia, deceased, and Juana López, a Portuguese Hebrew New Christian; married to Isabel Tinoco, born in Zacatecas, New Spain, and 16 years old. They had a daughter Meceda, three years old. His wife was the daughter of Catalina Enríquez and Diego Tinoco, both of Seville and Inquisition prisoners in Mexico, and the granddaughter of Antonio Rodríguez Arias and Blanca Enríquez. He came to Mexico in 1638 with letters of recommendation to Simón Váez as a prospective groom. He was tested for his knowledge of Judaism by Israel's grandmother. He contended that his religious observances were only to be able to marry Isabel. There were four publications of testimony against him before he made a full confession.

Reconciliation, 200 lashes, five years in the galleys as an oarsman without pay, and life imprisonment in Spain.

Manuel de Mella: born in Huelva, Portugal; resided in Guadalajara; 54 years old; a goldsmith; the son of Gregorio de Mella, a merchant of Zamora, Spain, and Violante Rodríguez of Ledesma, Spain, near Zamora. Manuel first had married Beatriz Rodríguez de Alba, a Jewess of Seville, in Utrera; she was the daughter of Portuguese parents and had been reconciled in Seville. He then married Violante Juarez, born in Lima and reconciled by this Holy Office. She was the "illegitimate" daughter of Gaspar Juarez and a half sister of Ana Blanca Juarez, both reconciled in this same auto. He came to New Spain in 1624 after the death of his first wife. He was reputed to be an excellent Jew; he stayed in Mexico and was friendly with many other Jews. He became famous as a zealous observer of Jewish rites and did a great amount of proselytizing. After his marriage to Violante, herself a very learned Jewess and an orthodox practitioner, they set up their home in Guadalajara, where they found it convenient to live because one could judaize more freely and there were many Jews there and in the surrounding areas. His home was like a synagogue because Jews came from far and wide to congregate there. He and his wife were regarded as blessed of the Law and were most charitable with his brothers of the Hebrew nation. He was known as *Letamca*, broom, and *Platero*, silversmith, in the cells.

Reconciliation, 200 lashes, and life imprisonment in Spain.

Micaela Enríquez: born in Mexico; 34 years old; the daughter of Antonio Rodríguez Arias and Blanca Enríquez; married to Sebastian Cardoso of Seville, reconciled by this Holy Office. She had begun practicing Jewish rites at the age of 12 years. She observed all Sabbaths, fast days, and holy days. [The proceso reports that she made Cro *(hecho el Cro)* on her knees, together with other Jews. Micaela vehemently labeled this a lie. *Cro* is an enigma to authorities consulted as well as to this author. In another part of the trial, reference was made to *Horcos*. G. García stated that she *Orcos, palabra de suma ignominia con que los desta incredula nacion motejan a los cristianos*, a most insulting term applied by Jews to Christians. The word may mean hell or damnation, but it must have been a greater vulgarity in those days.] She baked matzot for Passover and had all new crockery for this holiday. Certain prayers, not described, were recited by her and her mother over the first batch taken from the oven. She burned candles, i.e., wicks in oil, on Friday nights in an empty closet so that the slaves could not see them, and she permitted them to burn all night. When the Host was raised at Mass, she would make a fist with the thumb through the first and second fingers and she would spit. At other times when the Host was raised aloft, she would take her handkerchief and wipe her eyes and face in order not to see it or the chalice. Prior to her wedding, her entire family made a fast to insure a successful married life. At this fast, they squatted or sat close to the ground, and all the men and women kept their heads bowed and their hands placed on top of their heads. They remained that way for a long time while someone read from a Jewish book about the ceremonies and precepts of the Mosaic law. At the end of this ceremony, everyone arose content and confident that she would be well bethothed. Her mother arranged the match with Sebastian Cardoso because he was not Micaela's inferior in Jewish observances and was equal to her other brother-in-law. Micaela did everything possible during her testimony before the Tribunal to play down Sebastian's observances, even denying that he was a Jew, while confessing to everything she had ever done as a Jewess. [The word *aveluz* used in the proceso and in the relación is *avelut* in Hebrew, and means mourning rites.] The lapels of the men's jackets and the jackets, blouses, or dresses of the women were rent as a sign of mourning, and Jewish prayers were recited in a low voice. [It is probable that either the *Kaddish* or *El Mole Rachamim*, the prayers for the dead, were recited; this deduction is based on a study of the original proceso.] She was also noted for her witchcraft. She was known as *Boticario*, Apothecary, in the cells. During her incarceration, she and others conspired to undo the work of the Holy Office by bribery and other illicit means. They

also met to agree upon what should be revealed to the inquisitors and
to avoid any discrepancies in their testimony. Micaela revealed to some
of the prisoners that the inquisitors were using an unnamed Portuguese
as a "stool pigeon" and as a false witness to incriminate the Jews.
    Reconciliation and life imprisonment in Spain.
Rafaela Enríquez: born in Seville; 42 years of age; the daughter of Antonio
    Rodríguez Arias and Blanca Enríquez. She claimed to have received a
    dispensation from Rome to marry Gaspar Juarez of Lamego, Portugal,
    a merchant, her father's first cousin. Her mother had trained her as a
    Jewess when she was 12 or 13 years of age. She was sagacious in choos-
    ing those to dogmatize and in the manner in which she operated. She
    knew how to deceive others and had an explanation for her practices
    which might arouse suspicions about her faith. Prior to her incarcera-
    tion, the dinner parties at her home were held in the same style as in
    Leghorn, Pisa, Amsterdam, or other places where the Jews lived openly
    and freely. On the eve of the fast of the Great Day she would burn
    more than eighty candles for the living and the dead, and her house
    was lit as a gleaming Catholic altar on Holy Thursday. Prior to this
    day and as a Jewish ceremony and for penitence, she and her sisters
    would bathe in hot water, and they threw jars of cold water on each
    other's shoulders. Her husband, Gaspar, had been imprisoned by the
    Inquisition in Seville, as had many of his family. This caused him to be
    regarded as a great Jew among the Hebrew nation. Their home was
    used as a synagogue, and many Jews congregated there to study the
    law and fast. Rafaela arranged matches for her daughters, Ana and
    Blanca, when they came of age, with known and approved Jews. She
    admonished her daughters never to marry out of the faith. Her son,
    Diego Juarez, had died in 1641 in the loss of the Spanish ships off Santo
    Domingo. Manuel Alvarez de Arellano, however, survived the catas-
    trophe and wrote that she should be complimented and congratulated
    on what a wonderful son she had raised as a Jew, and his last words had
    been of his mother. She was accused of witchcraft, knowledge of pow-
    ders, and of being an expert mortician and knowledgeable of all fu-
    neral customs.
    Reconciliation and life imprisonment in Spain.
Rafael de Sobremonte: born in Guadalajara, New Galicia; 17 years old; cir-
    cumcized; the son of Tomas Treviño de Sobremonte and María Gó-
    mez. His father had circumcized him when he was young and he had
    been taught Jewish laws and customs. In 1643 he and his father, on
    horses, rose to Zacatecas, 240 miles from Mexico. While there from
    June to December he fasted every Thursday and on some Mondays.
    They bathed from the waist down and washed their hands and faces.
    Since these were Jewish customs, they could only perform these ablu-
    tions before going to bed in order to dissimulate. Even while they trav-
    eled, his father would stop next to a stream, wash his hands, cover his
    head with a cloth which he carried in his belt, put a prayer shawl on
    his shoulders, and recite some Mosaic prayers while standing. In 1644,
    he traveled to Guadalajara with his father, 270 miles from Mexico.
    Reconciliation and to be exiled after he had been taught Catholi-
    cism in a monastery.
Sebastian Cardoso: born in Seville; 56 years old; circumcized; a merchant; the

husband of Micaela Enríquez; the son of Diego Cardoso, an oil-seller, and Antonia Gómez, both of Marchena, Andalusia. He had judaized since he was 18 years of age. He had observed fasts in Spain and continued after he came to New Spain in 1628. He had worked as a secretary to Simón Váez.

Reconciliation and life imprisonment in Spain.

Simón de León: born in Mexico; 17 years old; a tailor's apprentice; the son of Duarte de León Jaramillo and Isabel Núñez. Ever since the age of 10 or 11 his parents had made him observe the Law of Moses. Since he had shown some obstinacy about saying what his parents wanted him to say about Judaism, they would make him wear coarse cloth and shirts such as slaves wore. Sometimes he would be tied to a ladder and lashed when he would refer to the Holy Virgin. His brother was Francisco de León and his sisters Antonia and Ana Núñez. He was known among his friends as a Jew and son of Jews.

Reconciliation, jail for one year, and exile.

Violante Juarez: born in Lima; 36 years old; illegitimate daughter of Gaspar Juarez; married to Manuel de Mella; resided in Guadalajara. She had left Peru for Spain with her father when she was a small child. She had been taught Judaism in Seville. Her stepmother, Rafaela Enríquez, had also taught her. She had no images or pictures of Jesus, Mary, or any of the saints. Her home was the synagogue in Guadalajara.

Reconciliation, 100 lashes because she had lied and twice deceived the inquisitors about the sincerity of her repentance, and life imprisonment in Spain.

Appendix B

Extracts of Inquisition Canons

The excerpts from the printed rule of the Holy Office reproduced below were taken from Jean Antoine Llorente's *The History of the Inquisition of Spain*, pp. 228-251.

6th.   In arrests for formal heresy, there shall be an immediate sequestration of all property of the denounced person.

9th.   The *alguazil* [jail warden] shall deduct from the sequestrated property a sufficient portion to defray the expenses of the food, lodging, and journey of the prisoner; he shall give an account of what he received when he arrives at the Inquisition. If any money remains, he shall give it to the cashier, to be employed in the maintenance of the prisoner.

10th.   The *alguazil* shall require the prisoner to give up his money, papers, arms, and everything which it might be dangerous for him to be in possession of; he shall not allow him to have any communication either by speech or writing with the other prisoners without receiving permission from the inquisitors. He shall remit all the effects found upon the person of the prisoner to the gaoler, and shall take a receipt, with the date of the day on which the remittance took place. The gaoler shall inform the inquisitors of the arrival of the prisoner, and he shall lodge him in such a manner that he cannot have at his disposal anything which might be dangerous in his hands . . . One of the notaries of the holy office shall be present and shall draw up the verbal process of the decree of imprisonment and its execution; even the hour when the prisoner entered the prison must be mentioned, as this point is important in the accounts of the cashier.

11th.   The gaoler shall not lodge several prisoners together. He shall not permit them to communicate with each other, unless the inquisitors allow it.

12th.   The gaoler shall be provided with a register, in which all the effects in the chamber of the prisoner, with the clothes and food which he receives from each detained person, shall be noted; . . . he shall not remit any food or clothing to the prisoners without examining them with great attention, to ascertain if they contain letters, arms, or anything of which they might make a bad use.

13th.   When the inquisitors think proper, they shall order the prisoner to be brought into the chamber of audience; they shall cause him to sit on a bench or small seat, and take an oath to speak the truth, at this time, and on all succeeding audiences; they shall ask him his name, his surname, his age, his country, the place where he dwells, his profession and rank, and the time of his arrest; they shall treat him with humanity, and respect his rank, but without derogating from the authority of judges, that the accused may not infringe the respect due to them, to commit any reprehensible act towards their persons. The accused shall stand while the act of denunciation by the fiscal is read.

14th.   The accused shall be afterwards examined on his genealogy. He shall be asked if he is married: if more than once, what woman he married: how many children he had by each marriage, their age, as well as their rank and place of dwelling. The recorder shall write down these details, paying attention to place each name at the beginning of a line, because this practice is useful in consulting registers, to discover if the accused is not descended from Jews, Moors, heretics, or other individuals punished by the holy office.

15th.   When the preceding ceremony has passed, the accused shall be required to give an abridged history of his life, mentioning those towns where he has made a considerable stay, the motives of his sojourn, the persons he associated with, the friends he acquired, his studies, the masters he studied under, the period when he began them, and the time that he continued them; if he has been out of Spain, at what time and with whom he had quitted the country, and how long he had been absent. He shall be asked if he is instructed in the truths of the Christian religion, and shall be required to repeat the Pater-noster, the Ave Maria, and the Credo. He shall be asked if he has confessed himself, and to what confessors. When he has given an account of all these things, he shall be asked if he knows or suspects the cause of his arrest, and his reply shall regulate the questions put to him afterwards. The inquisitors shall avoid interrupting the accused while he is speaking, and shall allow him to express himself freely while the recorder writes down his declarations, unless they are foreign to the trial. They shall ask all necessary questions, but shall avoid fatiguing him by examining him on subjects not relating to the trial, unless he gives occasion for it by his replies.

16th.   It is proper that the inquisitors should always suspect that they have been deceived by the witnesses, and that they shall be so by the accused, and that they should not take either side; for, if they adopt an opinion too soon, they will not be able to act with that impartiality which is suitable to their station, and on the contrary will be liable to fall into error.

17th.   The inquisitors shall not speak to the accused during the audience, or at other times, of any affairs not relating to his own. The recorder shall write down the questions and replies; and, after the audience, he shall read it to the accused, that he may sign it. If he wishes to add, retrench, alter, or elucidate any article, the recorder shall write after his dictation, without suppressing or certifying the articles already written.

18th.   The fiscal shall present his act of accusation within the time prescribed by the ordinances; he shall accuse the prisoner of being a heretic in general terms, and afterwards mention, in particular, the facts and propositions of which he is charged. The inquisitors have not the right of punishing an accused person for crimes which do not relate to matters of faith; but if the preparatory instruction mentions any, the fiscal shall make it the object of an accusation, because this circumstance, and that of his general good or bad conduct, assists in determining the degree of credence to be given to his replies, and serves for other purposes in his trial.

19th.   Although the accused may confess all the charges brought against him in the first audiences of admonition, yet the fiscal shall draw up and present his act of accusation, because experience has shown, that it is better that a trial, caused by the denunciation of a person who is a party in the cause, should be continued and judged at the prosecution of the denunciator; that the inquisitors may be at liberty to deliberate on the application of punishments and penances, which would not be the case if they proceeded officially.

21st.   At the end of his requisition, the fiscal shall introduce a clause, stating, that if the inquisitors do not think his accusation sufficiently proved, they are requested to decree the torture for the accused, because, as it cannot be inflicted without previous notice, it is proper that the accused should be informed that it has been required; and this moment appears the most convenient, because the prisoner is not prepared for it, and he will receive the notice with less agitation.

23rd.   The inquisitors shall give the prisoner to understand that it is of great consequence to him to speak the truth. One of the advocates of the holy office shall be appointed to defend him, who shall communicate with him in the presence of an inquisitor, in order to prepare himself to reply in writing to the accusation, after swearing fidelity to the accused, and secrecy to the tribunal, although he had already taken the oath at the time that he was appointed the advocate of the prisoners of the holy office. He must endeavor to persuade the accused that it is of the greatest consequence to be sincere, to ask pardon and submit to a penance if he acknowledges his guilt. His reply shall be communicated to the fiscal, who, with the prisoner and his advocate, shall be present at the audience, and shall demand proofs.

28th.   In the interval between the proof and the publication, the prisoner may demand audiences, through the gaoler. The inquisitors must grant them without delay in order to profit by the inclination of the accused which may change from day to day.

35th.   When the accused has replied to the publication of the depositions, he shall be permitted to consult with his advocate in the presence of an inquisitor and the recorder, that he may prepare his defense. The recorder shall write down the particulars of the conference which he considers worthy of attention. Neither the inquisitor nor recorder, still less the advocate, shall remain alone with the accused . . . It is sometimes advisable that learned and pious persons should visit the accused, to exhort them to confess what they obstinately deny, though they have been convicted. These interviews can only take place in the presence of the recorder or an inquisitor . . .

36th.   If the accused wishes to write, to fix the points of his defense, he shall be furnished with paper; but the sheets shall be counted and numbered by the recorder, that the accused may give them back again either written or blank. When his work is finished, he shall be allowed to converse with his advocate, to whom he may communicate what he has written, on condition that his defender restores the original without taking a copy when he presents his address to the tribunal. When there is an examination in the defense of the prisoner, he shall be required to name, on the margin of each article, the witnesses he wishes to call, that those who are the most worthy of credit may be examined. He must also be required to name as witnesses none but Christians of an ancient race, who are neither his servants nor relations, unless it is a case when the questions can only be answered by them. Before the address is presented by the advocate, if the accused requires it, it shall be communicated to him, and the inquisitors shall desire the advocate to confine himself to the defense of the accused in what he has to say, and to observe a strict silence on everything said in the world, as experience has shown the inconvenience of this sort of revelations, even in respect to the accused persons; they shall cause him to restore all the papers, without taking copies of them, or even of the address, of which he must give up the notes, if there are any.

39th.   When the inquisitors receive important information in defense of the prisoner, he shall be brought before the tribunal accompanied by his advocate; they shall inform him that the proofs of all the circumstances which might mitigate his crime have been received, and that they can conclude the trial, unless any other demand occurs on their part, in which they will do everything which may be permitted for the prisoner. If he declares that he has nothing more to say, the fiscal may give in his conclusions. It will be proper, however, that he should not do it immediately, that he may take advantage of every circumstance that may take place. If the accused demands the publication of the depositions in his defense, it must be refused, as it may tend to discover the persons who have deposed against him.

41st.   When the accused confesses himself guilty, and his confessions have the required conditions, if he is not relapsed, he shall be admitted to reconciliation; his property shall be seized; he shall be clothed in the habit of a penitent, or a Sanbenito . . . If it is proper that he shall remain in prison for an unlimited time, it shall be said in his sentence, that his punishment shall last as long as the inquisitors think proper. If the accused has really relapsed, after abjuring a formal heresy, or is a false penitent when he has abjured as violently suspected, and is convicted in the present trial of the same heresy, he shall be given up to the common judge according to the civil law, and his punishment shall not be remitted, although he may protest that his repentance is sincere, and his confession true in this case.

43rd.   If the accused is convicted of heresy, bad faith, and obstinacy, he shall be relaxed, but the inquisitors must not neglect to endeavour to convert him, that he may die in the faith of the church.

44th.   If the accused who has been condemned, and informed of his sentence on the day before the auto-de-fé, repents during the night and confesses his sins, or part of them, in a manner that shows true repentance, he shall not be conducted to the auto-de-fé, but his execution shall be suspended, because it might be improper to allow him to hear the names of the persons condemned to death, and those condemned to other punishments, for this knowledge and the report of the offence might assist him in preparing his judicial confession. If the accused is converted on the scaffold of the auto-de-fé, before he has heard his sentence, the inquisitors must suppose that the fear of death has more influence in this conversion than true repentance; but if, from different circumstances and the nature of the confession, they wish to suspend the execution, they are permitted to do so, considering at the same time that confessions made in such circumstances are not worthy of belief, and more particularly those which accuse other individuals.

45th.   The inquisitors must maturely consider motives and circumstances before they decree the torture; and when they have resolved to have recourse to it, they must state the motive; they must declare if the torture is to be employed *in caput proprium*, because the accused is subjected to it as persisting in his denials, and incompletely convicted in his own trial; or if he suffers it *in caput alienum*, as a witness who denies, in the trial of another accused, the facts of which he has been a joint witness. If he is convicted of bad faith in his own cause, and is consequently liable to be relaxed, or if he is equally so in any other affair, he may be tortured. . . . If he does not reveal anything in being tortured as a witness, he shall nevertheless be condemned as an accused; . . .

46th.   If only a semi-proof of the crime exists, or if appearances will not admit of the acquittal of the prisoner, he shall make an abjuration as being either violently or slightly suspected. As this measure is not a punishment for the past, but a precaution for the future, pecuniary penalties shall be imposed; but he shall be informed that if he again commits the crime for which he was denounced, he will be considered as having relapsed, and be delivered over to the secular judge;

49th.   When it is necessary to decree the torture, the accused shall be informed of the motives for employing it, and the offenses for which he is to suffer it; but after it has been decided, he shall not be examined on any particular fact, he shall be allowed to say what he pleases. Experience has shown that if he is questioned on any subject when pain has reduced him to the last extremity, he will say anything that is required of him, which may be injurious to other persons, in making them parties concerned, and producing other inconveniences.

55th.   The judges, notary, and the executioners shall be present at the torture; when it is over, the inquisitors shall cause an individual who has been wounded to be properly attended, without allowing any suspected person to approach him until he has ratified his declarations.

58th.   When the inquisitors release an accused person from the secret prisons, he shall be conducted to the chamber of audience; they shall there ask him if the gaoler treated him and the other prisoners well or ill; if he has communicated with him or other prisoners on subjects foreign to the trial; if he has seen or known that other prisoners conversed with persons not confined in the prison, or if the gaoler gave them any advice. They shall command him to secret these details, and all that has passed since his detention, and shall make him sign a promise to this effect, if he knows how to write, that he may fear to break it.

61st.　　When sufficient proof exists to authorize proceedings against the memory and property of a deceased person, according to the ancient instruction, the accusation of the fiscal shall be signified to the children, the heirs, or other interested persons, each of whom shall receive a copy of the notification. If no person presents himself to defend the memory of the accused, or to appeal against the seizure of his goods, the inquisitors shall appoint a defender, and pursue the trial, considering him as a party. If any one interested in the affair appears, his rights shall be admitted, although he should be a prisoner in the holy office at the time; but he shall be obliged to choose a free person to act for him.

65th.　　The inquisitors may take cognizance of several crimes which occasion suspicion of heresy, although they do not consider the accused an heretic, on account of certain circumstances; such as bigamy, blasphemy, and suspicious propositions. In these cases the application of the punishments depends upon the prudence of the judges, who ought to follow the rules of right, and consider the gravity of the offense. However, if they condemn the accused to corporeal punishment, such as whipping, or the galleys, they shall not say that it may be commuted for pecuniary penalties; for this measure would be an extortion, and an infringement of the respect due to the tribunal.

72nd.　　The witnesses in a trial shall not be confronted, because experience has shown that this measure is useless and inconvenient, independently of the infringement of the law of secrecy which is the result.

Notes

ALL TRANSLATIONS are by the author unless otherwise indicated. All Old Testament references are from *The Pentateuch and Haftorahs*, edited by Chief Rabbi Dr. Joseph H. Hertz (England), 5 volumes, London, 1940.

ABBREVIATIONS

ABEC Abecedario, an original Inquisition document at the Henry E. Huntington Library. It is an alphabetical index of cases before the Mexican Inquisition, and the pages are unnumbered.
AGN Archivo General de la Nación de México, Ramo de la Inquisición (Mexican National Archives, Inquisition Section).
AHN Archivo Histórico Nacional de Madrid (National Historical Archives, Madrid).
Exp. Expediente (file number).
f., fs. foja(s), leaf, leaves.
HAHR *Hispanic American Historical Review.*
JPS Jewish Publication Society, Philadelphia, Pennsylvania.
PAJHS Publications of American Jewish Historical Society, including the *American Jewish Historical Quarterly.*
Pro. Proceso (trial proceeding).
P/c Proceso contra (proceedings against).
TJHSE Transactions of the Jewish Historical Society of England.

INTRODUCTION

1. Lucien Wolf, *The Jews of the Canary Islands,* p. xxii.
2. Seymour B. Liebman, "Mexican Mestizo Jews," pp. 144-175.
3. H. J. Zimmels, *Ashkenazim and Sephardim.*
4. James Finn, *History of the Jews in Spain and Portugal,* p. vi.
5. Américo Castro, *The Structure of Spanish History,* p. 10. The Hispanic people constantly present a paradox. Yitzhak (Fritz) Baer, in *A History of the Jews in Christian Spain,* Vol. 1, p. 2, wrote: "The war

against the Moslem neighbors caused the Spaniards to become at once the most tolerant and the most fanatical people in medieval Christendom."

6. José Amador de los Ríos, *Historia social, politica y religiosa de los judíos de España y Portugal*, Vol. 1, p. 19.
7. Salvador de Madariaga, *The Fall of the Spanish American Empire*, p. 226.
8. Raphael Altamira, *The History of Spain*, p. xxx.
9. Ramón Menéndez Pidal, *The Spaniards in Their History*, p. 75.
10. Boleslao Lewin, *La Inquisición en Hispanoamerica*, pp. 121-125.
11. Salo W. Baron, *History and Jewish Historians*, pp. 12, 21.
12. Salo W. Baron, "Conference Themes," p. 137.
13. Peter Boyd-Bowman, "La Emigración Peninsular a América, 1520-1539," p. 175.
14. Herbert I. Bloom, *Economic Activities of the Jews of Amsterdam in the 17th Century*, p. 93, quoting from the Academie Royale de Belgique's *Bulletin de la Classe des Lettres*, VII (1905), p. 581.
15. Pro. Juan Franco, AGN 38, Exp. 1.
16. Vicente Riva Palacio *et al.*, *México a través de los siglos*, Vol. 2, p. 703.
17. José de J. Nuñez y Dominguez, "Los Judios en la Historia y Literatura Mexicanas," *Judaica* 139 (January, 1945), p. 35.

CHAPTER 1

1. Edward P. Cheyney, *European Background of American History*, p. 67, states: "We know now . . . that Spain was a hollow shell. After the reign of Charles V, population stood stationary or declined, and wealth decreased."
2. Seymour B. Liebman, "Spanish Jews in the 14th and 15th Centuries," p. 44; I. S. Revah, "Le plaidoyer en faveur des nouveaux chrétiens," p. 33.
3. Quoted by Elias Haim Lindo, *History of Jews of Spain and Portugal*, p. 294.
4. Andrés Bernáldez, *Memorias del reinado de los Reyes Católicos*, Chapter XXII.
5. Castro, *The Structure of Spanish History*, p. 519.
6. Abravanel is the preferred spelling according to the Spanish. See *Enciclopedia Judaica Castellana*, Vol. 1, pp. 19, 53; *Jewish Encyclopedia*, Vol. 1, p. 126; and Benzion Netanyahu, *Don Isaac Abravanel*, p. 261. Other spellings are Abarbanel and Ábrabanel.
   Isaac Abravanel left Spain with his coreligionists in 1492 and sired a famous family. One of those who claimed him as an ancestor was Francisco Rivas Puigcerver, a Mexican Jew who was born in Campeche, Mexico, about 1846 and died at the age of ninety-one.
7. Henry C. Lea, *The History of the Inquisition in Spain*, Vol. 1, p. 135 (hereafter cited as *Inquisition in Spain*); Heinrich Graetz, *History of the Jews*, Vol. 4, pp. 348, 351. On p. 351, Graetz reported that Abraham Senior converted because Isabella threatened "sharper measures against the Jews" if she lost his services. Ferdinand, Isabella, and Cardinal González de Medina acted as godparents for Senior and his family at their baptism. Senior later changed his name to Coronel. Coincidentally, in

Amsterdam, London, and the New World in the seventeenth century
there were several people whose patronymic was "Senior Coronel."
8. Lindo, *op. cit.*, p. 285.
9. Gregorio Marañon, *Antonio Pérez*, Vol. 2, p. 7.
10. Castro, *op. cit.*, p. 467.
11. Salvador de Madariaga, *Fall of the Spanish American Empire*, pp. 226, 227.
12. Lindo, *op. cit.*, p. 294.
13. Cecil Roth, *A History of the Marranos*, p. 30.
14. Gordon W. Allport, *The Nature of Prejudice*, pp. 56-58.
15. Yaacov Vainstein, *The Cycle of the Jewish Year*, p. 110.
16. A. S. Turberville, *La Inquisición Española*, p. 26.
17. William H. Prescott, *The History of the Conquest of Mexico*, p. 30.

CHAPTER 2

1. Alfonso Toro, ed., *Los judíos en la Nueva España*, p. 128.
2. Clarence H. Haring, *The Spanish Empire in America*, p. 29.
3. Eric R. Wolf, *Sons of the Shaking Earth*, pp. 29, 30.
4. Haring, *op. cit.*, pp. 10, 198, 199.
5. Silvio Zavala, *Spanish Colonization in America*, p. 89.
6. Ricardo Albanes, *Los judíos a través de los siglos*, p. 114.
7. Francisco Fernández del Castillo, *Libros y liberos del siglo XVI*, p. 584; Rafael Heliodoro Vallé, "Judíos en México," p. 225.
8. Nicolas López Martínez, *Los Judaizantes Castellanos*, p. 375.
9. Alfonso Toro, *La Iglesia y el estado en México*, p. 19, wrote: "Not only was the secular clergy venal, it was also profoundly ignorant. As Zumárraga in the last cited letter [pp. 17, 18 of the book] said, 'Your Highness should know that there is no clergyman in the entire city [Mexico] who knows the order of the Cathedral and in that which they should pursue. This is no small matter because they who have to lead are ignorant. And if they do not know their duties, how much less are they able to learn the Indian language so that they might strictly pursue their duties!'"
   Lesley Byrd Simpson noted in *The Encomienda in New Spain*, p. 11, that "The friars were too loose in their relations with the Indian women. One friar in Cuernavaca was reported to have got as many as eight Indian girls with child. . . . Fray Toribio de Benavente—the famous Motolina—was reported to have sent to Spain the sum of 700 *castellanos de oro*, and since he had no estate, he must have extorted the money from the Indians."
10. I. S. Emmanuel, "History of the Netherland Antilles," quoted from manuscript by permission of author. Publication due late 1970.
11. Hubert Herring, *A History of Latin America*, p. 221.
12. Seymour B. Liebman, "Research Problems in Mexican Jewish History," p. 170. See also A. Richard Konetzke, *La Emigración española al Río de la Plata durante el siglo XVI*, p. 15; R. de Lafuente Machain, *Los Portugueses en Buenos Aires*, pp. 52, 53; and letter from inquisitors to the Consejo dated November 22, 1611, AHN, Libro 1037, fs. 191v-191r.
13. Julio Jiménez Rueda, *Herejías y supersticiónes en la Nueva España*, p. 89.

14. Haring, *op. cit.*, p. 303.
15. *Ibid.*, p. 303.
16. Alfonso Toro, *Los judíos en la Nueva España*, p. xxvii.
17. Juan Friede, "The Catálogo de Pasajeros and Spanish Migration to America to 1550," pp. 333 ff.
18. Riva Palacio, *México à través de los siglos*, Vol. 2, p. 703.
19. Fernando Benítez, *Los Primeros Mexicanos*, pp. 274-275.
20. Lafuente Machain, *op. cit.*, p. 17.
21. Cecil Roth, *The World of the Sephardim*, p. 17.
22. Simpson, *op. cit.*, pp. 78, 79.
23. Seymour B. Liebman, *Guide to Jewish References in the Mexican Colonial Era*, pp. 13, 89 (hereafter cited as *Guide to Jewish References;* Toro, *Los judíos en la Nueva España*, pp. xxii, xxiii.
24. J. Horace Nunemaker, "Inquisition Papers of Mexico," p. 6.
25. Haring, *op. cit.*, p. 10.
26. William Harris Rule, *History of the Inquisition*, Vol. 1, p. 366.

CHAPTER 3

1. Benzion Netanyahu, *The Marranos of Spain*, pp. 26 *et seq.*
2. Nahum N. Glatzer, *Faith and Knowledge*, p. xiv.
3. Richard E. Greenleaf, *Zumárraga and the Mexican Inquisition*, p. 99 and Chapter VI.
4. George A. Kohut, "Jewish Martyrs of the Inquisition in South America," p. 119.
5. AGN 2, Exp. 2.
6. Liebman, *Guide to Jewish References*, p. 126. The practice of beating images and crosses with the figure of Christ was pursued in Spain and Peru, as well as in New Spain, by Negroes and slaves as well as Jews. According to Ricardo Palma, in *Tradiciones Peruanas, completas*, p. 362, the existence of many Portuguese Jews in Lima in 1635 was discovered by a porter who saw them lashing an image on a Friday night.
7. H. J. Zimmels, *Ashkenazim and Sephardim*, pp. 284, 285, 287.
8. *Ibid.*, p. 43.
9. Solomon Gaon, "Sephardi Character and Outlook," p. 103.
10. Liebman, *Guide to Jewish References*, p. 89, entry 968.
11. *Ibid.*, p. 89, entry 972.
12. AGN 337, Exp. 7; *cf* also AGN 77.
13. Milton Steinberg, *Basic Judaism*, p. 150.
14. Zimmels, *op. cit.*, p. 284; quotation from Ibn Verga, *La Vara del Judah.*
15. Cecil Roth, *History of the Marranos*, p. 276.
16. Palma, *op. cit.*, pp. 1218, 1219.
17. José Toribio Medina, *Historia del Tribunal del Santo Oficio de la Inquisición de Lima*, Vol. 2, pp. 75, 78, 79, 93, 221 (hereafter cited as *Inquisición de Lima*).
18. Julio Caro Barjoa, *Los judíos en España moderna y contemporánea*, Vol. 1, pp. 40, 41.
19. Roth, *op. cit.*, p. 16.
20. Abraham A. Neuman, *The Jews in Spain*, Vol. 2, p. 28.
21. Mariano Picón Salas, *A Cultural History of Spanish America*, pp. 31, 32.

22. Roth, *op. cit.*, p. 85.
23. Fernando Espejo, "The Santa Cruz Museum," *Oro Verde*, p. 21.

CHAPTER 4

1. Cecil Roth, *House of Nasi*, p. 4. This custom was observed by crypto-Jews in Italy. They told a boy at age thirteen that he was "of the seed of Israel." He was then taught the fundamentals of Jewish beliefs and practices.
2. Cyrus Adler, "The Trial of Jorge de Almeida," p. 34.
3. Abba H. Silver, *Where Judaism Differed*, p. 207.
4. Zech. 8:18.
5. Silver, *op. cit.*, p. 196.
6. *Ibid.*, p. 206.
7. I am indebted to Dr. Abraham S. Halkin for having told me that the Talmud reports a similar dispute almost 2,000 years ago. The dispute was over the date of the day to be observed. The disputants were the head of the Sanhedrin and one of the judges. The lesser judge attended on the day set by the *Rosh* (head), but not out of respect for the Rosh, but for the sake of unity in Israel. Some of the Jews of Guadalajara did not heed Manuel de Mella, who was considered one of the most knowledgeable in that part of New Spain. There were two factions in the Jewish community there at the time.
8. Lesley Byrd Simpson, *The Encomienda in New Spain*, p. 107.
9. *Pro. de Luis de Carvajal, el Mozo*, p. 304.
10. Lev. 12:2-4.
11. José Toribio Medina, *Historia del Tribunal del Santo Ofico de la Inquisición en México*, p. 111 (hereafter cited as *Inquisición en México*).
12. Abraham A. Neuman, *The Jews in Spain*, Vol. 1, p. 10.
13. Cecil Roth, *History of the Marranos*, p. 168.
14. In the prayer known as *Nishmat* which marks the opening of the section in the Hebrew prayer book for Sabbath and holy day prayers, appear the words ". . . were our hands spread out in prayer . . ." This prayer was well known in Talmudic times. There was a legend current in medieval times that the prayer was composed by the Apostle Peter as part of his alleged renunciation of the doctrine advocated by Paul. Maimonides denied the legend. J. H. Hertz, *Daily Prayer Book*, p. 416.
15. Joseph H. Hertz, *The Pentateuch and Haftorahs*, Vol. 5, p. 108.
16. AGN 309, Exp. 4, Zacatecas.
17. AHN 1736, Exp. 29.
18. Genaro García, *Documentos inéditos o muy raros para la historia de México*, Vol. 28, p. 243; AGN 397, Exp. 2.
19. AGN 417, Exp. 16; AGN 414, Exp. 9.
20. *Jewish Encyclopedia*, Vol. VI, p. 175.
21. Julio Jiménez Rueda, *Herejías y supersticiones en le Nueva España*, p. 93.
22. Eric R. Wolf, *Sons of the Shaking Earth*, p. 73.
23. Cyrus Adler, *The Trial of Gabriel de Granada*, p. 82.
24. Ricardo Palma, *Tradiciones Peruanas completas*, p. 362; Lea, *Inquisition in Spain*, Vol. II, p. 93. Negro slaves also followed this practice.

25. Liebman, *Guide to Jewish References*, p. 111.
26. AGN 694, Exps. 2, 3.

CHAPTER 5

1. George Ticknor, *History of Spanish Literature*, Vol. 1, pp. 406, 407.
2. Lea, *Inquisition in Spain*, Vol. 1, p. 78.
3. Henry B. Parkes, *History of Mexico*, pp. 28, 29.
4. Salvador de Madariaga, *Englishmen, Frenchmen, Spaniards*, pp. 42-52.
5. Cyrus Adler, *The Trial of Gabriel de Granada*, pp. 63, 85; Pro. de
   Duarte de León Jaramillo, AGN 381, Exp. 5; AGN 426, Exp. 7; cf
   Liebman, *Guide to Jewish References*, for individual references.
6. Margaret T. Rudd, *The Lonely Heretic*, p. 16.
7. Ticknor, *op. cit.*, Vol. 1, pp. 406, 407. See also Turberville, *La Inquisición Española*, chapters II, X.
8. Ticknor, *op. cit.*, Vol. 1, p. 407.
9. Raphael Altamira, *History of Spain*, p. 288.
10. Jacob Katz, *Exclusiveness and Intolerance*, p. 68, quoting from the
    Machzor Vitry (p. 179), the oldest printed book of liturgy for the
    Jewish New Year.
11. A book entitled *Alboraycos* was published about 1488 in Spain. It con-
    stitutes the appendix to *Los Judaizantes Castellanos* by Nicolas Lopez
    Martinez (Burgos, 1954). An even earlier book of the same nature was
    Jerónimo de Santa Fe's *Azote de los Hebreos* (Scourge of the He-
    brews), of which Amador de los Rios wrote, "The things gathered to-
    gether in this book could only have been . . . written in obedience to
    an intention of extermination" (Vol. 1, pp. 12, 16).
12. Reinhold Lewin, *Luthers Stellung zu den Juden*, *passim*. The Roman
    Church branded Luther and his fellow sectarians as heretics and Jews.
13. Salo W. Baron, *A Social and Religious History of the Jews*, Vol. 2, pp.
    45-46.
14. Benzion Netanyahu, *Marranos of Spain*, p. 35.
15. Ramón Santa María, "Ritos y costumbres de los hebreos españoles," p.
    181. These instructions were partially based upon a Jewish document
    in the municipal archives of Alcala de Henares, which Ramón Santa
    María paleographed and included in the cited article.
16. Lea, *Inquisition in Spain*, Vol. 1, p. 539. Cheyney, *European Background
    of American History*, p. 63, attributes the double expulsion to a desire
    by the Spaniards to achieve homogeneity in race and religion, a purity
    of blood and unity of belief, with the result that "Spain had little else
    than her orthodoxy to pride herself on."
17. Valeriu Marcu, *La expulsión de los judíos de España*, p. 97.
18. Lea, *Inquisition in Spain*, Vol. 2, p. 523. Jean Antoine Llorente notes in
    The History of the Inquisition in Spain that monks ravished virgins.
19. Haim Beinart discusses crypto-Jews in monastic orders in "The Judaiz-
    ing Movement in the Order of San Geronimo in Castile," p. 167.
20. Gregorio Marañon, *Antonio Pérez*, Vol. 1, p. 154.
21. Marcu, *op. cit.*, p. 98.
22. Liebman, *op. cit.*, p. 67.
23. *Ibid.*, p. 89.

24. Lea, *Inquisition in Spain*, Vol. 2, p. 91.
25. Abridgment, with slight changes, of translation by Lea in *Inquisition in Spain*, Vol. 2, p. 95.
26. Eduardo Pallares, *El procedimiento inquisitorial*, p. vii.
27. Altamira, *op. cit.*, p. 358.
28. F. D. Mocatta, *Jews of Spain and Portugal*, pp. 42, 44.
29. Antonio Puigblanch, *The Inquisition Unmasked*, Vol. 1, p. 11.
30. Lea, *Inquisition in Spain*, Vol. 2, pp. 539, 562, 564. See also Castro, *Structure of Spanish History*, p. 534. Castro quotes Juan de Mariana, a Jesuit historian of the fifteenth century, as calling the Holy Office "an unheard-of novelty . . . what was especially surprising was that children paid for crimes of their fathers, that the accuser was not known or indicated, nor confronted with the criminal, nor were the lists of witnesses" disclosed to the accused. This last was considered contrary to prevailing custom, and the death penalty was regarded as "a new thing." There were *malsines* (slanderers or informers) for the Holy Office. See also J. Hastings, ed., *Encyclopedia of Religion and Ethics*, article on discipline, Vol. 4, pp. 718 ff. (*Malsines* is *malsinim* in Hebrew.)
31. Anita Brenner, "Cavaliers and Martyrs," p. 8.
32. Puigblanch, *op. cit.*, Vol. 1, p. 193.
33. AHN 1737, Exp. 12.
34. Ricardo Palma, *Tradiciones Peruanas completas*, p. 1212.
35. Lea, *Inquisition in Spain*, Vol. 3, p. 142; Llorente, *op. cit.*, p. 110.
36. Puigblanch, *op. cit.*, p. 319.
37. José Toribio Medina, *La Inquisición en las provincias de la Plata*, p. 369.

CHAPTER 6

1. For additional data on Alonso and Morales, see Seymour B. Liebman, "Hernando Alonso: First Jew on the North American Continent," p. 291; Alfonso Toro, ed., *Los judíos en la Nueva España*, p. 17; and Richard E. Greenleaf, *Zumárraga and the Mexican Inquisition*, pp. 12, 90-92, 103, 113.
   I have drawn upon Greenleaf for many details of this period. Some scholars have appended "*Regaton*" to the name of Gonzalo de Morales. *Regaton* means merchant and its use merely reflected his occupation. Greenleaf, in *Zumárraga and the Mexican Inquisition*, p. 93, refers to a Jew eating "shark meat" (*tiburón*). Because they have no scales, the eating of shark is prohibited to Jews. The report may be in error due to poor reporting by the Inquisition secretary; *tiburón* may have had a different meaning or connotation in 1528; or else the Jew in question was not observant of Jewish dietary laws. Greenleaf errs in his translation of *pan cenzeño* as Jewish rye bread. It is matzot, unleavened bread; *centeno* is the Spanish word for rye.
2. Seymour B. Liebman, "The Abecedario and a Check-List of Documents at the Henry E. Huntington Library," p. 554.
3. Bernal Díaz del Castillo, *Historia verdadera de la conquista de la Nueva España*, p. 14.
4. Elkan N. Adler, *Auto de Fé and Jew*, p. 26.

5. Max L. Margolis and Alexander Marx, *The History of the Jewish People*, p. 506.
6. Roth, *History of the Marranos*, p. 70.
7. AGN 2, Exp. 2.
8. AGN 125, Exp. 5 and Exp. 7. Toro lists him as "Baca" in *Los judíos en la Nueva España*, p. 10, but correctly lists him on p. 113.
9. Greenleaf, *op. cit.*, p. 14. Arnold Wiznitzer, in "Crypto-Jews in Mexico in the 17th Century" (2 parts), p. 174, states that there were only fourteen trials of Jews. This is but one of numerous errors in his two articles, many of which are more serious and include citations unrelated to the text. The lack of diligent research appears in his comment that "Meat is never mentioned as the food of Mexican Judaizers" (p. 276). Obviously he did not know that landrecilla was practiced in accordance with Jewish ritual and he was unaware of the many cases that reveal women acting as slaughterers and draining the blood from the animals.
   Joaquín García Icazbalceta, in *Don Fray Juan de Zumárraga*, Vol. 2, p. 207, states that only ten Jews were tried, but he wrote in the nineteenth century when the existence of many documents bearing on this was unknown.
10. Richard E. Greenleaf, "Francisco Millán Before the Mexican Inquisition," pp. 194, 195.
11. AGN 395, Exp. 2.
12. AGN 399, Exp. 10.
13. Greenleaf, *Zumárraga and the Mexican Inquisition*, p. 99.
14. Liebman, *Guide to Jewish References*, p. 93.
15. Jiménez Rueda, *Herejías y supersticiones en la Nueva España*, p. 85. Many persons will doubt that Saña was English, since Jews had been expelled from England in 1290 and their return was not legal until 1664. Albert Hyamson, in *The Sephardim of England*, lists no such name. Although Jiménez Rueda and Alfonso Toro refer to this case, the original proceso is not where they note it (see Liebman, *Guide to Jewish References*, p. 93).
16. AGN 1A, Exp. 25.
17. *Pro. de Luis de Carvajal, el Mozo*, p. viii.
18. Harvey Gardiner, in *Martin Lopez*, p. 7, contends that "he was of at least nine clearly identifiable generations of orthodox Christians." He also wrote that Lopez was "religiously pious" (p. 15) and "must have been religious" (p. 176) but "was not a party to the hysteria which condemned the Conquistador and brigantine builder Hernando Alonso in 1528. Nor did evidence of bigotry appear in him when the Inquisition formally came in 1571" (p. 177).
19. I. S. Revah, "Fundo de manuscritos pour l'histoire des nouveaux chrétiens portugais," p. 293.
20. Jean Antoine Llorente, *The History of the Inquisition in Spain*, p. 254.
21. ABEC, year 1583.
22. Lea, *Inquisition in Spain*, Vol. 3, p. 243.
23. *Ibid.*, Vol. 3, pp. 235, 236.
24. Toro, *op. cit.*, pp. 168-177; AGN 4, Exp. 10. Corvera was acquitted after a brief trial. This proceso was in the possession of Francisco Fernández del Castillo and Julio Jiménez Rueda for many years, according to information given to Richard E. Greenleaf by Pablo Martínez del Río.
25. Alfonso Méndez Plancarte, *Poetas Novohispanos*, pp. xxii, xxiii.

26. Luis González Obregon, *México Viejo*, p. 93.
27. Vallé, "Judíos en México," p. 215.
28. Toro, *op. cit.*, p. xxxiii.

CHAPTER 7

1. Crane Brinton *et. al.*, *A History of Civilization*, Vol. 1, p. 504.
2. Preserved Smith, *Reformation in Europe*, p. 325.
3. Vicente Riva Palacio, *México à través de los siglos*, Vol. 2, p. 425.
4. Turberville, *La Inquisición Española*, pp. 103, 104.
5. Julio Jiménez Rueda, *Herejías y supersticiones en la Nueva España*, p. 89.
6. AGN 412, Exp. 2.
7. Alfred M. Tozzer, ed., *Landa's "Relación de las cosas de Yucatán,"* pp. 79-86.
8. AGN 89, Exp. 36.
9. Alfonso Toro, *La familia Carvajal*, Vol. 1, p. 25; Vitto Alessio Robles, *Coahuila y Texas en la época colonial*, p. 90; Jiménez Rueda, *op. cit.*, pp. 96-99; Pablo Martínez del Río, *"Alumbrado"*; Riva Palacio, *op. cit.*, Vol. 2, p. 441. See also Vicente Riva Palacio, *El Libro Rojo*, chapter on Luis de Carvajal, el Gobernador, and Seymour B. Liebman, "Hernando Alonso: First Jew on the North American Continent" for additional bibliographies.

   Lea, in his *History of the Inquisition in the Spanish Dependencies*, p. 208 (hereafter cited as *Inquisition in the Spanish Dependencies*) made numerous errors in his references to the Carvajals. He confused the governor with his nephew of the same proper name, and attributed to the governor's niece the ability to recite the Prayer of Esther and other Hebrew songs "backwards." Lea overlooked the fact that Hebrew is read from right to left and followed Paramo's *De Origene et Progressu Inquisitionius* (Spain, 1599).

   Roth, in *History of the Marranos*, uncritically followed Lea, who had done no original research in America but relied upon José Toribio Medina and Luis González Obregón.

   Toro's *La familia Carvajal* should be accepted with reservations, and classified as an historical novel. Toro errs in his dates and in citing the grounds for animosity between the viceroy (whom he names incorrectly) and the governor.

   Wiznitzer, in "Crypto-Jews in Mexico in the 17th Century," p. 184, relies on Toro and erroneously writes that the governor was jailed and "left to languish there for several years."
10. Toro, *op. cit.*, Vol. 1, p. 25.
11. J. A. Goris, *Etude sur les colonies marchandes meridionales*, Louvain Librairie and Universitaire, p. 582.
12. A. Richard Konetzke, *La Emigración española al Río de la Plata durante el siglo XVI*, p. 53.
13. Silvio Zavala, *Spanish Colonization in America*, pp. 60, 69. Clarence H. Haring, *The Spanish Empire in America*, p. 19, wrote: "The labor of discovery, conquest and settlement . . . was from the time of Christopher Columbus pre-eminently the achievement of private enterprise. . . . Very rarely did the king contribute to the cost of the undertaking."
14. Philip Wayne Powell, *Soldiers, Indians and Silver*, p. 172.
15. Jiménez Rueda, *op. cit.*, p. 109.

16. AGN 153, Exp. 9.
17. Medina, *Inquisición en México*, p. 97.
18. AGN 127, Exp. 3.
19. Alfonso Méndez Plancarte, *Poetas Novohispanos, passim.*
20. See P. Jesús García Gutiérrez, "La poesía religiosa en México: Siglos XVI a XIX," p. 33.
21. Toro, *op. cit.*, Vol. 1, p. 40.
22. *Ibid.* Toro cites Luis' defense before the Inquisition for the statement about the governor having "strong suspicions" about Rodríguez de Matos' faith and that he wanted to save people from persecution (Vol. 1, pp. 85, 86). Toro gives no page reference. My reading of the transcript failed to reveal any corroboration for this. Santiago Roel, in *Nuevo León-Apuntes Históricos*, p. 21, wrote: "Governor Carvajal had abandoned Judaism in his youth and had been an ardent Catholic for many years before coming to this area; and because of that which he did to his family, none of whom resided in the New Kingdom of León, except Luis, el Mozo, who accompanied him for a short time . . ."
23. Santiago Roel, *op. cit.*, p. 7. Gaspar Castaño de Sosa was Lieutenant Governor of Nuevo León. *Cf.* Dorothy Hull, "Castaño de Sosa's Expedition," *Old Santa Fe*, Vol. III, October, 1916, No. 12, p. 309.
24. Transcript of *Pro. de Luis de Carvajal, el Gobernador*, p. 175. See also Martínez del Río, *op. cit.*, p. 55.
25. Transcript of *Pro. de Luis de Carvajal, el Gobernador*, pp. 135, 182.
26. *Ibid.*, p. 209.
27. Robert Ricard, "Pour une étude de judaïsme portugais au Mexique pendant la période coloniale," p. 524 (hereafter cited as "Pour une étude de judaïsme portugais").
28. See Liebman, *Guide to Jewish References*, for citations and references concerning various individuals.
29. First printed in Hebrew in 1550. Thereafter, many editions followed in various parts of Europe, and the book was also translated into Spanish.
30. Leo Baeck, *Judaism and Christianity*, pp. 31-38. This chapter eloquently portrays the concepts of colonial Mexican Jewry vis-à-vis the Messiah and Christ, although Rabbi Baeck makes no mention of Jewry in New Spain.
31. Ramón Menéndez Pidal, *Los Romances de América*, p. 136.

CHAPTER 8

1. Joaquín García Icazbalceta, *Bibliografía mexicana del siglo XVI*, p. 449.
2. Abecedario, hereafter cited as ABEC. This unpaginated document was discussed in Liebman. "The Abecedario and a Check-List of Documents at the Henry E. Huntington Library," and references to it are made by years: 1577, Juan Heredia; 1594, Lorenzo Sánchez Pulido and Four Indians; 1561, Domingo Baltazar de Viana, Guillermo de Espinoza, and Juan, Negro Slave of the Warden; 1602, Francisco the Red; 1603, Juan Arias, the Scribe and Clerk of an Inquisition Official; 1605, Fr. José Pérez de Ugarte. I have not listed cases in later years which are equally abundant.
3. Codices—cedulario de Judíos, Vol. 121, 684 B-725, Cartas de Don Carlos.

4. García Icazbalceta, *op. cit.,* p. 449.
5. For a full account of Luis and pertinent facts about his family, see Seymour B. Liebman, *The Enlightened, The Writings of Luis de Carvajal, el Mozo.* The data on his life was gleaned from his proceso and the procesos of Justa Méndez, Manuel de Lucena, and many of the Carvajal family and contemporaries, all of which are set forth in the Selected Bibliography of *The Enlightened.*
6. AGN 153, Exp. 7.
7. AGN 152, Exp. 4.
8. Julio Jiménez Rueda, *Herejías y supersticiónes en le Nueva España,* p. 112.
9. Adler, *op. cit.,* p. 49.
10. Genaro García, *Documentos inéditos o muy raros para la historia de México,* Vol. 5, pp. 111-118, relates details of the trial procedures and the torture of Franco Tavares in 1601.
11. Ricard, "Pour une étude de judaísme portugais," p. 525.
12. AGN 151, Exp. 6. There were hundreds of cases before the Inquisition which involved non-Jews who said "simple fornicación no es un pecado" (fornication between two single people of opposite sexes is not a sin) or who made comments of a similar genre.
13. *Libro Primero de Votos de la Inquisición de México, 1537-1600,* p. 197. The dates of all votes and sentences are from this source.
14. Hubert H. Bancroft, *History of Mexico,* Vol. 2, p. 679.
15. "Ultimos momentos y conversión de Luis de Carvajal," pp. 64, 65. This is a paleographed copy made by Francisco Fernández del Castillo of the report in the Relación of Fray Alonso de Contreras. The original report is missing from the AGN. It may have been one of the AGN documents reputed to have been stolen in 1932.
16. Pablo Martínez del Río, "*Alumbrado,*" p. 189.
17. Alberto María Carreño, "Luis de Carvajal, el Mozo," p. 101.
18. Miguel León-Portilla et al., *Historia documental de México,* Vol. 1, p. 302.

CHAPTER 9

1. Julio Caro Baroja, *La Sociedad Criptojudía en le Corte de Felipe IV,* p. 23 (hereafter cited as *Sociedad Criptojudía*).
2. Robert Ricard, "Pour une étude de judaísme portugais," p. 522.
3. AGN 308, Exp. 1. See also AGN 223, f. 384.
4. See ABEC for data on Espinosa, Isabel de Medina, *et al.*
5. Lea, *Inquisition in Spain,* Vol. 3, p. 271.
6. A. S. Turberville, *La Inquisición Española,* p. 104.
7. *Ibid.,* p. 105.
8. Jiménez Rueda, *op. cit.,* p. 121.
9. AGN 279, Exp. 9; Liebman, *Guide to Jewish References,* p. 26.
10. P. Mariano Cuevas, *Historia de la Nación Mexicana,* p. 309.
11. Elkan N. Adler, *Auto de Fé and Jew,* p. 168.
12. Alfred B. Thomas, *Latin America: A History,* p. 144.
13. George A. Kohut, "Jewish Martyrs of the Inquisition in South America," p. 105.
14. Salvador de Madariaga, *The Fall of the Spanish American Empire,* p. 232. Madariaga states, quoting Cecil Roth, "Dr. Hector Núñez, one of

the most active merchants in the city [London] seems to have organized an elaborate information service in Spain and Portugal." Copies of Simon de Cáceres' plans for the conquest of Chile and other proposals to Sweden with respect to Jamaica are in Lucien Wolf, "American Elements in the Re-Settlement," pp. 95-100.

15. Public Records Office, London. *Colonial Papers*, Vol. XX, No. 202.
16. Pablo Martínez del Río, *"Alumbrado,"* p. 10; AGN 337, Exp. 7.
17. Cyrus Adler, "The Trial of Jorge de Almeida," p. 54. Adler wrote that Diego Díaz Nieto was "a native of Oporto . . . Portugal." But on p. 55, Adler states that he had "determined to tell the truth . . . he was born and brought up in the city of Ferrara, in Italy." The change of birthplace from Oporto to Ferrara must have been a ruse to avoid the jurisdiction of the Inquisition by denying baptism and the status of a heretic.
18. Cyrus Adler, *op. cit.*, p. 57. In a footnote, Adler states that a "Jacob Lumbroso was a physician and rabbi and writer in Venice" in 1607.
19. AGN 151, Exp. 6.
20. Medina, *op. cit.*, p. 171.
21. AGN 276, Exp. 14, fs. 412-483, relates the information about Jewish customs.
22. Medina, *op. cit.*, p. 171.
23. AGN 277, Exp. 2, in testimony of Pedro Jorge.
24. Robert Ricard, "Fray Fernando de Ojea," pp. 23-28. Ricard cites *Colección de documentos para la historia de Oaxaca, México*, 1933, pp. 18 ff.
25. Quoted by Cecil Roth in *Life of Menasseh ben Israel*, p. 47.
26. AGN 337, Exp. 7; I. S. Revah, "Fundo de Manuscritos pour l'histoire des nouveaux chrétiens portugais," pp. 276, 294; letter of August 28, 1962 from Cecil Roth to this author.
27. Letter of August 28, 1962, from Cecil Roth to this author.
28. Lea, *op. cit.*, Vol. 3, pp. 275, 286.
29. Cyrus Adler, "A Contemporary Memorial Relating to Damages to Spanish Interests in America Done by Jews of Holland (1634)," p. 46.
30. "The Jews of Amsterdam in 1655," TJHSE, Vol. 4, p. 224 *et seq.*
31. Charles E. Chapman, *A History of Spain*, p. 261.
32. *Ibid.*, p. 280.
33. Donald E. Worcester and Wendell G. Schaffer, *The Growth and Culture of Latin America*, pp. 205, 226.
34. There were three trials for Baltazar del Valle. AGN 380, Exp. 1; ABEC years 1626 and 1635; P. Mathias Bocanegra, *Relación del auto general de la fee celebrado 11 de abril de 1649.*
35. AGN 335, Exp. 86.

CHAPTER 10

1. Charles E. Chapman, *A History of Spain*, p. 31.
2. Solomon Grayzel, *A History of the Jews*, p. 512.
3. Proceso of Margarita Morera, Henry E. Huntington Library.
4. Salvador de Madariaga, *The Fall of the Spanish American Empire*, p. 231.
5. A few Jewish writers, particularly Americans of the late nineteenth and early twentieth centuries, attempted to trace descent and relationships among Iberian and other Sephardic Jews through similarities of patro-

nymics. George A. Kohut and Cyrus Adler appended many footnotes along these lines in their articles on New World colonial Jewry; we must remember, however, that names were changed and that children did not always bear their father's family name.

6. Medina, *Inquisición de Lima*, Vol. II, pp. 52, 54, 94, 135, 144.
7. See Liebman, *Guide to Jewish References*, for citations.
8. Cyrus Adler, "A Contemporary Memorial Relating to Damages to the Spanish Interests in America Done by Jews of Holland (1634)," pp. 46, 47.
9. Pro. de Manuel Alvarez Prieto, AHN 1620, No. 15.
10. In "Report of Pending Cases in the Tribunal of the Holy Office of the Inquisition . . . since the year 1642" there appears in the title the words "Pertaining to the Present Conspiracy" *(La Presente Complicidad);* AGN 426, f. 534.
11. Josephine Y. McClaskey, "Inquisition Papers, Part II," p. 4 and footnotes.
12. Lea, *Inquisition in the Spanish Dependencies,* pp. 210, 223, 229, 230-233, 234, 235, for fines and confiscations; Medina, *Inquición en México,* pp. 209-212; Clarence H. Haring, *The Spanish Empire in America,* p. 190 is a partial apologist for the inquisitors.
13. Quoted in Herbert I. Bloom's *The Economic Activities of the Jews of Amsterdam in the 17th Century,* p. xiii.
14. Medina, *Inquisición en México,* p. 210.
15. Transcript of *Pro. de Thomas Treviño de Sobremonte,* G. R. G. Conway Collection, Archives of the Library of Congress, p. 153.
16. AGN 390, fs. 369-377 vta and AGN 391, Exp. 1, fs. 3-13. These should be read in reverse order because the earlier testimony is in the second volume.
17. Transcript of *Pro. de Thomas Treviño de Sobremonte, op. cit.* Bibliographical data is based on A. J. Barker's two translations in the Archives of the Library of Congress; P. Mathias Bocanegra, *Relación del auto general de la fee celebrado 11 de abril de 1649;* and Gregorio M. de Guijo, *Diario:* 1648-1664, Vol. 1, pp. 42-44 inclusive.
18. Seymour B. Liebman, "Fuentes Desconocidas de la Historia Mexicana Judía," pp. 716, 717. This article has a genealogical table for Simón Váez Sevilla. See also AGN 398, Exp. 1.
19. AGN 419, fs. 310, 311.
20. AGN 416, Exp. 43.
21. AGN 397, Exp. 2.
22. From existing evidence this could not be the Chinese Jewish community, which was in the interior of China and in existence for over 1,400 years, described by Le P. Jerome Tobar, S.J., in *Inscriptions Juives de K'ai-Fong-Fu* (Shanghai, 1912).
23. Medina, *La Inquisición en México,* p. 113.
24. Alfonso Tejera Zable, *Guide to the History of Mexico,* p. 189.
25. Magnus Mörner, *Race Mixture,* p. 58.
26. Medina, *La Inquisición en México,* p. 204.

CHAPTER 11

1. Transcript of *Pro. de Thomas Treviño de Sobremonte, op. cit.,* p. 1.
2. In PAJHS, 17, p. 27, Cyrus Adler refers to Treviño as "a South American Martyr."

3. Gregorio M. de Guijo, *Diario: 1648-1664,* Vol. 1, p. 44.
4. José de J. Núñez y Domínguez, "Los judíos en la y literatura," p. 41.
   The poem was taken from Juan de Dios Piza, *Leyendas históricas, tradicionales y fantásticas de ciudades de México,* n.d.
5. AGN 409, Exp. 2; AGN 413, fs. 184-187, 239-246, 414, 417, 434.
6. Abba Hillel Silver, *Where Judaism Differed,* p. 206.
7. Nahum N. Glatzer, *Faith and Knowledge,* p. 20.
8. Genaro García, *Documentos inéditos o muy raros para la historia de México,* Vol. 28, p. 7.

CHAPTER 12

1. Joaquín García Icazbalceta, *Bibliografía méxicana del siglo XVI,* p. 456.
2. Elkin N. Adler, *Auto de Fé and Jew,* p. 159.
3. Medina, *Inquisición en México,* p. 114. The proceso of Francisca Tejoso is at the Henry E. Huntington Library.
4. Genaro García, *Documentos inéditos o muy raros para la historia de México,* Vol. 28, p. 245.
5. The American Jewish Historical Society owns one of the rare copies of the Relación, and a photocopy was purchased from them.
6. AGN 372, Exp. 21; AGN 404, Exp. 1.
7. AGN 378, Exp. 2.
8. *Ibid.*
9. *Pro. de Luis de Carvajal, el Mozo,* pp. 159, 160.
10. Medina, *Inquisición en México,* p. 192, quotes the letter.
11. AGN 409, Exp. 4. See the testimony of Gaspar Váez, witness number 8, who referred to her as his *"hermana vastarda" (sic).* This proceso reveals the existence of *baños de los japoneses* (Japanese baths), that single men lit candles on the eve of Yom Kippur, and that Jewish women would not even sew a button on a shirt on the Sabbath because it would be a desecration of the Sabbath.
12. AGN 419, Document 33 (an exception to *expediente*).
13. AGN 738, Exp. 4.

CHAPTER 13

1. AGN 400, Exp. 2.
2. There never was a female rabbi in Judaism. The only explanation for applying the title to her is that she was the spiritual leader of one of the communities after the death of her husband and served until the installation of Juan Pacheco as a replacement.
3. See Julio Jiménez Rueda, *Herejías y supersticiones en la Nueva España,* p. 113, for the complete prayer taken from the *Pro. de Luis de Carvajal, el Mozo,* p. 91.
4. Luis González Obregón, *Rebeliones Indigenas y Precursores de la Independencía Mexicana,* pp. 242-330.
5. Gregoria M. de Guijo, *Diario: 1648-1664,* Vol. 1, p. 111.
6. Lea, *Inquisition in the Spanish Dependencies,* p. 234.
7. AGN 435, Cholula f. 339.

8. AGN 416, f. 536 *et seq.*
9. Richard B. Morris, *The Peacemakers*, p. 65.
10. Charles E. Chapman, *A History of Spain*, Chapter XXVII.
11. P. Jesús García Gutiérrez, "La poesía religiosa en México," p. 54.
12. Clement G. Motten, *Mexican Silver and the Enlightenment*, p. 37.
13. Chapman, *op. cit.*, pp. 330, 333.
14. Luis Díaz, alias Joseph Jesurun Mendes, had lived in Surinam, then Recife, Brazil, and subsequently went to Amsterdam in 1654. He returned to Barbados, where he founded the first Jewish congregation in Bridgetown; *cf.* Wilfrid S. Samuel, "A Review of Jewish Colonists in Barbados in the Year 1680," p. 1. Días was a brother-in-law of Antuñez of Surinam.
15. Cyrus Adler, "Jews in the American Plantations Between 1600-1700," p. 105 ff.
16. Wilfred S. Samuel, "A Review of the Jewish Colonists in Barbados in the Year 1680," p. 1.
17. PAJHS, Vol. 4, pp. 53 and 47, respectively.
18. Quoted by Jakob Petuchowski in *The Theology of Haham David Nieto*, p. 48, from Nahum Sokolow's *Spinoza and His Time* (Hebrew), p. 255.
19. For detailed material I have used "Certificación de la visita de los procesos de fé," AHN 1738, Exp. 1, and "Cuestionaires de la visita de la Inquisición de México," AHN 1737, Exp. 12. See also Josephine Yocum McClaskey, "Inquisition Papers of Mexico, II, The Trial of Luis de Cruz," p. 3. Her footnotes are excellent. She indicates some errors of earlier writers. Insights are gained into some of the methods used by Jews in communicating with each other in and out of the secret cells. Miss McClaskey refers to Joseph do Zárate as a half-brother of María de Zárate. In the proceso of María, he is referred to as José de Sánchez, an illegitimate son of María's father, Juan Sánchez de Vargas, and María reared him.
20. Herbert I. Priestley, *The Coming of the White Man*, Chapter 3.
21. For a complete summary of the trial of López de Mendizabal, see Eleanor B. Adams and France V. Scholes, "Troublous Times in New Mexico."
22. ABEC, year 1667.
23. Medina, Inquisición en México, pp. 278, 280, 415; ABEC, year 1699.
24. AGN 520, Exp. 232; AGN 529, Exp. 12.

CHAPTER 14

1. Raphael Altamira, *The History of Spain*, p. 426.
2. A. S. Turberville, *La Inquisición Española*, p. 208.
3. *Ibid.*, p. 210.
4. Medina, *Inquisición en México*, chapters XVIII-XX, *passim*, for listing of some of the cases. Medina is not complete.
5. Hubert H. Bancroft, *Annals of Mexico*, p. 223.
6. Lea, *Inquisition in Spain*, Vol. 3, p. 302.
7. *Loc. cit.* For complete translation of the sermon, see Moses Mocatta, The Inquisition and Judaism, p. 1 *et seq.*

8. Monalisa Lina Pérez-Manchand, *Dos Estapas ideológicas del siglo XVIII en México*, p. 40.
9. *Ibid.*, p. 42.
10. *Ibid.*, p. 84
11. Frank Brandenberg, *The Making of Modern Mexico*, p. 168.
12. Howard F. Cline, *The United States and Mexico*, p. 114.
13. Medina, *Inquisición en México*, pp. 306, 420.
14. *Ibid.*, p. 295.
15. Gustavo Baez Camargo, *Protestantes enjudiciados por la Inquisición*, p. 9.
16. Liebman, *Guide to Jewish References*, pp. 83-88.
17. *Ibid.*, p. 88.
18. AGN 848, Exp. 12.
19. Medina, *Inquisición en México*, p. 306, errs in writing that Gil Rodríguez was a Spaniard. On p. 316, he gives his birthplace as Guatemala. I believe that there are a number of printer's errors on p. 306.
20. AGN 1416, f. 144.
21. Alan D. Corré, *Jewish Social Studies* 23 (1961), pp. 165-166.

CHAPTER 15

1. José Maier Bernadette, *Hispanic Culture and Character of Sephardic Jews*, p. 16.
2. Yitzhak Baer, *A History of the Jews in Christian Spain*, Vol. 1, pp. 2, 3.
3. Julio Caro Baroja, *La Sociedad Criptojudía en la Corte de Felipe IV*, p. 46.
4. Liebman, *Guide to Jewish References*, p. 107; ABEC, year 1647. He was the son of Fernando Franco and Ana Fernández and was born in Coruña, Portugal.
5. Cecil Roth, *Gleanings: Essays in Jewish History*, p. 119.

Glossary

abonos—the defense of good character (namely, being a good Catholic), one of the defenses available to an accused person.

abjuration—an oath of denial, disavowal, or renunciation. Abjuration was intended to instill fear of future sins, and was of two degrees (see below).

abjuration *de levi* (light suspicion)—a verbal oath administered by the inquisitors to heretics, proof of whose heresy had not been established beyond a reasonable doubt. The prisoner had to swear fealty to the Church as the symbol of the sole, true faith; loyalty to the pope; and promise to denounce opponents of Catholicism.

abjuration *de vehementi* (strong suspicion)—a written oath subscribed to by those convicted of heresy. Those taking this oath disavowed all future heresy, pledged eternal allegiance to Catholicism, and agreed to be considered a *relapso* if they ever again strayed from the Faith. A relapso, or second offender, was usually sentenced to the stake.

alborayacos—a pejorative name sometimes applied to Jews during the twelfth to fifteenth centuries. The term was taken from "El Borak," the gelding given to Mohammed.

aljama—an assembly of Moors. It also means a synagogue and a Jewish quarter.

Alumbrados—a sect also called Illuminati. They believed that recourse to all forms of immorality was a condition precedent to attaining enlightenment.

anusim—literally, forced ones (Hebrew). People converted by force, physical or psychological.

audiencia—a hearing by the inquisitors; part of the trial.

auto-da-fé—literally, act of the faith. Also auto da fé (Portuguese) and auto de fé (Spanish). *See also* auto general and autillo.

auto general—an open or public display of the penitents and the reading of their sentences. Also known as *auto publico*.

autillo—a closed or secret auto-da-fé usually held in the hearing room of the House of the Inquisition or the chapel of the Church of Santo Domingo across the street. Members of the clergy usually appeared only in autillos.

B.C.E.—Before the Common Era; synonymous with B.C.

buen confidentes—prisoners who have made complete and truthful confessions.

calificador—an Inquisition official who examined the preliminary evidence to determine if heresy or a crime against the faith had been committed.

cautelas—tricksters or informers planted in the Inquisition cells with other prisoners to try to extract confessions or incriminating evidence.

C.E.—Common Era; used in place of A.D. by most Jewish historians.

comisario—the agent of the Holy Office who operated in the provinces and rural areas.

con méritos—the complete reading of the digest of the trial and the sentence for each prisoner at an auto-da-fé.

contador—financial agent of the Inquisition.

coraza—conical hat, similar to a mitre, worn by penitents in the march to the place of the auto-da-fé.

criolla—a person born in the New World of white Spanish parents.

criolla negro—a black person born in the New World of Negro parents.

converso—a convert to Christianity.

diminuto—an incomplete or dishonest confessor or confession.

dogmatista, dogmatistador, dogmatistadora—a secret Jew who attempts to bring back to Judaism a New Christian or Hebrew Christian.

effigy—the dummy figure to represent, at an auto-da-fé, a prisoner who had escaped, one who had died in the cells, or a person who had been accused but who had never been captured.

familiar—an officer of the Inquisition.

farda—a tribute or fund collected by Jewish messengers, usually from the Holy Land, for the benefit of Jews residing in the Holy Land. The messengers were learned men who studied with members of the communities where they sought funds before they returned. The Moors had a similar practice for Moslems in the Middle East.

fiscal—the prosecuting attorney for the Tribunal of the Holy Office of the Inquisition; also the title of lawyers for the crown.

gachupine—a Spaniard born in Spain and residing in the New World.

garrote—a cord or iron collar used for strangulation at the stake as an act of mercy administered if the heretic expressed the desire to die as a Christian.

hebreo cristiano—a convert from Judaism to Catholicism.

hidalgo—the son of someone; an honorary title evidenced by "de" before the family name. Derived from *hijo de algo*, the son of someone.

in caput alienum—torture applied to make the Inquisition prisoner reveal the names of other heretics after he fully confessed his own heresies.

judaizante—one who observed or professed the Jewish faith or who believed in the "dead Law of Moses." Sometimes used as a synonym for a Jew.

judería—Jewish quarter or ghetto.

judío, judía, judaycas—Jews(s) or Jewess(es).

kashrut—the Jewish laws for slaughtering animals and preparing them for consumption.

landrecilla—porging; the removal of the thigh vein from slaughtered animals as part of kashrut.

limpieza de sangre—literally, purity of blood; a Catholic whose ancestors were all Catholics for three previous generations on both maternal and paternal lines.

marrano—literally, swine; one who professed Catholicism but secretly practiced Jewish rites.

mestizo, mestiza—a person of mixed (white and Indian) ancestry.

mordaza— a gag applied to the mouth of some prisoners on the way to or at an auto-da-fé.

nuevo cristiano—a New Christian; a convert from Judaism to Catholicism.

notario de azotaciónes—the man who kept count of the number of lashes administered to a penitent.

obraje—sweat shop.

penca—the leather strap used in administering lashes to a penitent.

pie de amigo—an iron instrument used to hold up the head of a person being publicly whipped.

potro—a wooden, bed-like frame with leather thongs instead of a mattress, on which Inquisition prisoners were tied while cords were tightened around their ankles, thighs, and arms.

proceso—the judicial records of a trial or hearing.

quemadero—the place where convicts were burned.

reconciliado, reconciliada—a heretic, first offender, who had been brought back into the Church; his property was confiscated and he was usually required to wear a sanbenito in public.

relación—an account of an event.

relapso—a second heretical offender; someone who falls back into criminal conduct.

relaxed *(relejado)*—the turning over of a heretic by the Inquisition to the secular authorities for burning at the stake.

sanbenito—a penitential garment worn over the outer garments for periods of time fixed by the inquisitors. Also sambenito.

sin méritos—the reading of a digest of an Inquisition sentence and the omission of the digest of the trial.

tachas—the defense used by the accused that the principal witness against him is his mortal enemy and, therefore, is lying.

vergüenza—literally, shame; the penitent being compelled to ride on a donkey wearing a pie de amigo in a public procession.

Bibliography

ARCHIVAL MATERIAL

Archival material appears in the numerical order of the volumes in the respective archives. Volumes in the Archivo General de la Nación de México are termed *tomos*, and those in the Archivo Histórico Nacional de Madrid are referred to as *legajos*.

ABBREVIATIONS

AGN   Archivo General de la Nación de México, Ramo de la Inquisición
AHN   Archivo Histórico Nacional de Madrid
ABEC   Abecedario, an original Mexican Inquisition document now at the Henry E. Huntington Library, San Marino, California. It is an alphabetical index of cases containing data on those penanced, and the pages are unnumbered.
Exp.   Expediente (file number of the document)
f., fs.   foja(s), the numbered leaf or leaves of a document.
Pro.   Proceso (trial proceeding).
P/c   Proceso contra (proceedings against)

AGN

1,   Exp. 2. Edict of 1523 barring the entry into New Spain of New Christians, Jews, Moors, and other heretics or descendants of those reconciled or relaxed by the Inquisition.
1A,   Exp. 25. Memorandum of children of those burned at the stake or reconciled in New Spain.
2,   Exp. 2. P/c Gonzálo Gómez.
4,   Exp. 10. P/c Juan Bautista Corvera.
30,   Exp. 8. P/c Francisco Millan.
38,   Exp. 1. P/c Juan Franco.
77,   Exp. 25. Acts of inquisitor Alonso de Peralta to learn about old and recent sanbenitos and the position of those remitted by the Santa Oficio.

38,   Exp. 36. Information against children of those reconciled or burned
           at the stake who were illegally in New Spain.
125,   Exp. 5, 7. P/c Juan de Baeza.
127,   Exp. 3. P/c Manuel de Morales.
150,   Exp. 1. P/c Jorge de Almeyda.
151,   Exp. 6. P/c Manuel Gómez Navarro.
152,   Exp. 4. P/c Catalina Enríquez.
154,   Exp. 1. P/c Justa Méndez. See also AGN 1495, Exp. 2.
159,   Exp. 2. P/c Diego Díez Nieto.
221,   Exp. 2. P/c Pedro de Silva Sauceedo.
223,   f. 384. Letter to other Tribunals in the New World re Gonzálo de
           Molino.
276,   Exp. 14. Declaration by Manuel Gil de la Guarda against many Jews,
           including Diego Díaz Nieto and Ruy Díaz Nieto.
277,   Exp. 2. Denunciation of Pedro Jorge.
279,   Exp. 9. Request to go free in accordance with the grace extended by
           Pope Clement VIII.
308,   Exp. 1. P/c Gonzálo de Molina.
309,   Zacatecas 4. Information against Cristobal de Herrera for teaching
           the Law of Moses to the Indians (1615). Additional material in AGN
           486, f. 68.
335,   Exp. 86. Draft of a letter denouncing the existence of a synagogue on
           Calle Santo Domingo.
337,   Guatemala 7. P/c Manuel Díaz Enríquez.
378,   Exp. 2. P/c Francisco Blandon.
380,   Exp. 1. P/c Baltazar del Valle.
381,   Exp. 5. P/c Duarte de León Jaramillo. See also AGN 426, Exp. 7;
           AGN 453, fs. 129-141; AGN 495, Exp. 14.
382,   Exp. 21. P/c Diego Nuñez Pacheco.
390,   Exp. 11. Testimony of Gaspar de Robles.
391,   Exp. 1. Testimony of Gaspar de Robles.
395,   Exp. 2. P/c Agustin de Rojas.
397,   Exp. 2. P/c Micaela Enríquez.
398,   Exp. 1. P/c Simón Váez Sevilla. See also AGN 414, Exp. 6; AGN 416,
           Exp. 24.
399,   Exp. 10. P/c Juan de Rojas.
400,   Exp. 2. P/c Juan Pacheco de León, alias Salomón Machorro.
409,   Exp. 2. P/c Antonio Caravallo. See also AGN 413, fs. 184-187, 239-
           246, 414, 417, 434.
409,   Exp. 4. P/c Pedro Fernándo del Castro.
412,   Exp. 2. P/c Luis Núñez Pérez.
413,   Entire volume. See *Guide to Jewish References*, pp. 51-53, for listing
           of expedientes.
416,   Exp. 2. Reference is made to Juan Pacheco de León in a letter to the
           Suprema concerning Jews who were to receive sanbenitos.
416,   Exp. 42. Letters dated May 24, 1649, and May 30, 1649, from the Mex-
           ican inquisitors to the Suprema in which Juan Pacheco de León is
           mentioned.
416,   Exp. 43. Memorandum concerning prisoners who had testified and
           who were exiled to Spain.
419,   Exp. 33. Letter from Francisco López to Simón Váez Sevilla.

435,   Cholula 43. P/c Jewish penitents in Puebla in 1650.
520,   Exp. 232. Denunciation of Manuel de Sosa y Prado. See also AGN 529, Exp. 11.
558,   Entire volume. P/c Isabel de Carvajal.
560,   Exp. 3. Petition of José de la Rosa.
848,   Exp. 12. Denunciation in 1733 against various Jews who practiced Catholicism in Veracruz.
1408,   Exp. 13. Application in 1802 by a vicar for the entry of Flavius Josephus' *Bello Judaica*.
1416,   f. 144. Denunciation in 1795 by the wife of an unnamed man for saying, among other things, that the best law was that of the Jews.
1429,   f. 59. Request in 1805 for the entry of two cases of books, among which was *Customs of the Israelites and Christians*.
1487,   Entire volume. P/c Luis de Carvajal.
1488,   Exp. 1. P/c Francisca de Carvajal. See also AGN 223, Exp. 2.
1488,   Exp. 2. P/c Leonor de Andrade.
1489,   Exp. 2. P/c Manuel Díaz.
1490,   Exp. 1. P/c Antonio López de Morales.
1490,   Exp. 3. P/c Mariana de Carvajal.
1495,   Exp. 2. Justa Méndez. See AGN 154, Exp. 1.

AHN

1620,   No. 15. Pro. Manuel Alvarez Prieto.
1736,   Exp. 29. Confession of Francisco de León.
1737,   Exp. 12. Report of visitador Pedro de Medina Rico.
1738,   Exp. 1. Certification of the examination of the procesos.

ABEC

The Abecedario is document number 2 in the Walter Douglas Collection at the Henry E. Huntington Library. For a description of the lengthy document see Liebman, "The Abecedario and a Check-list of Documents at the Henry E. Huntington Library," *Hispanic American Historical Review* XVIV (November, 1964), p. 554.

A microfilm of the document was presented to Don Wigberto Jiménez Moreno, Director of the Mexican Bureau of Historical and Anthropological Investigations, Chapultepec Castle, Mexico City.

A copy of the English translation of the document, made by this writer and rearranged in chronological order, has been presented to the General Historical Archives of Israel.

BRITISH MUSEUM MANUSCRIPT DIVISION

Additional 29.868. E. Mendes da Costa, Jewish Inscriptions

PUBLIC RECORDS OFFICE, LONDON

Calendar of State Papers. *Colonial America and West Indies*, 1675–1676, Vol.

88, pp. 419-422. Letter of Gov. Sir John Atkins to the Lords of Trade and Plantations, July 4, 1676, Barados; *Idem*, Vol. 90, letter of June 11, 1681, Sir Richard Dutton re Barbados.

Colonial Office, Vols. 324, 355, 356, containing lists of persons that were naturalized in His Majesty's Colonies in America pursuant to Act-13° George 2nd; 140/30 Council, Council in Assembly; CO 140/31.

PUBLISHED MATERIAL

ABBREVIATIONS

HAHR *Hispanic American Historical Review* (Durham, North Carolina)
JPS   Jewish Publication Society (Philadelphia, Pennsylvania)
PAJHS Publications of the American Jewish Historical Society (New York)
TJHSE Transactions of the Jewish Historical Society of England (London)

Adams, Eleanor B., and Scholes, France V. "Troublous Times in Mexico." *New Mexico Historical Review* 2 (January, 1927) and successive volumes to 1936.

Adler, Cyrus. "A Contemporary Memorial Relating to Damages to Spanish Interests in America Done by Jews of Holland (1634)." PAJHS 17 (1909):45.

Adler, Cyrus. "Jews in the American Plantations Between 1600-1700." PAJHS 1 (1893).

Adler, Cyrus, ed. *The Trial of Gabriel de Granada*. Translated by David Fergusson. PAJHS 7 (1899).

Adler, Cyrus. "The Trial of Jorge de Almeida." PAJHS 4 (1894).

Adler, Elkan N. *Auto de Fé and Jew*. London: Oxford University Press, 1908.

Adler, Elkan N. "The Jews of Amsterdam in 1655." TJHSE (Sessions 1899-1901) 4 (1903):224.

Aguirre Beltran, Gonzálo. *La Población Negra de México, 1519-1810*. Mexico, 1946. Consulted at the University of Veracruz, Jalapa, Mexico.

Albanes, Ricardo. *Los judíos a través de los siglos*. Mexico: privately printed, 1939.

Alessio Robles, Vito. *Coahuila y Texas en la época colonial*. Mexico: Editorial Cultura, 1939.

Allport, Gordon W. *The Nature of Prejudice*. Garden City, N.Y.: Doubleday & Co., 1958.

Altamira, Raphael. *The History of Spain*. Princeton, N.J.: Van Nostrand Co., 1949.

Amador de los Ríos, José. *Historia social, politica y religiosa de los judíos de España y Portugal*. 3 vols. Madrid: Aguilar, 1960.

Baer, Yitzhak (Fritz). *A History of the Jews in Christian Spain*. 2 vols. Philadelphia: JPS, 1961.

Baez Camargo, Gustavo. *Protestantes enjuiciados por la Inquisición*. Mexico: Casa Unida de Publicaciones, 1961.

Baeck, Leo. *Judaism and Christianity*. Philadelphia: JPS, 1964.

Bancroft, Hubert H. *Annals of Mexico*. Publisher unknown. Consulted in the Ben Franklin Library, Mexico, D.F.

Bancroft, Hubert H. *History of Mexico*. 6 vols. San Francisco: A. L. Bancroft & Co., 1883-1888.

Baron, Salo W. "Conference Themes." PAJHS 46 (March, 1957).

Baron, Salo W. *History and Jewish Historians*. Philadelphia: JPS, 1964.

Baron, Salo W. *Social and Religious History of the Jews*. 3 vols. New York: Columbia University Press, 1937.

Beinart, Haim. "The Judaizing Movement in the Order of San Jeronimo in Castile." *Studies in History, Publication of Hebrew University of Jerusalem. Scripto Hierosolymitana* 7 (1961).

Beinart, Haim. "The Records of the Inquisition as a Source of Jewish and Converso History." *Proceedings of the Israel Academy of Sciences and Humanities* 2 (no. 11, 1967):211.

Benítez, Fernando. *Los Primeros Mexicanos*. Mexico: Biblioteca Era, 1965.

Bernadette, José Maier. *Hispanic Culture and Character of Sephardic Jews*. New York: Hispanic Institute, 1952.

Bernáldez, Andrés. *Memorias del reinado de los Reyes Católicos*. Madrid: Bibliotecas Reyes, 1962.

Bloom, Herbert I. *The Economic Activities of the Jews of Amsterdam in the 17th Century*. Williamsport, Pa: Bayard Press, 1937.

Bocanegra, P. Mathias. *Relación del auto general de la fee celebrado 11 de abril de 1649*. Mexico: Santo Oficio, 1649.

Book of the Wisdom of Solomon. Edited by William J. Dean. London: Oxford University Press, 1891.

Boxer, C. R. *The Dutch in Brazil*. Oxford: Clarendon Press, 1957.

Boyd-Bowman, Peter. "La Emigración Peninsular a América: 1520-1539." *Historia Mexicana* 13 (Oct.-Dec. 1963):175.

Brandenberg, Frank. *The Making of Modern Mexico*. Englewood Cliffs, N.J.: Prentice-Hall, 1964.

Brenner, Anita. "Cavaliers and Martyrs." *Menorah Journal* 16 (January, 1929).

Brinton, Crane; Christopher, John B.; and Wolff, Robert Lee. *A History of Civilization*. Englewood Cliffs, N.J.: Prentice-Hall, 1955.

Cantero, Francisco. "Review of the Marranos According to the Hebrew Sources of the 15th and 16th Centuries." *Sefarad* 24 (1964):15.

Caro Baroja, Julio. *Los judíos en la España moderna y contemporánea*. 3 vols. Madrid: Ediciones Arion, 1961.

Caro Baroja, Julio. *La Sociedad Criptojudía en la Corte de Felipe IV*. Madrid: Imprenta y Editorial, 1963.

Carreño, Alberto María. "Luis de Carvajal, el Mozo." *Memorias de la Academia de la Historia de México* 15 (January-March, 1956):87-101.

Castro, Américo. *The Structure of Spanish History*. Princeton, N.J.: Princeton University Press, 1954.

Chapman, Charles E. *A History of Spain*. New York: Macmillan, 1918.

Cheyney, Edward P. *European Background of American History*. New York: Collier Books, 1961.

Cline, Howard F. *The United States and Mexico*. Cambridge, Mass.: Harvard University Press, 1961.

Cuevas, P. Mariano. *Historia de la Nación Mexicana*. Mexico: Talleres Tipográficos Modelo, 1940.

Díaz del Castillo, Bernal. *Historia verdadera de la Conquista de la Nueva España*. Mexico: Editorial Porrua, 1960.

Emmanuel, I. S. *History of the Netherland Antilles* Forthcoming.
Enciclopedia Judaica Castellana. 10 vols. Mexico: E.J.C., 1948.
Espejo, Fernando. "The Santa Cruz Museum." *Oro Verde* 8 (1968) p. 21.
Fernández del Castillo, Francisco. *Libros y libreros del siglo XVI.* Mexico: Publicaciones del AGN, 1914.
Finn, James. *History of the Jews in Spain and Portugal.* London: Gilbert & Rivington, 1841.
Friede, Juan. "The Catálogo de Pasajeros and Spanish Migration to America to 1550." HAHR 31 (May, 1951).
Gaon, Solomon. "The Sephardi Character and Outlook" in *Essays Presented to Rabbi Israel Brodie.* London, 1967.
García, Genaro. *Documentos inéditos o muy raros para la historia de México.* 28 vols. Mexico: Libreria de la Viuda de Ch. Bouret, 1910.
García Gutiérrez, P. Jesús. "La poesía religiosa en México: Siglos XVI a XIX." *Cultura* 11 (1919).
García Icazbalceta, Joaquín. *Bibliografía mexicana del siglo XVI.* Edited by Agustín Millares Carlo. Mexico: Fondo de Cultura Económica, 1954.
García Icazbalceta, Joaquín. *Don Fray Juan de Zumárraga.* 4 vols. Mexico: Andrade y Morales, 1881.
Gardiner, Harvey. *Martin Lopez.* Lexington: University of Kentucky Press, 1958.
Glatzer, Nahum N. *Faith and Knowledge.* Boston: Beacon Press, 1963.
González Obregón, Luis. *México Viejo.* Mexico: Editorial Patria, 1959.
González Obregón, Luis. *Rebeliones Indigenas y Precursores de la Independencia Mexicana.* 2nd ed. Mexico: Ediciones Fuente Cultural, 1952.
Graetz, Heinrich. *History of the Jews.* 6 vols. Philadelphia: JPS, 1894.
Grayzel, Solomon. *A History of the Jews.* Philadelphia, JPS, 1947.
Greenleaf, Richard E. "Francisco Millán Before the Mexican Inquisition." *The Americas* 21 (October, 1964).
Greenleaf, Richard E. *Zumárraga and the Mexican Inquisition.* Washington, D.C.: Academy of American Franciscan History, 1961.
Guijo, Gregorio M. de. *Diario: 1648-1664.* 2 vols. Mexico: Editorial Porrua, 1953.
Haring, Clarence H. *The Spanish Empire in America.* New York: Harcourt, Brace & World, 1963.
Hastings, J. ed. *Encyclopedia of Religion and Ethics.* 13 vols. New York: Scribner's, 1908-1927.
Herring, Hubert. *A History of Latin America.* 2nd ed. New York: Knopf, 1964.
Hertz, Joseph H. *The Pentateuch and Haftorahs.* 5 vols. London: Soncino Press, 1940.
Hyamson, Albert. *The Sephardim of England.* London: Methuen & Co., 1951.
Ibáñez, Muriel Yolanda. *La Inquisición en México durante el siglo XVI.* Mexico: Imprenta Universitaria, 1946.
Jewish Encyclopedia. 12 vols. New York: Funk & Wagnalls Co., 1901-1907.
Jiménez Rueda, Julio. *Herejías y supersticiones en la Nueva España.* Mexico: Imprenta Universitaria, 1946.
Katz, Jacob. *Exclusiveness and Intolerance.* New York: Schocken Press, 1962.
Kohut, George A. "Jewish Martyrs of the Inquisition in South America." PAJHS 4 (1894):119.
Konetzke, A. Richard. *La emigración española al Río de la Plata durante el siglo XVI.* Madrid: M. Ballesteros y Beretta, 1951.

Bibliography
Lafuente Machain, R. de. *Los Portugueses en Buenos Aires*. Madrid: C. de la Real Academia, 1931.

Lea, Henry C. *History of the Inquisition in Spain*. 4 vols. New York: Macmillan Co., 1907.

Lea, Henry C. *History of the Inquisition in the Spanish Dependencies*. New York: Macmillan Co., 1922.

León-Portilla, Miguel, *et al*. *Historia documental de México*. 2 vols. Mexico: Imprenta Universitaria, 1964.

Lewin, Boleslao. *La Inquisición en Hispanoamérica*. Buenos Aires: Editorial Proyección, 1962.

Lewin, Boleslao. *Los Marranos: Un Intento de Definicion*. Buenos Aires: Colegio Libre de Estudios Superiores, 1946.

Lewin, Reinhold. *Luthers Stellung zu den Juden*, as quoted in Bonvetsch, Gottlieb Nathaniel, *Studien zur Geschichte der Theologie und der Kirche*. Leipzig: Bonvetsch und R. Seeberg, 1897-1908.

Libro Primero de Votos de la Inquisición de México, 1537-1600. Introduction by Edmundo O' Gorman. Mexico: AGN and Universidad Nacional Autónoma de México, 1940.

Liebman, Seymour B. "The Abecedario and a Check-List of Documents at the Henry E. Huntington Library." HAHR 64 (November, 1964).

Liebman, Seymour B. *The Enlightened: The Writings of Luis de Carvajal, el Mozo*. Coral Gables, Fla.: University of Miami Press, 1967.

Liebman, Seymour B. "Fuentes Desconocidas de la Historia Mexicana Judía." *Historia Mexicana* 14 (April-July, 1965):707.

Liebman, Seymour B. *Guide to Jewish References in the Mexican Colonial Era: 1521-1821*. Philadelphia: University of Pennsylvania Press, 1964.

Liebman, Seymour B. "Hernando Alonso: First Jew on the North American Continent." *Journal of Inter-American Studies* 5 (April, 1963):291.

Liebman, Seymour B. "Mexican Mestizo Jews." *American Jewish Archives* 19 (November, 1967):144.

Liebman, Seymour B. "Research Problems in Mexican Jewish History." PAJHS 54 (December, 1964):165.

Liebman, Seymour B. "Spanish Jews in the 14th and 15th Centuries." *Alliance Review* 19 (Winter, 1965).

Liebman, Seymour B. "They Came With Cortés." *Judaism* 18 (January, 1969):91-103.

Lindo, Elias Haim. *History of the Jews of Spain and Portugal*. London: Longman, Brown, Green & Longman, 1848.

Llorente, Jean Antoine. *The History of the Inquisition in Spain*. London, 1826.

López Martínez, Nicolas. *Los Judaizantes Castellanos*. Burgos, Spain: Publicaciones del Seminario Metropolitano de Burgos, 1954.

Madariaga, Salvador de. *Englishmen, Frenchmen, Spaniards*. London: Oxford University Press, 1928.

Madariaga, Salvador de. *The Fall of the Spanish American Empire*. New York: Collier Books, 1963.

Marañon, Gregoria. *Antonio Pérez*. 2 vols. Buenos Aires: Espasa-Calpe, 1947.

Marcu, Valeriu. *La expulsión de los judíos de España*. Buenos Aires: Libro de Edición Argentina, 1945.

Margolis, Max L., and Marx, Alexander. *The History of the Jewish People*. Philadelphia: JPS, 1938.

Martínez del Río, Pablo. "*Alumbrado*". Mexico: Porrua Hnos, 1937.

McClaskey, Josephine Yocum. "Inquisition Papers of Mexico, II: The Trial of Luis de Cruz." *Research Papers of the State College of Washington* 15 (March, 1947).

Medina, José Toribio. *Historia del Tribunal del Santa Oficio de la Inquisición de Lima.* 2 vols. Santiago de Chile: Fondo Histórico y Bibliográfico J. T. Medina, 1956.

Medina, José Toribio. *Historia del Tribunal del Santo Oficio de la Inquisición en Chile.* Santiago de Chile: Fondo Histórico y Bibliográfico J. T. Medina, 1952.

Medina, José Toribio. *Historia del Tribunal del Santo Oficio de la Inquisición en México.* With additional notes by Julio Jiménez Rueda. Mexico: Ediciones Fuente Cultural, 1952.

Medina, José Toribio. *La Inquisición en las provincias de la Plata.* Santiago de Chile; 1906.

Méndez Plancarte, Alfonso. *Poetas Novohispanos.* Mexico: Ediciones de la Universidad Nacional Autónomia, 1942.

Ménéndez Pidal, Ramón. *The Spaniards in Their History.* Translated by Walter Starkie. New York: W. W. Norton Co., 1966.

Mocatta, Frederick David. *The Jews of Spain and Portugal and the Inquisition.* London: Longmans, Green & Co., 1877.

Mocatta, Moses. *The Inquisition and Judaism* [with translation of "A Sermon . . . at the Auto-da-fé in Lisbon, 1705]. London: J. Wertheimer & Co., 1945.

Mörner, Magnus. *Race Mixture in the History of Latin America.* Boston: Beacon Press, 1968.

Morris, Richard B. *The Peacemakers.* New York: Harper, 1965.

Motolinia, Fr. *History of the Indians of New Spain.* Translated and edited by Francis Borgia Steck, O.F.M. Washington, D.C.: Academy of American Franciscan History, 1951.

Motten, Clement G. *Mexican Silver and the Enlightenment.* Philadelphia: University of Pennsylvania Press, 1950.

Netanyahu, Benzion. *The Marranos of Spain.* New York: American Academy for Jewish Research, 1966.

Netanyahu, Benzion. *Don Isaac Abravanel.* Philadelphia: JPS, 1968.

Neuman, Abraham A. *The Jews in Spain.* 2 vols. Philadelphia: JPS, 1942.

Nunemaker, J. Horace. "Inquisition Papers of Mexico." *Research Papers of the State College of Washington* 14 (March, 1946).

Núñez y Dominguez, José de J. "Los judíos en la historia y literatura mexicana." *Judaica* 19 (1945):41.

Pallares, Eduardo. *El Procedimiento Inquisitorial.* Mexico: Imprenta Universitaria, 1951.

Palma, Ricardo. *Tradiciones Peruanas completas.* Madrid: Aguilar, 1961.

Parkes, Henry B. *History of Mexico.* Boston: Houghton, Mifflin Co., 1950.

Pérez-Marchand, Monelisa Lina. *Dos Estapas ideológicas del siglo XVIII en México.* Mexico: El Colegio de México, 1945.

Petuchowski, Jakob. *The Theology of Haham David Nieto.* New York: Bloch Publishing Co., 1954.

Picón Salas, Mariano. *A Cultural History of Spanish America.* Translated by Irving W. Leonard. Berkeley: University of California Press, 1963.

Powell, Philip Wayne. *Soldiers, Indians and Silver.* Berkeley: University of California Press, 1952.

Prescott, William H. *The History of the Conquest of Mexico.* New York: Random Press, n.d.

Priestley, Herbert I. *The Coming of the White Man.* New York: Macmillan Co., 1929.

Procesos de Luis de Carvajal, el Mozo. Mexico: AGN, 1935.

Publications of the Hugenot Society of London, located in Public Records Office, vol. 24, pp. x-xiii.

Puigblanch, Antonio. *The Inquisition Unmasked.* 2 vols. London, 1816.

Revah, I. S. "Fundo de manuscritos pour l'histoire des nouveaux chrétiens portugais." *Boletín Internacional de Bibliografía Luso-Brasilera* 2 (April-June, 1961).

Revah, I. S. "Le plaidoyer en faveur des nouveaux chrétiens." *Revue des Etudes Juives,* 4th series 2 (102), Parts 3, 4 (July-Dec., 1963):279-324.

Ricard, Robert. "Fray Fernando de Ojea." *Abside* 8 (August, 1937):22-28.

Ricard, Robert. "Pour une étude de judaïsme portugais au Mexique pendant la période coloniale." *Revue d'Histoire Moderne* 14 (August, 1939).

Riva Palacio, Vicente. *El Libro Rojo.* Mexico, 1867.

Riva Palacio, Vicente. *México à través de los siglos.* 5 vols. Mexico: Publicaciones Herrerias, n.d.

Riva Palacio, Vicente. *Monja y Casada.* Mexico: Editorial Porrua, 1958.

Roel, Santiago. *Nuevo León—Apuntes Históricos.* 8th ed. Monterrey, Mexico: Ministerio de Educación, 1958.

Roseman, Kenneth D. "Power in a Midwestern Jewish Community." *American Jewish Archives* 21 (April, 1969):58.

Roth, Cecil. *Gleanings: Essays in Jewish History.* New York: Hermon Press, 1967.

Roth, Cecil. *History of the Marranos.* Philadelphia: JPS, 1959.

Roth, Cecil. *House of Nasi.* Philadelphia: JPS, 1948.

Roth, Cecil. *Life of Menasseh ben Israel.* Philadelphia: JPS, 1945.

Roth, Cecil. *The World of the Sephardim.* London: Wizo, 1943.

Rudd, Margaret T. *The Lonely Heretic.* Austin: University of Texas Press, 1963.

Rule, William Harris. *History of the Inquisition.* New York: Scribner, Wilford & Co., 1874.

Samuel, Wilfred S. "A Review of the Jewish Colonists in Barbados in the Year 1680." *TJHSE* 13 (1932-1935):1-111.

Santa María, Ramón. "Ritos y costumbres de los hebreos españoles." *Boletín de la Real Academia de la Historia* 22 (Feb., 1893).

Schwarz, Samuel. *Os Christaõs Novos em Portugal.* Lisbon, 1925.

Sicroff, Albert A. "The Marranos—Forced Converts or Apostates." *Midstream* 12 (October, 1966):71-75.

Sierra O'Reilly, Justo. *La Hija del Judío.* 2 vols. Mexico: Editorial Porrua, 1959.

Silver, Abba Hillel. *Where Judaism Differed.* New York: Macmillan Co., 1945.

Simpson, Lesley Byrd. *The Encomienda in New Spain.* Berkeley: University of California Press, 1929.

Smith, Preserved. *Reformation in Europe.* New York: Collier Books, 1962.

Soldaña, Quinteliano. "La Inquisición Española 1478-1808." *Criminalia,* año XXVIII (Nov. 30, 1962), no. 11, pp. 632-690.

Steinberg, Milton. *Basic Judaism.* New York: Harcourt, Brace & Co., 1962.

Teja Zable, Alfonso. *Guide to the History of Mexico.* Mexico: Ministry of Foreign Affairs, 1935.

Terrejoncillo, Francisco de. *Centinela contra judíos puesta en la torre de la Iglesia de Dios, con el trabajo.* Pamplona: Juan Nucon, 1691.

Texeira, Anthony J. *Antonio Homen e a Inquisião.* Coimbra, 1902.

Thomas, Alfred B. *Latin America: A History.* New York: Macmillan Co., 1956.

Ticknor, George. *History of Spanish Literature.* 3 vols. 3rd ed. Boston: Ticknor & Fields, 1863.

Tomson, Robert. *An Englishman and the Mexican Inquisition.* Edited by G. R. G. Conway. Mexico: privately printed, 1927.

Toro, Alfonso. *La familia Carvajal.* 2 vols. Mexico: Editorial Patria, 1944.

Toro, Alfonso, *La Iglesia y el estado en México.* Mexico: Publicaciones del AGN, 1927.

Toro, Alfonso, ed. *Los judíos en la Nueva España.* Mexico: Publicaciones del AGN, 1932.

Tozzer, Alfred M., ed. *Landa's "Relación de las cosas de Yucatán."* Cambridge, Mass.: Peabody Museum, Harvard University, 1941.

Transcript of *Proceso de Luis de Carvajal, el Gobernador.* G. R. G. Conway Collection, Archives of the Library of Congress, Washington, D.C.

Transcript of *Proceso de Thomas Treviño de Sobremonte,* G. R. G. Conway Collection, Archives of the Library of Congress, Washington, D.C.

Turberville, A. S. *La Inquisición Española.* Mexico: Fondo de Cultura Económica, 1950.

"Ultimos momentos y conversión de Luis de Carvajal." *Anales del Museo de Nacional de Arquelogía* 3 (1925).

Vainstein, Yaacov. *The Cycle of the Jewish Year.* Jerusalem: World Zionist Organization, 1961.

Vallé, Rafael Heliodoro. "Judíos en México." *Revista Chileana de Historia y Geografía* 81 (Sept.-Dec., 1936).

Wiznitzer, Arnold. "Crypto-Jews in Mexico in the 16th Century." PAJHS 51 (March, 1962).

Wiznitzer, Arnold. "Crypto-Jews in Mexico in the 17th Century." PAJHS 51 (June, 1962).

Wolf, Eric R. *Sons of the Shaking Earth.* Chicago: University of Chicago Press, 1959.

Wolf, Lucien. "American Elements in the Re-Settlement." TJHSE 3 (1898): 76.

Wolf, Lucien. *The Jews of the Canary Islands.* London: Spottiswoode, Ballantyne & Co., 1926.

Worcester, Donald E., and Schaeffer, Wendell L. *The Growth and Culture of Latin America.* New York: Oxford University Press, 1956.

Zavala, Silvio. *Spanish Colonization in America.* Philadelphia: University of Pennsylvania Press, 1943.

Zimmels, H. J. *Ashkenazim and Sephardim.* London: Oxford University Press, 1958.

Index